D1144865

CHASING THE LIGHT

BOOKS BY OLIVER STONE

A Child's Night Dream

Oliver Stone's USA
(contributor, essays edited by Robert Brent Toplin)

On History: Tariq Ali and Oliver Stone in Conversation

Responses to Oliver Stone's Alexander
(contributor, essays edited by Paul Cartledge and Fiona Rose Greenland)

The Untold History of the United States
(with Peter Kuznick)

The Putin Interviews

CHASING THE LIGHT
OLIVER STONE

BAINTE DEN STOC

WITHDRAWN FROM
DÚN LAOGHAIRE-RATHDOWN COUNTY
LIBRARY STOCK

monoray

An Hachette UK Company
www.hachette.co.uk

First published in Great Britain in 2020 by Monoray, an imprint of
Octopus Publishing Group Ltd
Carmelite House
50 Victoria Embankment
London EC4Y 0DZ
www.octopusbooks.co.uk

Published in the United States by Houghton Mifflin Harcourt Publishing Company,
3 Park Avenue, 19th Floor, New York, New York 10016

Text Copyright © Ixtlan Corporation 2020
Copyright © Octopus Publishing Goup Ltd 2020

All rights reserved. No part of this work may be reproduced or utilized in
any form or by any means, electronic or mechanical, including photocopying,
recording or by any information storage and retrieval system, without the
prior written permission of the publisher.

Oliver Stone asserts the moral right to be identified as the author of this work.

ISBN 978-1-91318-318-9 (Hardback)
ISBN 978-1-91318-354-7 (Trade)

A CIP catalogue record for this book is available from the British Library.

Book design by Chloe Foster
Cover design by Yasia Williams

Printed in Great Britain
10 9 8 7 6 5 4 3 2

Excerpts from *Stone: The Controversies, Excesses, and Exploits of a Radical Filmmaker*
by James Riordan. Copyright © 1995 by James Riordan. Used by permission of James
Riordan. All rights reserved. *Conan* script excerpts © Edward R. Pressman Film
Corporation, Inc. Used by permission. *Scarface* script excerpts included courtesy of
Universal Studios Licensing, LLC. All rights reserved.

"Calmly We Walk Through This April's Day" by Delmore Schwartz, from SELECTED
POEMS, copyright ©1959 by Delmore Schwartz. Reprinted by permission of New
Directions Publishing Corp.

All photographs courtesy of the author unless otherwise noted.

CONTENTS

CHASING THE LIGHT

INTRODUCTION

I 'm moving swiftly through the cobblestone streets of a small, sixteenth-century Mexican town complete with churches, plazas, and
stone bridges over a meandering stream traversing this small gem of
a location.

Hundreds of extras and technical people, as well as actors, are waiting
in the heat for me to decide where, when, how. I'm in the middle of Zapata
country, in Morelos state, two hours south of Mexico City.

On one street, I have 150 Mexican army soldiers dressed as Salvadoran
troops circa 1980. On another street, neighing and pawing the pavestones
impatiently are seventy horses with riders gathered from the best vaque-
ros in the state, a rebel cavalry. I've decided they're going to charge over a
bridge onto the main plaza for a final overwhelming of besieged government forces. There will be multiple explosions which we've set along the
line of the charge. Between the two sides are several dozen villagers, civilians gathered as extras, who will scatter in all directions on cue.

My principal actors, playing journalists, are going to be right in the middle of this charge, watching the cavalry pound down the side of the street
right at our cameras. I'll stay with my nervous star because he's terrified of
getting hurt with this crazy director who's nearly gotten him killed several
times already (according to him), and whom he doesn't trust because he
thinks I'm this gruff veteran of another war (in Vietnam) who believes that
all actors are namby-pambies. He thinks entirely, of course, of his face and

our imminent gas bombs, any of which could disfigure him and ruin his career when they're detonated.

The sun is high and hot. I'm ready to call "Action!" After some fifteen years of trying to direct a film like this, today is a dream come true — the vision of a six-year-old boy under a Christmas tree loaded with toy soldiers and electric trains — my very own world. I am the engineer, and I have the power to decide today who dies and who lives in this theater of my making. It's everything that made the movies so exciting to me as a child — battles, passionate actions, momentous outcomes.

And yet, as exciting as it is to be a god for a few days, behind our film's props, scenery, and manpower is a forbidding dilemma. We're out of money. Fifty or sixty of us, foreigners, are stranded in Mexico, living off credit and borrowed time. We started six weeks ago on a vast enterprise requiring ninety-three speaking roles in two languages, some fifty locations, tanks, planes, and choppers to shoot an epic-scale movie about the El Salvador civil war of the early 1980s. We're working in three different states in Mexico, separated by great distances, shooting, among other things, a massacre outside a large cathedral in Mexico City (standing in for San Salvador), death squads, the rape and murder of nuns, and this scary horse charge — all this for a ridiculous fantasy sum of less than $3 million! Truly, we'd been crazy to start this.

And now the money people are driving out from Mexico City to basically take control of the film from me and the producer, because we're clearly over budget — by how much no one yet knows — with two weeks left to shoot. Authority has to be reestablished. The people in LA are calling in the "bond company"(Urgh! The very words terrify most producers), who've guaranteed "completion" of the film as an insurance company might value a human life until its death, which we're fast approaching. Despite my exhilaration at getting to this moment, I am also massively depressed that this might be my last setup on a movie on which we'd gambled so heavily and now seem to have lost.

"Action!" I yell so they can hear me several blocks away without the radios. "Charge!" The orders are repeated in Spanish over bullhorns by my assistant directors.

Then comes the growing sound of pounding hooves on those old cobblestones — four metal shoes to a horse, 280 coming from a distance, heading ultimately for our camera crew. I'm praying no one falls off his damned horse in these narrow streets; he'd surely be trampled to death.

"Get ready!" I yell out, unnecessarily, to the two actors playing journalists with their 35mm cameras perched to shoot the oncoming charge. My lead is jittery. The other actor is solid, though, and determined to shine as the first of the riders appear around a corner, roaring toward the bridge, firing rifles as they ride all out. Brave men. The first horses are now flying over the bridge, a fiery red explosion to their side. Two or three men fall off in choreographed spots without injury. The horde keeps coming. The momentum of the cavalry charge is the most important thing, and I know we've got it. I can feel the violence of this moment. It's too good, too real.

Then, with seventy horses over the bridge, my lead actor bolts. A little early perhaps — the riders are still fifty yards away — but who wouldn't be scared? Like a giant wave coming down on a ship, the noise alone is enough to terrify even the hardiest soul. And yet the supporting actor, motivated by a moment of greatness, stands firm as a rock, "photographing" this classic moment. At thirty yards I scream at him to run — "Get out of there!" — as my brave cinematographer and I know we won't escape unless we do it now, sprinting out of the path of the horses. We go!

At twenty yards, my intrepid and nimble second actor jumps to safety just in time. It's chilling. The sound alone and the jittery images will work. It'd be a spectacular moment on film. Too bad the first actor left a little too early, but . . . that's his "character" emerging in the movie. Not exactly a Hollywood hero.

"Cut!" I scream. A tremendous energy is expired before the horses and the crew reassemble, breathing hard, the horses' flanks heaving, instructions in Spanish yelled out between crew members, many adjustments made.

Now that we've broken the ice, I call for a second take. We're on a roll; over the next two hours, we do the charge four more times, covering all kinds of angles as the cavalry swarm over the government troops (mostly Mexican stuntmen), turning the tide of the battle in favor of the rebels.

That is, until — in the film — the United States embassy, on alert, intervenes by phone in this crucial battle of this civil war and authorizes the newest tanks and weaponry from America to be released to the government side. With three tanks, some air cover, and artillery, there's enough firepower to turn back the temporary rebel tide and ensure a government stabilization. We're planning to shoot this over the next two days as we try to complete the battle before our financial lifeline is cut. But I tighten when I see my producer walking toward me with his perpetual frown of worry. With British understatement he quips, "I'm not frowning, am I? . . . We got the million."

Wow! Life. Breath! A million dollars from a Mexican investing syndicate friendly with his Mexican wife. They've saved our film from the evil bond company, which has now arrived in the form of two representatives — one a version of the Grim Reaper, the other an affable Scot who looks like an IRS agent — walking the edges of the set, counting everything. But thankfully, they've been called off by some higher-up on the phone from Los Angeles.

The problem comes on the next day, when the Mexican money doesn't show up after all. Dozens of phone calls now follow — wires from the bank in Amsterdam to Los Angeles, to Mexico City, and finally to us in Tlayacapan, the end of the line. Some cash is gotten — from whom exactly is unclear to me, but by this time I'm too tired to care.

So we keep shooting the battle, one foot in front of the other. The six inches in front of my face are all that matter to me — to finish this film. I've risked so much. How many times have they said I couldn't direct? I've had two film failures. I'm nearing forty. I've been trying to make my own movie since I was twenty-three. I'd written more than twenty screenplays by this time — but this was the break point. Hollywood hadn't supported me, they didn't believe in me or believe that a film about a "shithole" country like Salvador would have any interest for an American audience, much less a film with revolutionary sympathies. In their eyes, I was washed up at forty. And I knew it. I'd made too many enemies, burned too many bridges with my provocative personality.

We shoot until our forty-second day — exhausting six-day weeks. The Mexican crew goes on strike more than once. They're right; the money is generally late, the whole production has been chaotic, near impossible, and on this day we abandon Mexico as quickly and surreptitiously as we can, leaving a trail of creditors and unpaid craftsmen behind. These debts would eventually be paid off, but for now we have a film — I think a great one, but in hundreds of pieces that need to be edited. I knew it'd always been a passionate story, written by me and a journalist friend who'd lived through it, but it needed desperately to be finished.

Back in the US, more funds are needed to shoot our preplanned eight days in San Francisco and Las Vegas. We'd saved the beginning and the end for last, figuring the money would have to come in to complete the film in order to save it. We come up with the last few hundred thousand dollars and barely get our last must-have shot at 7:42 p.m., just as the light flees below the mountain overlooking this broiling desert outside Vegas.

Thus my book title — *Chasing the Light*. It seems all my life I've been doing just that.

Such was the making of *Salvador* in 1985, released in '86, my first true film which I'd made from beginning to end with no studio behind me, no distribution arrangement at all — made on pure faith and the backing of two gutsy British independent producers who would best be described as gamblers — or, more nobly put, pirates looking for the big score, and willing to risk death by hanging.

The resulting picture was shockingly violent, outrageously sexy, colorful, and "too much," but in limited theatrical distribution, and especially in the new format of video, it eventually found a large audience of people who liked it and talked about it. A "new" filmmaker was being discovered, supposedly repudiating the previous version of himself. Out of it came two Academy Award nominations for Original Screenplay and Leading Actor — he being the nervous one we saw at the cavalry charge. And with those same gamblers, right on the heels of finishing *Salvador*, plunging right into the Philippine jungle, came the chance to make another low-budget film with outsize ambitions, which, though rejected dozens of times for ten years, now miraculously struck the American mood at the right time in 1986, in the heart of a conservative presidency. It was called *Platoon*, and America, in fact the world, was ready for this gritty, real depiction of a nightmare war I'd experienced firsthand. And as in a fairy tale, in the very same year as the nominated *Salvador*, this low-budget film was shockingly honored in April, 1987 with the Oscar for Best Picture and, as to myself, an equally shocking first Best Director award.

My life after that would never be the same. I'd work for real studios, with real money. I'd go on to have an up-and-down career like most of us, each film widening my view of the world as I went; actually, the films were shock absorbers, marching me through decades of an intense, almost insane American experience. Some hit, some missed — success, failure, "equal imposters," as Kipling said. The constant strain of a dog-eat-dog film business geared to make money can wear any good soul to the bone. The movies give, and they destroy.

But this isn't a story about that, or about those later years. This is a story about making a dream at all costs, even without money. It's about cutting corners, improvising, hustling, cobbling together workarounds to get movies made and into theaters, not knowing where the next payday is coming from — or the next monsoon or scorpion bite. It's about not taking "no" for an answer. It's about lying outrageously, gritting it out with sweat and tears, surviving. It goes from a magical New York childhood to the Vietnam War and my struggles to come back from it, ending at the age of forty in the making of *Platoon*. It's about growing up. It's about failure, loss of confidence. And it's about early success and arrogance too. It's about drugs, and the times we lived through politically and socially. It's about imagination, dreaming up what you want and going out to make it happen. And of course it's full of deceits, betrayals, crooks and heroes, people who bless you with their presence, and those who destroy you if you let them.

The truth is, no matter how great my satisfactions in the later part of my life, I don't think I've ever felt as much excitement or adrenaline as when I had no money. A friend who came from the underclass of England once told me, "The only thing money can't buy is poverty." Maybe he really meant "happiness," but the point is, money gives you an edge, and without it, you become, like it or not, more human. It is, in its way, like being back in the infantry with a worm's-eye view of a world where everything, whether a hot shower or a hot meal, is hugely appreciated.

Many people tell me time is the most valuable possession we have. I'm not sure I agree, because no story is ever straight. In traversing our life from youth to old age, we truly live outside time. There are certain ordinary moments, and then there are highlights that your consciousness treasures forever. Some good and some horrible moments, but indelible. And for me at least, trying to get from cradle to grave is too long a time, too much happens, too many characters to cherish, too much forgotten or remembered falsely. Baby steps are required to understand these moments outside time and what they mean. That's the greatest pleasure I take in writing — re-appreciating, loving all over again. My intermittent diaries in this regard have been most helpful in reconstructing what I was thinking in any particular moment. No greater satisfaction exists now than a paragraph well written in honor of something you value more and more the older you get.

By the time I got to forty, I finally surpassed the success I so wanted in my chosen field of play. And I realized no matter how far I'd go in the future, I'd already achieved what I'd first dreamed up in my concept of a life. So this is what this book is about — that dream, the first forty, those years "whose margins fade for ever and forever" as we move. As a young man I never understood what that beautiful phrase from Tennyson meant. That was the one thought in the whole beautiful poem "Ulysses" that eluded my grasp. Now I know why.

1

Child of Divorce

I was coming up on thirty, and I was broke, but I didn't want to think about that anymore. Here I was, like tens of thousands of tourists from Jersey and Long Island, gawking at some two hundred–plus ships, all shapes and sizes, circling New York Harbor. The sun was bright, a whiff of Atlantic breeze alleviating the heat, ruffling the lush white sails on the sixteen "Tall Ships" at the center of it all. It was the Fourth of July 1976, and America was drunk on itself, celebrating its two-hundredth birthday with, of course, TV cameras everywhere. To Americans, two hundred years was a huge deal. To older civilizations like China and Europe, it was just part of the tapestry. I say that because I'm half American and half French, and thirty years ago, on this very river — the Hudson — with its graceful Statue of Liberty greeting refugees from all over the world, my mother came across freshly pregnant with me. It was the hard winter of January '46, and my soldier father was proudly accompanying her to a new home in this vast land. And today, thirty years later, we were here assembled, witnesses to history, a beast of a million eyes, stacked in the streets and windows of Lower Manhattan, drawn to the memory — in our bones — of freedom, of the promise of a better world.

Promise? The world was built on it. The Democrats were coming to town the next week for their presidential convention, the city jumping with money fever — stores, bars, hotels, restaurants. Some twenty thousand of them at Madison Square Garden would be screaming for Jimmy Carter, the peanut farmer from Georgia with the beaver teeth and shy smile. He was going all the way; we sensed this was destined because, even with Gerald Ford in office, people were still sick of Nixon and his secrets and lies. Reform was in the air. The Democrats back in power meant money in people's pockets. And money meant freedom, and freedom meant sex. This crazy country was ready to "PARTY!" Barry White's dance music would be our God and Donna Summer his Goddess. "*Yeah! Give me some . . . mmm, mmm!*" No more crackdowns. No more scary talk of "law and order" while giving us high crimes and mass disorder. Vietnam was over. Fuck this Nixon "War on Drugs" shit! America was on the move again. We're gonna get high. Like in the '60s before it got so heavy. The late '70s were going to be Fun! Fun! Fun!

I was drifting through the thick crowd to the bottom of this $24 island, past the barbeque families waving little flags back at the ships, lugging their ice chests and folding chairs, my eyes picking out the girls of summer, so many of them, R. Crumb–like caricatures of midwestern corn-fed Amazons in their shorts and sandals. Summers in New York were sexy. The heat travels up through your feet into your loins as the sidewalks steam with a humidity that rips the shields off everyone; people walking around half-naked like they were at home and nobody was looking. It's so hot somehow that who you are and what you do isn't so important anymore; your identity, like candle wax, blurs and drips into someone else's.

Wiry rat-faced vendors were making big bucks today, slipping through bodies, peddling orange sodas, hot dogs, and souvenirs destined for garage sales. I noticed an Albanian's cash roll as he changed a fiver, maybe $300 or $400 there already, $700 to $800 by tonight. (And I'd made thirty-five bucks the last night I drove a cab.) Religious fanatics pitching "Jesus" and "The End of the World," bald Hare Krishnas chanting cult rhythms were duck-dancing through the crowd. Screams of kids and their anxious moms chasing them like pecking pigeons. The dads were always here at these things on holidays — dependable working stiffs, humble and happy just to have a couple of kids, a wife, and a job, Jesus, a good job, which might not be there in the years to come. Even if you had nothing to say to them, it was nice to just hang with your bloodlines. They did it around the caves from the very beginning. I missed that. I missed a family.

In the harbor, I can now imagine my mother's eyes, coming from a terrible war that nearly destroyed human civilization, sailing past on that icy deck, staring up at the giant island before her. It must've been so powerful, like Cleopatra arriving in Rome in the first century BC. She must've wondered who were these barbaric creatures who built these granite towers so high into the sky? Or those sailors and fur trappers who long ago went upriver into the dark and dangerous forests along the Hudson, looking for the ends of the earth, to plunder, to rape, to be free of kings and paupers. People here were not scared and poor like they were in Europe. These people were free. They were gods because, according to the histories written by the victors, America won this global World War, now known as Two, which for some 70 million departed souls and 20 million refugees looking for new homes had been an apocalypse — sealed when America dropped never-before-imagined atomic bombs on two Japanese cities. As 100,000 people burned, we danced in the New York streets in victorious joy as we knew that nobody — nothing — could stand up to America. We were the mightiest country ever — and the best!

My mother, like so many French, fell in love with the American movies of the 1930s. Their women — Crawford, Hepburn, Shearer, Garbo, Davis — became her role models. And when she read Margaret Mitchell's massive best-selling novel, majestically called *Gone With the Wind* (*Autant en Emporte le Vent*), she dreamed of seeing the 1939 movie all America was talking about, its timing perfect — a vision of pre-bellum America. Oh, to be Scarlett O'Hara, as embodied by Vivien Leigh; fiery and independent, she'd go through hell to keep her family's plantation, Tara. At first in love with her fiancé, the indecisive, noble southern aristocrat, Ashley, she'd fall for the outsider, the northerner Rhett Butler with not a trace of nobility, treating her like the spoiled child she was; he'd be embodied by her very favorite male, the mustached, grinning Clark Gable, the man's man of American cinema at its peak, its Golden Age vanishing (the movie not screening in France till 1950) just as the war engulfed Europe. Great creativity and great destruction grow side by side, needing each other — in all things.

My mother was a natural rebel, finishing at eighteen her baccalaureate at Sainte-Marie de Neuilly. Her parents' years of toil had saved enough to invest in a modest old five-floor hotel with forty rooms on the rue des Quatre Fils (Street of the Four Sons) in Le Marais, then hardly fashionable but one of the oldest sections of Paris. It was called "L'Hôtel d'Anvers — Tout le Confort Moderne," which meant a bathtub on each floor, hot water when ordered, and a sink and a bidet in each room. They'd rent the rooms on a long-term basis to middle-class locals and expatriates who'd fled other, poorer countries like Poland and Romania. My grandparents, "Mémé" and "Pépé," as they were called by the family, provided their only daughter the best of what they could, more than their only son. She had willpower, this girl, she wanted to rise above her class origins, and somehow she managed to wrangle a membership at the exclusive Racing Club of Paris in the Bois de Boulogne, where the favored of Parisian society were admitted.

Once there, Jacqueline Goddet rode and jumped horses, swam, played tennis, went ice-skating; she dated, went to movies, cafés. It's hard to really know who your mother is when you know her only from a certain age on, but there were hints in the old photo albums that she was "une coquette," as the French fondly call it, a young woman who enjoyed the attentions of several sophisticated men, whom the French termed "des boulevardiers." Mom told me several times of her dramatic shock at seventeen, when, preparing to go out, she wore lipstick for the first time, and Pépé, shocked by her audacity, whacked her hard across the cheek and made her wipe it off and stay home. In France, there was a lot of slapping and hitting of the young, which was acceptable then, but my mother never forgot this particular humiliation. Hewing to her mountain stock from the Savoie region of southeast France, she was tall and big-boned, healthy in the Ingrid Bergman mold, a real in-the-flesh beauty with a charismatic smile that, throughout her life, attracted many friends. Sometimes, it seemed to me, too many, but that's another story.

She wrote years later in the grandmother's book she prepared for my children: "My ambition was to be married. I was raised to be a good wife. — cooking-embroidery-languages — to run a house, etc. Very old-fashion. Help my mother, take care of the dogs, take care of my room and clothes, respecting them, have good manners. Be polite and nice to humble people, and stay simple at all times with a king or a servant." After graduating from the lycée, she enrolled at a cooking academy which later became famous, Le Cordon Bleu, and also took courses in "puericulture" — taking care of babies, the French way, "comme il faut": "the right way." Sometime in that period, she became the fiancée of a handsome young tennis champion at the Racing Club, from a good family in the commodities business; it was another step up to a better life, and her parents were very proud.

Her strapping, adventurous father, six-foot-two-inch Jacques Goddet, had moved up to Paris as an ambitious trainee in the cooking and hotel management field. By 1912, he made it to America as a sous-chef at the exclusive Waldorf-Astoria in New York City. But he returned home to take up arms against "les sales Boches" (the filthy German Huns) in what was then called "La Grande Guerre," which began as a Balkan operetta in 1914 but did not end till 1918 with half an entire French generation between eighteen and thirty-five killed or wounded in the most brutal slaughter ever witnessed. Pépé started at the Marne in '14 and served all the way through '18 in the trenches cooking for the troops. He'd tell me stories about the war, the gas attacks most vivid to me, when I was a child, sitting on his lap. He married my grandmother, Adele Pelet-Collet, from the same Savoie region, after the war, and they stayed inseparable for the rest of their lives.

The next generation of Germans, reaping their vengeance from the First War, marched into Paris that May of 1940, just as my mother was turning nineteen. A strict curfew was imposed, snuffing out any semblance of gaiety and nightlife. All supplies, especially of meat, were rationed; any gatherings of friends were discouraged; waiting in lines was commonplace; and perhaps worst of all, no real news of the outside world was allowed. The Germans were polite, cold, smart, and above all methodical; they scared the French. They came regularly to check the papers of her family's hotel guests, sniffing out the problematic ones, those of mixed blood and Jews. Her parents warned her repeatedly, "Don't ever talk to the Germans, cross to the other side of the street, make sure you always take your 'carte d'identité.'" Avoiding makeup, she wore clothes with no fashion sense and ugly cork-soled shoes. For four full years this went on. She despised the Germans as she would a disease, and one day she'd get her revenge for the lost years. By having fun. So much fun.

The tide of war began to shift in '43 with the shocking Soviet victory at Stalingrad. The Red Army began pushing the Germans back across Russia into eastern Europe, while the Allies bogged down in Italy. Finally, in June of '44, the Allies made their D-Day landing in western Europe and in August liberated Paris. The world was spinning suddenly on a new axis; all the rigid rules were being broken. With their money, nylons, cigarettes, and easy laughter, the Americans were gods to the poor French. But the war still had nine hard months to run, and with the Allies moving in from the west, and the Russians, at great cost, destroying the German war machine from the east and then taking Berlin block by block, the Nazi empire crumbled into ruins in May of '45.

In that month, on a day redolent of the smell of spring, my father, Lieutenant Colonel Louis Stone, saw my mother on a bicycle heading to her Racing Club in a city still free of automobiles. On an impulse — always the best way, I think — he took off after her on his own bike. Somewhere in the Bois de Boulogne he deliberately ran into her, apologizing and pretending to be lost, asking directions. I would've loved to have been there to record those first words. At five feet, ten inches in his impressive uniform with his bull-like carriage, dark good looks, and his gap-toothed, Gable-like insolence, he was hard to say no to for a romantic twenty-four-year-old French girl; as part of Eisenhower's staff in Paris at SHAEF (Supreme Headquarters Allied Expeditionary Forces), how could he not have an advantage over any native living on ration cards? Speaking a passable French, he was bold, insisting on meeting again, and managed to procure her street address, although she found him much older at thirty-five than her fiancé in his twenties.

Much to her surprise, on the following afternoon, in the days before telephones were realistically available, he came calling directly — very Rhett Butler — introducing himself to her surprised family, sweeping aside any protestations on her part of a fiancé. Next came gifts from the PX; he brought an entire ham, coffee, chocolate, as he totally charmed these French "peasants," who were most impressed that he was an officer on "le général Eisenhower's" staff. And because English was an easy language to acquire, as Churchill boasted, "to conquer the world," their daughter spoke just enough to communicate the basics of life with a charming accent, but not enough to share an interest in the other ideas that preoccupied my father's attention, such as finishing a war which he didn't think had really ended in 1945.

America was inheriting the world's strongest economy by far, undamaged by bombing, and was the clear moral victor. The Russians were disqualified by their strange language and supposed crude behaviors against the "civilized" German female population — as well as a long-standing distrust of their 1917 Bolshevik Revolution. My father, who'd worked on Wall Street before being assigned to the G-5 financial branch of SHAEF, was sent from France on to Germany. In 1943 he'd sympathized with the underdog struggles of our allies the Russians, who now were our co-occupiers of Germany. But by 1945, he was joining the old struggle against communism. He denounced the poverty-stricken Russians as "cheating bastards" who were probably counterfeiting our currency in massive quantities throughout western Europe; he later told me they'd stolen our printing plates. He began to believe in General Patton's unrequited ambition to push east against our "ally" to take Moscow and destroy communism once and for all. Many, though hardly all, shared this thinking but knew, if even achievable, it would've been at great cost and loss of life. The world was clearly beginning to divide, and my father naturally intended to stay on the right side of that rich-poor equation.

He later told me the French were "different" to him. He'd had girlfriends in New York, Washington, and London, but he found "les Françaises" more maternal, family-oriented, with their accents, their "savoir faire," and they knew the allure of a woman's perfume and clothes. Essentially, they dressed better than the English girls he'd known in London, who took wartime austerity as either an excuse or a vow. A French woman would always be vain enough to find a way to be wanted, and "look good." Back in Paris from Germany, wooing my mother, he was now thinking of his future. He was adamant; according to my mother, he told her bluntly, "I want you to be my wife. I waited thirty-five years to find you. I don't want to lose you." And with those words, a pear-shaped diamond of ten carats, rolled in a piece of silk paper, suddenly appeared out of his uniform pocket.

On my mother's side, if you're a respectable Catholic girl, engaged to an attractive young Frenchman of good family, you simply *do not* break your vow to marry and suddenly run off with an unknown American soldier to an unknown country. In later years, when I came to know her fiancé, Claude, I never sensed she loved him as he had loved her. And so, discarding the noble Ashley, Scarlett committed to Rhett six months after the close of the war, and in December 1945, Jacqueline Pauline Cézarine Goddet and Louis Stone (born Abraham Louis Silverstein) went ahead and made possibly the greatest mistake of their lives — to which I owe my existence — and were wed at the mayor's office in Paris. My mother wore a red dress from Jacques Fath with a coat of red wool lined with taffeta and a red feathered hat. The ceremony was attended by her family and American officers, as well as her fiancé, Claude, who she wrote "came hoping I'd change my mind." I'm sure her parents were concerned, as they really didn't know the American, but they did know their daughter well enough to recognize that, even if they were opposed, she'd roll over them. By this time, my mother's knowledge of English had improved significantly, if not her charming accent, which, her family and I noted over time, she managed to carry to her grave without any marked improvement.

They spent their magic first night at the Ritz Hotel in the Suite Royale with white flowers tied everywhere on the drapes, furniture, and chandelier; the white silk sheets were embroidered with their initials. They honeymooned, with the privileges of a high-ranking American officer, in the South of France, and then moved into the Hôtel San Régis in Paris, where I was probably conceived between café and croissants amid white, fluffy, good French linen. And in January '46, off they sailed for the New World with seventeen pieces of luggage, according to my mother, on a returning troopship with twenty thousand GIs — starring herself as the only female aboard, although she said she was a "stowaway." It sounds like a movie, but my father, who was adamantly honest about my mother's "exaggerations," confirmed this tale. It was a freezing winter, one of the worst in memory in a desolate Europe, and the voyage intolerable in the gales of the North Atlantic. The bride threw up ceaselessly for some twelve days, not yet registering that she was pregnant, but if your first consciousness is violent and storm-tossed, I'm sure notice was taken by her surprise visitor.

From the railing at Battery Park in 1976, now imagining thousands of cheering GIs on the ship making its way past the Statue, I could equally imagine my young mother wondering, in a kind of innocence, not only what future lay in store but who *really* was this man next to her whom she'd married and whose baby she was now carrying. She later told me she found America to be an overwhelming and strange place, that my father's Jewish family was "cold" and was unlike French families, where everybody knew almost everything about one another, because, for one thing, they were poorer and they shared smaller spaces, and their nature was open and emotional. My dad's people had "secrets" and they judged, she said. They'd come from an intellectual tradition; some had been learned rabbis in Poland, their offspring emigrating to New York in the 1840s, while his mother's people emerged from unknown parts of eastern Europe. They would pay "visits" to the East Side of Manhattan to see this French girl, Jacqueline, but they kept to themselves and their preferred Upper West Side.

So it was into this situation I was born on September 15, 1946, in a tempest of blood and pain. It was so difficult a birth, apparently, by way of forceps, that she'd never achieve it again — and I'm told I narrowly made it. Mom took a picture of me at six months beaming in her arms at the camera, where I seemed to be yelling "ba ba" or something similar; she later invented my dialogue in the picture — "Je suis fort!" (I am strong!) I was a happy baby, she said many times, even if I "looked Chinese." Dad being a nonpracticing Jew, and she a naughty Catholic, it was somehow right that I'd be raised Episcopalian in the American tradition, attending Sunday school until I was fourteen — rich, healthy, and loved.

For my father, whom I grew to know far more gradually than my mother, as fathers often wait to confide in their sons, the war was an especially intoxicating time, and as the years went on, he'd wistfully say they were "the best years of my life." Civilian life, the long forty years after World War II, could never match it. Born in 1910, he grew up in the 1920s into a rich manufacturing family in a new era of illegal "speakeasies," women liberated by the First World War, Babe Ruth, Jack Dempsey, and Lindbergh crossing the Atlantic. The four siblings, three male, one female, decided to change their family name from Silverstein to Stone, and were admitted, in spite of the Jewish quotas, to Princeton, Harvard, Yale (my father), and his sister to Wheaton. He was smart, mathematically inclined, and could write well. Being darkly handsome no doubt helped him.

The first of three major shocks imploded his life when, in October 1929, the stock market crashed. His father, Joshua Silverstein, had sold his

Star Skirt Company and invested the proceeds in the market on so much margin that his savings were quickly eroded, except for a few low-renting Harlem properties. Thus my father graduated in 1931 from Yale into the heart of this Depression and was fortunate to find a job, at $25 a week, as a floorwalker in a department store. He often told me how shaken he was by this sudden reversal of fortune, but in another year's time he'd found his way into a back-office research job on Wall Street, and by 1935–36 was licensed as a stockbroker. When the Second World War broke out, his connections secured him financial staff jobs in the army in Washington, DC, and then London in 1943. He continued to live quite a bachelor's life in these cities without commitments, affirmed by several telling pictures of him with attractive women, but clearly no one stood out. It was his tall, graceful mother whom, by all accounts, he loved deeply; in fact he adored her almost as a saint who bore five children (one died), each of whom she lavished her attention on.

In what became the second shock of his life, with no forewarning, his mother perished suddenly of a heart attack in her early fifties in 1941, when he was thirty-one. How it affected him I can tell only from the way he talked about her, which is to say, *never* with any detail. Given that we generally criticize our parents for perceived hurts at the least, it's quite surprising that about Matilda ("Tilly") Michaelson there was not a word, an anecdote, something human. Grief, such as he might have felt, was summarily rejected, I sense, as "self-pity," his emotions stunted at a deeper level than any of us ever knew. I believe a part of him died with her; a certain coldness, a remoteness that my mother and I both felt, ran through his heart. In my mother's memory, he never cried, not once over anything; he always seemed in control, the model of a father figure, and his mother sacred, distant. I don't think, for that reason, my mother would ever decipher the man she married.

In a poem from 1932, my father expressed his longing for something that would last and his belief that life's destiny was arbitrarily dark:

> "And Beauty, be it sight or sound or thought,
> Was never meant to be a lasting thing.
> It must be glimpsed, not stared at or embraced.

We will devise a way of ending it."
They did.
Their doctrine is perhaps all wise.
The man is thankful for his glimpse of beauty.
He goes his way, a vision in his eyes.

I believe the war saved my father from his darkness, allowing him to escape his past — for a while. But he'd always be tainted by his financial fears
born from the Depression. After the war, when the Republican Congress
came to power in the midterms of '46 on a "fear ticket" and the Cold War
was beginning, Dad turned against his earlier positive opinions of Russia and fought with many of his liberal Jewish friends who defended Roosevelt, who wanted a postwar peace enforced by the United Nations and
the "four policemen" (America, Russia, Britain, and, if united, China). My
father, on the contrary, despised Roosevelt with passion, forcefully arguing
that his New Deal had corrupted our society and not solved the unemployment problem — only the war had. And that in order to avoid another Depression, we had to keep fueling the military-industrial state that'd grown
so strong in 1941–1945. By the time of the Korean War of 1950–1953, his
argument was a given, and we never looked back after his hero and former
boss, Dwight Eisenhower, took office in '53 and the military numbers grew
more gigantic and irreversible. America had moved from a Hot War to a
Cold War with hardly a pause to reconsider. The unemployment fears of
the Depression were no longer a problem, and any opposition was buried
by J. Edgar Hoover, Joe McCarthy, Truman's loyalty oaths, and the nation-
alistic media.

In the following twenty years, until the end of the Vietnam War, even
when my father was making big money, he never really relaxed. He refused
to own anything if it could be rented — an apartment, a New York town
house, land, a painting, not even a car once leases became available. "I'm
just passing through, kiddo," or "Huckleberry," as he called me, after the
greatest creation of his favorite writer, Mark Twain. He particularly enjoyed Huck's drunken father scenes, possibly because of the father's complete irresponsibility; his favorite picture of himself as a young man was
one taken after he went missing for a few days and reappeared disheveled

and unshaven as a hobo. Perhaps that's why he didn't want to own any-thing; it involved Pride, which came before the Fall. "Into this world I came with nothing, and out of it, etc." — which included me, of course, his sole heir. "No one gets out of here alive" and "life's no bowl of cherries" were the dark maxims I heard throughout my youth.

Lest I give the wrong impression, my father did have a sharp, self-dep-recating Jewish sense of humor, and it was appreciated by many; he also could tell wonderful bedtime stories, the main character from his dark side being "Evil Simon" — I'd say a predecessor to Lemony Snicket — who could assume innumerable forms and disguises to come after me, at times kid-napping me; Evil Simon terrified me as much as the Russians. In any event, my father made it quite clear I shouldn't count on anything, as he presum-ably had before the '29 crash. He'd put me through college, as his father had done him, and that was it. Although he was devoutly secular and would ridicule the insular behavior of Brooklyn's Hassidic Jews — "Why can't they act like Americans!" — he was more Old Testament than he'd ever admit. If he drove the insecurity of this life into me early and often — combined, of course, with his terrorizing me about the Russians infiltrating the country — it was partly because, I believe, he feared I might adopt my mother's extravagant, "show-off" French mentality.

So then why did he marry his opposite? As a self-denying, discreet Jew in a white Anglo-Saxon-controlled society and a rational man under most circumstances, he must have known that marrying a French girl from "peasant" stock was a gamble. Or perhaps he recognized that marrying outside his tribe might paradoxically revitalize a tired gene base. His wife wasn't bringing family money, breeding, education, or business connec-tions to this union. She was outside the New York–Washington power structure that would come to dominate the world, and into which, even as a Jew, he could have penetrated with his Yale and military background. Mom was an outcast, a charming unknown to the high-powered women who decided these things. When I asked him why, Dad said quite candidly that he'd married her "because she'd make a good mother," and in so saying would never admit the possibility of his loving her, and if pressed, would actually confess with unsettling honesty, "The only woman I ever loved was Mother" — his own.

It was sex, not money, that derailed my father. Sex, in fact, was the bête noire of that World War II generation. The hypocrisies of modern life were dramatized in the cutting-edge plays of Arthur Miller, Tennessee Williams, William Inge, later Edward Albee, and in the novels of Salinger, Mailer, Bellow, Roth, Updike, James Jones, and others. In the New York world of the later 1960s I would come to know, divorces from long, traditional marriages became an acceptable, almost inevitable second act. My mother later told me she ignored the infidelities, but by 1949, around the time the Soviets blew up the American bubble of being the sole possessor of the atomic bomb, the balance of power also suddenly and dramatically shifted at our home when my father was found out. She claimed she broke a mop on his back, and they'd had a terrible fight. Exaggerated and wild things were said, but Mom, in repeating this mop story over the years, made sacred her revolt, a French revolutionary now declaring that her husband had betrayed her and their marriage — and that if he misbehaved this clumsily, other people must've known, and now that her humiliation was public for both of them, then things could no longer be as they were: "the king is dead . . ." She'd been rejected. It hurt her deeply, her American dream shattered. But of this I knew nothing.

As many do, she tried to make things better by having another child, which my father and I both wanted. But carrying me had taken a severe toll on her system, and late one night, when we were guests at a house in East Hampton, I heard a disturbance from downstairs. Through the banister I saw medics taking my mother to the hospital, and then, I believe, I saw an aborted and bloody fetus of five or six months being carried out in a blanket, but I cannot be sure, it was so like a horror film.

With my father continuing his wandering ways more discreetly, and my mother playing the plucky heroine — hadn't Scarlett also been rejected by Rhett? — she made the best of it. She decamped to France in the summers, sometimes with me when I wasn't sent to some camp with an Indian name on a freezing cold lake in Maine or upstate New York. In France in the '50s, my mother was treated like a movie star, bringing hard-to-find blue jeans, cosmetics, and electronics, and dropping me off with her parents in the peasant countryside east of Paris. Meanwhile, she'd be off to her richer friends' country houses outside Paris, or the South of France, where she tasted a life of European sensuality, which in time, with America's modern conveniences, would evolve into the new international "jet set."

My French grandparents were the antipode to my parents. I'd spend several summers with them. Mémé always seemed old to me, stout and warm in the way of women raised at the turn of the century, down-to-earth, her handkerchief often pressed to a stye over a drooping, watery eye, which shut down part of her vision. Mémé was usually worried about something — the upcoming dinner, the food available, money, or when it wasn't her daughter or son or one of the boarders, it was us — the grandchildren. "Quel souci!" was Mémé's version of "Oy vey! Now what!" Or a singsong "Oh la la! Qu'est ce qu'on va faire!" (What are we going to do!) And yet she always saved something special for us, "un p'tit bonbon" or two tucked away somewhere in her vast armoire of clothing, a tin of sweets or luxury chocolates, and sometimes a little pile of crisp paper francs with writers and soldiers colorfully printed on them — big, bold postwar money to send us happily to the movies or the comic book store.

Because there was not enough space in their cramped Paris hotel, as the favored one, "l'Américain," I'd sleep in Mémé's bed with Pépé, and she'd tell me stories of "le Loup," the wolf who haunted the rooftops of Paris — and could climb down chimneys while people were sleeping and, without the parents knowing, snatch an errant child right out of bed. France had a strong mythology of wolves; there'd supposedly been roving packs of them in the Middle Ages, and there still were rumors of them in the big forests. Invariably I would shiver and grab Mémé, as in the French fairy tale "Little Red Riding Hood" — remember what the young girl found when she arrived at her grandmother's house? I looked closer at Mémé. In the dark it was hard to see, but her mouth was certainly not a long, hairy snout with sharp, terrifying teeth. It was just Mémé, and her soft smile reassured me forever as she pressed me to her warm breasts. I could love her in ways more traditional than I could love my mother. It was simply that Mémé was always there for me, and Mom was . . . well, exciting but tempestuous and inconsistent.

Pépé was quick, in the French way, to spank misbehaving children, but now in his sixties would more often just growl like an old dog cozy by the fire. He was a loving man who, as I said, told me stories of the Great War.

The nature of life was accepted stoically by these two — and, I noticed, this was true of most of the French; they'd seen enough of war. What I've grown to love about older people is their indifference to passing time and style and ideas. That's the core strength that age gives us. Pépé was made better by Mémé, who stood by him, loyal to the end of their days. Together they were a rock. I never understood the observation I'd been told as a child — that a man may wander in his ways, but the woman must be firm in her allegiance — until much later in my life. Without a moral center — and it takes only one firm soul — there can be no strong family. And without family, we one and all suffer. I was to learn these hard lessons from my parents, whom I loved deeply.

It seemed when I was young, children from families with the means were stored with other children in schools, churches, camps, sitting down to meals at other tables and times than the adults, disciplined to be seen and not heard. And my mother, with her nervous temperament, could be as tough as her father had once been with her, which I believe shaped her strong and rebellious nature. It was the French way — "une bonne gifle" to my cheeks or my backside with a hard open hand, electrified by anger, could settle things very quickly with a misbehaving child. Strong, emotional words could be screamed, but they did clear the system without lingering guilt on either side. Several times over the years, my mother chased me around our apartment in a red rage, sometimes with a riding crop, and let me know who was boss. My father, though, was unable to raise a hand to me, but he could scold me harshly with words whenever he saw a C on my report card.

Many years later, Mom told my son a story that, when I was eight years old, I came to her crying, "You don't love me anymore!"

"Why do you say that, darling?" she asked.

"Because you don't spank me anymore."

She told my son, "You see, children like to be corrected and told wrong from right. Remember that for your own children." Like an addicted child, I missed my mother and loved her all the more, always watching for her return — or if I was lucky enough to spend time with her, then it was better at one or two in the morning, when she'd return from some party to give me a kiss good night. Emitting the overpowering allure of her perfume mixed with the alcohol she'd drunk, she'd cuddle with me, a sexy good night you see time and again in older European films but I see little of anymore. A Madonna and child portrait. My mother had a healthy, natural way about her, in sex and all matters. She'd walk around naked in her bedroom, and as a child, I'd see her often in the shower or on the toilet, no need to feel shame. After all, France had been so deprived during the war years — good soap was hard to come by, and showers were certainly an American luxury, along with amazing flush toilets — that intimacy in all things became habitual.

Thus my mother made me aware early that women were earthy human beings, and not the big-titted goddesses whose image so many men distort and fall prey to. Hers seemed a far healthier attitude than the repressed feelings in Anglo cultures. Yes, it's true, her "sexy" manner may have given me a hidden desire for my mother, but did it distort my values? Possibly I adored her too much, but I'd prefer this fate to the cold, queer dislike or distrust of women I see in some men. Nor was she ever the shrew out of Tennessee Williams plays — castrating, bossy, loud. Selfish and self-dramatizing, yes, passionate and punishing at times, but always with a sense of love. "I'm punishing you, but I love you" is human to me. "I'm punishing you because I love you" is not.

I'm convinced our intimacy repelled my father, who I doubt ever saw his mother naked. He didn't want to know more about women; he preferred them as fantasies in black nylons, although he enjoyed the company of women in social situations. And women, as I could tell in later years, certainly liked him.

I was sheltered from this ongoing dynamic the first fifteen years of my life. In my mind at least, the three of us were one — and the World was outside. I was loved by parents who clearly loved each other, and to make things even rosier, they were attractive, responsible adults with means. At primary school, I was so proud when my mother could actually find the time to come visit in her fashionable clothes — with that accent, asking questions of my teachers, the other, plainer mothers charmed to speak with her, and at the same time monstrously jealous of her style. Second grade, eighth grade, it didn't matter. When she showed up, the other kids noticed, every-one noticed. You couldn't miss Jacqueline Stone. In a movie, it would be Jeanne Moreau, with that animal warmth she shared with all. Yes, she was *there* for me, and yet she wasn't; it was more like she was on display. Later in life, I equated our relationship to "either a close-up or a long shot, rarely a medium shot."

But I'm being unfair because of what happened after. In those first fif-teen years, aside from a terrifying hospital operation, I had a blessed life; I wholeheartedly adored my sexy mother, trusted and respected, sometimes feared, my hardworking and loving father. I had complete access to two cultures, two languages, able to think and speak in both. I was able to read everything I wanted, and to devour as much of this new television as I could, and my mother often snuck me out of school to go to double fea-tures at the movies, which she adored, and then covered me with written excuses; in short, I could have my ice cream and toy soldiers too. I never could've surmounted the obstacles I'd face later without that fundamental sense of optimism instilled by my mother into my nature. It became a basis to face life.

All was still well, even when they sent me off, at fourteen, to freshman year at boarding school in an isolated Pennsylvania town where we were allowed to return home only at Thanksgiving, Christmas, spring break, and of course the long summers. This was the next step on the ladder I had to climb to reach the "right" levels of East Coast society. Trinity, my first school at 91st Street and Columbus Avenue in New York, was fine through the eighth grade but would never do for the secondary years — although most of my class stayed on there till college. The Hill School in Pennsyl-vania, by contrast, with five hundred boys going through stormy growth pains, was suddenly "serious," all hard discipline, nothing comfortable, sensual, or French. It had an American mindset, more like the marines in the sense of schoolwork and athletics, especially its famed wrestling and swimming programs. The motto of the school was "Whatsoever things are true," and unlike in primary school, cheating was dealt with harshly, and a significant percentage of the class, for one reason or another, was thrown out during my four years. We were up by 7 a.m., freezing in the winter, fixed hours for chapel and dining hall, poorhouse food, five classes each day till early afternoon, mandatory athletics, early dinner, then three to four hours of study, and lights out by 10 or, in the upper classes, 10:30.

Nothing I'd done at my previous school seemed good enough. I'd been spoiled by New York, and if I wanted to get into Yale, like my father, I had to grow up fast. So I lived for four years in anxiety about not being good enough. Though miserable in many ways, I was getting the hang of it by the middle of my sophomore year, when, in the winter of '62, I received the biggest shock of my life. It began with a cryptic note in my mailbox from our headmaster: "Your father called me. I'd like to see you at 2:30 today." He signed it "Ed Hall." He was a towering figure in our world, highly respected as a strong leader with Yale connections, as well as a macho image from coaching the hockey team. I was scared of him and had no desire to see him alone. He didn't know who I was. My grades were good, my demerits insignificant, yet something was obviously wrong. Why would my father call? Something to do with my mother? An accident? Could she be *dead*?

Long-distance communication was not simple then. From one of the two old phone booths in the school's main hall, I dialed my father's office. Mary, his faithful longtime secretary, was anxious, I could tell; I can always tell when something's off in a telephone voice. My father couldn't talk now. He was in "an important meeting," he'd call me tonight "from his hotel" — hotel! What was he doing in a hotel? Alarm bells were going off. Mary knew he'd spoken with my headmaster, and she asked if he'd seen me yet. It was getting worse every minute. I had no intention of going to see Ed Hall. I didn't want him to know anything about my personal life, especially if there was some failure in it. But my mother was okay — or Mary would've told me. It was something else.

My 2:30 appointment came and went. I was now officially "in trouble" because I was not showing up as told. Suffice it to say, my mind was a blur. I reached my godmother, Suzanne, who was also French, in New York within an hour or two. She'd known both my parents from the war and had always seemed well liked by both. She didn't tell me much, but enough to know it was serious, as I suspected. They were "separating." What did that mean — separating? Not final, then? Temporary? She wouldn't say more because she really didn't know more. My father would explain. I asked her, where was my mother? I'd called the house and no one was answering. Suzanne reassured me that Mom was okay, but she didn't know where she was now. It was the "now" that threw me. Yes, something had changed — and as I sensed, it was forever. All things change, I learned in time. And generally, if serious, they change for the worse.

Finally, I spoke with my father that evening at the hotel he was now staying in. It was a conversation, as I suspected, that would change my life. In hindsight, I see it now as the third and last great crisis of *his* life — the loss of security in '29, his mother's death in '41, and now this break in '62. He was sad, bewildered, stricken, not at all like himself — he was partially, only partially, in control. He asked if the headmaster had seen me. No, I told him. He paused.

"Oliver, your mother and I are getting a divorce."

That was enough. I heard the rest along the way, I'm not sure in what order.

"She hasn't been the same for a long time now."

"She's been crying every morning."

"She's in love with another man."

"I can't stand it any longer."

"I don't know where she is right now, but I think she's going to France for a while. She'll call you, I'm sure" — but he wasn't really sure.

"Who, who is this man?"

"A hairdresser she knows. Miles Gabel."

This was simply unbelievable! Miles was my mother's "friend." I'd spent part of the previous summer with him. Dad had rented a modern house in West Hampton with a big lawn, a pool, tennis court. Miles had been a hairdresser before, but now, with Mom's help, had set himself up as a photographer with a small studio. He was a thirty-five-year-old man whom I'd come to really like that summer — movie star handsome, dark, dangerous, Siamese green eyes, earthy Queens Jewish accent, he loved life, women, dogs, his MG, and his beloved camera. He'd become an older brother to me, a link between my generation and my parents'. As my father stayed mostly in the city that summer, Miles would come out for stretches of time as a "houseguest," Mom conspiratorially telling me not to mention this because "your father doesn't like him"; I understood this explanation because

Mom often liked people whom Dad didn't like. It'd been such an exciting summer. Miles, who'd once been a lifeguard, was the physical father I never had, building me up in the ways of men, teaching me how to work out and lift weights and how to handle girls — *but fucking my mother?* It never once occurred to me; they were *friends!*

"He's a bum!" my father's voice rose emotionally. Miles's temper was volcanic, my father said, unpredictable — he'd hit my mother. There'd been one time, yes, when I'd noticed a bruise on her face. My father went on. Mom was giving Miles money — Dad's money. He was a "gigolo." It'd been going on now for almost two years! Mom was acting wildly, crying each morning because she was "in love with this guy." There was nothing Dad could do about it, it made him sick. He'd given her so many chances to get him out of her life, but she couldn't. It was as if he realized, for the first time, that he'd lost my mother's heart and couldn't believe it, couldn't accept that it might have been through his own negligence. Now his decision was set, and everything I'd believed up till then about my life — that there could be security, love, and happiness between people — turned out to be a lie. There was no more love in Dad for Mom, I knew that on the phone. His mind was made up. He wanted me, but didn't want her anymore. He'd now keep the "family" idea going only because of me — their only child. Now that I'd reached "the age of reason," I was presumably old enough to understand these things. Perhaps that was why they'd sent me to boarding school, they'd sensed this was coming.

He told me the town house — our home — had already been sublet to the founder of a huge cosmetics company, whom he knew; all my things, my personal items, pictures, baseball cards, comic books from years past, toy soldiers, had been moved out of my bedroom in boxes. I found out later that my mother had been "locked out," her credit cards canceled.

The divorce was settled over the next few months while I stayed in school, custody of me going to my father as the responsible party, as my mother had no means of support, and, most damningly, had been profiled in a psychiatric report, agreed to by her. My dad later told me the psychiatrist had described my mother as "still a child, living in a fantasy world, quite unable to function as an adult with a child."

Mom never spoke of this psychiatrist. But she later told me the ends to which my father went to obtain the divorce, including hiring a private investigator to track her in Los Angeles, where he'd sent her to "recover her senses." He set her up at the Beverly Hills Hotel, and the detective hired a photographer, who got pictures of my mother and Miles, who'd secretly accompanied her, together in the hotel room. The blackmail worked, and she acquiesced to the settlement terms he offered. My mother's Scarlett O'Hara prewar fantasy had come true in ways she'd never envisioned. Her home — Tara — was wrecked. She was wiped out, but she'd get up on her feet again, and she'd get it back! But not now.

Yet neither of them could come and tell me any of this in person? It was bizarre, hearing it all long-distance. Couldn't my dad take a day, or two, and come down and see me? Or bring me to the city in person? The headmaster had told him it was not a good idea with the workloads the students carried, that I'd get too far behind or something like that. Dad said he was worried for me, yes, but he'd explain everything in detail in three weeks' time at my spring break; he'd arrange a trip for the two of us to Florida, where we'd play tennis, be "bachelors" together, we'd talk, and we'd bond. And my mother would quietly recede to the edges of my life — a marginalized semi-adult.

But where was my mother? She hadn't even called. She'd tell me later she was in shock; everything in her world had crumbled so suddenly. She was "embarrassed." She didn't have any money, and had to borrow $1,000 from a close friend. As I'd seen in the movies with Lana Turner or Joan Crawford, Mom was now a woman living in shame. In another century she'd have had a scarlet letter on her breast. Most of my parents' respectable New York business community friends dropped her. Increasingly, she replaced them with new friends of her own, society's outcasts — artists, fashion people, "faggots" then, gays now, divorcées, libertines, friends from Europe who wouldn't judge her by American standards. She ended up returning to France for six months each year to be in their company — and also, so I gather, to avoid some taxes in the United States that my father would otherwise have had to pay. It made sense for him to keep her abroad.

But it was all really a lie. Dad, I found out, had been having affairs since the marriage began — with models, the wives of several of their friends, hookers, and even our chunky Swiss housekeeper/nanny when I was a boy of seven or so ... which my mother said she knew about; she eventually told me stories of all those "girlfriends" who came to our house for dinner parties or canasta or bridge games, or were at the country houses where we were hosted, or the "old friends" from the war — Dad had fucked them *all,* it seemed! He was a satyr. Even so, my mother was "liberal," not a scold. She was French, they understood "l'amour." Men had that thirst in them, and to go against it and make a public scandal was ridiculous — as well as "against nature." I gathered later from her own partners that my mother was naturally expressive and experimental in sex, exploring lesbianism among other adventures. But for my father, aside from some threesomes (two women, one man) he asked her to participate in, the sex with his wife wore off, as sex generally does, and he'd return to his chosen archetype of the tall, cold, leggy fashion model from the 1940s. He didn't want his sex too realistic or too earthy; he preferred cerebral fantasies, which I guess is another way of saying my father never really let my mother fully into his heart.

It was a time of Billy Wilder's Oscar-winning *The Apartment* (1960), which uncovered cynical truths Americans were not yet comfortable in admitting. Mom, on her side of the equation, instead of discreetly having an affair with a younger man or woman, as some of her married friends did, actually had to go and fall in love with and support this young aspiring photographer. And she was emotionally way too honest to hide her feelings — and now, as a result, at forty-one, her life was falling apart faster than she could control.

Why, I still wonder, didn't my mother put her taste and talent to work earlier in her life? She'd been ambitious as a girl to always better herself. From a Savoie peasant girl, she'd become a sophisticated woman of the world — in Manhattan, no less. She organized for charities and was also a wonderful cook, hostess, and housekeeper who knew how to do the things she'd hire others to do. She was practical, could fix things, and could be counted on to find a baseball lost in the bushes. She'd gone to interior decorating school in the early '50s but, after two years of study, never followed up; she said once, "I'm sorry I didn't go through with it. I had talent." But again and again, she helped her friends decorate their houses without asking to be compensated. She cared about fashion, dispensing sought-after advice to several known designers. She had painters, actors, writers as good friends; she had taste in everything — in art, parties, houses, cooking, design — but not in lovers apparently.

But she'd tried, I believe. As she wrote in her grandma book, she'd always wanted to "be a good wife, to run a house, very old-fashion." And I believe she would've been, if my father had been like her father — had been straight and true with his heart, which he was not. He was twisted. The truth is Scarlett tried to keep her side of the bargain, but Rhett, for his reasons, let her down in the end. And the door closed on her when she tried to make things work with younger, sexy men.

In the big picture, which no one really thinks about in the middle of a storm, it was the end of a family. I had no brother or sister to share the blow with. We were suddenly three different people in three different places, and if my parents didn't even care enough about me to see me or pull me out of school, then what did I really matter to them? Well, then, I'd make myself matter to me — *somehow.* I'd have to become harder now, be on my own, not give in to grief or weakness or self-pity. I was also deeply ashamed. Something was wrong with me, considering that most of my classmates had solid families; very few divorces occurred outside the East Coast big city world, and for the most part, these were the "troubled" students who most often were expelled. The very next day, I was further embarrassed to be bawled out by Headmaster Hall for not respecting our appointment time. His consolation was telling me to find my "character" and overcome this adversity.

Three weeks later in Florida, I received one more tremendous shock. My father, reliving his Great Depression moment, told me flatly, disgusted, that he was "broke" and "$100,000 in debt," which was a great deal of money then — and he blamed it on Mom, who'd seriously overspent, "pretending she was rich, always pretending to be something she was not." He'd objected so many times, so many arguments, but it did no good. But I wasn't to worry. He'd go on working, making a living, pay this off, and have enough to put me through college.

Mom would later defend herself, saying, "Your father was small. I made him think big. Lou made more money with me than he ever made. I introduced him to rich people; we had to entertain — to show them they could have confidence in your father." This was only partly true, as Dad did have his own clients, some quite substantial. Mom began thinking of the marriage as the failure of an experiment that Dad didn't have the courage to carry through with. "If only Lou had taken the chance and bought things instead of always renting them," she said despairingly, he might've emerged on the other side as a big man in New York society. But I'm not sure he had that in him, or that he would've been happy in that role; later in life, he echoed my mother's sentiment: "I'm a small man, kiddo, never was a big one."

This profoundly affected me, because he was past the age of struggle — and seeing things differently. So Mom was right in a certain way, and he was terrified in another. And insofar as I hadn't even been able to identify the phenomenon of a young man fucking my mother while I was sleeping in the other room, inured to all the signals, what could I ever trust myself to know? My naïveté at fifteen stupefies me. It's a story that's taken me a long time to process, if indeed I have. It's a consciousness that is shared by most children of divorce. That our lives, our being itself, is the creation of many lies. If my parents had truly known each other before they were married, they would never have united, and I would never have existed. Children like me are born out of that original lie, and living a false front, we suffer for it when we feel that nothing and nobody can ever be trusted again. Adults become dangerous. Reality becomes loneliness. Love either does not exist or cannot survive. And my past, my fifteen years on earth, was a "fake past" — a delusion.

In November 1963, my last year at Hill School, President Kennedy was assassinated. All of us watching the black-and-white TVs, stunned, understanding nothing but the surface of things, the explanations handed down to us by our chief priests. Nor did we have any concept of the changes going on in America's foreign policy as we moved closer to a war in Asia. After four long years, I felt like an overworked clerk, always under obligation to do what I was told rather than having a genuine curiosity over any subject matter. I was more robot than human, with excellent grades and varsity letters in grueling cross-country in the fall and gentlemanly tennis in the spring — and thus, with relief more than joy, I was admitted to Yale, my father's alma mater. To which I went in the fall of 1964 and . . . oh, it's difficult to explain why you come to a full stop. High achievement was expected of me; it was bred into my bones. American life is geared to upward motion; the only response to adversity I knew was "Never Give Up. Never. Never." But suddenly I did — because I was "burned out" but didn't even know it. You never do, as the psychological aspects of stress in those days were not acknowledged. I had no one I could talk to, no one I trusted. My father would only think it a lapse that could be corrected. And my mother . . . ? Truly, I needed her then, because I had no place to lay my heart down and I was scared, more scared than I'd ever been — and lonely. But at that place and time, I was hardened against her as a weakling who'd betrayed our family.

I negotiated with the dean at Yale to take a year off, something that was rare then. On a bulletin board was an offer from a Catholic Church group in Taiwan, strongly anticommunist, which had a school in Vietnam that needed teachers. As long as I could get myself there, the salary was low but livable. My father, devastated, nonetheless accepted my desire to go, assuming I'd return to Yale.

So in June 1965 I began teaching several large classes of English-speaking high school students in Cholon, an overcrowded Chinese suburb of Saigon. I'd never seen so many people in my life, every inch of space taken, squabbled over, prized — faces, smells, sex, and a mindset wholly different from the American one. Meanwhile, US military were filtering into the city in larger groups as the war expanded. Terror-bombing attacks were on the rise, but life was pretty good in general, as I whipped around on my motor scooter to all kinds of strange places at night without fear. I grew a beard and got as far away from the person I'd been as I could.

After six months and two school terms, I resigned and traveled alone around Cambodia, Thailand, and Laos, then joined the merchant marine back in Saigon. I'd always been fascinated by the sea from literature, and in those days they'd book non-union personnel out of foreign ports to replace crew members who'd go missing in war zones in search of higher contractor pay, or a woman, or whatever. My job was that of a "wiper," which is the lowest skill on the ship and the dirtiest down in the engine room, blowing boilers twice a day and cleaning out the gunk.

I traveled back to the States on a hard, storm-tossed thirty-seven-day voyage, which killed any further desire to go to sea. And once on dry land in Oregon, with my savings I took off for Mexico, where I holed up in a hotel room in Guadalajara. Here, to my surprise, I began writing day and night, in longhand, about all my new experiences. Really, I was pouring out my innermost feelings, because I *had* to. They flooded out of me like tears, beautiful, long, lush, looping sentences calling attention to myself — me! For the first time in my life, I existed not as someone else's projection but as a person who was *right there* — on paper at least.

This was a glorious release, the strongest emotions I'd ever had. Rarely leaving my monk's cell in that small hotel with a flowered balcony overlooking a church, an alley, and a barking dog, I spent the next four weeks vomiting up a raw two-hundred-page semiautobiographical "cry in the night" from the perspective of a young man. I called it "A Child's Night Dream," and it read big and bold, and feverish like a dream; certainly pretentious in areas, but confirming an independent existence.

Reading much of the literature that I'd missed as a young man, I reentered Yale in September of '66. But my heart was not in it. My interest in this parallel universe outside New Haven had only deepened, and I kept at my novel with the same fervor I originally felt in Mexico. My course load of six classes seemed to slip away as I sat in my room most of the day and shaped what I'd written in blood into a more organized second draft.

So when the midterms came around, another dean called me in to inquire if something was wrong. After all, there was no record of my attendance at any of my classes. He presented me a document, and I remember staring at a long column of F's — or was it zeros? I'd reached another breaking point, a terrifying choice I had to make. I can still hear the clock on the wall in his office ticking on this dreary fall afternoon, and the shouts of young men playing touch football in the distance. I could get to work right away and make it up, the dean said, or I could withdraw for a second and final time from Yale; but this time I could never come back. I imagined my father's anger about both the tuition money gone up in smoke and my clear failure of will to become a Yale man and join the societal mainstream.

It's a moment I'll never forget. In a resigned voice I nodded to the dean and said, "I'll leave." He was surprised and asked me if I was sure, and I repeated what I'd said. I couldn't waste words. I was numb, depressed. I didn't know what I wanted to do as much as I knew what I *didn't* want — and that was to be my father, whom I loved — but destiny is never clear when it arrives. Sometimes we just refuse to do what we no longer feel good about doing. These moments are mysteries in our lives, but we know everything will change.

With Dad's grudging consent (what else could he do?) I returned to New York and, in my bedroom at his apartment hotel, feverishly kept writing, praying in my heart to be delivered from this self-imposed hell by a publisher who'd accept the book. I was just twenty, and I worked ceaselessly and guiltily to show Dad my resolve, and within three more painful months, my book was two hundred pages longer. On the streets in midtown Manhattan, I'd depressingly see people hustling, making all kinds of money in a new era of prosperity, and here I was into my own solitary narcissism. I hated myself for doing this. But I was after something else and it was important, but what?

The novel went out through a friend of my father's to, I believe, two potential publishers. One replied in the negative right away, but surprisingly, the esteemed Robert Gottlieb at Simon & Schuster considered it carefully for several weeks, or so I'm told. In his decision, I thought, lay the balance of my life; if he said yes, I'd happily become a novelist in New York, and I'd stay.

When he finally said no — well, I'd expected that, but I took it very hard as a sign of my lack of worth. I'd overreached, flown too close to the sun, like Icarus, writing selfishly on and on about myself. I was filled with exaggerated shame and self-loathing. I gave up on myself, romantically assuming my heart was "broken," however it is that a heart "breaks"; there were very dark thoughts propelling me, something stronger than me. Those of you who remember what it's like being nineteen or twenty will recognize it as a dangerous time, even if adults in those days didn't take adolescence seriously. If I didn't have the courage to take my own life, perhaps God, in whom I was raised to believe, would take it for me in payment for my "sin" of hubris.

That's why I went back to Vietnam in the US Infantry — to take part in this war of my generation. Let God decide. I "volunteered for the draft" in April of '67, which was a way to go into the army as a draftee and spend two years instead of the three required of regular army. Nor did I want any special treatment, specifically insisting on infantry in Vietnam at the lowest possible level—as a private, rejecting Officer Training School, which would've delayed my wishes by several months. I was in a rush to get to the front lines before this war was over, which the media were telling us would happen soon. I wanted to be like everybody else, an anonymous infantryman, cannon fodder, down there in the muck with the masses I'd read about in John Dos Passos. My mother and father were truly puzzled but not overly worried, as, given their life experiences, Vietnam did not seem like a real war to them.

After six months of basic and advanced infantry training at Fort Jackson, South Carolina, on the eve of September 15, 1967, I was shipped back to Vietnam . . . to find my answers. Ironically, my twenty-first birthday vanished into the blue Pacific when the clock skipped forward at the international date line to the sixteenth of September.

It'd be a long journey before I'd return. None of us, when we went, reckoned with the aftereffects. Odysseus thought he would return home when he left Ithaca. I wasn't sure of anything . . .

The long, exhausting day was now setting over the New Jersey wastelands, a murmur of excitement stealing over the crowd, the temperature cooling just enough to leave the humidity sticky and sexy. The first fireworks shot out over the piers to the extended "oohs" and "ahhs" of the moms and dads, their children screaming above it all. BOOM! POW! POP! POP! "Oh, Say Can You See!" America at war. Kicking ass. Two hundred years old! The Tall Ships were now sailing in the glow of red, green, blue, white, and purple lights riding the shoulders of the past, the great cult goddess Liberty holding her torch at the center.

It was so beautiful. The populace adoring the soft pop of giant pyrotechnic flowers exploding into all shapes and sizes, fingers reaching down from the heavens in ecstatic glory. I wanted to believe like them, the million people around me, but I didn't feel it. I felt the awe, but also a profound terror. Because I'd been here before. On a night like this, I'd seen the most spectacular fireworks of all—the real thing. An all-night battle where the artillery, the gunships, the tracers, the bombs never let up — not once — from midnight to dawn. And in the flash of those explosions, I saw bodies in such extremes of rigor mortis, they could've been sculpted by Michelangelo. Such power, so much death in one place at one time. Never to be forgotten.

2

Strange Days

Nineteen sixty-eight was a year most people of my generation remember. For us, it started with a real bang on January 1. We'd been out patrolling on the Cambodian border for close to two weeks, chasing Apaches without much luck. We never saw more than two of them at the same time. We called them "gooks" because we feared or hated them, sight unseen. But we knew they were there, because we were finding stores of weapons, rice, maps, "order of battle" paperwork — but never "them." We were locking into a two-battalion perimeter, about a thousand to twelve hundred active troops, which is a big deal because we were in a hot zone interdicting North Vietnamese Army trails coming from Laos through Cambodia toward Saigon, the capital, 150 kilometers to our southeast; in fact, we were right in the enemy's crosshairs but had no idea.

We dug our foxholes on the edges of the jungle, leaving a large treeless area in our center for our helicopter pad and a heavily bunkered battalion command post with wires and antennae running off it and mortar pits dug around it with heavy sandbagging. Surprisingly, we had armored personnel carriers (APCs) and powerful M24 tanks parked in the tree lines on only half of the perimeter, our infantry on the other half. I didn't understand the strategy, but in the army, you don't want to think about these things too much or you get in trouble. I mean, why not spread out the APCs evenly over the 360° perimeter so that the infantry would be supported? But I didn't go to West Point, and I guess we had so much firepower even with this configuration, it didn't matter. There was some kind of truce going on because it was our calendar's New Year. And actually, the previous night, New Year's Eve, we'd gotten loaded, four of us in a foxhole, on whiskey and beer, which was a rare event "in the field." Today we were hung over, and were pulling inner-perimeter duty, which is a way of saying "take a night off."

With the light softening toward the end of day, our night ambush patrol headed out, about ten to twelve men; nothing was expected, as the truce was still in effect. The onset of evening was always a peaceful time, some food, rest, chores mostly done, foxholes dug and sandbags filled; it'd be a time to reread our mail from home, which had been delivered for the holidays.

It started not long after we were chowing down on hot food instead of the usual cold C rations. The unmistakable pop and rattle of distant fire coming from the same direction our ambush unit had taken, now maybe five hundred yards out, told us immediately that something was wrong — somebody was shooting, somebody hadn't heard about this truce. And when the firing went on and on, we knew it was serious. But we couldn't make out the radio noise, and before long, the firing dropped off — to silence. Information was relayed to our command post but rarely came back to us.

About fifteen minutes later, to the south and east sides of the perimeter, something was sighted moving toward us — "Tango two come in," we heard from a whispery, unidentified voice on the radio. "We got movement out there." Then nothing. A mystery sound of static. After all, this was the jungle. But where were they? The enemy never made a frontal attack, much less at night; we had too much firepower in the perimeter. It wasn't their style. Nonetheless, we grew anxious, thinking ourselves surrounded; the mind goes quickly to these things. Then suddenly, from twenty or more miles away came the whistle of 155mm shells out of our howitzers, spinning and whirring toward us and then hurtling down just over us — exploding out there somewhere, not very far. But still no signs of them. Reports of small arms fire seemed to be picking up at certain spots in the perimeter, yet it was hard to tell if it was incoming or outgoing — us or them. A crucial signal.

Directly across the perimeter, about two to three hundred yards away, the loud bark of a 50-caliber machine gun on an APC jumped us. Had they seen, heard something? More firing now from another sector. Rumors spreading on the radio — "Movement spotted in the perimeter! Two! Three . . . Victor Charlies, between Bravo and Charlie Company, can you see them, out . . ." Where? The thought of them inside our lines was terrifying.

A human shape was approaching our position. Couldn't see his face. A dark silhouette, moving cautiously. Too big to be one of them — or not? He called out something . . . his platoon, name, rank. We guided him in. A sergeant. He tried to sound calm, but he wasn't. "You see anyone coming through here, password is . . ." I forgot what it was. Before moving on to the next position, he said something like "We're gonna fire some beehive rounds, so stay low." And then he ominously added, "I heard they're hand-to-hand down at Charlie Company. Stay alert." We looked. Charlie Company was maybe three hundred yards to our side, which in the dark is a long way. The sergeant ran on. "Hand-to-hand" meant close — close enough to see them — bursts of fire, grenades, entrenching tools. Eye to eye. Jesus. And beehive rounds were designed to stop human wave attacks. When fired, a thousand pellets would spread like shotgun blasts and, coming from a tank, carried the sonic power of a pressurized bomb that could sweep men off their feet. What the fuck was going on! No one was saying.

The firing was picking up elsewhere in the perimeter, but not around us. An hour, maybe forty-five minutes crawled by, and then "Puff the Magic Dragon" arrived. The giant CH-47 helicopter, with 50-caliber machine guns and rockets firing from all its pockets, sailed overhead, spitting red tracer fire. The drilling noise it made was intense, otherworldly, like the roar of some ancient monster.

As I struggle to piece together the chronological events, we were finally ordered to move out to reinforce another position. On command, a group of us assembled and began humping across the inner perimeter. Flares were by now lighting most of the sky to a sort of moonlit day effect, making us visible targets. There were more and more explosions in all directions; it was nearly impossible to hear anything. But at that point I heard the blast first because it was so loud, then felt the beehive round coming from a tank behind us, maybe a hundred yards away. Why? It didn't matter why — someone fucked up! It engulfed us like a giant wave that swept us maybe ten or twenty yards through the air, maybe more. I blacked out, but I have no idea for how long, much less where I landed.

Moments later — again, perhaps five, ten minutes, perhaps longer, I'll never know — I woke as if inside a dream. I was probably concussed, but I didn't know that either. I struggled to my feet, couldn't see anybody from my group. But I was moving all right, no blood I could see, nothing broken. I felt I was okay, although a week earlier, I'd seen a man in my platoon walk into a medevac chopper, wounded in the gut, relieved to be getting out of the bush, and then the next day we heard he'd died from "internal bleeding," a form of death I'd never imagined. And the poor man thought he was lucky.

Rifle in hand, I was running toward an area I thought I recognized from the daytime. The jiggling sound of my equipment was banging loudly in my ears. There were more distant explosions now, one right after the other. Who knew what was happening? I'm not sure anyone did. I finally ran up on somebody from my company who was screaming, but I could barely hear, probably because my eardrums had been stunned by the beehive.

I was ordered to head into the jungle with two or three others to reinforce another section of the perimeter. There we found a soldier in his foxhole, alone, without a helmet, who was really scared, maybe in shock, yelling, pointing, "I seen 'em! They're here." But where? What time was it? Someone said "two" — middle of the night. It seemed that a few minutes ago, it was ten.

And now there was an enormous roar, like I suppose the end of the world sounds. So quickly, like a shark cutting through water, an F-16 jet fighter was coming in very low over our perimeter out of the lit night sky. So low, that doomsday sound — we were all going to die. This was crazy — they were going to drop their payload on us! I jumped into the scared man's foxhole and buried myself as deep as I could in the earth, which trembled and shook as a five-hundred-pound bomb dropped somewhere close. Somebody was being shredded to pieces, my God! There's nothing quite like a five-hundred-pound bomb to terrify any human being.

There was nothing for me to do really except stay alive. Our greatest fear was encountering a North Vietnamese shoulder-fired RPG, which could take out any of our bunkers from twenty to fifty yards out. I'd already seen bodies torn up by their RPGs; we were all scared of them, partly because we had no similarly efficient shoulder-fired rocket, and for that matter, their AK-47s were better than our toylike M16s. There were phosphorus shells from our artillery now hitting the jungle, burning white fire, incinerating trees and bushes and whatever stood in their path. The smell was chemical and horrific. Still no one. Then suddenly, the noise subsided. It was eerie.

The quiet continued for some time with occasional sounds of distant rifle and machine gun fire, but the volume was dropping off. What time was it? Around four? How could it be? It'd just been two. The next hour hung there in the torpor, the sweat of the jungle. Nothing. Nobody moving. Soldiers, dazed, appeared here and there. Some quietly talking. Daylight reasserted itself slowly, as if unsure. There's *been* a battle. "They'd" been here, that's for sure, but I hadn't seen a single one of them.

And then, I believe, we were moving back toward our platoon command post just inside the perimeter. Helicopters were coming in to evacuate the wounded, who were far more than I'd imagined — maybe 150 or more men taken out in various stages of distress — as well as our dead, they said about twenty-five, but I didn't see them. Though I think I was still concussed, I was assigned to "recon" the perimeter and bury the "gooks," who were beginning to stink up the jungle with that awful intimate smell all of us could recognize.

Full daylight revealed charred bodies, dusty napalm, and gray trees. Men who died grimacing, in frozen positions, some of them still standing or kneeling in rigor mortis, white chemical death on their faces. Dead, so dead. Some covered in white ash, some burned black. Their expressions, if they could still be seen, were overtaken with anguish or horror. How do you die like this? Charging forward in a hailstorm of death into these bombs and artillery. Why? Were you terrified, or were you jacked out of your fucking mind? What kind of death did you achieve? It was frightening to contemplate, and yet, I wasn't scared. It was exciting. It was as if I'd passed on from this world and was somewhere where the light was being specially displayed to me in a preview of another life. Soldiers might say it was hell, but I saw it as divine; the closest man would ever come to the Holy Spirit was to witness and survive this great, destructive energy.

In the next hours I grasped the extent of what had happened. Most of the dead were fully uniformed, well-armed North Vietnamese regulars. Some said they were Chinese troops disguised as NVA, but I didn't think so; they looked Vietnamese. Those who were relatively intact we brought in on litters, walking out some fifty to a hundred yards to find them, or pieces of them. A bulldozer had been airlifted in to dig mass burial pits. I helped throw the bloating bodies into the giant pits late into that day. The gaseous stink was so bad, even covering our noses and mouths with bandannas made little difference. There were maybe four hundred of their dead. We worked in rotating shifts, two men, three men, swinging the corpses like a haul of fish from the sea. Later we poured gasoline on them, and then the bulldozers rolled mounds of dirt over them, so they'd be forever extinct.

No person should ever have to witness so much death. I really was too young to understand, and thus I erased much of it, remembering it in this strange way as a stunningly beautiful night full of fireworks, in which I hadn't seen a single enemy, been fired on, or fired at anyone. It'd been like a dream through which I'd walked unharmed, grateful of course, but numb and puzzled by it all. It reminded me of passages in Homer of gods and goddesses coming down from Mount Olympus to the bloody battlefields at Troy to help their favorites, wrapping a mist or cloak around them and winging them to safety.

Almost a year later, in November 1968, I left Vietnam. By this time I'd served in three different combat units in the 25th Infantry in the southern sector of the country and in the 1st Cavalry Division in the northern sector. I'd been wounded and evacuated twice — the first a piece of shrapnel (or possibly a bullet) clean through my neck, nearly severing my jugular in a night ambush; the second a daylight enemy ambush where the shrapnel from a satchel charge planted in a tree penetrated my legs and buttocks. In another firefight, I was awarded a Bronze Star for heroism, which I'll come to later. I'd been in some twenty-five or more helicopter assaults, been promoted to Specialist 4th Class, and although I was experienced, I tried to avoid any higher responsibility such as taking charge of a squad. I extended my tour three months, on the front lines in the 1st Cavalry, so I could be discharged three months shy of my two-year obligation, which meant I wouldn't have to do six months of stateside duty. Some in my platoon thought this was a foolish risk to take, but I hated the army's rules and regulations so much that I preferred the danger and freedom of the jungle. I also became a devotee of the powerful Vietnamese weed I discovered there with, for the most part, my fellow black soldiers, who baptized me into a new way of thinking and seeing; of that too, later.

They finally released me at Fort Lewis, Washington, where I was made a civilian again, and I really thought going home was the end of it, the beginning of something else. What would I do now? Go back to college? I'd taken some correspondence courses in the army. There was talk with a Tennessee buddy still over there of putting together a construction company, big talk. But first I'd relax a little.

Suddenly on my own, in a khaki uniform, I took the Greyhound bus south with a duffel bag and a lot of cash and walked aimlessly around San Francisco, as if looking at everything for the first time. Suddenly I missed my companions from the army. I don't think any of us ever reckoned with coming home. I took LSD in Santa Cruz, bused down to Los Angeles, and, after several dreamy, stoned days, crossed into Tijuana, terrified already of the country I'd just returned to. I was quite alone — no direction home. I hadn't called my father or mother, anyone. I was happy to "disappear." No one could get ahold of me. I didn't want to think. All I wanted to do was party, drink, and find myself a Mexican woman, like any sailor or soldier boy. With a two-ounce bag of strong Vietnamese weed I was carrying, I was feeling no pain, top of the world, no fucking officers or sergeants to tell me what to do anymore, never again — free! And stupid. One night, after midnight, I grew depressed and bored with the seedy Tijuana scene and, gathering my few belongings, wandered back across the border into the US. What was I thinking? Did I have a screw loose? I did. I was only twenty-three.

At the near empty border crossing, an old, nervous customs agent asked me to step into the station. It must've been easy — I looked the part. Had I drunk too much beer? Did I not remember there were rules, even in civilian life? Within an hour I was handcuffed to a chair, being interrogated by two FBI agents who were fresh after my collaborators in this smuggling scheme I was working out of Mexico. Clearly, I should have left the damn Vietnamese weed in some footlocker in the US. But then again, I wasn't thinking too much, and hardly knew where I was going next. Maybe I'd just keep wandering south in Mexico. I didn't know.

They knew. Within a day or two I was processed into the downtown San Diego County Jail with a capacity of about two thousand beds, but which was now occupied by around four to five thousand mostly tough black and Hispanic kids, many of them gang members, jammed into this overcrowded space; many of them were still waiting for trial after six months inside. No money, no bail, nothing. Within a few days, I was chained to eight or nine other young guys, marched in our prison uniforms through downtown San Diego streets, eyes down to avoid the stares of the civilians on the sidewalks, ashamed, led into a courtroom where I was indicted on federal smuggling charges, facing five to twenty years.

It was a lot like my first days in Vietnam; no one told you shit. But I found out from my fellow prisoners. There were two judges: Monday/Wednesday/Friday I had a chance at three years, and with a Vietnam service record, might get parole and do no time. Tuesday/Thursday I'd get five years, which meant I could be out in three with parole. It was a cold situation, and on top of that, my court-appointed lawyer was not showing up — it'd been some six or seven days now. I barely got a mattress in a cell built for two, now holding five. Toilets weren't working too well. The guards were icy. I hadn't even gotten to make my one call. I wrote a note to my captors, pleading, "Vietnam vet. Just back. I've been gone 15 months. My family doesn't know I'm back. Please let me make my first call." Put the note, folded up, in a slip box attached to the cell; the guards pick it all up end of day; the guards' faces change each shift, but nothing happens.

Prison. A faceless experience. What the new underground papers were calling "Amerika" with a K was here to be seen. Nixon hadn't yet been inaugurated, so the War on Drugs hadn't officially started, but I could tell many of my young cellmates, any of whom could've been in Vietnam, didn't give a fuck about it: "Shit, ain't my problem — they fuckin' with me right *here!*" Though white, I felt their anger; it was pervasive, but I was scared too. Would I ever get my call? I'd still be sitting here in six months. I wrote another note.

I was figuring out a routine now — how to wash, some yoga stretching in a tiny space, don't mess with the wrong guy, don't use somebody's soap bar by mistake, don't ask anybody a question that can come back to hurt you, don't tell anybody too much about yourself, and don't look for compassion here, because *nobody* in here's guilty. And anyway, drugs were cool. The "sickos" were on the outside, in DC, killing hundreds of people every day, bombing the shit out of them, and now incarcerating everyone who might revolt, who could lead the rebellion against them. This was truly another war I had stumbled into — a badass "civil war" at home — the corollary to our war abroad, the thing Malcolm X said about the JFK assassination, that "the chickens are coming home to roost."

Finally the jailers allowed me to make my call. There was one number I knew by heart — my father's. Thank God he answered, because if he hadn't, it might've been days till they'd get me to a phone again. His voice, the familiar solid sound of it, gave me a burst of hope, the operator telling him he had a collect call from San Diego "from a William Stone" (that was my service name). "Will you accept the charges on this call?"

I was thinking of Dad's favorite O. Henry story, "The Ransom of Red Chief," where some incompetent crooks kidnap a spoiled brat who no one wants back. Would the perversity in my father just say no? "Go ahead," the operator said, and clicked me in.

". . . Dad?"

"Kiddo, for Chrissake, where've you been! Two weeks ago — they told me you got out in Fort Lewis?"

Hearing his voice, I felt a surge of warm emotions. I was so relieved to know he was really there. It was *his* voice. There was no way to apologize for not calling. I could go on about flight availabilities, international time zones, my orders, but I just said, "Dad, listen — I'm in trouble."

A silence. He was waiting, thinking the worst. Years later I'd try to capture this moment in the scene in *Midnight Express* with Billy Hayes's father in Long Island gushing over his son in Turkey, assuring him that this disinterested slob of a Turkish lawyer would take charge now that his father was here. (Unfortunately, the actor in the film was a ham and overplayed the scene, looking to cram every bit of significance into the few moments of screen time he'd been given.)

I had to hurry. The phone in that shithouse could have cut out at any moment, and then what? Anyway, I told him where I was and why and what might happen to me, and it'd be good if he could get in touch with this "public defender" whose name and number I carefully gave him in the hope that he could reach him on the phone, because I sure couldn't, and maybe he'd get me out on bail, because the longer I stayed in this place, the other dudes were saying, my chances were getting worse.

My dad sighed noticeably, and I could visualize his expression — really not surprised, because I think he always suspected I'd end up like this. So, what'd he say? I've heard it's the most overused expression in the English language, something you think just as you see the other car coming too fast, and you know you've bought it.

"Oh, shit!"

My lawyer, a jolly, well-meaning fellow, who earned $1,500 upfront and $6K more on the back end, did finally show up and got me out within a day. I had to stay "clean" around San Diego, which was essentially a military town then, for almost a week while the charges against me were mysteriously processed and "dismissed in the interests of justice." Ah, the power of money. I was extremely lucky, and when I got to New York that December, I was coiled and tight, a jungle creature, ready for anything, living 24/7 on the edge of my nerves, even when I slept. I was a hard man, harder than I'd ever been. I was so numb I couldn't recognize it, like waking up anesthetized after an operation in a hospital. An operation that lasted fifteen months. What had really happened in Vietnam? I didn't know one other combat vet in New York, and found myself out of my depth in a sea of civilians, rushing around, making a huge deal out of money, success, jobs, all kinds of personal shit, which to me was still petty daily stuff compared to surviving. When the media started talking about "posttraumatic stress disorder" — PTSD — I didn't believe it. I thought it was bullshit, 'cause if it were true, there were millions of civilians running around with it. They were nuts, stressed out over nothing, but still they were suffering the same way I was. But I didn't want pity, I didn't want some lame excuse as a Vietnam vet to ask for extra money and all that whining crap I hated in the complainers, the groaners; there were so many of them in the army.

I was confused, in no shape to go anywhere — either to college or to start up any construction company or whatever else with a fellow vet. I'd be gripped with sudden rages when people would talk about protesting the war and Nixon, who'd just been elected and was going to continue it. I'd read about them going on in newspapers, or see them on television, and I'd be so angry at the futility of protest — frothing at the mouth, telling them to "shut up and just go fucking *do* Nixon! Kill the motherfucker. Get some guns and go after that whole fucking gang — the whole inner sanctum. They're all pigs!" But no one understood me. My rage was talking to me faster than my mind. I was unhinged, and others could sense it; they avoided me. I became more isolated, more paranoid. I didn't want to go back to college, and Yale was certainly finished with me too, and fuck them anyway! While still enlisted, I'd applied to the University of California, Santa Cruz just because it was peaceful and beautiful to look at, barefoot girls brushing down horses and all that, but they'd already turned me down as an out-of-state dropout, which was a blessing because I would've turned into some other kind of man if I'd gone there — maybe even a nice "California guy" with a tan and a car, UC grad you know, detached from the passions of his time.

With my combat bonuses and the extra three months I'd put in, I had significant savings, and I didn't spend much of it on a series of cheap apartments downtown. There was a dump on East 9th Street between Avenues B and C, in those days a junkie ghetto. I painted the walls a deep emergency red — and, for good measure, the ceiling. Red for blood, red for creativity. Maybe the war had made me that way. I bought some screenplay books out of curiosity. I had an urge, a nervous reflex, really, to write again. It was, frankly, the only way I could express myself — not through music or drawing, in neither of which I'd shown any particular talent when young. Certainly the memory of writing that damn painful book that had cost me my career at Yale lingered with the taint of defeat. But screenplay writing was new, sexier, far different from the old navel-gazing novel.

So I channeled these feelings inside me as a screenplay and called it "Break"; it was about Vietnam, and it fit right in with the mood of my weird apartment. It had nothing to do with the reality of what I'd been through, which wasn't interesting to me; it was too specific. Who cares, there were enough stories about the war on TV and in the papers. No, this was something mythic, the real thing that was going on in our culture. It was about a Jim Morrison "hero." "Break On Through" gave me the script's title. This was about a kid I recognized from the Doors' "Unknown Soldier" and "The End," who rebels against his divorced, weirdly abstracted parents living in "the City."

"The Time is the Future. The White World has split apart, many of its young people have migrated to the Forests of the East, where they live in tribes. The reactionary White World, as in the past, has invaded the East to destroy these outlaw white races . . ."

Thus began my intro to the first scene, where Anthony, the main character, burns all his student possessions and runs away from school. Confronting his father, an "intellectual liberal out of touch with the world of action":

FATHER: I raised a pyromaniac for a son.

ANTHONY (PAINED): *What* does that mean?

FATHER: It means you're sick.

ANTHONY: I disappoint you?

FATHER: Yes.

ANTHONY (SHRUGGING): I'm sorry.

FATHER: Anthony, I love you, you're my boy.

ANTHONY: These are words, Dad, just like your word "pyromaniac."

Arrested and sent as a soldier to the East, Anthony is involved in a battle where the American invaders, despite all their technology, are massacred with spears, rocks, bows and arrows; he's wounded, taken prisoner, and switches sides. He joins the jungle resistance, led by a beautiful, sexy goddess — Naomi — with whom he mates in the presence of snakes.

NAOMI: You're not scared of snakes, are you, handsome one?

ANTHONY: Not anymore.

NAOMI: You're not scared of me, are you, handsome one?

ANTHONY: My eyes have seen you . . . dreamt you . . . dreams.

NAOMI: Take your clothes off, dreamer . . . beautiful creatures run free. Who are you?

ANTHONY: Anthony.

Portentous dialogue, but intense to me at the time. Through Naomi, Anthony becomes conscious — a Dionysian leader who's killed at his next encounter with the overwhelming invading force. He doesn't die in the normal sense, and lands in a version of the Egyptian Underworld, where he's judged by hybrid animal-like beings, and then reemerges, surprisingly, in an American prison in California full of blacks, Latinos, and rebel whites. There, fueled by his yearning for freedom, he leads a successful prison break! People in those days wanted, at all costs, to be *"free."* Jim Morrison was breaking taboos and crossing all the barriers — till he died in 1971. Singing about killing his father and fucking his mother, my God. Nothing was sacred — it was all possible — we were all going to "break on through to the other side!"

Did we? Critics who police popular culture discount the '60s with safe dismissal; you can't believe in it too much or you're a fool to your colleagues. But they miss the point. It was a massive breakthrough, and still is. That's why *Avatar* in 2009 became the highest-grossing film of all time — with a similar, almost mystical theme of a change in thinking about our civilization. Its writer-director, Jim Cameron, though insisting the antagonist was not the American empire, was on to something big — an over-industrialized, war-motivated world that regresses into our original, primordial nature. The common man protagonist evolves his consciousness, like my hero in "Break," but has to fight the Old World desire to exploit and, if necessary, destroy the population of this New World.

It was hard to write in that Avenue B dump. Fleet-footed robbers, mostly desperate junkies, were spotted coming down from the roof through the fire escape into my windows; more than once they emptied out my apartment, which had nothing in it anyway, not even a radio. Then a young mugger tried to rob me in the doorway of the building, but I stared at the knife in his hand like I was having a traumatic flashback and backed away, silent, horrified. He didn't know what to do — something was off about this guy he was robbing. Another New York psycho? He cursed and walked away empty-handed (something you never see in the movies).

I was weird, vaguely on the lookout for death. I moved next into a walkup at Mott and Houston Streets with heating problems. It didn't matter that winter, as I got used to freezing, and sometimes six inches of snow would accumulate next to my kitchen table when I left the window open. I kept writing "Break" and then started another screenplay called "Dreams of Dominique," wanting to re-create my mother's world as Fellini did with his wife in *Juliet of the Spirits*. It began with her landing in New York in '46, then her unraveling, and finally her reconciliation with her son.

I'd so missed her when I was fifteen — at boarding school, then later, living a bachelor life with my father, so dry in my heart, like the kid in *The Catcher in the Rye* — where was the love I cried out for? I realized belatedly my mother had been my true lifeline, but today . . . a veil hung there between us. Now nearing fifty, my mother was getting her mojo back, living in a cozy apartment on the East Side, like an older Holly Golightly in *Breakfast at Tiffany's*. She worked for almost a year on a gay friend's successful new cosmetics line, but visiting retailers around the country selling perfume to department store buyers was not for her. The great disruptor of her life, the dark and dangerous Miles, had exploded somewhere off camera — too much fury, heat, divorce. It all conspired to destroy what was probably impossible in the first place — a love affair built on passion. Living on alimony in a new '60s world of fashion people, artists, and party animals, she divided her life between Paris and New York. A younger lover had lately moved in with her — a gentler soul, a Harlem-raised Italian American trying to make a living as a painter and later an interior decorator, who needed Mom's strength and financial support. And later, when Mom moved on to still other lovers — all younger, black-haired, generally Mediterranean — she remained his friend, her basic nature one of loving-kindness.

I advised her to marry one of the rare rich, straight bachelors who came to these parties she attended, but she denied them the same respect she had for my father. Some had asked, but they'd either inherited their fortunes and were hopeless drunks or were simply lacking the character of her ex-husband. As much as she admired her, she could never be a Jackie Kennedy and remarry for the money. Not to say she didn't like money, but she had her pride, Mother — not to chase after money, not to stoop to needing it. It was supposed to be "provided"; a man, in her era, took care of a woman, and it was her responsibility to "be wanted." With age, her outlets narrowed and her nights, in the French style, became more devoted to dressing up, going out to dinner and parties, dancing, and sex — or just an ordinary evening at home with her lover and the TV.

And the telephone. In her time on earth, my mother may well have spent a third of her waking day on phones, being kind to the hordes of people she met whom she really didn't know. Or responding to the urgent needs of friends in trouble, seeking out the always available and sympathetic Jacqueline. I never knew her to say no to anyone, and years later, during the AIDS crisis, she gave many, many hours and days to those who needed it. I still had to struggle for her attention, and I felt, at times, like just another guest at her party — but what a party! I understood better now her intellectual limitations than when I was younger. She wasn't really interested in history, art, literature, the things I was wrestling with; she was into people, friendship, the guts of real life. The interaction was what excited her to no end, and because of that she was a firecracker and lit many a spark in other people's lives. As well as mine. But to be the son of such a person is not simple, and I could never satisfy her as a son or as the engine in her life. Certain mothers seek out such a quality, so in love with their boys, overprotective to the point of being destructive, that they want to be "the one" in their son's life. My mother had too much going on in her life to limit herself to that role, so I accepted my status and cherished the times we had alone, or else, too frequently, scolded her for being who she was.

Her elegant gay friends, some quite decadent, would devour me with their words and eyes at the parties she took me to. There was a possibility — a rumor — that I might lean in that direction; after all, I was not often seen with a girl, and if so, rarely twice with the same one; sometimes I'd head off to bed with a European or South American woman closer to my mother's age whom I'd met at one of these soirees. I was willing to go way beyond my earlier parameters as a shy adolescent, and these older women were experienced in the ways of sex and taught me how to be comfortable, at least what I could remember when I wasn't stoned. Getting stoned was my best defense; I didn't have to be responsible, I could hide behind the "high."

But always there was that dark thought — Vietnam. Her friends would wonder, "Why on earth did you go?" It was a question I couldn't answer glibly. "Seriously, Vietnam?" A disappointed look. "What are they *doing* in that silly war!" Yes, everyone in the world, at least in New York City, knew it was a silly war — except for the boneheaded generals straight out of Stanley Kubrick's *Dr. Strangelove* who were fighting it. Or those French generals sending men to be slaughtered in his World War I epic *Paths of Glory.* The makeup, the hair, and the peacock clothing on the gay men and all my mother's female friends' faces at the parties, smiling, stoned, were the stylized masks in what was now my Fellini-Kubrick universe. Years later I put some of that mood into *The Doors,* evoking my disorientation in a strange new world.

My father had wanted to write plays when he got out of college, like Arthur Miller. They were now stacked in a drawer in his desk — never produced. His heart, part of it, resided in that drawer. As he went to work almost every day of his life down on dark, depressing Wall Street, and later in towering corporate glass buildings in midtown with escalators and rushing people, he made money to survive, never to own, but to rent in a dog-eat-dog society. His writing ability was transferred into the esteemed *Lou Stone's Monthly Investment Letter,* which was translated at its peak into more than a dozen languages, his counsel sought by wealthy clients. Of Vietnam, he wrote in 1966 in his *Letter:*

> War is always a tragedy to those who do not survive it . . . From a cold-blooded military point-of-view, however, the war in Vietnam is not all bad, and in some respects, it has certain advantages . . . [E]very time that a ship or plane or a gun goes into action, it adds to the store of our military expertise, which will save lives in the future and lead to the development of new and improved hardware . . . [T]he lives being lost in Vietnam are not being lost in vain; they are the price required for the contain-

ment of communism, and the battle-trained veterans who survive will be the cadre of a force that very well may be needed in
the years to come . . . We aren't there to win, because there isn't
anything to win . . . [I]f it were not for this policy of resistance,
or containment, the well-organized, highly-disciplined communist conspiracy would move into every place in the world
where there is either economic weakness or a political vacuum,
and that means most of the world.

In the latter part of his *Letter,* he would recommend a list of defense stocks
to buy.

In May of '67 he wrote in the same *Letter,* "A philosophy of personal
protest is no substitute for a foreign policy; Joan Baez and Bob Dylan are
no substitutes for McGeorge Bundy," Lyndon Johnson's national security
adviser, adding, "Let's keep the hippies out of Congress."

Of course it was bitterly ironic that he had a long-haired time bomb of
a son, wearing beads and amulets, in his own living room in 1969, using
ghetto dialect he despised: "Wow . . . Cool . . . I can dig. What's happenin'?
Whatcha doin'?" and the ubiquitous "man" along with the hand signals.
"You turned into a black man!" he once said to me. Naturally, I despised
his way of thinking. I'd been in combat, my father never had, yet he never
expressed interest in the details, nor did I really want to tell — because it
was not something I was really proud of. He dismissed the Vietnam War
as a "police action" — as the Korean War had been officially categorized
by Truman's administration earlier; after all, what were 34,000 Americans
dead in Korea or 58,000 in Vietnam compared to World War II's 417,000?
— and on top of that, there was simply no progress in this war. Vietnam
was "a mess," and implicitly I was part of that "mess." I was on the road
to becoming what he always feared — "a bum." How could he even begin
to understand me? He'd been an officer at the headquarters of the "Greatest Generation," where he could only see a "Big Picture" full of maps and
projections, where war made sense, if such a thing can be said. War, to my
mind, was weather, accident, confusion, human nature, the basic malfunc-
tioning of a rifle and ammunition, and a certain brutality in that nothing

ever quite worked the way you thought it would in real combat. Or as Mike Tyson aptly put it, "Everybody got a plan till they get hit in the face."

He couldn't begin to understand that in some ways I'd gone quite mad. I'd been a good combat soldier who could be counted on not to fold in a fight. I'd learned to hate the enemy in a professional, non-emotional way, and I was able to engage them without hesitation. I was primed, and when the monsoon rains came heavy, I could smile about it and fertilize in the moisture along with the rest of the creatures of the forest — the wetter the better. Big, ugly, slug-like insects would spread and bloat at night in the moist jungles. Leeches could grow fat around my wet groin or underarms; they liked the warm places, and I'd enjoy burning them off with the smoldering tip of my cigarette. I was twenty-two then, I shit jungle mud, I could live in a hole anywhere. Because I was READY for ANYTHING in this fucking jungle, in this life. I sleep on hair-trigger alert. I react. I am 24/7 on the edge of my nerves. Even when I sleep — which I don't. That's a man — a hard-nailed man, not a movie bullshit hero! There were better soldiers than me, no question — but I showed up when the shit hit the fan.

Which is why, like many guys over there, I took to dope when I could. I needed to relax. Without it, I would have snapped, done something stupid. I couldn't have taken the pressure *all* the time. I needed some space outside the jungle, time with music and smoke and the laughter of those crazy black soldiers who could dance in a tribal group, snapping fingers to Smokey Robinson, Sam Cooke, the Temptations, or jazz, or anything with a beat. It looked feminine, yes, their voices falsetto, but they knew how to "cool it." I'd never interacted with black people before I went there. Occasionally at school there'd be the well-behaved athlete on a scholarship. But Vietnam was a head-on plunge into a new world, discovering people from the poorest uneducated backgrounds from the South, or cities like Chicago, who saw the world in completely different ways. Some I found alienated and alienating, even hating "honky" white people, but most became friendly if you opened to them, and would share just about everything in such a compressed situation. As time went on, I found these were the people I wanted to spend my time with, because I understood their distrust and their rebellious attitude toward "the man" and the army and "this fucking war," which they endured like they endured most everything in the genes. It was the music that started it — and the grass naturally followed from that.

And crazy as it sounds, these men, these "heads," we called them — as opposed to the "straights" or the "juicers" — taught me a feeling for real love, the love that exists between human beings, and that's the most important thing any soldier can keep in war — *his humanity.* Without it, we're beasts; I saw that Beast in play many times over there. And now I was learning the Beast could take a more sophisticated form in civilian life, but I could recognize it *anywhere.* And my father's mind was part of that Beast, praising this military-industrial complex he'd helped build.

There were times, yes, I wanted to kill him. I wanted to extinguish this mind that condoned war as necessary. And one day out on Long Island, I actually slipped a strong tab of orange sunshine LSD into his scotch rocks to blow that mind. It was at a dinner party he'd invited me to, where I was among twelve other guests, so I couldn't be singled out. But after his initial awkwardness when he realized he was "on something," he surprisingly announced to the suspects around the table that, whoever had given this to him, he was actually enjoying the "trip"; after all, he'd drunk a lot of whiskey in his life, and it takes more than one trip to change a strong mind. In that regard, I was younger when I was exposed to LSD, grass, mushrooms. I was able over time to essentially reexamine and question almost everything in my life, every mental feeling and perception. Having been under my father's strong influence, I found it was quite a change in consciousness.

In truth, my father was as much a victim as he was a perpetrator; at sixty, as a vice president at Shearson Lehman Brothers, he was struggling inside a dynamic and changing economy by trying to "stay even," because, as he often repeated, his '62 divorce, brought on by my mother's extravagances, cut his knees out from under him — and eight years later, he was still in debt for the same lousy $100,000. It was like a bad dream. A hundred thousand dollars may not seem like a backbreaker these days; students run up loans of that size, and modern entrepreneurs routinely go for millions of dollars of debt. But my father came from the Depression, where, after 1929, the fear of buying anything on margin was embedded like a thorn in his fate, and like Sisyphus with his taxes and alimony, the conservative investments of an aging clientele, along with the reduction of the commissions permitted by the Stock Exchange, my poor father, as in the worst of Dickens, wore himself down without getting any closer to trimming that searing $100,000 number. It was as late as 1983, almost fourteen years later and not long before his death, that he said to me one day without much satisfaction and certainly no joy, "It's paid off." He sounded like a man coming out of jail after twenty years, too old now to start fresh.

Capitalism, in effect, had chewed my father up and spit him out. Despite the fact he'd made millions of dollars after forty years of work, the capitalist system of wars, greater and greater profits to meet shareholder demands, and the exploitation of "lesser" people had left him hollowed out, beaten. He finally realized the pointlessness of a Cold War that required endless amounts of weaponry when, in fact, just a fraction of it on each side was enough. Dad began to change his views as he hit his mid-sixties, when one night out of nowhere he said to me, "What's the point of all this buildup when a Russian nuclear sub can be just off our coastline?" And then, in the early 1980s, when President Reagan was rallying the country once more into a renewed Cold War against the "Evil Empire," my father dismissed him as "a dope" who'd ruined his once admired Republican Party.

Nor did he understand a new Wall Street that was conglomeratizing his world. His new employer, the mogul Sandy Weill, was the avatar of mixing credit card, travel, and insurance companies with brokerage firms into larger and larger entities, leaving no firm or job secure. The old Wall Street was surely dying, and with it, my father was suffering the death pangs. It was a true revolution, much more dangerous than what Roosevelt had wrought, as he once feared. His nemesis turned out to be the excesses of a capitalism he thought could be contained. But it couldn't, and it brought, ultimately, the deepening structural crises leading to 2008 and beyond.

Yet I don't believe it was this, the destruction of his ordered world, that most depressed him. I believe it was the failure of his marriage, because Dad, despite his sarcasm and occasional disparagement, truly wanted a strong family unit, and at that he failed. He'd failed in his relationship with his wife, my mother. Or perhaps, as he hinted, he was never meant to be a family man. Some men are not.

But who was I to point the finger of judgment? What had I done with my life? My education was spotty and not paying itself off. My experience was interesting, but my skills were blowing a boiler on a ship, handling weapons, walking and bivouacking in a jungle, rolling a joint, getting fucked up, what else? By the time I was thirty — my self-imposed deadline to succeed — I'd expected to be established, starting a career, taking care of myself. I wasn't so sure anymore; it was going on a year now since I'd come back from the army, and I was quite lost in a spiral of feelings, writing half-baked scripts, taking LSD and grass, angel dust, and engaging in sex, a lot of lust, New York parties, random girls young and old. I was drifting.

To Dad I was the idiot son who'd never amount to much. But he'd love me nonetheless, because he'd married Mom on his hunch she'd breed strong children. To his mind, he'd lost that bet, but his natural Jewish pessimism could allow for that. By comparison, his brother's oldest son, my cousin Jimmy, would be teaching economics at Harvard at twenty-five, and then become the youngest appointee ever to chair the Commodity Futures Trading Commission, under President Carter; and after that, he would found a large private insurance company in Massachusetts and become a multimillionaire. Next to him, I seemed pointless.

It was this same uncle, Henry, who asked me what I had for "plans." Without any real thought, I said I was thinking about acting, which evoked a pained look from him. In the New York social whirl, there were many "actors." It was an acceptable way of life in a city of intense pretensions. I began attending two different acting schools downtown, one teaching the stricter Stanislavski Method, the other the practical workshop-oriented HB Studio on Bank Street, where there were a variety of interesting teachers — Uta Hagen, Bill Hickey, Aaron Frankel among them. But I had a problem with my acting. To be an actor, to bring myself intensely, exhaustively into another person's soul, was something I thought I could achieve with more insight when I wrote.

In certain ways, actors reminded me of Harry Houdini, the famous magician, who, time and again, dared death and escaped at the last moment. You transcend your own self through acting out someone else's life. Frank Langella, with whom I worked years later, told me Laurence Olivier, when asked once to explain his motivation for acting, cut through all the bull-shit and barked, "Look *at me*. Look *at me* — that's my bloody motivation!" Meaning, there's something childish about it all, isn't there, and "if you're looking at the other actor, I've failed." Not a bad response, really, but I ba-sically didn't like relying on my expressions or my looks. I wanted to *be* my looks, have my own ideas, live in my body, not rent it. I had ego, but unlike a good actor, I couldn't locate it. I didn't know who the hell I was, and that mystery drew me inward, searching.

Maybe by connecting my own dots, I could help not just myself but others to see things they hadn't seen before. I could, as a playwright or director, bring actors to realizations they could not find on their own. The writer can become the hand-holder of the actor's dreams; the writer brain-washes an actor into feeling *the script's words* are *his* own feelings. Perhaps I was being arrogant, but toward those goals I was driven to stumble with a blind and zealous faith.

My own acting, in any case, was muffled and thought-bound. I couldn't get out of myself — fly like a bird, be *free!* Once I got stuck in the pompous role of Thomas Becket, my Russian-born teacher scolding me constantly, until one night I dropped LSD and stopped by the class and played the shit out of this old twelfth-century archbishop. She applauded wildly, told me I'd finally arrived at its meaning, and praised me to the class. Yet on the LSD I had no idea what I'd done. I just *did* it. But how could I repeat the performance? I had no clue.

Studying Chekhov, drawing upon and evoking domestic issues at that stage of my life seemed boring and bourgeois. I wanted action. Jim Mor-rison action, girls, sex. Sam Peckinpah was the guy. And in France, in a wholly different way, Jean-Luc Godard, no prude, was the other guy for me because he appreciated the sex and violence of cinema. In *Pierrot le Fou* in 1965, he could montage eight or ten shots of a burning match, a gun, a drunk American cowboy, a French chick wearing a Vietnamese rice hat, a Viet Cong flag, this, that, and a voice-over with American artillery sound effects, and you could take a metaphorical leap into Vietnam — it was stunning. What Sergei Eisenstein had done for silent films, Godard was doing with modern cinema. Luis Buñuel, in the same vein, could take an ordinary dinner party in *The Discreet Charm of the Bourgeoisie* (1972) and turn it inside out — so that, as both participant and observer, you saw with an acid trip's clarity the folly and irrationality of this life, which always seems, despite our best efforts, to interrupt our plans, and in case you don't understand, the curtain comes up and there's an audience out there laughing at your dinner party. Those were the kinds of scripts I was writing. I could not appreciate the realism and rationality of Chekhov, Arthur Miller, Tennessee Williams, or Edward Albee (whom I admired and wrote a thesis on in boarding school). But I didn't want their realism. I'd just come back from Vietnam, and it was so intense, so far from the normal social intercourse, that civilian life *was* smaller to me, a farce, with people running around worried about careers, money, who loves who — who gives a shit! I was really an anarchist at this time.

Although I met a lot of girls my age, slept with a few of them, I was too strange, and I thought some of them were psychotic, I mean crazier than batshit with their neuroses, which is why I preferred older women. For instance, you're with a girl alone, you've both been giving all the right signals, and although you don't really know each other, and you're supposed to take the initiative because you're the guy, and you're holding her and kissing her, and then, all of a sudden, she flips the switch and doesn't want to go any further — just simple stuff like "Do I really want to be with this guy?" — that sense of doubt that many women project, and then, before you know it, you're picking up on it and feeling guilty as shit, like, "Wow, am I projecting too strongly? Is she scared I'm gonna try to rape her?"

And before you know it, back to her — "Who is this guy? I'm not comfortable."

And so forth. Everyone's getting real paranoid, and if she's even higher than you, she's running out into the New York street about to get killed, screaming, "Go 'way! Leave me alone!" One time it was, "No, no, no! I don't wanna live! I don't wanna live!" Insane, exaggerated dialogues, or as Jim Morrison wrote, "weird scenes inside the gold mine." Yeah, you meet strange people in the City.

A former schoolmate told me I could go to "film school" and get a college degree. For what — "going to the movies"? That seemed ridiculous because, like most everybody else in America, I never had a problem going to the movies. So almost a year after my return, in the fall of '69, I enrolled at NYU's School of the Arts, undergraduate, not really with a defined purpose, but because maybe there was something to this. And the GI Bill was paying about 80 percent of the tuition. I got to see numerous films and took a production course wherein we'd rotate as director-writer, cinematographer, editor, actor on 16mm black-and-white short films from one to five minutes long. The teachers were committed, serious. There was Haig Manoogian, their leader, a wisecracking, humane fiftyish New York street intellectual who always wore a tiny porkpie hat; Dean Oppenheimer, the head of the program, a majestic cultural figure; Charlie Milne, an eccentric Zen-seeker given to a day of silence each week, who ran the valued equipment department, making sure we all had fair access; and Marty Scorsese, NYU's star graduate, then in his mid-twenties, who'd made some celebrated short films and was struggling through various stages of a low-budget feature, *Who's That Knocking on My Door?* He'd soon make *Mean Streets,* which would become his entrée to Hollywood. Marty sported greasy hair down to his shoulders and a very fast, high-pitched, nervous New York accent. He'd generally be a mess in our morning class, as he'd stay up sometimes till dawn to watch old movies on television, because in those days before videocassettes, there were a limited number of repertory theaters in the city. I'll never forget his spontaneous lecture on the greatness of Josef von Sternberg's expressionistic madness in *The Scarlet Empress* (1934) with Marlene Dietrich. Marty clearly worshiped cinema as intensely in his way as the young protagonist did God in Robert Bresson's *Diary of a Country Priest* (1951), and his classes were fun, punctuated by rapid-fire dialogues, irreverence at every level, but at the same time, he understood the sacred stakes we were playing for and that very few of us in these classes would succeed. I know I felt this, perhaps because I was older than most of my classmates.

At NYU there was this instinctive distrust of the people who'd been in the military and gone "over there." I rarely volunteered to anyone that I was a vet, but some figured it out. There was no welcome home for us. It was simply in the air. The way they looked at me, I was apart. Had I killed in Vietnam? I had a vague dread of that question. Most of the students were left-wing, radical, Marxist, anarchist — and some were just out to make a buck in commercials, whatever. This was New York City, and their reactions, for the most part, were based on what would later be called "political correctness," and their dubious judgment of me was made without knowing what I'd been through in Vietnam.

Najwa Sarkis was a striking, olive-skinned Lebanese woman with a polished, somewhat haughty British accent. Although she was raised Christian, her face belonged on a fourth-century Phoenician vase, so I ignored the accent. With holes in my jeans, stoned, insolent, pretending indifference, I met her at an uptown party my mother invited me to. She was intrigued by me, so different from the civilized crowd she was accustomed to. More important, she came to accept me as I was, this jungle animal, dangerous to myself and potentially to her. All I wanted was her warm, brown Mediterranean body. That sea was in my genes too — through France, through Odysseus. The first time we made love, all that pretentious New York veneer vanished, as we ripped each other's clothes off like two junkyard dogs going at it. She was twenty-eight to my twenty-three and a rational woman integrated into the world with a job as the chief assistant to the Moroccan ambassador to the United Nations, with a decent salary and a rent-controlled apartment in the East 50s. She was independent of me, my father, my mother, NYU, all that had gone before, thus a new force unto herself, and she allowed me gradually — by trusting me, by loving me — to pretend once again that I could believe in the customs of New York society, circa 1969–1975.

Eventually, at her invitation, I moved uptown from my hole to her place. Incongruities persisted. I'd be walking down a New York sidewalk with Najwa in daylight when a car would suddenly backfire and I'd plunge to the pavement. She was quite slow by my standards as she looked casually for the source of the sound, then turned back, wondering where I'd gone. It took her a while to understand how much my instincts and fear controlled me.

This actually helped me in film school, where I was beginning to learn a trade, a real trade. It wasn't writing I was learning; that had already been a part of me for as long as I could remember, since my father began assigning me twenty-five-cent weekly themes when I was seven or so. Not a bad idea; it didn't make me want to write, but because I wanted the money, I accepted, little by little, the literary impulse he was teaching me. Only later did I realize it was a skill which I could use to make far more money than either my father or I could ever have dreamed of. Dad would say, "I'll give you a quarter, kiddo. Write about anything you want. Make it two pages, three, just tell a story. Let's say by Saturday?" Dad had always been a terrific bedtime storyteller when I was young. And twenty-five cents in the early '50s was enough to buy a hamburger or a Classic Comic — "Rob Roy," "Count of Monte Cristo," "Ivanhoe," "Ulysses," "Tale of Two Cities" — which excited my imagination in ways only classic novels could; I don't remember Jane Austen or Henry James being illustrated. I wrote several stories based on movies I'd seen of the Indian wars — a lot of killing, of course, because that was okay in the American culture. Killing was acceptable. Massacres were even better. That and money. Money was power. That's what children learn the fastest — the meaning of Power.

Dad also infrequently took me to good movies, at least ones he wanted to see, like Kubrick's *Paths of Glory* (1957), or his favorite, David Lean's *The Bridge on the River Kwai* (1957). He objected to Elia Kazan's *On the Waterfront* (1954) because of Marlon Brando's incessant "mumbling," which was rare in those days; no longer. But even at nine, I knew this movie was different; it set a new standard of realism in which life in my hometown was actually gritty and scary. My dad would always ask me as we were walking out of the movie house, "So kiddo, what'd you think?" I'd say something like, "I really liked it," or not, and he'd say, "But did you notice that [this thing] was wrong, and because that happened, [this other thing] didn't make sense?" And I'd ask, "Why doesn't [this] [that] make sense?" And we'd go into this chess game of what made sense in a movie. My dad was logical, and he'd generally end up smiling and saying, "Well, you know, we could've done it better." Without either of us realizing it, he gave me my first encouragement to be a screenwriter.

Going to film school was a different experience, because now I had a new acquired savagery from seeing it for real in Vietnam, an instinct I'd learned, and I knew in my gut that this savagery was necessary to *see*. To *feel*. To *hear*. Everything! Above all — the six inches in front of my face. My senses were now joined with this new thing — this 16mm camera, Bolex,

Arriflex, Eclair, whatever you could get from the school equipment store
— which would become my eyes and ears to record everything around me.
My eyes had grown omnipresent and nervous in the jungle. They'd become
360°, ears attuned to the slightest shift in sound. You have to blend with the
jungle, smell like it, see it from the inside out; you're the snake crawling on
the jungle floor, or the giant spider weaving its thirty-foot web between
primeval trees. You pay attention at all times to survive in the most visceral
sense of the word. In other terms, you're a camera, and with that camera,
you take the same time and space, no matter how ordinary, and tear it
apart as if you're fucking, penetrating this reality with all your senses, but
primarily your *eyes* — and creating on film, out of pure instinct, something
fresh and new. That was the thrill for me.

By the same token, I never gave up, or took for granted, my interest in
writing; in fact, I was one of the few students from the production side who
consistently, over the two years, attended the courses offered in screenwriting, which surprisingly at NYU were not a requirement. The European
"New Wave" had killed off respect for screenwriters; writing and directing were considered two different professions. Writers were grim, wormy
backroom creatures; filmmakers were dashing, bold, frontline creative;
they were inventing on the day of the shoot with the actors, and screenplays were closer to treatments. After a few efforts working this way, I never
really believed it, and over time, clearly the screenplay has reemerged as the
equal, if not dominant, player.

During those two years, I watched many movies with this new eye, and
learned as much as I could about making them. One of the first basic lessons in filming is chasing the light. Without it, you have nothing — no exposure that can be seen; even what you see with your naked eye needs to
be shaped and enhanced by the light. New York in winter was a short day,
and as the sun dropped, you intensified everything to get the last shots
you needed, because you couldn't afford artificial light or coming back and
shooting a second day. This condition persisted throughout my career,
even on the most expensive films. Every day knowing I was chasing the
sun, I'd be running from the first shots through the lunch break, avoiding,
if I could, the ugly midday light, rehearsing and trying to do as much as
possible to "get the day" between 4 p.m. and 6 or 7. It was always an over-

riding question of pacing myself to get the shots I needed. If I made a shot list of, let's say, eighteen shots that day, under the pressure of the shooting I'd find out by 3 p.m. that I only really needed twelve — or just nine shots. The point was, I was doing some of the best work, or at least necessary work, in that last hour or two. "What do you really *need* to understand the scene? Not 'want' — what do you *need!*" was the mantra. Marty brought to the class John Cassavetes, who'd made *Shadows* and now *Husbands* with NYU-style low budgets; he was a warm, open individual whom we deeply admired for his independence. He encouraged us to find our reasons — our *need* — for making films, and by way of showing us, ran acting exercises with us and assigned us different roles in which we'd improvise together. "Don't waste time as an actor — get to the point. What do you really *need* from this other person in the scene? Approval? Money? Sex? Love? What?" Talk about keeping it personal, here was a man who literally sacrificed his health for his films.

Near the end of my first year, I made a short film, which I called *Last Year in Vietnam*. There was no dialogue, and I shot it in crude 16mm black and white with some 8mm color intercuts; I intended those to be a stand-in for the Vietnamese jungle, which I was contrasting to the black-and-white cold concrete New York streets of winter. But it worked, as I portrayed a young veteran living in New York alone, waking up on an overcast morning, still trying to adjust to civilian life. Played by me without much expression, the character evokes an aura of uncertainty and loss. Spontaneously he packs all his personal memorabilia, medals, and photographs in a bag, the idea growing that he has a problem with his past. The Vietnam photographs I used had been my first baby steps in cinema. In the last months of my tour, I'd bought a Pentax at the PX and kept it waterproofed in a plastic bag. By comparison, writing anything on paper was useless, given the amount of rain in the jungle; taking photos was the only way to keep a record.

The young vet hops the subway downtown, his gait in rhythm with a cane, his leg damaged by the kind of shrapnel that'd taken me down the second time. He boards the Staten Island Ferry, and once out on Lower New York Bay, as the music of Borodin's "In the Steppes of Central Asia" surges through his consciousness, he literally throws the bag full of memories into the churn of the surf from the ferry's engine, gone now, purging himself of the past. To add to the intensity, I laid Najwa's cultured voice reading flatly in French from Céline's *Journey to the End of the Night,* which comes together in a rough sort of exorcism of the young man's pain. It made no sense really, but it had a curious power. When the film ended after some eleven taut minutes and the projector was turned off, I steeled myself in the silence for the usual sarcasm consistent with our class's Chinese Cultural Revolution "auto-critique," in which no one was spared. What would my classmates say about this?

No one had yet spoken. Words become very important in moments like this. And Scorsese simply jumped all the discussion when he said, "Well — this is a filmmaker." I'll never forget that. "Why? Because it's personal. You feel like the person who's making it is living it," he explained. "That's why you gotta keep it close to you, make it yours." No one bitched, not even the usual critiques of my weird mix, sound problems, nothing. In a sense, this was my coming out. It was the first affirmation I'd had in . . . years. This would be my diploma.

Marty's sense of the "personal" was married to a rich Italian American subculture of gang brotherhood and lethal violence. My sense of the personal to date was invested in my growing up in sheltered conservative America and contradicting that with the shattering madness and violence of Vietnam. But it would still take time for my vision to mature and emerge.

When I finished film school in May 1971, there wasn't much to celebrate. There were no jobs waiting, much less any interest in our work. A BFA degree in film meant nothing but another certificate on the wall alongside my Bronze Star. I had no illusions. Several of us went into cab driving, which was the steadiest work I could find; working the night shift from 6 p.m. to 2 or 3 a.m. allowed me to keep writing screenplays in the daytime. It paid about $30 to $40 a night with tips included, which was okay money then. With Najwa's salary and rent-controlled apartment, we could make ends meet.

I'll never forget my desolation when walking back crosstown from the taxi garage at two or three in the morning, buses few and far between; I'd be sparsely dressed in a sweater, fatigue jacket, and thin jeans that couldn't stand up to the fierce blasts of cold air blowing off the Hudson right down those big-ass New York canyon walls. You could die from hypothermia right there on the empty streets and no one would care, not at that hour. My teeth chattering, I'd count the blocks to Najwa's apartment, my little shelter in the world. After that forty-five-minute hike into the wind, I'd arrive chilled and shivering for several minutes. I'd climb quietly into her bed and embrace her warm toaster of a body. I was the toast. She would stir, and sometimes we'd make silent love.

Najwa was finding her way to love me. When things started to deepen between us, she visited her gynecologist, and he recommended I visit a doctor to check myself out. The verdict out of NYU Medical was most painful and abrupt. The doctor said I'd *never* have children; my sperm count was so far below normal, he didn't think it warranted further investigation. I could have been visiting a 1950s insane asylum, asking them about depression and being told I needed a lobotomy. Were there any remedies? Not really. It's hard for me to believe how final this verdict was, but I accepted it. Depressed, yes — "never to have a child" felt like *1984*. It seemed my mother's woes, having one child with complications, were to continue into the next generation. I attributed my shortcomings to my rough forceps birth or the operation at six that had been sold to me as an "appendectomy" but was really the removal of an undescended testicle.

But there was another possibility in this miasma: Vietnam. It was the first time I connected chemical warfare to hearing my grandfather Pépé's stories of the gas attacks in World War I. We'd used great quantities of Dow Chemical's "Agent Orange," which had severely damaged the genes of Vietnamese civilians and poisoned much of their land. We'd patrolled these areas frequently, never worrying about it. The concept of Agent Orange was just then starting to be investigated as a medically liable by-product of that war. What a strange bargain, if it'd been so, that as an infantryman I did not lose my life but lost my future. I went to another doctor for a second opinion, but his prognosis was no different. My father took the news stoically, while my mother thought it was bullshit and assured me I'd have a child one day — of course, she was superstitious and had always supported me.

Most important, Najwa didn't seem to mind, which made me wonder if she truly wanted children of her own. Not that we could afford one, at this time, but in any case Najwa adapted quickly to this conclusion and rarely mentioned having kids again. This led me to believe she took her greatest satisfaction from her embassy work and her strong connections, especially as a loving aunt and sister, to her extensive family in Lebanon.

What Najwa did want, after almost a year of living together, was to get married — or else, she was candid, we should probably break this thing up. The uncertainty for her could not continue. As I had no real prospects, feeling like an abandoned samurai in a Kurosawa picture, I agreed to marry, although I was still too young to realize the consequences. We were wedded in a small civil ceremony at City Hall, attended by her beloved boss the ambassador, his wife, my mother, hopeful, and my father, skeptical. To my mom, as much as she liked Najwa, she was never the "right one," and to Dad, well, she was sort of a secular bus stop on the road to whatever hell I was going to.

In time I became more comfortable, my rough edges smoothing out. I was defanging. I can't say the marriage, from my side, was built on love, but rather on comfort and caring for each other. And for much of it, I was very happy with this refined woman who was solid, more mature than me. She also appreciated the work ethic; I managed almost two original scripts a year, in addition to long story treatments. Besides my taxi driving, I found spot work here and there as a production assistant, and with the help of one of Najwa's friends, the founder of a major trucking company, put together with two young producers a very low-budget film shot near Montreal.

Seizure, originally titled *The Queen of Evil*, was based on a most vivid nightmare I had, which I turned into a screenplay, in which I was a writer of supernatural tales that I also illustrated, living in a rather large old house in the countryside with a wife and young son. My guests that weekend were of different social styles and classes, an eclectic group I was comfortable with; there was nothing forced in the dream. But then evil things began to happen. A window broke. The housekeeper disappeared. The intruders began to show themselves in increasingly frightening ways, and my guests were disappearing one by one. I couldn't do anything. In the grip of some malevolent force that in a dreamscape always seems to leave you utterly passive, I saw a gigantic dwarf figure in medieval clothing with huge, calloused hands crash through a window. There was a stunning black-haired woman who seemed to be guiding events, but she was sociable and fit right in with the guests . . . until she didn't. Horrible scenes continued to unfold mysteriously, mostly out of sight, until I was the last one left alive except for my young son; the others, including my wife, were presumably dead. And now a choice had to be made — this woman was demanding an answer. It was either my life or my son's. So in my dream life, I can't tell you how ashamed I was to abandon my son there to the monsters and flee into the forest for my survival!

Not that this awful woman kept her word, either. Because her gigantic dwarf was thrashing after me in the forest, catching me, and with his tremendous grip was strangling me to death in some bog. I was gurgling, protesting, a muffled "agghhh" barely clawing its way out of my throat as I woke, terrified, in New York City at 4 a.m. Najwa was a shadowy lump next to me — or was she? Was *she* that black-haired woman! I jumped, startled from my side of the bed. Yes, I'd woken, but I was still stuck in this nightmare! And she was here — the malevolent woman from the dream! The Queen of Evil herself.

I couldn't be sure. Slowly I checked. Now I was in real life, it seemed. And thank God it was Najwa next to me, not the other one. I realized it had all been a dream. But where was this cowardice coming from? What was I scared of? In the dream, the writer was bringing this fate down upon himself, his family, his friends. In the dream, he even tells one of his friends he's dreaming the events up, but he can't stop it — which smacks of Greek family tragedy wherein Orestes tells of his being doomed by the Furies.

It was most exciting to make this film, even if my eyes were bigger than my stomach. Najwa helped my two novice producers and I to raise funds, but after a frustrating year of chasing, we didn't have enough money, and from that dilemma arose many problems. I learned a great deal, including not to insist that some of the actors live in the same house where we were shooting. In other words, how to avoid chaos on a movie set. It was a memorable first film experience with a wonderful bouillabaisse of actors, drawn both from the theater — Jonathan Frid (famous as Barnabas Collins in the hit TV series *Dark Shadows*), Annie Meacham, Roger De Koven, Louis Zorich — and from pop culture, sexy Martine Beswick, the outrageous knife-throwing French dwarf Hervé Villechaize, Warhol's Mary Woronov, Troy Donahue (a box office name), and egomaniac Joe Sirola. I changed my title to the less corny *Seizure* partly because my protagonist terrifies himself into a coronary when he finds, after all he's gone through in the dream, that it *is* the Queen of Evil in his bed. There is a double entendre in this title as well, because in our chaotic post-production, in a raid with a bailiff by our side, we had to legally "seize" the film back from our French Canadian director of photography, who owned the production house, and we barely escaped with the film back across the border to the US. *Seizure* was finally released by Cinerama in 1974 in action houses on double bills, did minor business, and, after so much hope and effort, did nothing for my career as a filmmaker.

Through another of Najwa's friends, an important advertising executive, I lucked into a steady-paying job at a baseball sports film company promoting itself as a production house to the big Madison Avenue advertising agencies. But I was hopeless as a salesman, with no real love of advertising or the agency life, and nothing much came of it except that I kept writing, furtively, in the company's backrooms, guilty over taking a salary. And when I was finally, politely, "let go" after almost a year, I was relieved to find myself again on the unemployment line, free of responsibility. That became my financial base whenever I qualified in those years. Down by Wall Street, standing in lines up to an hour and more in a gloomy, run-down official building with fluorescent lighting at its worst, we were treated impersonally by the weary New York State employees; it was nothing I hadn't seen in the army, especially the lines for everything and the indifference of others, but it was definitely something I didn't want to get too familiar with.

Exacerbating these fears, I was reading George Orwell's *Down and Out in Paris and London,* based on his sour 1930s existence trying to write while slumming as a waiter, dishwasher, vagabond; being the realist he was, he made the strong and depressing point that the "workers of the world" were all snagged in this dog-eat-dog economy and could never get out of their bind, thus behaving in even more unkind and ungiving ways. Tough stuff. Orwell himself was spared only because of his past connection to a man he met from his own social class. If not for this deus ex machina, Orwell was implying, there would have been no hope.

The problems with this way of life, as any writer will tell you, was that there is no honest measure of time or effort in such a crazy dream except through rejection, and there was plenty of that. I grew a file with dozens, probably hundreds, of written turndowns, a dossier of shame, from which I drew hurt and a perverse pride in being able to take rejection. Yet my wounded ego interfered with my ability to understand the reasons for these rejections. It's too easy to blame the buyer and not yourself. Beyond the paper world of rejection, there was also the in-person wound of being told no in face-to-face meetings — when they could be had — the hard-to-come-by lunches, the unreturned phone calls. Hope would spring up like a weed inside every word or slight quiver in tone; an eye glancing in an elevator or a lobby off a face you might know, looking for leads *anywhere, anything* — but *without* being obvious. It was, overall, humiliating, the news generally depressing, but with fantasies of succeeding getting me through the days.

Then suddenly my own deus ex machina moment appeared. One of my forty-page treatments, "The Cover-Up," was optioned by an Italian producer, Fernando Ghia, who was dating a pretty Australian model I knew, who, without reading it, suggested he read it — kismet? Fernando, an intellectual, was partnered with the celebrated screenwriter Robert Bolt, who was one of the most admired dramatists of his generation, having created *A Man for All Seasons,* both play and film, and then, for David Lean, *Lawrence of Arabia* and *Doctor Zhivago.* I'd written a story about the recent Patty Hearst kidnapping (1974), calling attention to the little-discussed fact that the leader of the abductors, a black ex-convict named Donald De-Freeze, had a criminal record and was reportedly an FBI informant, which led to all sorts of complications. Although I wasn't politically driven in my screenplay writing, this was a good hook for a story. Could the government deliberately be doing these illegal things? True, my father had been my greatest political influence, but I was moving away from him. I'd loved Costa-Gavras's *Z* as a film student in '69, although that was about Greece. We all worshiped *The Battle of Algiers* (1966) at the school but still didn't connect it to our American belly button. Peter Davis's documentary *Hearts and Minds* in 1974 hit home, yet it was closely focused on Vietnam, which was still far away to most. Emile de Antonio, who'd done a wonderful documentary on the McCarthy era, was the oddball in dealing with US government madness.

Women were also being heard from, and loudly, but most of the liberals at that time—Gloria Steinem, Bella Abzug, Betty Friedan—stuck to female empowerment issues, not the mendacity of the US government in domestic and foreign affairs. The outlier was Jane Fonda, whom I secretly admired for her balls, because she was challenging the government at a high level, even if she seemed to me at that time too radical.

Conspiracy films were newly in the air, such as Alan Pakula's *The Parallax View* (1974) and his forthcoming *All the President's Men* (1976), and Sydney Pollack's *Three Days of the Condor* (1975). For once my timing was right. My treatment was optioned for $5,000 against $40,000 if the film was made, and I was brought out to Los Angeles for a script conference. Bolt, as a dedicated socialist, saw the point of my treatment probably more clearly than I did—the rise of the American security state long before 9/11 —and the idea that "terrorism" could be used to strengthen and monetize the state excited him. He gave this project great urgency and pushed me to flesh out the treatment into a full screenplay.

Although it was exhilarating to be working at this level, and my knowledge of screenwriting was accelerating, writing for Bolt became a baptism by fire, and the fire was constantly being quenched. With him, I was swinging back from the free form of the NYU filmmaker world to the strict screenwriting art, in which the movie is laid out in some detail on paper, so that the money people can oversee their investment more closely. You're not writing a movie as much as submitting an architectural blueprint. I'd give Bolt pages as I went, and like the schoolteacher he'd been for many years, Robert red-penciled a great deal of it while explaining, elaborating, and often writing between the lines. He found the work "a bit careless . . . but I'll punch it up in London for these cunts who'll read it. It won't be a shooting script." The process became even more torturous with him back in the UK requesting more rewrites and more questioning. My script pages were going back and forth over the course of the next three months, but I never felt I could please Robert. In England, he always had "doubts." Then again, he was known to take years sometimes to write a screenplay; such was *The Mission*, which he worked on for almost ten years. To me it became a lesson in overwriting. We're not writing a play but making movies. We need speed and action, not too heady. When *The Mission* finally came out in 1986 it was brilliant, yes, sophisticated, issue-oriented, and yet it failed at the box office because it missed the element of sheer excitement that I wanted for our film.

And so "The Cover-Up" was again traversing that slow, dull passage of time that tells you there is no film, and there will be no film, and we're really going to funerals for the dream we never lived. It was, in the end, a quality political thriller, half Bolt, half Stone, well written, recommended at the studios, but dulled by its polish, and with a glum ending, its commercial prospects weren't appealing to financiers. A series of actors and directors turned it down. My last hope was Robert Shaw, who was achieving leading man status after *Jaws,* but he too passed. I was heartbroken, but used to it; the patterns of struggle and failure in life tend to repeat themselves.

I also knew a similar honesty was now required in my life with Najwa. We had to end the Lie that had become our marriage. My spirit was simply expiring; you can't hide that. I came back from Los Angeles on what was likely my last trip for "The Cover-Up" and went straight to the apartment and told her that I couldn't go on this way. We fought, our voices went up, both of us acting out our deeply hurt roles. Yes, Najwa would grow fiercely jealous of any woman I talked to at any party, but she also knew I'd never seriously pursued an affair with another; there'd been a tumultuous interlude in Canada with my *Queen of Evil* star, but that had lasted a month and, like film melodramas, had died off. The love and passion of my life, if there was to be any — that woman was still out there in the cosmos. And Najwa sensed it.

But she thought it was Los Angeles that was twisting me, that I'd been deeply hurt by this setback on "Cover-Up." But if I stuck it out, she was sure my career would gather heat and I would succeed. She loved my talent. She'd grown to trust it. And she'd grown to love me as her husband, and when I looked around, it was so comfortable in that little apartment, my things laid out in their proper place, my writing desk, my library, watching TV together, the warmth of another's body to sleep with at night or talk to after making love.

"Comfortable" was the killer word. In a few more years she'd be forty, I'd be thirty-five, still living in this rent-controlled apartment, no children, occasional weekends on Fire Island or in the Hamptons; maybe we'd share a summerhouse with other couples. Occasional vacations and trips back to Lebanon. And maybe I'd sell a screenplay or treatment here and there. Or if not, well, there'd be so many international people coming through New York and asking for business favors from Morocco that Najwa could potentially find us a spot in one of these ventures. With her Lebanese instincts guiding the ship, I'd sharpen my own business acumen. And one day, with fortitude and patience, perhaps we'd even be rich. Comfortable, for sure. But who was I in this? I still didn't know. But I knew that's how people stop believing in their dreams.

Nor was Los Angeles, which was increasingly in my sights as a route of hope, ever in consideration as a place to live for Najwa. New York was her true home, and although she was in her prime and could certainly have attracted a quality man who could take far better care of her than I, she had never come to New York looking for a sugar daddy. I believe she came to love her job more than she'd ever love a man. This sounds severe, but I think of all the strong women I've known working in jobs so long — thirty or more years — who moved beyond the need for a husband.

Because she was older than me, some people said I'd married my mother, which hurt me. Nobody said it out loud, of course, but I could feel it. And there was some truth to it. My mother certainly must have thought of it immediately, and I'm sure was flattered — "Oliver needs a woman like me . . . I raised him, I know what he likes! Of course, Najwa's nothing like me, but she keeps him happy. She loves him like I loved Lou. She's good for him."

There's nothing ultimately wrong with men loving their mothers, absolutely not. In fact, it's a healthy sign. But the truth was, I'd started breaking my "jones" with my mother during those years in Vietnam. Now I was being "cared for" by my older wife, but that was okay from Mom's point of view. The flaw was that I hadn't grown into my own man. This I knew in my gut — that I hadn't yet been successful as a writer because I'd failed to complete the journey I started when I went to Vietnam. I hadn't held my own and stood alone; I'd settled for the comfort of a bourgeois marriage with a good woman who could give me a home, give me sex, share her friends, and make well-cooked fish. She had loved me in her way, but who was I really? I would never know.

As I left the apartment that night with two suitcases, it'd been almost five years I'd been sleeping here, but I'd never felt this was my home. I told Najwa I'd come back for the rest of my things and kissed her lightly on the cheek, saying as gently as I could, "Take care of yourself, Najwa. We'll talk." I was relieved to get out of there before something worse happened, like an emotional thunderstorm. But then she said quietly, as if she knew I wouldn't come back this time, "Stay my friend . . . ?"

This hung there in the air; it stopped me, the tremor of the question in her voice. It was heartbreaking, because she needed my energy, my vibrations. She needed *me*. She loved me deeply. How could I be just "a friend"? What could I be but a bastard! Break hearts. No, not really. But I was a child of divorce, yes. Why not, it's the way of the world. Didn't you meet my parents? Didn't you see this coming — that great mistake they committed when they married and begat me? I brushed one of her tears away and left her without the love I could not give. The door closed on her broken expression, and feeling coldhearted, I walked down the hall, down the stairs, and into the street, where I inhaled the first fresh breath of air that I'd had in . . . years.

I'd loved Najwa to the degree that I could, but in that blurry, constrained manner when we know we are not being honest with ourselves; you could say I didn't understand what love was, because it's an overused and overdramatized word, but nonetheless as powerful an explanation for the universe as we have. I read once in an Eastern text that love could be known only "by its absence." We take away, we subtract, reduce — and there it is finally. In its simplicity, you love. No bells, no whistles, just good old love, like an old sweater . . . I didn't know who — but I'd meet her someday.

Not surprisingly, forty years later, Najwa remains in her lovely "rent-stabilized" apartment, going to the same job she still loves. Seven, eight ambassadors later in time, it makes no difference. Najwa serves the Royal Kingdom of Morocco. And even the damn king has changed, but not Najwa, bless her. She remains very close to her family, adores her sisters, nieces, nephews. I still visit with her, not without sadness, and cherish what we can of our memories together.

• • •

Past midnight now, the Fourth of July fireworks were winding down. Hours had slipped by. The waves were lapping quietly at the Statue of Liberty's little islet, her soft face still visible in the light of the last explosions.

"Time is the fire in which we burn," the poet Delmore Schwartz wrote. Things had gone wrong for my mother and father; they never fit, and I too, as their sole product in temperament, was destined for divorce. It'd been a lie. So had Vietnam. So had most of my life. The Lie had infected everything, and I was still numb from it. Because I'd basically never woken up. I was so lost. I wasn't sure of anything. In that story I'd read long ago, where was the thread Theseus had found to get out of that huge Cretan labyrinth?

With a silent nod of hope mixed with despair, I bade farewell to my goddess and headed for the uptown subway — and in that way, my Fourth of July 1976 drew to a close.

3

The Land across the Sea

L ooking, I suppose, for a thread to anything, I started to peck away at a story based on my memories of January 1, 1968. What had I really remembered of that battle except the bodies and the fireworks? Eight years ago was a long time — details, faces were blurring. Ten screenplays and maybe five real-time years of my ass connected to a chair — and nothing to show for it. This story might possibly speak some truth about our failure in Vietnam because it'd be bigger than just "miserable old me." A first draft shouldn't take so long, or I'd end up like a crazed Robert Bolt, researching and writing for years. Cut your losses. As I understood Norman Mailer's directive on writing, we are governed by a secret pact to do it each day, to store and carry the residue of the previous day into our unconscious, to sleep on it, and then continue that mindset through the next day. It's a rhythm you don't break, and if you do, you wasted your preparation, never to be regained the same way.

After leaving Najwa, I moved into a friend's third-floor walkup for almost a year. It was like living at a YMCA — a small, shabby room overlooking the rumble of trucks day and night down Second Avenue. I was happy here in my little room, no obligations, no rent to pay. My friend Danny Jones, in his forties, a divorced five-foot-five Englishman of sardonic wit and generous heart, held a stable and creative job as an art director at a top New York advertising agency, but he also had a huge appetite for drugs and alcohol and, like many New Yorkers, was living every two weeks from paycheck to paycheck. Being a bachelor again with an eccentric host, I found the gloom of George Orwell's poverty was dispelled, and I discovered a side of New York no cab driver would ever find on his map, the world of Henry Miller's 1930s Paris, transposed to 1970s New York — an underdream of aspiring musicians, filmmakers, actresses and models, photographers, artists of all stripes, Wall Street hustlers, Park Avenue heiresses, divorcées, widows, teachers, nurses, doctors selling speed, drug dealers, immigrants, all new, all on the make. Every night turned into an adventure; waking up in different places, I don't think I've ever had as much fun in my life, maybe because being young and single is more fun without money, and maybe because the only thing money can't buy is poverty. Money gives you an edge, but without it, you become more human. In some ways it was like being back in the infantry, with a grunt's worm's-eye view. Everything is seen by looking up. Every gift, every kindness is appreciated as much as any dollar.

Sometimes, for the majority of the day I'd walk alone through the streets, exploring or dreaming. There was unemployment money, but that eventually ran out. And I felt no guilt at being a bum, not responsible to my father, or Robert Bolt, or anybody. I still felt destined for higher things, but was enjoying, day by day, the rent-free shelter given me by an older Falstaff in return for my collaboration with him on two promising screenplays. Let me add that with his remarkable Celtic constitution, Danny went to work each morning sober, as I would write up our ideas at his tiny kitchen table. But this writer's journey of hope and heartbreak does not bear repeating, except to say that I was now totally responsible for myself, and since I'd gone on this unique journey, I knew I was going to the very end of my talent — *if* I had any.

But after six months, our co-written screenplays were languishing in purgatory, and I sensed nothing was going to happen with them — again. "Nothing" is the most frustrating feeling in the world. *Nothing*. After that Fourth of July night, I began writing alone again, quickly in longhand, three pages here, four pages there, building a muscle of memory mixed with some imagination. I called it simply "The Platoon."

War in reality is dull. So much boredom and dead time. Spiritual death too. A realistic version of my time in four different units, three of them combat platoons, would not make an interesting movie, and I was a screenwriter by this time, even if without success; I had at least gotten to know the form and the feel for it. The movie culture by the '70s was moving off the success of *Midnight Cowboy* and *Easy Rider* in 1969 in a neo-realistic, antiheroic direction. Dustin Hoffman, Jack Nicholson, Bob De Niro, Al Pacino, and Women's Liberation were contradicting the traditional roles movie heroes and heroines had played. Nonetheless, movies had historically, to my mind, stood for action, spectacle, resonance — above all, a feeling that life had a meaning. Even failure had a meaning. And now I had to find meaning in that shitty little war if I was going to write a movie about it.

I didn't want it to be an allegory like "Break," my 1969 effort to deal with Vietnam. This was not going to be just about me — it would be about all of us who went on that journey without an ending. It was not hippies or college boys but lost working-class men whose future in contemporary America would be increasingly bleak. And I'd be the observer, if such exists. My alter ego in the script would be Chris Taylor — an anodyne white Protestant name for a young man who volunteered and just wanted to be anonymous over there. After all, in the army I'd resorted to using, as in boarding school and the merchant marine, my official baptismal name, William. My middle name, which my parents settled on — Oliver — was too effete and European for rougher American accents. So Chris would have no family history to haunt his flesh, and there'd be a distant but obviously important grandmother to whom he writes letters from the battlefield:

> Well, here I am — anonymous alright, with guys no one really cares about — they come from the end of the line, most of 'em towns you've never heard of — Pulaski, Tennessee, Brandon, Mississippi, Pork Bend, Utah . . . Two years' high school's about it, maybe if they're lucky a job waiting for them back in a factory, but most of them got nothing, they're poor . . . they're the backbone of this country, grandma, the best I've ever seen, the heart and soul . . . I found it, finally, way down here in the mud — maybe from down here I can start up again and be something I can be proud of, without having to fake it.

This would be a movie with young men who looked older than their years, not men in their thirties and forties playing young GIs like in many Hollywood war movies. It'd be a dirty war, as it was—men who rarely slept, their nerves bent out of proportion, jumpy, hateful, playing to some of their baser instincts of racism, white, black, and yellow. And at its worst, it'd be about murder most foul, as in a Greek drama. But their faces would be pure rural or inner-city American. It'd be a modest, low-down grubby movie, but with a venomous sting.

Watching antiwar demonstrations in New York brought up a fury and contradiction in myself over something in the American air that was so deeply hypocritical; we marched for peace but somehow wanted war, wanted to release its aggression. After all, I'd wanted to go, hadn't I? And I felt again the pure futility of my quest, alongside that of our expeditionary army. I was back in *The Iliad* with those Greeks camping on the shores outside the walls of Troy, with the divisive bickering and feuds. Like the Greeks, I felt, the Americans had great hubris embodied by an undeserved arrogance of victory left over from World War II. As our "Dr. Strangelove," Henry Kissinger, summed up the problem, "I refuse to believe that a little fourth-rate power like Vietnam does not have a breaking point." We were so proud, and then, when we couldn't achieve victory, we had to lie like we all do when we deny what we know is true—that we lost, and lost big-time, and all those technology-loving Pentagon warriors were at last revealed as failures, and those determined little Vietnamese had licked us. So America came up with its "Peace with Honor" public relations campaign, and then later intensified it with its "Bring Home Our Missing POWs" mission to mask the Vietnamese denial of our will to win. Never lose, never. This exceptionalism was stamped all over the arrogance of *Patton,* embodied by George C. Scott in the hit movie of 1970. The horrible truth was Americans loved this Patton, the movie and the man, a sick man who'd gone too far. We loved killers. Why was I raised seeing killers on almost every TV show? Isn't that why I made *Natural Born Killers* later in life—to show that madness in our culture?

In my script, I'd model my alter ego on Odysseus, the wanderer struggling to find his way home. A young man without identifying traits beyond a vague educated-class status who goes innocently into hell and comes out the other side — a man darkened by his experience. I'd read Edith Hamilton and Robert Graves and loved the actions and fates of the multiple characters that appeared in Greek myth, which had essentially disappeared from our culture. That's why Professor Tim Leahy at NYU, whose class I'd taken outside the film school, struck lightning with me in a classical drama course; he'd rage about the fate of Odysseus.

"Why," he'd thunder, "did Odysseus alone return to Penelope after nearly twenty years? Why him of all the heroes that went off to Troy?"

He waited for his answer — silence. "Nine years! On the beaches at Troy, and nine more years returning to Ithaca. No one else in his crew made it home. Why? Why Odysseus?

"Consciousness!" he wrote, as his fist banged the chalkboard, his voice carrying. "Because he had consciousness," he repeated. "That, people, is what kept him alive. That's the difference between each one of us — how conscious can you remain in this hard world? How often do we forget because we . . . what? We want to —" He banged the board where he'd written the word *"LETHE"* in big block letters. "Sleep! Lethe. Forgetfulness." In the silence that followed, I sensed several of the students were already practicing their form of "lethe" in this sparsely attended class.

"What are the Lotus Eaters about? Why are men turned into swine by Circe? Because they forgot they were men. They became beasts. But not Odysseus. Why does he order his men to tie him to the mast, no matter how much he'd plead to be released? Because, while his men stuff their ears with wax, he wants to *hear* the voices of these sirens! Knowledge — that is what Odysseus is after." He was gone deep into the recesses of Odysseus's mind. No one was taking the bait, most of them terrified of interrupting this intense man. He was so loud, I imagine people in Washington Square eight floors below our open window could hear him.

"Because he *wants* to *know!* To hear — *to know all things!* To go to the end of things. Consciousness, people, consciousness. *That* is the difference between life and death. This is what makes the modern man. Pay attention, I implore you!" It was sad to see this really great teacher using all of his life breath to pour the honey of Greek myth into the overstuffed minds of these bored and jaded NYU students.

Who would listen? This is the question. I understand now that I was lucky to be there, because I did recognize, if not yet completely, the importance of what he was saying, and that the Word and the Memory are what connect us through time; and one solitary young man hearing Leahy in that classroom might carry on that memory as if it were a torch passed down from Homer himself to the end of his own life — and perhaps, through my passing it on to others, ennoble the meaning of the Greek myths. Not only does Odysseus have the hugely difficult problem of surviving the Trojan War, and then nine more years of travails, but also, once he manages to get home, lo and behold, he's facing dozens of cocky young men from a new generation thinking him long dead, now lusting after his wealth and his beautiful widow's consent in marriage. That he, weary from all his wanderings, actually accomplishes this homecoming by pretending to be a poor beggar and slaying these aggressors and reclaiming his wife, son, and island is the most glorious of his actions — and a deeply satisfying climax to one of the greatest stories we have.

Remember that many of the most famous warriors — Hercules, driven mad, Ajax, a suicide, or Agamemnon, murdered by his wife and her lover — could not resolve this abyss at the end of their outsized lives, whereas Odysseus, despite his enormous suffering, did. When Tennyson described him in his famous poem as an older man still wanting "to seek, to find, and not to yield," it's the ultimate Victorian compliment to our ability to rise above our circumstances. To my mind, Odysseus is a Western hero parallel to Gautama Buddha in the Eastern tradition. But it's telling that to the Western mind, killing your rivals and reclaiming your wife and property has far more resonance than the story of Buddha's life, which embraces nonviolence. And that's why, in my own life, I kept coming back to Odysseus as an example of conscious behavior. I drew sustenance from it. If he could stick it out, so could I.

Given, then, that the mythic in all of us is hiding behind the ordinary, I searched for my equivalent Achilles, Hector, and Odysseus. Leahy made me understand the people I'd been with in Vietnam had more weight than I'd felt at the time — several heroic, some cowardly, most in between.

I especially remembered two soldiers who stood out; both were sergeants, whom I encountered in two separate units of the 1st Cavalry Division. "Sergeant Barnes," as I renamed him in the film, had the pride of

Achilles, an avatar of war, quiet and dangerous, darkly handsome, prominently scarred, his wound running an entire half of his face from forehead and eye to jawline. Compact at five foot seven, he was as close to a leader as any of us in the infantry ever saw. With his four stripes — three above, one rocker below — he was really a staff NCO acting as a platoon sergeant because we were usually short-handed. I carried his radio for a stretch, walking directly behind him through the bush, keeping in contact with our platoon and company command posts. He was left-handed, a natural shooter, so smooth in his movements. It seemed fitting he hailed from Montana someplace, a nineteenth-century fur trapper type with black eyes and a bushy black mustache, seemingly scared of nothing. When he spoke, you obeyed.

One morning, out on an irregular early patrol around seven, he froze, signaling for silence. We waited. The faintest whiff of cooking fish came from the bush. He moved quickly, quietly ahead, motioning us to stay still. No distractions. A long silence followed, then some sudden shots, then nothing. Barnes came back, no expression, told me to get our patrol up here. He'd killed two Viet Cong, young men carelessly eating their breakfast, never suspecting the Americans would be out so early. They paid with their lives. Most of us were pretty excited whenever we actually, but rarely, saw the enemy, much less killed them. But Barnes was cool, so cool, no big displays ever. Having reported the incident, and stripping the dead men, he soon had us under way, no credit taken, looking for further action ahead; considering there had already been contact, the likelihood of more that day was in the air. Whereas some of us were not looking forward to such an encounter, the thought excited Barnes. He was a great soldier, probably on his second or third tour — but why? Why would he come back after a facial wound like he had? I never asked, and he never told.

You hear things in the army, as in all society, and some kind of narrative emerges; in this case, the story was that he'd been literally shot or sustained shrapnel in the face, skull, head, requiring a major reconstruction job as the scar branched deeply around his eye, nose, and cheek; even his lips were affected. And as he had clearly once been a handsome man, the scars perversely heightened his visage into a Phantom of the Opera echo — a man distorted, perhaps, by anger or revenge, or really a question mark.

What was he about? He never hinted in all the time I was around him. I watched him with both curiosity and trepidation; he'd get back to the rear after we'd been out in the field a week or more and relax with booze, poker, cigarettes, sometimes a cigar. It was said he'd been in Japan in the hospital about eight months, rehabbing from the wound. And there he'd "married a Japanese gal." And now he was back. Sort of an Ahab looking for his White Whale. And here I was, like Ishmael, walking five or ten steps behind him, always expecting that something was going to break because, like a fly, he smelled the blood of war.

As good a soldier as he was, I was relieved when he got rid of me as his radio operator. I don't know what line I'd crossed in his mind; never said much, maybe he just didn't like my face, maybe I was thinking too much, and you don't want to think too much when the shit hits the fan, but I was happy to go back to "point" or "flank," as just another grunt. Why? Because anyone who knows the infantry knows to keep your mouth shut, do what you're told, slowly if you can, don't volunteer for nuthin', and don't get singled out. Barnes was trouble, a magnet for action — and walking behind him was definitely dangerous. I was seven months in at this point, and with two wounds, I'd learned a few lessons.

I'd actually been exempt from further combat with my wounds, and was first sent from the 25th Infantry in the south to an auxiliary MP unit in Saigon, guarding billets and buildings all night — a deeply boring assignment that could turn deadly in a flash. The master sergeants (six stripes and a diamond in the center) were the true gods of the army, as close to generals as we'd ever see. They were "lifers," guys in their forties, fifties, with twenty to thirty years' service from World War II and Korea, many of them ballbreakers who knew better than to come out in the field and risk their life when they had a nice pension coming due; so most of them stayed in the rear with cushy "administrative" jobs and, depending on their badass nature, would fuck with you accordingly when you came back to base. Sometimes it was the uniform or your bedding, your rifle, sometimes it could be dope, or booze, or "attitude," but whatever it was, it was bullying. My master sergeant busted me for "blousing" my trousers either inside or outside my "dirty" boots, as well as talking back to him. He charged me with an "Article 15" infraction, a common means to punish disorderly soldiers short of a court-martial. Assuming I'd lose the case, I volunteered to return to the field. This sergeant was more than happy to get rid of me, and soon enough I was ordered north to the 1st Cavalry, not far from the DMZ line between North and South Vietnam, for the rest of my fifteen-month tour.

My relationship with the master sergeant race remained dubious throughout, and I barely mention officers, because we didn't see much of them. Platoon lieutenants were the closest to us, some good, some bad, most okay and forgettable. The platoon sergeant, like Barnes, was the boss. Sometimes a standout captain at company level, yes, but most of them had nothing to do with the bubble in which you lived. When you're spread out in the jungle, or even the rice paddies, imagine how the lieutenant and captain disappear in the foliage or the formation itself. Majors were rare, remote, never talked to; I saw them only during large-scale, battalion-size operations, and above that, maybe once or twice a lieutenant colonel or, very rarely, like spotting a polar bear or an eagle, a general. Nor, for that matter, did I run across those much-written-about war correspondents who preferred hanging with the marines, who loved their publicity and consciously worked them. Our "regular army" lacked glamour; very rarely a story that got attention back in "the world."

If Sergeant Barnes was a mythic Achilles, Sergeant Elias was Hector, noble but doomed. I'd come to know him in my previous unit — the Long-Range Recon Patrol (LRRP, nicknamed "Lurps"). Elias was a squad sergeant, three stripes, no rocker; it may not mean much to a civilian, but each stripe in the noncommissioned ranks meant differences in money, privileges, and sometimes life and death. Elias should have been, in experience alone, a four-striper (platoon sergeant) like Barnes, but clearly he'd been busted for some infraction. There were quite a few of these combat vets who'd been demoted. You could tell from the pride Elias had in his washed-out uniform, the rolled-up sleeves and lapels, the silver Indian-made bracelet on his smooth forearm, the Buddhist medallion he wore over his hairless chest. Like Barnes, he was compact and lithe, about five foot eight, with strong black dancing eyes, full of life like Jim Morrison on his first album cover; you're not supposed to use the word "beautiful" for a man, but he was — a beautiful Apache from Arizona someplace, mixed with Spanish blood. In the way rumors spread, he'd "done time" back in the world, and probably made a deal with a judge to join up; he was now on his second tour. Bear in mind, guys like him could save up a good deal of money with combat pay in Vietnam, which he needed, as I'd heard he had a fucked-up marriage of some kind, with a young daughter.

Elias's future, no doubt, with his spotty background, would be as a "lifer" in the army, that is, if he could make it through the twenty years. This was where the money was for him. Considering what I've read about the old-time Apaches, they could run circles around the regular cavalry and never be seen. But the reservation wore them down, as a system of gradual oppression always does. No one could resist the white man's system — its clever use of money as reward and bribe — ensnaring all of us in a giant scheme of corruption.

Elias just loved going out on a scout. That's what the Lurps did — take chances. They were the guys who went deep into the jungle in small groups of five to twelve and came back with the news that was supposed to make a difference. Sometimes they went into the Ashau Valley to stake out on trails or mountaintops overlooking North Vietnamese regulars moving down from Laos or North Vietnam on the Ho Chi Minh Trail. But the idea was *not* to engage, just spot and report, maybe call in artillery or just silently withdraw. Some of the nightmares were more rumored than experienced. "No one coming back alive" was usually an exaggerated claim; most of the time, nothing happened.

Anyway, as you might deduce, once I got to the 1st Cavalry in the north, I was "washed out" of the Lurps for "an attitude problem" by another prick master sergeant with a handlebar mustache much too big for his skinny, tattooed, grizzled drunk frame, another overdecorated six-striper who'd guzzled more whiskey than most broken-down fifty-year-old cowboys; you could always tell from the huge "hungry ghost" gut hanging out on a skinny frame of bones, his whiskey-soaked brains no longer able to digest food or thought. These are the guys who, when hung over, would love to hear themselves yelling at some "dumbass FNG" (fucking new guy).

I did get to know Elias a little, and he was fun to be around; everyone seemed to like him, no one had a beef going with him. He smoked dope in the rear, loved music, and could talk jive. Whereas Barnes was hard and real, Elias was dreamy, a movie star. With Barnes, you knew he'd walk out of this war alive; after all, who could kill Barnes if a bullet through his head hadn't achieved its purpose? But Elias . . . different cat, different destiny. Far more vulnerable, feminine. Whereas with Barnes I'd be wary, with Elias I wanted to be assigned to his squad, I wanted to shine and show off for him. I wanted him, above all, to like me. But because of that master sergeant, I never got the chance.

After I was dropped from the Lurps, I moved down the road to a regular outfit with the 1st Battalion, 9th Cavalry Regiment, where I first encountered Sergeant Barnes, who ran that show. And it was there, about a month later, where I first heard it. The news came casually, like a baseball score on an overheard radio — Sergeant 'Lias from the "Lurps up the road" was KIA on patrol. Something stupid, even demeaning, had happened to him. A grenade had accidentally gone off. It wasn't clear, but it was one of ours, not even an ambush or firefight. A man as good as Elias "wasted" by someone's mistake. My God, I even imagined that asshole master sergeant who had it in for me had maybe gone out on some easy mission to make his quota of combat time and set something off like that, a loose grenade. But what, besides my prejudices against master sergeants, did I really know about what happened? I tried to find out, but getting the truth in a war is nearly impossible. And reading any after-action report, if you can get it, is devious.

A firefight breaks in the jungle, and at first you don't know who's firing in or out or where it's coming from, and because of the varying angles in a jungle, you often don't know where your own men are. There's shooting, the smoke, and the screaming on the radio; and even then, there were numerous times you knew your own men were firing past you toward the supposed enemy. That's not a fun feeling. Death comes 360°, from *all* directions.

No one in my new unit, including Barnes, knew him. Only me, and that made it tougher. I knew Elias's worth as a man, but I had no one to share it with. And in time, with other events happening one upon the other, the Elias story was layered into a nest of memories. It was equally unfair the way they chopped up the units with replacement troops and moved us around with orders in such ways that we lost track of one another. Perhaps it was intended to lessen the effects on morale by keeping things anonymous and forgettable, but still we found things out through the grapevine. I never could believe the sloppiness in the reports on Elias. I always sensed something worse had happened. I tried to get down the road to my old unit and ask some questions, but opportunities like that when we were in base camp were rare. In the same vein, it wasn't too long before Sergeant Barnes disappeared one day without fanfare, his tour apparently up; no explanations. That was the army.

Seventeen years later, in 1985, I visited the newly constructed Vietnam Veterans Memorial in Washington and caught up with Elias. He existed —I wasn't crazy. He was inscribed as Juan Angel Elias from Arizona. And when I used his real name in my *Platoon* film to honor him, and mentioned him in interviews, I received another kind of confirmation when his daughter wrote me and came to Los Angeles to find out who her father was, because she sure as hell didn't know. I didn't either, so I couldn't help her much. She'd been a child when he was killed, and she was fragile, struggling in her life. He was so young; we all were back then. And yes, so many of the vets and their families were struggling, not just her. War breeds that struggle. Her mother, it seems, had a stormy marriage with Elias, a lot of tough things happened to him — the law, always "the law" in America. Being from New York, I used to hate the abundance of cop shows on TV, but I recognize now that the law, the sheriff, the sense of frontier justice is embedded in the American soul, as fundamental to our thinking as the need for a gun. Forget about such a thing as class; most Americans know what jail is and what "the law" is better than they know school. People in America get into "trouble"; that's the way it is, and then it becomes a song on a guitar. Elias was defying the odds from the beginning — too much free spirit for his own good. And Barnes, in his way, was that sheriff and would dispense that frontier justice.

But what if Barnes and Elias were in the same platoon? My imagination was kindled by the possibility. They'd be the alpha leaders of this imaginary platoon; both men, as in real life, were sexual magnets to the naked eye. The story would have a basic, striking duality in which I, as the newcomer Chris Taylor, would be attracted to different sides of myself—my father's strong, "realistic" masculine attitude in Barnes in conflict with my mother's rule-breaking rebel in Elias. It intrigued me. And what if it ended up with one man destroying the other? As Achilles did Hector.

As I kept writing, my memories were expanding, and I began to understand my experience in Vietnam on a deeper level. Ours had been a battle of man and his corruption in a system that demanded every man there had to lie, which, in a sense, was a form of dishonoring ourselves. The war there was one of the many manifestations of the Lie, which I'd first experienced during my parents' divorce. There were three lies I saw. The first was "friendly fire," which had killed a man I'd liked and admired — Sergeant Elias. As defined by the rules, "friendly fire" was death by our own weaponry — bombs, artillery shells, grenades, rifle and M79 fire in close combat. It included "accidents" that happened all the time — gunships opening fire on us; artillery coordinates that were a few degrees off in a jungle; an F-16 flying in low and fast, operating off shifting coordinates; even a guy who didn't read directions so good might point his Claymore mine inward instead of outward and, instead of blowing up NVA soldiers on his perimeter, would make a mess of himself when it went off in his face.

The Pentagon, which years later turned down *Platoon*'s initial request for technical assistance (calling the script a falsification and distortion of service life), doesn't talk about it much, but "friendly fire" might have unofficially killed and wounded, I believe, at least 15 percent of the boys in Vietnam, probably more. The military has cut it out of the official records and Hollywood movies as much as they can, because they don't want thousands of poor parents or wives getting upset about their loved ones dying so stupidly. Imagine — 15 percent of the American KIA in Vietnam amounts to almost nine thousand; and then there are the three hundred thousand wounded, seventy-five thousand of them severely disabled. Ron Kovic, in his searing memoir *Born on the Fourth of July*, wrote a profound chapter about how he shot one of his own men by mistake. After Ron's marine CO refused to accept his declaration of culpability, Ron allowed this incident to build into a mountainload of guilt that led to Ron essentially offering himself as a sacrifice — and ending up sealed in a wheelchair the rest of his tormented life. I have no proof either, but I'm 75 percent sure an incompetent squad sergeant in the 25th Infantry early in my tour almost killed me in my first ambush action at night when, from behind me, he carelessly threw his grenade "short," close to my position, and blasted me into unconsciousness. I was, in fact, very lucky to survive. Another inch in, and the shrapnel would've severed my jugular. This goes on all the time, and is, I think, one of the great secrets of modern war.

The second lie involved killing civilians — by bomb and artillery mostly, but also by infantry. We were careless. The My Lai massacre in March of '68 had decimated several villages, resulting in a body count of more than five hundred civilians — without *one* enemy bullet being fired. We heard about it, and knew this killing arose from the frustration of losing men to mines and never seeing the enemy. Villagers then replaced the enemy in many GIs' minds. And as the summer of '68 progressed, it grew uglier. Between missions into the thickly covered Ashau Valley, we'd run "recons" as well as "search and destroy" missions on villages up and down the coast around Quang Tri and Hue. We were angry much of the time, because our sergeants made us look for VC in holes, pits, bunkers, and you never knew what the fuck was down there — would it blow up in your face? You'd yell, "Get the fuck out! Get out!" into these hidden spaces, and sometimes one or two villagers would slowly pop out, terrified. Then you'd find weapons, and arms, and rice stores all around these villages. So you hated the civilians, because you felt they were supporting them, the enemy. I felt sorry for the villagers too, because I knew they were getting pressure from the other side. I didn't know where their real political sympathies lay; I don't believe most of them had them. They were into survival, just like we were.

We might be walking up on a village one day, and there'd be an old lady walking away down a trail. A grunt, in a bad mood and just fucking with her, would yell, "Hey, gook, come here. Hey, you — 'didi'! You — get your ass over here!" She might not hear, or she wouldn't want to turn around because she was scared. She'd just keep walking a few more steps. The guy wouldn't ask her a second time, he'd just raise his M16 — *boom, boom, boom.* No questions asked. She hadn't come when he told her to. He wouldn't have done that with an officer around, or a sergeant with authority, but it happened.

One time I came close to losing it. It was a blindingly hot day, and I was sick and tired of Vietnamese villagers protesting, denying, moaning in self-pity, lying to us, hiding things from us, it didn't matter. I was just sick of the whole thing — our role in this, their language, their smell, their anger at us, and my own fear and anger all mixed up. And when a stubborn old farmer started yelling at me accusingly, I snapped. I fired several rounds right at his feet, screaming at him to "shut up and dance, motherfucker! Shut the fuck up!" I wanted to kill him, and I could've gotten away with it. We were spread out in pockets, two or three men around me, no sergeants with us. The other soldiers were busy searching other parts of the village. But I didn't kill him; there was the thinnest of lines that prevented me, the thinnest thread of humanity in me that didn't break.

In a different village, I broke up a group of three soldiers harassing two Vietnamese teenage girls; the tension was growing into a clumsy rape. Some men in my platoon turned on me for that. Another time, a dumb eighteen-year-old kid in our group boasted quietly that he'd killed someone; he'd bashed in the head of an old woman with the stock of his M16, then burned her hooch down to wipe out the crime. Nobody saw it because the village was spread out; he was arrogant and stupid, and no one took him seriously, but who really knows what he did? You see, it was a kind of game if you could fuck "them" up without getting caught; some of the guys were like naughty kids with rifles getting away with something — that's how crazy it could get. We were always pushing them, shoving them, treating them like lower beings, animals. We were bullies. There was just no telling what happened in a village that was spread over several hundred meters.

I became an acknowledged killer one day that summer when we ran into a mean little ambush in a beach area not far from the ocean on the outskirts of a village; we lost a lieutenant and a sergeant as well as our scout dog, a German shepherd I'd taken quite a liking to. It was one of these strange little firefights that grew from single random shots into a raging storm of bullets. Two of our platoons were spread out over approximately a hundred yards, confused by the directions on the radio — when suddenly there was new fire from inside our own positions, which created even more confusion. This was highly dangerous, and it would've been a calamity for us to enter into a crossfire situation where we were shooting each other; the enemy was often known to plan ambushes so that would happen. I was under no obligation to do anything but keep my head down and let this thing work itself out. Yet I strongly felt I had to deal with this confusion myself or no one else would, and a disaster would happen today. I *had* to do something. Maybe I was really cold and angry about that police dog's death, or the futility of it all, or maybe, like Camus once described, I just had a headache and the sun was burning too hot in my eyes. Who the fuck knows these things? I did know one thing — that *this* was my moment in time to act, and if I didn't . . .

Exposing myself, I rushed a spider hole from which I sensed someone had fired and taken cover. Without further thinking, I threw my grenade from about fifteen yards away toward the tiny hole. This was very risky, because if I'd overthrown the grenade, it might've easily wounded or killed our own men crouched ten yards beyond the hole, unsure of what to do. But it was a perfect pitch, and the grenade sailed into the hole like a long throw from an outfielder into a catcher's mitt — followed quickly by the concussed thump of the explosion. Wow. I'd done it! Warily I moved in closer, thinking he might still be alive, but when I looked down into the hole, the man was mauled, torn, and very dead. It felt good. I actually saw the man I killed, which was rare in this jungle warfare. I was proud. Barnes would've been proud of me too if he'd been there. His efficiency was now mine. The dozen men who saw the action were astonished — and grateful. Somehow word got around, and I was quite surprised a week later to be told by the lieutenant I was going to get a Bronze Star. For what? Doing what I was supposed to do — which, in truth, a lot of people didn't do under battle pressure. But still — I'd prevented what might've turned out to be a bloody mess. My description of it might seem callous, but it isn't — that moment will stay with me the rest of my life. I see the moment again and again in my consciousness. Why? I don't know why. I feel no guilt. He's dead. I'm alive. That's the way it works. We all trade places, if not in this life then in another time and place.

You can get away with "friendly fire" casualties, you can get away with killing civilians, but the third lie — saying you're winning a war that you're losing — was too big to hide. I think back to the enemy attack the night of January 1, 1968. Even at our level in the infantry, we recognized that we'd just been through a major "probe" a few miles from the Cambodian border by an NVA regiment (two to three thousand men) moving toward Saigon. The "probe," in the official Pentagon report, apparently came in three waves, beginning with a mortar attack at 11:30 p.m., another wave at 1 a.m. infiltrating the perimeter, and a third one ending at 5:15 a.m. Now, as I said, they never tell you shit in the infantry, but this I saw with my own eyes. We counted some four hundred dead NVA, whom we buried in mass graves. You had to pay attention, because the NVA, up to that point, had rarely wasted men on frontal attacks of this size against a heavily armed US battalion.

For weeks now, our patrols had found caches of stored rice, weapons, even "order of battle" maps that were indicating some kind of operation under way. This information was taken back by US intel officers to General Westmoreland's MACV headquarters in Saigon. Who was looking at this vast trove of information? Interpreters? Translators? Who was really seeing the big picture? Certainly not the CIA, which was, in reality, telling our generals what to do. Instead of alertly preparing for what became a gigantic attack four weeks later on every provincial capital in the country, what did we do? Well, the story got around that Westmoreland had actually come out to visit the site of our New Year's battle a couple of days after my company was rotated back to base camp.

Westmoreland was a great-looking military man, six feet, three inches, perfect uniform, trim salt-and-pepper hair; he probably could have run for president. But my Lord, he had the dumbest eyes, the same kind I'd seen on so many other six- and seven-stripers. He was imposing, no doubt, he could talk better, but what did he say when he came out to the field? Westmoreland, as unimaginative as the French generals in World War I, apparently wasn't interested in the conclusions that could be drawn from the battle that night, but rather focused on the sloppy state of our uniforms and the troops' lack of haircuts. The 25th, at this point, had a spotty reputation because we carried a lot of draftee replacement troops like in the 4th and 1st Infantries. But the truth was we'd been out in the bush a long time, many of us pretty regularly since September, and there'd been a constant upsurge in movement by the enemy heading south and east. Why wasn't he paying closer attention to that? Why was the focus of the American media at that time intent on our marines up north at the siege of Khe Sanh, which, while deadly and dramatic, was in truth a diversion? The NVA never even made a frontal attack. The real knockout punch came against Saigon in the south. Classic move—fake with the left, hit with the right, that's what the Vietnamese did, and General Giap, the brilliant North Vietnamese commander, later confirmed that. His objective was to cut the country in half at the South Vietnamese capital.

In any case, when NVA troops materialized, division-size, at the Tet Offensive in late January of '68, in far greater numbers than were ever estimated, and then again in a second, smaller offensive in April '68, the troops knew for sure the brass was lying to us big-time. It was all PR bullshit—the inflated "body counts," the unwavering faith that our technological supremacy would triumph was crap. All that bombing—for nothing! We were losing because we weren't winning; you can't relocate an entire peasantry on new land in artificial villages with no respect for tradition or history. Nor, for that matter, could you import Las Vegas–sized army bases with all the latest PX material goods and all the dollars they represented into an extremely poor nation without destroying the values of our so-called Vietnamese "collaborators." How could you not *pretend* to like Americans with their money—"GI number one! VC number ten!" How many hookers did I get to know who told me this kind of bullshit, and yet you knew that even the worst black market hooker, selfish, mean, vengefully hating men, still had a bump in her heart for her nation and for Ho Chi Minh as a fighter for their independence. Yes, many of them were looking for the quick buck or marriage to an American, but they all knew the GIs would not stay in Vietnam; it was the Vietnamese who would stay in Vietnam. The reckoning was coming, and the Americans would not be there to save them. Same was true later in Iraq, Afghanistan, wherever we set our occupations. There was no faith in us, and why should there be?

In any event, Westmoreland's war was falling apart that year. President Lyndon Johnson was running from it in March, when he announced that he'd not seek another term. You think soldiers are so stupid that they're going to risk their lives when their commander in chief cuts and runs? And then in April, less than a month later, Martin Luther King was shot down in Memphis, and blacks turned their hard anger on white folks both in our home country and in the platoons out in the field. Barely two months after that, Robert Kennedy was assassinated in another ridiculous scenario of incompetent protection and cover-up lies, and America was really on fire. Riots that summer of '68, cops with sticks beating kids and blacks, law and order — the country was falling apart. And at the same time, a conservative counter-element was being born in disgust at the new freedoms assumed by this '60s generation, the "love it or leave it" mentality of redneck culture. Shades of Barnes and Elias. The civil war that we'd helped start in Vietnam was coming home.

The Lie in our culture was the root of our failure. Perhaps it's our love of exaggeration. In combat reports, in movies, we made everything bigger than it was — counting civilians as soldiers in the body counts, after-battle reports that glamorized ordinary reactions. I'm not saying there wasn't unusual heroism out there, but it was far rarer than our media and Pentagon salesmen would have us believe. Not having come close to suffering the casualty rates of the Germans, Russians, and Japanese in World War II, we really have no concept of the parameters of true disaster. Most of our generals who've worked their way up the Pentagon pole are tough guys, sure, with competitive egos, but it's a way of life that encourages obedient, conventional thinking; it's far easier to get along than question what we're doing and why. These professional men, in their lust for promotion, for "action," grow far too eager to hype or inflate any kind of risk into a "major threat" to our nationhood. Who doesn't exaggerate their own importance, especially when it comes to their payday? But from this individual inflation comes this "national security" madness of $700 billion–plus budgets for our military to prevent anything "bad" from happening to us. And yet every one of us knows from our individual experience of life that it doesn't work that way. You can't insure yourself against what you fear, because the more you do so, the more fearful and insecure you become. The result is a form of insanity, looking for total security in a world where security can never, for any individual, be certain. The hypocrisy — and more, corruption — sickened me then and now, which is one of the reasons why I got into so much trouble later on, criticizing our way of life — because we lie to ourselves, and we've confused the ordinary citizen who worries that terrorists are hiding in his barbeque pit, or that Russia is subverting our "democracy" with insidious forms of hybrid warfare, or Chinese economics are eating our lunches with their chopsticks. In my seventy-plus years from 1946 to now, the chorus of fear-mongering bullshit has never ceased — only grown louder. The joke is on us. We're the clowns. Ha Ha Ha.

I had my story, I realized. I was no hero. I'd slept on my consciousness. My whole country, our society had. But at the least — if I could tell the truth of what I'd seen — it was better than . . . what? Nothing — the void of a meaningless war and waste of life while our society was stuffing its ears with wax. Odysseus, lashing himself to his mast to preserve his sanity, had insisted on hearing the Sirens, and remembering it. Whereas I was honored for my service to my country, the truth was I'd soiled myself when I could've resisted, exiled myself, gone to jail for it like the Berrigans, the Spocks, and some 200,000 others. I was young, yes, and I can say that I didn't know better, that I was part of the unconsciousness of my country.

I didn't really wake up until I was thirty years old — in 1976. I was not the kid I thought I was. I was really the child of two fathers — Barnes and Elias, who represented this dividing war for America. I was darkened. A part of me had gone numb there . . . died, in Vietnam, murdered. My story would be about the lies and war crimes, which were committed not just by one platoon but, in spirit, by every unit. The specific crime in this case would take place in a village with the lead sergeant, Barnes, murdering a villager in frustration because he feels they are collectively helping the enemy to destroy his men. The other sergeant, Elias, lesser in rank, would turn on him and resist. This man would own his honor and integrity, which says do *not* kill the civilians caught in this war. He would take the other road and bring charges of a war crime against Barnes.

Elias, in an intimate moment, would reveal his feelings to Chris Taylor in a foxhole one night: "You know, we've been kicking other people's asses so long, I guess it's time we got ours kicked." He would talk about "politicians selling us another used war," and he'd say that it's up to the veterans, people like us, to remember and never to forget: "That's why the survivors remember. 'Cause the dead don't let 'em forget." And that's why Elias, in my mind, would be one of those who died. He would be sacrificed by us because he was what was left of a good America.

America was more Barnes than Elias, and in his quiet cunning and animal instinct for survival, Barnes would kill his mortal enemy, Elias, under the cover of a "friendly fire" incident. If he didn't, he'd be prosecuted, cashiered, his military career destroyed by Elias's charges. I think, truth be told, a lot of Americans would agree with Barnes. Kill the whistleblowers. They're traitors, undermining our cause.

At the real battle, as I've said, I'd walked through that incredible night and seen absolutely nothing of the enemy. In the film, I had my character Chris Taylor do a horrible but honorable thing. He'd witnessed Barnes killing Elias, and it would sear his heart. Using the all-night battle as his cover, he'd avenge the betrayed ghost of Elias and slaughter Barnes, already badly wounded and now descended to his basest animal state, crawling through the bloody mud of the jungle floor, begging for death. Taylor would pull that trigger and do the Beast a great favor by putting it out of its suffering.

Or would he? Should he? Should Chris Taylor *not* kill Barnes? Walk away? Leave his miserable soul in hell? In movies the hero is never supposed to stoop to the level of the villain — never. It's a rule instilled in theatrical dramaturgy and, more viscerally, in movie blood. And yet, in the screenplay, I left myself both choices. And when it came time to shoot the film and edit it a decade later, I did what the brutality in me *demanded*. I killed him. I killed the bastard because I wanted to.

Why? Because, as I've said, that war had poisoned me too. Because a piece of Barnes was in me. I believe my decision shocked quite a few members of the audience when the film was finally seen in 1986. Letters were written calling for my prosecution as a war criminal. The truth, though not admitted by the majority of those who'd served there, was that Vietnam had debased us all. Whether we killed or not, we were part of a machine that'd been so morally dead as to bomb, napalm, poison this country head to toe, when we knew this was not a real war to defend our homeland. No honest American could ever look himself in the eye and say this was akin to our World War II effort against German Nazi fascism or Japanese imperialism. I wanted the audience to feel the shame that I felt, and that we all should have felt — the truck drivers, the clerks in the rear, and, yes, the civilians paying their taxes in the USA — for having participated in that war *as a nation*. Having left Vietnam, Laos, and Cambodia in bombed-out shreds, toxins and land mines everywhere, 4 to 5 million of them dead, hundreds of thousands maimed and poisoned, countless refugees — was this not a pure Holocaust created out of American firepower? Though there've been many great things that have been accomplished in my country — a resourcefulness, a progress, a relative social and racial integration, and I obviously could go on — and though we've convinced ourselves again and again of that greatness, there is darkness that still lurks at the edge of town, in the nights without sleep.

I finished the first draft of my script in a few weeks, calling it simply "The Platoon." I knew it was good, solid work — maybe some of the best stuff I'd done yet. Maybe it was even the fabled lotus flower sprung from the mud and shit of that awful war. But I was by now enough of a realist to know it'd be a tough sell. There'd been no movie made from the grunt's point of view about Vietnam, and it was still a highly unpopular war, "a bummer" to the American imagination. No one, I was made to believe, wanted to know more about it. I wasn't optimistic.

Shortly after, my mother called from Paris to tell me my beloved grandmother, Mémé, to whom I'd written from Vietnam, had died in her arms in Paris at eighty-four. Could I come right away for the funeral? My father would pay my expenses.

The funeral was only three days away when, on a gray afternoon on a quiet street in the suburbs of Paris, I approached Mémé's pre–World War I apartment building, where she'd moved after Pépé's death. It was strange. The dead were calling to me from the past — Vietnam, now France. I thought about how Odysseus went to the Underworld to find Tiresias for a prophecy about when and how he'd return home to Ithaca. And once in the Underworld, he recognized his mother, Anticlea, who, like the other shades, had come to him to slake herself at the pool of sheep's blood he sacrificed to get there.

I climbed the creakiest of stairs and shared sparse words with a gloomy female neighbor with a mustache who was supervising the visits of my grandmother's relatives. I was alone, the apartment was musty with bric-a-brac and pictures of a lifespan back to 1890s France. I made my way down a dark, narrow corridor into a simple bedroom. A crucifix was on the wall over the bed where she lay. It was still a shock; the dead I'd seen had violent expressions, but Mémé was at peace, listening, watching; she was a presence in the room, no question, motionless like an oracle, her awareness in the air as if someone else besides myself was hearing the ticking of the mantelpiece clock. They close the eyes of the dead, but after a while you expect them to open; you always remember a person's eyes when they're alive. I thought of that scene from *Last Tango in Paris* where Marlon Brando sits next to the bed and grows angry with his dead wife, cursing her memory. Movies can help, but not this time.

I drew my chair closer to be with her, like we'd been when I was young, cuddled in her big bed as she told me the stories of the wolves in Paris who'd come down the chimneys to snatch the children who'd been bad. Of all her grandchildren, she'd treated me as special because I was "l'Américain," and she'd secretly give me extra francs and candies from her stash in her giant armoire. I knew I could get away with almost anything with her; and my cousins were jealous of that intimacy.

Forty years with her beloved Pépé, married from 1918 to his death in 1958, each experiencing two harsh wars, but she never complained or expected much more from life other than the basics — and some love. The First War took so many men from that generation — you sobered in the presence of the old France of Mémé and Pépé. For my mother, the postwar period had devolved into being about having fun, but for Mémé it had always been about duty. Yet she naturally forgave my mother, as she did me. For Mémé, family was everything.

I stayed in the bedroom a long time. There was the silence of "la mort," and then the October light began to drop. No one else knocked or visited. Just me. And you, Mémé — and that something listening between us. Not long ago I'd been twenty-three. You were so happy when I'd returned in one piece from over there. I'd tried to pay my debt to society. We all have one, we don't live only for ourselves. But I still felt uneasy and Mémé did too. What did Vietnam have to do with saving our civilization when it only made the world more callous? You never asked me for an explanation. Three wars in your lifetime . . .

The American experiment? It had started so well. What went wrong with this generation? You stayed married, you and Pépé. Now the world is going crazy with too much — sex, cars, TV, money — people are spoiled, unhappy, like rats drowning on a sinking ship of their desires. There are no excuses anymore, it's too late.

Your daughter, now divorced, living an unmoored life, no proper partner, had she really achieved, in the end, the independence she so desired? And her only son? At least I'd survived, but I was floundering. I'd been home seven years, and as I saw my life through my father's eyes — which were still my eyes — I'd done nothing. I'd achieved nothing. Therefore I was nothing. All through my twenties I'd made various deals with Time — as if Time really made deals with anybody. And now, at thirty, all those heaps of inner dialogue were coming to a hard-crashing dead end, because I never listened or changed — as a student leaving college twice, quitting several jobs, quitting my marriage, forever angry with my idealized self, losing friends because they did not live up to . . . and seeking solace in romantic notions of suicide, Vietnam, and movies. You racked it all up like a bill in a restaurant and it sounded awful.

I was crying but didn't know I was until I felt the tears. I hadn't cried in so many years — I was a hard boy. I had to be, I felt, to survive. I was raised to believe men don't cry. But this time it feels fresh, like a rain. But who am I crying to? Not you, Mémé — you're not the one judging me. You never have. Is it my self I'm crying to? My self, but *who* was that? I could not see myself. I was ugly, hiding.

I could cry myself dry with self-pity. All this pain, so much pain. Yes, I feel it now — feel sorry for myself, it's okay — so raw, all my lies, my embarrassment naked for the dead to see, naked to the whole world! No one loves me, no one will ever love me. Because I can't love anyone — except you, Mémé, and you're gone now. Can I . . . can I learn to love? How can I start? By just being kind, like you were? Can I be kind — to myself? Can I learn to love myself? In my mind, I heard Mémé reply: *"Try — you're a man now. You're no longer seventeen sitting on the sidelines of your life, judging. You've seen this world, tasted its tears. Now's the time to recognize this, Oliver, Oliver, Oliver"* — my name, invoked three times to rouse myself, to wake myself from this long slumber. Do something with your life, I demanded, all this energy bottled up for years, hopeless dreaming and writing, no excuse, you can do better. Stop fucking around.

Mémé continued speaking to me so gently. That soft voice: "Mon chéri, mon p'tit Oliverre, te fais pas de soucis pour rien ... toutes mes bêtises, mes soucis, à quoi ça sert? Regardes moi maintenant — comme je suis." (My darling, my little Oliver, don't be miserable for nothing ... All my worries, what good did it do me? Look at me now — the way I am.)

I looked and saw. Nothing but her silence. In it was her answer.

"Fais ta vie. Fais ce que tu veux faire. C'est tout ce qu'il y a. Je t'embrasse, je t'adore." (Make your life. Do what you have to do. That's all there is. I embrace you, I adore you.)

The other shades were approaching now, smelling the blood, so many young men groaning. They envied me. I thought I saw Elias among them but wasn't sure; others I barely recognized, limbs, faces distorted in death. There was whispering, many voices. "Stone, hey man, don't forget me! Where you goin'? Gimme some! Hey, tell my girl you saw me, will ya? Remember me, will ya? ... You got a joint?" Mémé wanted me to go — quickly, before it was too late. I couldn't hear, but it was clear what the shades were saying: We, the dead, are telling you — your lifespan is short. Make of it everything you can. Before you're one of us.

I rose and kissed Mémé's face one last time, inhaling her smell as best I could, recalling the perfume she wore and the feel on my cheek as a boy of her cashmere-covered breasts. "Au revoir, ma belle Mémé." And I walked out — as she looked away and began slaking her thirst with the others.

The gloomy neighbor with the mustache managed a nod of recognition on the way out, closing the apartment up; today was the last visiting day. French stoicism was implicit in her shrug of "Eh ben, ta grand-mère était une bonne femme. Quoi d'autre peut-on dire des gens?" (Well, your grand-mother was a good woman. What else can we say about people?)

I walked the silent streets to the Metro. Like in a dreamscape, there were no living people. Maybe that's the reason we die. It makes us want to live again.

I went back to New York with a certainty about what I had to do now. Over the next month, I worked another draft of *Platoon* relatively quickly and sent it out to the usual suspects. I told my host and roommate, Danny, I was going to Los Angeles for good, "to give it a last shot." He recognized that our collaboration hadn't worked out, but most things didn't work out; he also knew he'd be lonelier without me than I without him. Youth still had the legs of hope. There were not too many other good-byes to share. There'd be a somewhat cold, embarrassed meeting with Najwa; our divorce papers had been filed as inexpensively as possible and, because of New York State law, would take a year to become final. My mother wasn't around. It's funny how she drops out of the play at a time like this, a missing leading lady in act two. Unlike my father, she always believed I'd be something in my life, which of course meant a lot even if it was an unconscious faith.

New York was near death, in deep debt to its bondholders, services slashed, garbage piling up in the streets. President Ford, in the words of an infamous tabloid headline, had told New Yorkers to "DROP DEAD!" And it almost did for a few years, before it was reincarnated as the "Big Apple" tourist mecca of the world in a brilliant public relations campaign designed by savvy real estate developers. The same New York, but rediscovered. Old bones, new flesh. Everything replenished. I never saw it coming.

Dad hoped I'd at least end up with a job inside "the system" — at a studio, reading scripts, on a set . . . *something*. He didn't like *Platoon* when he read it: It was ugly. Who'd want to see it? "Why can't you give people hope?" he complained.

But there was hope, I said. "In telling the truth of what happened. In being honest."

"People don't want to know the truth," he countered. "Reality is too tough. They go to the movies to get away from all that."

How could I argue with him? He was right. In a way. He'd always counseled me growing up, "Kiddo, don't tell the truth, you'll only get yourself in trouble." I would certainly find that out for myself later.

But now it was fitting I go west to start another life. Like Jim Morrison sang, "the West is the best." I flew out on an economy ticket with two suitcases, my expectations minimal, resigned to whatever would happen. When you're a newborn, hands you don't know hold you, guide you, someone feeds you, sticking you on a tit . . . then some woman's face looms up, makes soft sounds, and tells you . . . suckle, my baby, suckle.

4

Midnight Express

*Dog eat dog, Hayēs . . . You fuck other man before he fuck you.
And you must fuck last.*
— Turkish prisoner, *Midnight Express*

The Midnight Express was a code word used by foreigners, signifying the dream of escape from a Turkish prison; according to the author of the memoir *Midnight Express,* Billy Hayes, there was a train each night that whistled past the prison walls, behind which he had been unjustly sentenced to thirty years of his life. In these years, I identified strongly with that sense of imprisonment. Then suddenly, from a slow-motion jail cell, you jump on this train and just know you're going somewhere! That's really what a movie is. At a set time, it starts. If nothing happens, you don't have a movie; go home, back to prison . . . but not now. I was going somewhere.

Hollywood, aka Los Angeles, on first inspection lay flat, shapeless, and ugly as my jetliner drifted down toward it in a harsh, polluted afternoon light. Just another day down there. The hand-me-down architecture of freeways and affordable housing was more like Flushing, Queens, than paradise, but the sea, the mountains, and the climate did make it special. And so far away from everything — East Coast, Europe, Asia. It had no palpable connection to another culture, or really to the past itself. Everyone came here to be reborn.

On closer inspection, LA looked like a seventy-year-old hooker, her thighs having engulfed how many screenplays buried in her vault, long forgotten, lost lives squandered in fantasy — writers, actors, directors, producers murdered by rejection, suicides by despair, or just living on as walking zombies in small apartments with thirty, maybe fifty years of diminishing hopes behind them, never having sold a treatment or a screenplay, not even an "option," in all those decades. And yet they go on and tell anyone who asks, "I'm working on a screenplay." I actually got to know a couple of these unrequited souls, and each one was still *convinced* he was about to score. There were so many aspirants ready to repeatedly plunge their faces between the old girl's thighs, because she was simply there, so open, so generous. Surely, then, there was enough for a thousand snaking tongues, all flicking at the same time. The gorgon might have the face of a seventy-year-old extra, but you never saw it once you closed your eyes and sucked the juices of this California orange.

At Rent-a-Wreck, for something like $150 a month, I got a fairly reliable white '68 Oldsmobile and checked into the Montecito in East Hollywood, a ten-story hotel dating back to the '30s where many actors, some quite old now, lived on a $350–500 per month basis. I had enough for a month, then I still had enough to go weekly, for a total of six weeks. I was shown a clean apartment suite with high ceilings and simple solid furniture; I could write here, staring out at a liberating view of Hollywood Boulevard, sweeping south onto the freeways. It was the '70s, and nightly, newly formed SWAT teams would stream out with their endless helicopters, searchlights, and loudspeakers, looking mostly for black criminals loose in the wild streets of Los Angeles. Somewhere in the hills lurked two terrifying white men collectively dubbed "The Hillside Strangler," who liked to pick up girls in a car pretending they were cops and, after torturing them endlessly back at their garage, would flaunt their defiance, leaving them naked, strangled, and spread-eagled on a desolate Hollywood hillside.

When my money ran out, I'd finally do what I'd always dreaded — become a waiter. It was a doable thing, you could find a job, and if I could get on nights, I could write during the day. And if I could clear $1,000 to $1,500 a month, I could hang on. You see, here I was already negotiating with myself for another year or two of writing — and then what? That pit-of-the-stomach fear that I'd become that older waiter you've seen in so many restaurants, still smiling at life. What had he or she been at thirty? What dreams, expectations? And then, at forty . . . fifty? How do dreams freeze or die or just corrode? Or do you simply shrug, forget, and get on with it? It's a living. It gets better every year. And if you do it well, with love, people will know that and appreciate you more and more. And if I'm working, I don't spend or drink. And I like the nights. I like people. My mother always did. It could be my natural calling. I was never made for my father's world of business.

It didn't turn out that way. Los Angeles was shockingly generous to me, beginner's luck in a casino. A memorable moment. Two weeks in, the phone in my '30s hotel room rang. Daytime. I was writing. It was my new, conscientious William Morris agent, Ron Mardigian, who was representing me because of Robert Bolt's strong recommendation to Stan Kamen, the most powerful agent in Hollywood at that time; William Morris was in its last years as an omnipotent power. Ron, a no-nonsense, straight-shooting Armenian American with a designer wife and three kids, lived in Pasadena, his tone always upbeat.

"Hey, Oliver, guess what?"

Uh-oh. No, I didn't want to guess.

"Marty Bregman read *Platoon*. Loved it. He wants to option it, $10,000 in cash upfront. Against $150,000 if he makes the picture and five percent of the net. How's that sound?" What do you think? "He wants you back in New York right away to meet with Al Pacino and Sidney Lumet. He wants this to be his next picture."

Imagine the thunder and lightning of these words. "Pacino and Lumet" — New York institutions — *and they like your script.* These words, whatever the outcome, changed my life. How many miles does a writer crawl in a desert mirage to hear that? And a mirage it most likely is, but you don't know it at the time, because you've never heard these words before. Yes, once with Robert Bolt and "The Cover-Up," there was promise, but this was more real to me because these were New York people.

I suddenly had somewhere to go. The Midnight Express was calling, and I jumped on for dear life. Bregman, originally Pacino's manager, was a respected New York independent producer of his films, as well as those of Alan Alda, also his client. He had a rich deal at Universal. He paid me, flew me back to New York first class, set me up in a modern company apartment close to his office in the 50s off Lexington, not far from where I'd just spent the last few frustrating years with Najwa. I was impressed with his busy secretaries, accountants (for his tax and money management business), and the massive electric door that opened only from the inside when he buzzed me in to his private office. He stood up, wearing leg braces; while the effects of his childhood polio were not as severe as Roosevelt's, it no doubt made getting around difficult. He reeked of authority with a commanding, no bullshit New York sensibility. He brought in Al Pacino from a secret back office, who, like his *Godfather* persona, was restless, edgy, sensitive, and tough to read; he didn't really look me in the eye, and I felt nervous. He didn't speak much. He was sizing me up like he would a boxer in training. All that mattered was the part, "the play." Everything else was "hanging around."

Marty invited me to join him at the well-known Elaine's restaurant uptown, introduced me with conviction as a coming young writer, and the conversation with his celebrity friends dazzled me. Marty was genuinely trying to make *Platoon,* but it was uphill all the way. Sidney Lumet, who'd directed Al in *Serpico* and *Dog Day Afternoon* with Marty producing, had been sent the screenplay and said that as good as the script was, he was too old now to chase around a jungle like he'd done earlier in his life (which in fact he'd never done). He was a man of the New York neighborhoods through and through, a man of interiors and raw dialogue; *12 Angry Men* (1957) was his first film. And Al, well, he was already in his mid-thirties, not close to the *Platoon* protagonist's twenty-one. Marty, in that first phone call to me, had done his job well as the producer; he created excitement, which is crucial to birthing a project. But in this case, excitement was all there would be.

Platoon was being "read." No question it had impact. "John Frankenheimer wants to meet." "We're setting up a meeting with you and Clint Eastwood." "Fred Zinnemann wants you for something he wants to develop — he's waited thirty years to do this project!" And on and on. My head was spinning with possibilities and, for the first time ever, a choice — a real choice. Some writers, I found out painfully, really have no choice in their lives. They're destined only to do a certain thing — a personal experience, one book, one life, and that's it; the rest is beating around the bush.

Nowhere in this process did a studio ever offer to actually buy *Platoon*. To them, my life, my most personal story, was a "read," a sample to taste for my talent. There was no interest in actively filming *Platoon*. It was a "bummer, too depressing, too real. But Stone's got something — he's young, exciting." My script was now circulating widely to A- and B- and even C-level producers. It seemed like it was everywhere. It was embarrassing to be so naked. I tried to develop a stronger protective skin; people were now talking about me when I wasn't there.

The train was moving fast, and off my Bregman disappointment, I was quickly hired by a dynamic thirty-five-year-old Irving Thalberg type — Peter Guber, a young prince at Columbia with a music partner in Casablanca Records, who had the then hip late-'70s disco queen Donna Summer and the king, Barry White, along with electronic composer Giorgio Moroder all under contract. Peter had just delivered a $50 million hit in *The Deep* with Nick Nolte and Jacqueline Bisset. He'd go on to make millions off the gigantic *Batman* series, and numerous other films, and then run Columbia for Japanese Sony when it bought the studio, and once satiated with films, he'd become a co-owner of four sports teams, including the basketball champion Golden State Warriors. Several people had told me the same thing — "Peter gets things done!"

I walked into his office at the Burbank Studios, which was decked out *Casablanca*-style with fake palms. He was a Boston-accented working-class guy who started mid-sentence to share his excitement over a kid he'd seen on TV — Billy Hayes. "You see this Long Island kid? He was on the news, landed at Kennedy, mom, dad crying, the works. So this kid escapes from a shithole Turkish prison where he's doing thirty years for smuggling this tiny amount of hash back to the States." (Actually it was two kilos.) "Make a little money for college. Innocent kid basically, knows nothing, first trip outside the country, right? They beat the *shit* out of him! Everything in the world happens to him — and then he escapes from this island prison on a rowboat . . . that's right! A rowboat, believe it or not. Gets back to the mainland, then runs through a minefield across the Turkish border into Greece — right? Unbelievable! Great story! Tension — like you wrote *Platoon*. Every single second, you want to feel that tension!" Guber stared me right in the eyes, sharing his willpower. He knew I could do it. He put a book in my hand. "Had this written. I own it" (by which he meant the rights to the story). He pointed to it, written by Hayes and a professional ghostwriter, William Hoffer. "Go home, read it, tell me you want to do it — you got the edge this needs, dark, hard!" Pause. He took a breath.

"Then I want you to meet the director I want for this. He's coming in day after tomorrow. From England. Alan Parker. Did *Bugsy Malone*. Lots of talent. Right?" I hadn't seen it, but I certainly agreed with him. "Then you go meet Billy in New York, get some face time with him, then go to England, write it there." It was exciting to be in a room with Peter, even if you couldn't get a word or two in; fifteen minutes and you were out the door, and he was into his next meeting.

I read the book. Very interesting story as told by Hayes. At the Columbia studio, I screened popular prison films to explore the structures — *Cool Hand Luke, Papillon, The Great Escape, Brute Force* . . . A day or two later I was ushered into a room at Columbia with the British team — Alan Parker, his producer Alan Marshall, and Peter's choice for the executive in charge of this film, David Puttnam, handsome, suave, a Tony Blair–like politician. Peter liked his class. Apparently I'd already been rammed down their throats, and they were cautiously positive, frosty in the British manner, and later, apart from Peter, expressed their collective relief to be out of this nonstop maniac's office and looking forward to working in London, as far away from Hollywood as possible.

Parker was a top British commercial director who'd won acclaim for his first film, *Bugsy Malone* (1976), an eccentric movie featuring a young Jodie Foster, in which all the characters, 1930s gangsters, are played by child actors; Parker had co-written it — so he seemed capable of backing me up if necessary. We'd all meet again in England. A deal was struck, and I was back on a plane to New York, to the Regency Hotel. Over the next three or four days, I went over the story's details closely with Billy Hayes. Having experienced my own terror over being buried in a prison on my return from Vietnam, I felt great empathy for Billy as he told me his tale of innocence lost. Trying to make a little extra money for college and for his supposed girlfriend, he'd made a huge mistake, and he was sorry for it, but he'd learned a hard lesson. His experience in prison was both horrifying and oddly humorous. The Turks at that time were notorious in Amnesty International dossiers for an infamously corrupt prison system. On one hand, you could live like a king behind bars; on the other, without money or connections, you'd rot away. And Billy was a foreigner without money; at his nadir he was actually resentenced from four years to thirty for two kilos of hash. All my antennae were firing in his defense. But the truth was, I never really examined the things Billy told me in depth. I assumed it was all true because this boy had been through so much suffering; I wanted it to be true.

I left for England, rented a flat in Kensington, and without much ado set to work at Alan Parker's Great Marlborough Street office in Soho — a glum Charles Dickens workhouse with huge windows looking out onto a grimy courtyard where it often rained. Parker was a cold man, matching the sun that rarely showed up during a bitter winter of union strikes and general discontent. Like many who have grown up in the social class system of England, Parker seemed to have a serious chip on his shoulder, both despising the upper classes and wanting their accolades. In our brief conversations, he was frosty. Whatever his personal feelings about me, it was clear from the outset I was there only to work, starting early mornings in his shop, an hour off for a sandwich lunch along Wardour Street, and then back to the typewriter into the evenings until 8 or 9 p.m. Sometimes, to catch a play, I'd leave earlier as Parker stared at me through the glass partitions. I was being paid the princely sum of $30,000 (against $50,000 if the picture was made). The cherry on top was the per diem of $100 a day in cash, which was then a small fortune in inexpensive London; it was the first time I had cash to burn, and burn through it I did — clothes, meals, theater, nights out, dinners with beautiful women when I could find the time, which I did. And eventually a British lover who actually enjoyed having sex.

But Parker continued to treat me as if I was Guber's emissary, and I never felt welcome. I later heard from a friendly source in his office that they were thinking I'd be gone soon and replaced by Alan or someone English who would make it into a truly British-only production. The only obstacle was the material itself: it was essentially American, and Billy Hayes was Long Island, and I was what I was.

Going through that cold winter in this depressed pre-Thatcher England, I worked lonely, long hours, excited by the script, and turned out a first draft I liked in five weeks, which I handed over to Professor Parker on a Friday, then went out and got pissed during "pub hours" on their powerful "special import" beer. I'd done my best, but if I'd known how precarious my situation was, it would only have hurt me deeply. I'm glad I didn't. Actually, Alan's longtime producer from commercials, the hard-faced Yorkshireman Alan Marshall, talked to me several times as a human being; he was working class in a warmer way than his director. Also Alan's veteran secretary knew him well and sometimes gave me some helpful information — and hope. But everyone treaded softly around the boss.

When I showed up Monday morning for my expected scolding, Parker met me right off, looked me straight in the eye, which was rare, and said with a hint of happiness, "It's good." Which meant, in his shorthand, "It works." Both Puttnam and Marshall fully agreed, surprised that I'd delivered. With Parker more involved, I went back to work for another three or four weeks of revisions, wherein the script grew to a fat 140 pages, over which Parker now glowed with pride, saying to me more or less, "You've done your job. You've given us a script we can finance. You're done."

That weekend Alan actually invited me to his home in the country outside London for lunch in a large house with his wife, kids, dogs — a dream world; he was kinder to me, and seemed genuinely happy for once. The next time I saw him, several weeks later, he was in LA on the edge of a "greenlight" from Columbia, asking me to do another set of revisions over some two weeks that brought the script to a manageable 110 or so pages. The budget was tight, around $2.3 million, Columbia's lowest one that year, a definite dark horse, but we had a new gambling studio head in Danny Melnick. And at that price, it was approved for shooting in Malta. The catch was that the elaborate ending, with a sea and land chase to the Greek border, had to be eliminated and replaced with a less interesting, almost accidental self-defense killing by Billy of a brutish prison guard who has hounded him from the beginning; Hayes then changes in to a guard's uniform and walks out the door to his freedom on a street in Istanbul. In real life, Hayes never killed anyone, but this made for a strong "movie vengeance" ending. I far preferred the original, in which he doesn't take a life, but yielded to the pressure to get it made. If I hadn't, Parker would've written it himself. Guber was hot, so was the script, and "this kid Parker's got a great eye" was the mantra in Hollywood. The forces had aligned. The Midnight Express was rolling!

I wouldn't be invited to the set in Malta or, for that matter, to the film's spectacular international premiere at Cannes the next year. The screenwriter must learn the art of detachment, which is difficult when strong emotions are involved. I buried myself quickly in another project, which was offered to me as soon as I finished. Word was out that *Midnight* was good. I was wanted. I was golden, "on the come" in Vegas terms. For someone who grew up with the only child's insecurity and doubt of my family life, this was quite a reversal and an affirmation, and so necessary to balance the toxic effects of continual rejection.

The offer to write *Born on the Fourth of July* immediately came from Marty Bregman in New York. Although he hadn't made *Platoon,* Bregman knew in his bones *Born on the Fourth* was right for Pacino, and he knew I was the one to write it. Marty was a great salesman, a 1930s Jewish kid from the Bronx who hauled his polio-weakened legs around on braces and wielded his cane like a weapon of war. His strength was clear, compounded by his New York accent and an edge of anger: "Don't cross me, kid, or I'll break you." He was also dark and handsome like Bugsy Siegel — altogether a dramatic persona you don't forget. He'd become a major figure in my life, both good and bad, but right now I was "his boy." He felt he'd discovered me with *Platoon,* and he'd test me to my limits with *Born.*

He'd optioned the book by Ron Kovic in the centennial year of 1976, when it emerged to a front-page rave in the *New York Times Book Review.* It followed the agonizing story of an all-American Long Island boy who grows up in a large family defined by an unthinking patriotism, joins the marines, and is terribly wounded in Vietnam. The heart of the book is about how Kovic adjusts to his life turned upside down. There'd already been an adaptation developed by a hot young writer who'd never lived through something similar, and it skewed in all the ways "intellectuals" think of war. I knew I could do it, but I didn't want to. I was scared. I didn't want to identify with this boy's suffering. And besides, the writing of it, the production itself, would be so traumatic and difficult to achieve — I foresaw rewrite after rewrite under the painstaking Bregman. You suffer too much with a producer like that, but sometimes — not always — you get to a higher place. And sometimes you end up a broken, masochistic lump of despair. Marty was good with a script, no question, but he was also, less happily as I would find out, a major "control freak."

The story was epic, encompassing 1950s suburbia through Vietnam and Kovic's return into the 1970s — twenty years of American life. I actually had written a return from Vietnam story in '69–'70 about a young one-armed veteran who gets into trouble with the law — "Once Too Much." It was a cautionary screenplay with Sam Peckinpah–like violence. But it wasn't right, too melodramatic; the truth was better. When I first met Ron Kovic in his wheelchair on his thirty-first birthday, July 4, 1977, at the Sidewalk Café in Venice, California, he was like his book — painfully blunt, poetically so, his words softened by his gentle voice and tender eyes. He was a handsome man with a thick black mustache like my French grandfather's, and piercing black eyes full of sensitivity and perception, his mind on fire. His compassion was mixed with great anger. I realized *here* was the story — a tortured monument of a human being right in front of my eyes. This would be Al Pacino. We talked for two hours, and I knew he was my anchor for the screenplay, that I could be "safe" with Ron — that I wouldn't fail. Coincidentally, when I first arrived, Ron had been talking to a group of veterans on the busy terrace, among them an Irish American journalist who'd been in Vietnam and told me a little of his own amazing story. Richard Boyle was a personality as outsized as Ron; I would file his tale away and, years later, actually return to it as the basis for my film that became *Salvador*. Two films were born that propitious day.

When Billy Friedkin fell in as the director of the Kovic movie, all the pieces fit. Along with Francis Coppola, Friedkin was in the top tier of new Hollywood directors. Apart from the older quality filmmakers like Kazan, Jewison, Pollack, Lumet, George Roy Hill, Mike Nichols, then on everybody's list, there was a new breed of films around with directors like Spielberg and Lucas — but Friedkin and Coppola were then working at higher altitudes with no net. After making two monstrous successes with *The*

French Connection and *The Exorcist,* Friedkin had suddenly failed at the box office in 1977 with the expensive *Sorcerer,* and *Born on the Fourth of July* was the perfect choice, to my mind, for him to do his penance. Bregman flew me to Paris, where Friedkin, along with his wife, the great French actress Jeanne Moreau, was licking his wounds as many offers were being thrown at him.

Friedkin came to our suite at the luxurious Plaza Athénée, the preferred base for film-centric Americans abroad. He seemed like a lanky, basketball-playing teenager, determinedly American with his Chicago accent, intent, concentrated. It was that famous concentration I sensed in his films. You can know a director's mind by watching his film unfold — the pace, the reasoning, the emotion. In two long sessions, Billy lived up to his reputation for analysis, getting to the dramatic point on our second day. Kovic's book was written in a dreamy, time-fractured, impressionist style, like Kurt Vonnegut's *Slaughterhouse-Five,* beautiful on paper and very moving, but probably disorienting and confusing to an audience trying to absorb the visual story points; the audience never really knows the story as well as the filmmakers do, and they can lose the surface thread easily if they have to think "Who is this? Where am I? What happened to that other character?" while still trying to follow the basic storyline.

Friedkin exclaimed, "Oliver, forget all this jumping around in time — tell it in order . . . literally. Just cut the bullshit. The film's corny Americana — but make it good corn." And that, in essence, solved my dilemma. Because it made me back up and start at the beginning — in Massapequa, Long Island, in the backyard, playing baseball in the 1950s, the long summer days.

I returned to my new one-bedroom condominium with a small terrace on the twenty-fourth floor, overlooking West Hollywood and Sunset Boulevard in all its laid-back decadence. It was clean, modern, sterile — but it was *mine.* I was offered $50,000 against $100K on *Born* with a small net backend, and I prepared myself to write, going to screening rooms (in pre-video days) to watch classics such as Kazan's *On the Waterfront* (1954) and Wyler's *The Best Years of Our Lives* (1946). Additionally, *Midnight* began shooting in September of '77, which brought in more money, and for the first time, I was deluged with offers to write quality material for directors like Richard Lester and Fred Zinnemann — six quality offers in my first ten days back in LA. I soon found a business manager for life in Steve Pines from the Bronx, who guided me in how to handle an abundance of money I'd never seen before. There was reason to be optimistic. In 1976 my income had been $14,000, but in 1977 it shot up to $115,000. What a year I'd had. This train was moving fast.

I worked faithfully for months with Kovic, reliving his rise, fall, rise again. It was at times so difficult for him; he'd act out entire scenes for me in his head, sometimes crying quietly from the pain remembered. His young life on Long Island, the isolation of the veterans' hospital, the alienation of coming home, the lack of contact with his past, his old friends from school, a desire to flee to Mexico. A scene with his devastated Polish Catholic mother and working-class father, or confessing he'd shot his own man. He'd go there in his eyes; I'd follow. It was difficult to watch and share. Every moment anchored to that wheelchair was an echo chamber for Ron, every sound, every feeling existing "from here to eternity." He was obsessed, overly so I felt then, because in my American upbringing, strong emotions were supposed to be kept in check. One couldn't make *everything* in a movie hyper; proportion was necessary. But what else could Ron be? He'd been driven crazy by this wound to his spine — half-dead the rest of his life. When later I studied Buddhism and they talked of "mindfulness" as a supreme virtue in this life, I thought of Ron and the necessity of staying in his mind to survive. So many vets in wheelchairs died early because they wanted so badly to get out of that confinement through drinking, drugs, excess, whatever. I would have. I would have died.

Clearly I was deeply influenced by Ron — his power, his integrity. He was far more mature than I; he had to be after a thousand nights in a Bronx hospital bed. Despite some major setbacks, he'd stayed sane through his suffering and become the most compassionate human being I'd yet met. My father's sarcastic side, which had rubbed off on me, didn't always register with Ron until he began to understand me. The first time we went to his hometown, Massapequa, Long Island, and I saw the cramped rooms he grew up in, I was taken aback by the low-cost 1950s postwar housing, which was built far smaller than I was accustomed to. I gently mocked his favorite restaurant in town — Tony's, a meatball and spaghetti joint, red tablecloths and dripping wax candles. I'd dined in some better New York

Italian places, and when I took "Ronnie," as I came to call him endearingly, to these places, he made sure to tell me he preferred Tony's in Massapequa.

Ron was everything I hadn't been growing up in 1950s New York—a Boy Scout, baseball star, wrestler; he had several brothers and sisters, his dad was a grocery store manager at the A&P, his mom regularly went to church and hung crucifixes on the walls of their home. He was a true believer, and the call to serve from President Kennedy's inauguration speech in 1961 deeply moved him. So much so that when he graduated from high school, he volunteered for the marines in Vietnam. In contrast, I'd admired Barry Goldwater, the conservative candidate in '64, for his straight-talking ways—a by-product of my dad's influence. He had preferred Nixon in 1960 and thought Kennedy was another untrustworthy "egghead" Democrat without solid experience.

Ron, among others, changed me. His story, unlike my own, was mainstream American and could touch the world if there was such a thing as a collective heart. Ron introduced me to a network of veterans living in Los Angeles, helping one another. There was a lonely desperation to these men. I had avoided them; the reunion thing chilled me, as well as the thought of getting together with other vets to feel sorry for ourselves. But to my surprise, these raw encounters allowed me to feel truly the collective experience we'd been through. This calmed me, and in later years I made an effort to go to my own school reunions, as well as reconnect with several veterans in different states. I was, in my way, exorcising Vietnam by talking about it with others, not dismissing it as I had for years. The films I would make helped that process, and as time went on, I'd meet veterans and others in national political groups, speaking openly about the folly of that war. There was hope at that time in the 1970s—it seemed there'd be no more Vietnams. It was possible we could actually learn something from that war. And until Reagan in 1980, no leading figure would defend its purpose.

Meanwhile, word of mouth for *Midnight Express* was growing in Europe. The film was shown to an electric response at Cannes in May '78, where it became an immediate scandal when audiences were shocked by its intense and unpredictable violence. The Turkish government objected loudly and formally to its depiction in the film. (Turkey's tourist revenue, in fact, would end up taking a significant dive.) Critics were divided, but the ones who loved it gave it box office reviews. I wished I'd been invited to Cannes, but clearly Parker did not want me there. But even from afar, it was my first experience of a "hit" of any kind — it goes faster than I'd ever imagined. The moment it was shown in Cannes, and then all the little screening rooms in all the cities worldwide where prints and labs existed, it was talked about, whispered about, it was hot — it was on lips and in eyes. Movie exhibitors and distributors took up the echo: "Have you seen *Midnight Express* yet?" And without waiting for an answer, the person on the receiving end knows — good or bad, it's simply "to be seen." This is the role of *"Did you see?"* It's rule number one, I've come to learn, and it isn't logical. It never is. Every filmmaker knows if he's experienced it, and at the same time, every one of us knows, no matter how hard you've tried, it makes no difference whether someone likes it or doesn't like it, as long as they see it and are talking about it. And not some praiseworthy film no one really wants to see. People wanted to see *Midnight Express* because it was simply on fire.

Back in the US, in spite of this heartening news from abroad, I'd failed to anticipate the difficulties in store for *Born*. Pacino and Friedkin both professed to "love" the script. But there was a pause as the studio read it. "Was it commercial? A wheelchair film? Even with Al Pacino?" There was another Vietnam film in the pipeline, Jane Fonda's *Coming Home,* which many thought was a similar story, especially as the filmmakers had interviewed Ron Kovic extensively before his book was published. But *Coming Home* was a relationship movie with Fonda as the puzzled, hurt wife of Bruce Dern, returning from combat, unrecognizably alienated, and committing suicide; parallel to this storyline is Fonda's growing attraction to Jon Voight as an angry paralyzed vet at the hospital where she volunteers. It was a strong film from Hal Ashby, and it won acting Oscars that year for Fonda and Voight — but it wasn't going to make any money, and that is the cruelest bottom line in Hollywood, always has been. You can "talk" all you want about a film, but it's just "talk," not money. And who really wanted to see a paraplegic veteran who can't fuck Jane Fonda and yells out his anger at a world that's betrayed him?

Friedkin gave up early on the making of *Born*. Perhaps he knew something I didn't — that Marty Bregman couldn't get it properly financed. He chose instead to direct Dino De Laurentiis's *The Brink's Job* about an armored car robbery, which turned out to be forgettable. I was furious at Billy for giving up and "selling out," and wrote him a passionate note asking him to reconsider. Sadly, he never rose again to the heights of his early success.

I poured my remaining hopes into Al and Marty's replacement director, Dan Petrie. He was a compromise choice, a veteran mostly of TV films who would later make the excellent *Fort Apache, The Bronx* (1981) with Paul Newman, but he had the placid personality of an insurance executive putting out fires — no crisis here. So with Petrie in, Bregman had gone out and successfully raised German tax shelter financing of some $6 million, and on that basis Universal agreed to distribute the film.

We plunged into rehearsals, theater-style, for two long weeks with Al and a fully cast film in a Broadway-area studio. As with Robert Bolt, I went back to Screenwriting 101, forcing myself to reexamine each word, nuance, scene, at times embarrassed by my work, constantly rewriting to accommodate Dan and the actors. Best of all, I watched a white-hot Pacino doing a modern version of Richard III in a wheelchair, ripping the world apart for its robbery of all he held dear. Al was truly a remarkable actor, and Lindsay Crouse was powerfully real as his girlfriend; she made the written words come off the page in ways that surprised me ("Did I write that?"). The same was true of Lois Smith as his mother and Steven Hill as his father. I was so proud, so excited, yet I knew, without acknowledging it, that Al was now a thirty-eight-year-old man. He was, in truth, a theatrical Ron Kovic. It would certainly have worked for the film's later scenes, but he'd never be seventeen or twenty-one again.

We were so close — a week or two from location shooting in Massapequa — when the German tax shelter financing collapsed. It often happens like that on a film, dramatic throughout. But to see everything actually crash down and disappear *in a day* after months of intense work is devastating. Suddenly, our cast and company were wandering around in a daze as we somehow expected Bregman to find an alternative source of money. But it wasn't happening. I took it personally, so ashamed. No one wanted this film, even with the magnificent Pacino. No one had seen what two dozen of us had seen in that rehearsal hall, how brightly, despite his age, the light of true greatness had shone on Al, who never felt he was too old for the part.

Stories had it that Al had lost confidence in Dan as a director; in those days, Al was extremely suspicious and tough on directors he hadn't previously worked with, trusting mostly his own instinct. Soon we all stopped coming to the rehearsal hall, and the prep week to start locations on Long Island was canceled. Al playing seventeen and going to the prom was going to be a stretch anyway. Our company, which had been so close, simply dissolved. Nothing to do, no place to go in the mornings, no film. Marty's office was a tomb. He'd aged a lot in these weeks. Al was then rumored to have accepted Norman Jewison's . . . *And Justice for All* (1979) as his next film. Nor would he return Ron's or my calls. Nor, for that matter, did he return Bregman's calls. It was over.

Ron was broken apart for weeks — months, really — and couldn't help but turn some of that rage on me for giving him hope. And truth be told, Ron had become a little "glamorized" by his Hollywood hopes, and at times I'd grow irritated with him for "falling for this shit" where you believe a picture's made before it really is. One night, back in Los Angeles, we argued ferociously. Pissed, I walked away. He screamed at me like a possessed wraith, and chased me in his wheelchair down the Venice boardwalk. He scared me. Days later, when he was calm, I promised him, "Ron, if I ever make it in this business, I'll come back and make this damn movie!" Ron always remembered that and reminded me years later. To him, it became prophetic. To me, it was a dead weight. My heart, already crushed by the gloomy fate of *Platoon,* was like a mother's stillborn baby, ready to be vacuumed out. I hated this town so much — such cowards! They don't like, they don't want my films! They don't want the real Vietnam!

But the worm does turn, and 1978 was actually signaling, unrecognized by me, the *start* of a Vietnam wave. *Coming Home* was followed by *The Deer Hunter,* a film from a relative newcomer, Michael Cimino, which came out of the blue, out-shocking *Midnight Express* with its violence and American homeland message. It became the film of the year. And *Apocalypse Now* would follow at Cannes the next year, in 1979, and then Stallone's Vietnam veteran in the *Rambo* series (1982 and 1985), and Chuck Norris looking for American MIAs in the *Missing in Action* series (starting in 1984), all moneymakers. But to me it seemed the Vietnam excitement was coming and then going, and *Platoon*, as well as *Born*, were just not fated to be the right films at the right time. I was stoic; "my Vietnam" had burned out. No self-pity here. But *Platoon* had opened doors for me, and I was grateful and busy.

Unlike Ron, I had *Midnight Express* to attenuate the pain. The film opened in October 1978 to glorious business all over the country, as well as in Europe and Asia. Columbia was shocked and pleased as the film ultimately grossed worldwide something close to $100 million. The Golden Globes was the first stop on the Oscar path, to which we were clearly headed to compete for Best Picture against *Deer Hunter, Heaven Can Wait, Coming Home,* and *An Unmarried Woman.* Some critics were scathing, inflicting personal pain. Pauline Kael destroyed Parker and me for having made a "mean-spirited, fake visceral sadomasochistic porno fantasy"; Kael went on at great length to express her hatred. I felt misunderstood, but looking at the film years later, I recognized the ruthless sense of violence in myself. Yes, because I'd been there — in war, in prison, in the merchant marine, at various times in civilian life I'd seen some of the worst of the human race. Why not show it? This was not "fake" at all. I was partly a beast — because I'd served "the Beast" over there. I'd killed in its name. Why deny it? I didn't condone it, but if I'd been as oppressed as Billy Hayes was in that prison, I knew I would use any weapon I had to get out. And I'd yell at the phony judges at the trial, condemning me to thirty years. And I'd bite out the tongue of the man who'd betrayed me! I had, since Vietnam, so much bottled up in me for years, I felt justified in releasing my unexplored rage — my own "wrath of Achilles." In the film, Billy Hayes, arbitrarily resentenced from four years to thirty, explodes in the courtroom:

> I just wish you could be standing where I'm standing right now and feel what that feels like, cause then you'd know something that you don't know, Mister Prosecutor. Mercy. You would know that the concept of a society is based on the quality of

that mercy, its sense of fair play, its sense of justice . . . but I guess that's like asking a bear to shit in a toilet. For a nation of pigs, it sure is funny you don't eat 'em. Jesus Christ forgave the bastards, but I can't. I hate. I hate you. I hate your nation. And I hate your people. And I fuck your sons and daughters, because they're pigs. You're a pig! You're all pigs!

Excessive, over the top? Yes, let alone talk like that in court. No one would have the guts. According to the real Billy, he "forgave them for what they did," which he revealed much later, after the movie was released, and which, considering the source, sounds suspiciously Christ-like. But the point is, my lines *shocked* the audience in an unaccustomed way. In movies, the protagonist being sentenced for his innocence cannot attack; he must accept the injustice of this world. This supposedly makes him vulnerable, human. But with the director's approval, I defied convention. I wanted Billy to be raw, human, and vulnerable, and lose his temper, get angry, really angry. The hell with good taste! As for Billy at the time, he wanted the film to be made at all costs and expressed no dissatisfaction with the script that I heard about. I had an instinctive confidence the audience would know these feelings because we've all suffered injustice. We've all been in some way Jean Valjean — and Inspector Javert as well. And for sure, that court-room scene, as well as several others, is still remembered for its shock value alone. Once you see it, you cannot ignore or forget the feelings and images in *Midnight Express.*

The backstory to the Oscars competition is the misery that hunt entails for everyone. Back then it was a "big deal," but nothing compared to what it became in the 1990s, when Harvey Weinstein and Miramax took the art of promotion one step further. There was always the unfounded rumor of "buying votes," as there's a lead-up chain of events beginning with the Golden Globe awards in early January. The Globes are given out by a co-terie of foreign journalists in Hollywood. A rather meaningless group of publicity-creating writers without real readership in their home countries, they had nonetheless accumulated "standing," which all producers chased after as a signifier of social popularity, like a high school election. There were also the film critics' awards in New York and Los Angeles. They had their own signifiers among themselves, mainly self-contained, I believe, until "Harvey," as Weinstein was always known, penetrated that circle. They often skewed to the less commercial films, or to put it another way, films not necessarily waiting to be seen by a real audience. *Midnight* was way too vulgar and successful for their consideration.

Deer Hunter was, as I said, the big shocker of 1978, with its definitely mythic and unrealistic characterization of American POWs being tortured by the evil Vietnamese, incessantly jabbering in harsh, guttural exclamations. This irked Alan Parker and David Puttnam, who were riding into town as the avant-garde of the new wave of British directors and their films — Ridley Scott (*The Duellists*), Hugh Hudson (*Chariots of Fire*), Franc Roddam (*Quadrophenia*), Adrian Lyne (*Flashdance*), and Roland Joffé (*The Killing Fields*). The British were good, sprung from the world of commercials, their camerawork brooding, smoky, different, their actors superb, and they could do it cheaper. And here with *Midnight,* Parker and Puttnam had pulled off something highly exotic with a new Middle Eastern aura and atmosphere, our senses magnified by the whiny tension chords of Giorgio Moroder's music. And yet here were the Americans again, with *Deer Hunter,* self-involved with their bloody Vietnam syndrome. Had we, Parker and Puttnam thought, not suffered enough at the hands of super-mogul Peter Guber's gigantic ego or that screenwriter with the damned *Platoon* script? Enough already. Theirs was a deep-seated, particular dislike for things American (except for the money, of course), and over time, Puttnam's career was damaged by his criticisms of the Hollywood system.

The January night at the Golden Globes took a peculiar turn for me. There'd been several parties in the days leading up to the ceremony where I finally met Brad Davis, the hot new star of *Midnight Express;* he seemed a volatile, angry young man who grew in the part. He was close to the real Billy Hayes, and the three of us ended up sharing alcohol, quaaludes, and some cocaine, which was making its reappearance in Hollywood as a party drug back in vogue, I believe, for the first time since the 1920s. There were always private users, but this was a popular, just-below-the-surface public thing with younger actors beginning to enjoy it. It was sexy, innocuous enough, and fun. It sparked great energy and laughs, and was nothing more to me — at first. A terrific burst of "friendly fire," yes, but I already had great energy. So I'd do it here and there, including at the Globes, which was known as a fun and unexamined party, not at all like the Oscars.

So as the speeches and the television awards dragged on for three hours before the big film awards in the last hour, the three of us, Billy, Brad, and myself, did cocaine in the men's toilets of the Beverly Hilton ballroom; several other parties of people were also stepping in and out of stalls that night. And at our table, front-center, first row — thank God this was in the pre–live TV broadcast days — we were laughing among ourselves, having a great time as Parker glared at us. He was, as I said, not a happy man, and I suppose the prospect of waiting around for Cimino to win the director award for *The Deer Hunter* further darkened his view of the world.

So it was after a few hits of coke, a quaalude or two, several glasses of wine over three hours, that finally my name was called for screenwriting adaptation. Not that I was surprised, because many people had told me I'd win. I felt like a racehorse they were betting on, and I'd come in on a two-to-one bet. The applause was tremendous in my ears, the ballroom floating in the pure joy of this moment. My rebel side had been restive the whole night, or perhaps since I'd seen Parker's glum face earlier, and it reminded me of all the indignities he'd piled on me. Who knows? The devil was in me that night. And here we were, at a ceremony with all the people who'd rejected *Platoon* and *Born on the Fourth of July* and lavished applause on a bunch of television cop shows up for awards. I'd seen the shows, disliked most of them, representing the triumph of Nixon's "law and order" world, jailing the underclass, the black, the Spanish as "bad guy" drug dealers, outsiders. All these actors and producers being lauded for fawning over cops. I hated the whole self-congratulatory air of the night.

There was something else growing inside me, but I couldn't articulate it. I'd seen it in Vietnam. That the US was always quite ready to lecture others on how to behave, be it about drugs or human rights, while ignoring our own giant appetite for drugs at home. I'd always despised bullies, at school, in war, and now I was finding them here, in my dream city — Hollywood. But far more subtly. The biggest bullies quietly control the airwaves, the content, the attitude, and you do not veer too far from what is "thinkable." So when I got to center stage to accept my Golden Globe and have my moment, I started to explain to the audience what I was really thinking, which wasn't necessary, but certainly Brad's and Billy's faces were egging me on. I was trying to say something like this, which is far more articulate, probably, than what I said.

"Our film's not just about Turkey . . . but our society. You know, we arrest people for drugs, and we throw them in jail . . . and we make heroes of the people who do that . . . and . . ." It was going on. Seconds. It wasn't clear. My tongue was dry and heavy in my mouth, and I was trying too hard to explain my concept of how we condemned people to jail without recognizing what we were doing to ourselves as a nation. But it got so lost because I hadn't written it in advance, and I was more zonked than I thought. I was losing them. I now heard a dead silence in the room . . . then the hissing started, and it grew.

The next thing I recognized was the exit cue music as co-hosts Chevy Chase and Richard Harris, both formidable partiers in their own right, were coming from stage left and right to get me, that is to "accompany" me offstage as quickly and politely as possible — as the hisses and boos rang out in an ascending chorus. My message was clearly lost. I was embarrassed when I walked back to our film's table, which was, as I said, front and center. I was not uncomfortable with what I was *trying* to convey, and perhaps some had understood me, but they were silent as the awards pounded on to their conclusion. Parker, flushed with red wine, glared at me, while Puttnam and Guber avoided my eyes. Brad and Billy just smiled neutrally and moved on to the next round of applause.

Cimino indeed won Best Director for *The Deer Hunter*. Then *Heaven Can Wait* received Best Picture–Comedy, which brought Warren Beatty to the stage in his peak splendor as producer, co-director, co-writer, and actor. And then, surprisingly, *Midnight Express* upset *Deer Hunter* for Best Picture–Drama. That shocked us, and Peter Guber and David and the two Alans, Parker and Marshall, took their turn on stage. And then the music wound up the exit cue, and after three long hours, the tuxedoed crowd stood up to leave.

Parker wasted little time coming right up to me, vindicated. "You just blew it, Oliver. That was your Oscar. The worst thing is — you hurt the film." He was so palpably angry, wanting to punish me; the actor Tom

Courtenay could have played him perfectly as the class-hating communist commissar in *Doctor Zhivago,* or the overbearing British POW in *King Rat* — same voice, characteristics, and look, with all the meanness of a British school and class system that could eat at the soul. Puttnam chimed in something like "this is really going to hurt us," and even Peter Guber, to whom I felt more loyalty than to the others, stopped and, though delighted by the picture's win, commiserated without personalizing it: "I wish you hadn't done that. Congratulations anyway."

The room emptied, no one seeking me out. I went home sad and still ashamed. The Oscars were still two and a half months away, but I *had* blown it. For our picture, perhaps. I'd certainly destroyed my own chances, but that was okay. I hadn't gone up there, as Parker thought, to fish for an Oscar. I wanted to share my feelings; what a mistake that was. Feelings. So dangerous when you express them.

My agent made light of it the next day. There was actually a kinescope made of that night, in the years before the show was telecast widely around the world, which I saw twenty-five years later on YouTube, although it's since been removed. It made me laugh. What a fool I was. Not for what I said but for saying it so badly. But Hollywood at that time was actually far less hysterical and more tolerant than it's become. The incident was simply noted in *Variety* and the *Hollywood Reporter.* I was talked about — "Stone must've been high!" — but it was funny, part of the general loosening mood with a younger generation coming on in the later 1970s — the "Young Turks," as Jane Fonda labeled us. And with no TV broadcast, there were, after all, only about a thousand people in that ballroom, so it never grew into a shaming event, as it would today.

And I kept getting offers of real money. I was being chased. Producers who once considered me with the attention span given an insect were now looking right at me, valuing my thought process. The glamour and fast lane of Hollywood were intoxicating. At a party given in their New York town house by Arthur Krim, head of Orion Pictures, and his wife, Mathilde, a pioneer in AIDS research, I was amazed that all these known faces — Yul Brynner, Dustin Hoffman, Faye Dunaway, Barbra Streisand, Rex Harrison, Julie Andrews, Liza Minnelli, William Holden, Natalie Wood, and so on — could all be here, in the flesh, at one time.

To me, movie stars you see in Cinemascope frames are not quite real. They should rarely come down to earth, stay hidden, unreal. So I'd meet them, shy, intimidated, and drinking more to calm my nerves, probably made a repeated fool of myself trying to be witty or provocative in order not to be considered boring. Then they'd drift on. Who knows what they thought? Do people really listen at these things? I wonder. But first impressions are given and taken — often wrongly, which is ridiculous in itself. Any person needs a few "takes" at the least. Now that I'm older, when I meet someone at a party, I tell them frankly, "No, I don't remember you, but that's good. It gives us a chance to try again. I'm Oliver. Now who are you?" Parties are indeed minefields.

Arthur Krim and his partners were the highly respected owners of United Artists since the early 1950s, then sold it to a huge insurance company (Transamerica), and broke away to form Orion Pictures in 1978, which became the industry's foremost independent distributor, with full access to the Warner Bros. network of theaters. And they were the first to offer me an opportunity to write and actually direct my next picture. I was in heaven.

A group of Armenian American investors was also offering me a small fortune to write a big-budget genocide film set during the First World War; the millions of Armenian deaths were a terrible, little-known tragedy of that era, but the investors' filmic intentions were marred by their hatred for Turks, for which they wrongly admired me as a result of *Midnight Express*. I couldn't possibly go back to another Turkish horror story.

I took meetings with people such as Jane Fonda, one of my idols for her outspokenness on Vietnam. She'd defied every convention of that era and come back from "exile" with *Klute, Julia,* and now *Coming Home,* and had her own determined way of doing things, including a production company run mostly by like-minded females. I wanted to work with her; in fact, I was probably goo-goo-eyed in love with her image when we met. Her strong face and voice echoed Henry Fonda's iconic charisma, and now she wanted to adapt Paul Erdman's *The Crash of '79* about the end of our financial system. And she really wanted *me* "specifically"; at the least, a good actor makes you feel that way. I so wanted to do anything to be closer to her, but when I read Erdman's book, I knew I could never make it work; it was fascinating, informative, but not dramatic. How could I commit this form of suicide for Jane? She was married to Tom Hayden anyway. Reluctantly I passed, and of course she forged ahead with her remarkable willpower and made the costly and messy *Rollover* (1981) with Kris Kristofferson. I watched Fonda from the sidelines over the years as she spoke out on so many issues, engaged in different lifestyles, an icon of this era. I felt so publicly conservative next to her; my true feelings were still subversive and slow to gain confidence, but I was getting ready to explode against the rules of that time.

Barbra Streisand, the queen of Hollywood in terms of her wealth and status from albums and movies, invited me out to her gigantic Malibu ranch one Sunday with her boyfriend Jon Peters, who was restless and somewhat uncomfortable in the role of second banana; that was clear. A former "star" hairdresser, he'd produced, with Barbra, the successful *A Star Is Born* (1976) and was hungry for more, and actually, to my surprise, I'd be in business with him shortly. Barbra was clearly one shrewd, sharp-eyed woman, yet I was somewhat surprised at her delight in showing off her property, exterior and interior, to her half-dozen guests, especially in displaying her antiques and particularly her jewels, which she fished from various boxes. She had that Jewish mother's delight in shopping and talking of the great bargains she'd found, not that she needed to; it was simply in her blood. Unknown to some of us, she had directorial ambitions that would soon emerge — quite successfully. Like Jane and other Hollywood actresses, she possessed the quality of "being powerful" — and possibly dangerous for your soul — which I found exciting and sexy to be around.

John Frankenheimer, a groundbreaking, tempestuous, highly emotional man then struggling with his career, had made some of my all-time favorites in *The Manchurian Candidate* (1962) and *Seven Days in May* (1964). I was invited to his studio office, and when I provocatively questioned his latest choice in making a bad horror film, he blew up and told me to get out. It was embarrassing, of course, and I felt terrible. Years later, after we got to know each other and I'd made a few films which he told me he much admired, he humbly asked me to present him with a career achievement award at the film editors' annual banquet. I delivered a heartfelt speech not long before his death, which clearly touched him and his wife. I meant every word of it.

The meticulous, patient Austrian director Fred Zinnemann (*High Noon,* 1952; *Julia,* 1977) wanted me for his dream project on mountain climbing, which was his primary hobby. Fit and lean in his sixties, he was so . . . how do you say, punctilious, methodical in his filmmaking, as if he were step by step climbing that mountain. But his story, from the novel *Solo Faces* by James Salter, was hopeless as drama, lacking the primary tension that a movie, unlike a book, needs. I had to say no, and when he finally made that film with Sean Connery (*Five Days One Summer,* 1982), it died. He came back to me later for another project he'd wanted to make for some thirty years — André Malraux's *Man's Fate* — but that too seemed more dream than reality. Actually, I believe Michael Cimino also wanted to make it, and had secured the rights. But when Michael's next film, the unusually expensive *Heaven's Gate* (1980), bombed miserably in theaters, he never got to make it. There were so many dashed dreams in Hollywood.

I was now a commodity in demand. Even my name, the ring of it — O-L-I-V-E-R S-T-O-N-E — was coming back at me like an echo. It's remarkable the way words take on another meaning. I was starting at times to wonder: Am I still in this body, is this a real trip now? Was LSD consciousness coming back at me? I had become, without thinking about the business side, one of the sought-after new names you wanted to get on your screenplay in order to get it made. I heard the words "brilliant," "genius" behind my back, and it made me feel great, surer of myself. For the first time in my life, I could walk into a Hollywood party and immediately people would know who I was. It's quite something, if you've been a cab driver or a GI in Vietnam who was expendable for sure, to have a party stop — for just that moment. "Who's that? Oh — yes! That's Herman Melville. He did *Moby Dick.* He's a genius. What's he doing next? *The Odyssey,* I think." Whew! "Respect, mang," as Tony Montana would say. Can't buy it? Fuck the rich millionaires! We were the creative ones. You had to earn the recognition, and the less they knew you, and the newer you were, the greater you became. It was a "fabulous" (and I use the word in all its sincere and superficial flattery) entrée to another act in my life.

I always wondered what was it like to be introduced at the court of Versailles to Louis XIV. Well, Hollywood in the late 1970s was my Versailles. Nothing ever came close again. It marked a sort of social peak in my life. Until then, I'd lived in hope and penury, and shame too, and near death. So forgive me for getting as high as a kite, to use a metaphor that accurately conveys my state of mind.

The parties would go from showy business events to intimate and naughty. There was a night at a small dinner party of drinking and drugs I remember for its novelty of watching the brilliant, witty Gore Vidal try to seduce Mick Jagger, whom he wanted to star in the movie of his new novel *Kalki,* which of course he wanted me to adapt — and suggesting we might have a threesome. I could write it at his villa in Italy in Ravello. Surely, why not? Cocaine was flourishing. It came in with the disco scene of Barry White and Donna Summer, it was fast and smart like the music business; movies, if anything, were too square, unhip. Cocaine sparked great energy and laughs, and there didn't seem to be a real downside. Not then. We were young, and we had money to burn. This is what my mother dreamed would be her life — in fantasy. And she certainly lived it out in parties after her divorce. But she was never satisfied, and she would, in coming years, come out to parties with me.

There was a part of me that truly enjoyed the style, the bubble of it all. Witty conversation with knowing people, the possibility of a deal, the excitement of money, the seduction of a new subject without the actual work. Subtly dangerous females who smile at you, slinking up out of the background; so many beautiful young women were always migrating to Hollywood like new flocks of birds, struggling for winter's warmth. What was glamorous at night might easily turn sad in the morning. With partying and flirting, like my mother, I could never be satiated. But my father's side beckoned me back to work, which was sometimes hard after a long night. Mostly I managed each day, six days a week, alone in my apartment, to adhere to a writer's schedule.

The nights I stopped by a Sue Mengers dinner party were a social experiment in her blunt New York style of being so outrageous as to provoke amusing reactions from her favorite guests, as well as the occasional outsiders she'd allow in, to study their reactions as if they were fish in a bowl — like me. She was the queen super-agent of her time. Around her tables would be Streisand, Jon Peters, Ryan O'Neal, Candice Bergen, Ali MacGraw, Goldie Hawn and Kurt Russell, Ray and Wendy Stark, a young Robin Williams, Neil Simon, Walter Matthau, Gore Vidal, and on and on; many of them were her clients. Sue would arrange for one of them, Michael Caine, to star in my first Hollywood-directed film, *The Hand,* for which he would be handsomely paid, or, as he put it later in time, "I needed to put two more rooms over my garage." Although Caine was one of the best raconteurs I ever heard, Matthau was the champion storyteller; he'd add vinegar to all his comments. To hold a table of these stars and make everyone laugh is, believe me, a supreme art of conversation to be admired, although oddly Neil Simon, who was probably the most successful comedy writer of his time, hardly ever spoke or facially reacted, a surprising bore. Robin Williams, on the other hand, perhaps out of nervousness, would deliver hilarious monologues and skip the conversation part. In that regard, Matthau and Caine would've survived and thrived in Richard Brinsley Sheridan's *School for Scandal* drawing rooms of eighteenth-century London, which, I believe, were as tough as it got for wit. And Sue was, by her own admission, a vicious gossip with a tongue that could destroy reputations, but people loved her nastiness and feared her for it. I would see her over the years, right up to her death in 2011, and I'd certainly commit several social faux pas, which she tolerated from me because she continually courted me to join her as a client. I never did. I was somewhat scared of her. I would never have survived eighteenth-century England, undoubtedly run through in one duel or another.

In the week of the Oscars in April 1979, Barry Diller, the freezing-cold head of Paramount, gave a glittering party. I was still nervous, unsure of myself, when Diane Keaton, who was another one of the top female stars at that time, warmly welcomed me, so unassuming and kind. And then of course there was her then partner, the man who knew the power of appearances, indeed was the ringmaster of all of them. Remarkably handsome, six foot two with those sparkling eyes, Warren Beatty knew he had the gaze of the whole room and could play that for all the genuine, adorably fake shyness he layered into his performance. At that time his bouffant hair was out of Jon Peters's *Shampoo* — today it'd make you laugh, but then it was stunning — as he was heading for the Academy Awards for his film *Heaven Can*

Wait. The stars were aligned, and he was already setting Barry Diller up to make his great historical epic *Reds*, which would almost break Paramount.

A cool, casual hello came out of him, shared with a possible competitor in *Midnight Express*, and then "Jack," his buddy, was in my line of sight . . . just ineffably "Jack," the guy next door. Everyone knew Jack from New Jersey, or thought they did. But in all the times I'd meet and talk to him, and be fascinated by him, never did I think I knew him — or, for that matter, comprehend the meaning of his beat, Jack Kerouac dialogue. Literally. As close as I'd pay attention, I never understood his long, loopy spiels. And although I'd see people listen and laugh, I'm sure most of them didn't understand what he was talking about either. That's the power of Jack Nicholson's mystique.

When the Academy Awards finally arrived on that Sunday night in April, it was a new peak. I was on Mount Olympus, nervous because everyone, despite my Golden Globes fiasco, told me I'd win — hot, sweaty in my tux, slipping in and out of my chair to check my appearance in the downstairs men's lounge as the ceremony dragged on into its third hour. I was in my thirty-third year and self-conscious. Christ had supposedly died at this age, thus creating in my mind a dividing line beyond which you aged in mortal fashion.

It was glamorous from beginning to end, the afternoon pickup at my apartment building by the limousine, the drive downtown, the enormous outdoor red carpet, television interviews, cheering fans, the music roll, the beginning of the Fifty-first Academy Awards! It felt like an intersection of time that night, a changing of the guard. It was a fantasy to see Cary Grant, Laurence Olivier, and John Wayne all at once. Grant, as impeccable in real life as he was on the screen, smiled warmly to me, as if he knew me. And the long-lashed Olivier received an Honorary Lifetime Oscar and, trying to outdo Shakespeare, for once undid himself, giving a flowery, over-the-top, poorly written imitation of Shakespeare. But who cares — he was Laurence Olivier. And then at the end, to present Best Picture, came his opposite — John Wayne, striding alone onto center stage. He was still a big man — six foot four. Dying from cancer, wearing a bad wig, his lungs wheezing with difficulty, he remained a monument of a man; everyone in the room knew it. And by this time, any resistance to his woeful politics was gone. Big John mispronounced most every name and title of the Best Picture nominees. He particularly mashed the name "Cimino" into something that sounded like "Simoncitto," some immigrant off the boat from Sicily, and then gave the Oscar to the dark *Deer Hunter* to thunderous applause. It was the chosen one that night, and I was oddly torn. The moment was beautiful, the vision complete; and for me, I guess the Hollywood version of Vietnam — with Jane Fonda and Jon Voight winning the best acting awards for *Coming Home,* and *Apocalypse Now* coming out the following year — was now complete. Clearly, neither *Platoon* nor *Born on the Fourth* would ever be made, nor did it seem necessary to make them any longer, and that was okay with me. Vietnam was buried — I was at peace with it. It was a glamorous ending to this chapter of my life.

My turn came up earlier. Lauren Bacall, accompanied by Jon Voight, regally walked on to bestow the awards for screenwriting, both adapted and original. She put me back into the Bogart-Huston era, still looking like a lynx with those slits for eyes and that 1940s smoker's voice. My nerves couldn't help but take a quantum leap upwards. God help me now. Remember, this audience doesn't want a lecture on the War on Drugs; anyway, most didn't agree with me, or they wanted a crackdown on drugs, or they just didn't want to think about it. On the contrary, the US was clearly drifting toward an expanded prison system, and the fight against crime and terrorism was a popular theme. So be cool, man, say what you gotta say quickly and get off. This was on TV now, going out to hundreds of millions across the globe. Don't fuck this up, Oliver. *Midnight* had won only one Oscar so far — for Giorgio Moroder's tense, driving score. Neil Simon, sitting close by, the most financially successful dramatist of his time, was my competition for adaptation of his own play, *California Suite;* sitting separately were Elaine May and Warren Beatty for their rewrite of the original *Heaven Can Wait.*

"And the winner is" — that grand cliché of a pause as Bacall opens the envelope — "OLIVER STONE!" Wow. Cheers breaking all around. I knew this moment was special. I memorized it. I planted it in my heart — like a tree that would grow. I started walking toward the stage. Nothing fancy. Just walk up there, don't stumble on these stairs.

Mom was at Studio 54 in New York, partying with a coterie of gay friends who went wild. She'd taken me faithfully to the movies throughout my youth, the young French girl still dreaming of American cinema. Now her only son had achieved this pinnacle of success. She enjoyed it far more than I, which irritated me then but makes me happy now. Dad stayed home to watch, but had fallen asleep and missed it; it was way past his bedtime, bless him.

My speech this time was considerably better delivered than at the Globes, but the meaning again was botched, as I naïvely wished for "some consideration for all the men and women all over the world who are in prison tonight." Considering that this generality includes some genuine psychopaths and cold-blooded killers was beside the point, because who really listens or cares? I was just another writer up there making a case, my hair tumbling messily down to my shoulders, and presenting a slightly stoned, out-of-it expression. But I was young enough to strike a chord and briefly be remembered in a profession in which, I would discover, writers are profoundly interchangeable. I thanked my colleagues and got off. Lauren and Jon stayed on to give the screenwriting prize for originals to Waldo Salt, Nancy Dowd, and Robert Jones for *Coming Home*.

Backstage was brutal, nothing like I expected. Lauren abandoned me, stars were moving left and right to get ready for the next number. Cary Grant smiled at me again. There was Audrey Hepburn! Then Gregory Peck! Then Jimmy Stewart was congratulating me, the warmest of men. Then fifty photographers were popping flashbulbs in my face in one room, and in the next, another fifty reporters were throwing tough questions at me like grenades. I did my best and, soaked like a sponge with sweat, gratefully returned to my seat for the finale with John Wayne.

I went on to the Academy Ball and other parties, giddy, drinking, ending up quite high and drunk at a Hollywood Hills mansion where so many people congratulated me it became a blur. Alan Parker's face loomed up somewhere that night. A begrudging congratulations. Nothing more needed to be said between us — for years. I remember chatting with a cerebral Richard Dreyfuss, who'd won the acting award the year before for *The Goodbye Girl*, then being embraced by Sammy Davis Jr., who was hugging me and "spreading the love, baby!"

And then, out of the smoke and music, near three in the morning, emerged a goddess, now older but still desirable, her voice strained and hoarse enough to seduce any Odysseus shipwrecked on her island. Kim Novak was Circe, able to turn men into swine, but alas, she preferred her dogs and horses on her Northern California ranch, where she lived in reclusive splendor. As I talked with her quietly on the couch, she seemed to me a woman who, never satisfied with men, had found her lonely island. I yearned for her without saying it, and felt her isolation. She was amused by men, accustomed to being desired, but could never be mortal. She preferred her dream.

Three short years ago, I'd been in the gutter. Now I was on a mountaintop I'd never thought possible. And in three more years, I'd be back in the gutter.

5

Downfall

An extraordinary thing happened in 2017, almost forty years after *Midnight Express* was made. In a documentary about himself, Billy Hayes, the author and protagonist of *Midnight Express,* seemed amused, almost proud of the fact that he'd been arrested on his *fourth* trip smuggling hash out of Turkey. He saw himself as an early warrior against Nixon's War on Drugs in the '70s.

I was stunned. When we'd met in New York so many years ago, having read his book, I assumed the smuggling was Billy's first time, and in all his dialogues with me, he never contradicted that impression. He conveyed that innocence as well to producer Peter Guber, to the American co-author of his book, and to the English team that made the film. In an interview with the *Los Angeles Times* when the documentary was released, Hayes played the victim card again, saying the filmmakers had distorted key things in his life. This angered me, and when I wrote a letter to the paper in July of 2017 raising the issue of his three previous drug runs, which none of us had known about, Hayes responded in a follow-up letter that his "admission of said trips constituted major felonies," so "I was advised by my lawyer that I could not speak or write about them in my book." Oh. Now he tells us. But considering that Billy had long since escaped from Turkey by the time we made our film, I highly doubt he had intentions of returning there to face its justice system. His reasoning served to obscure the truth, which is that he knew the film would *not* have been made if the facts had been known.

There was a second issue, this about his sexuality. I presumed he was heterosexual, as his book placed significant importance on his girlfriend back on Long Island, and how much he missed her; in the film we showed him rejecting the advances of a handsome Swedish prisoner — but now he said things to the contrary, fully embracing his homosexuality. As a result, the film was accused of sanitization and exploitation, in addition to the distortions about his smuggling. When you find yourself in a maze woven by an opportunist, there's no exit.

The film, made for reportedly $2.3 million, grossed close to $100 million worldwide, and to this day plays regularly on television, instilling in parents fear for their children in foreign countries. In effect the drug smuggler got away with it, escaped from prison, and conned his own country into seeing a movie where he is portrayed as the innocent kid who made a mistake. And goes on to make a life out of being "Billy Hayes," whoever that is. Now over seventy, Billy still tours in a one-man show riding his five years on the "Midnight Express."

How do you live with yourself? I have no problem believing he can. He's justified himself. But does he think I could have written the script the way it was, knowing these facts about him? Or would Peter Guber, the biggest promoter of Billy, much less Columbia Pictures, have made it? Yet when the truth came out, except for those critics who despised the movie, no one really cared. It was another lesson to me in a long learning curve of lies. Do lies matter? You could say, "The truth be damned, this is the movies" — and be rewarded for it.

But still I believe this is an evasion of responsibility, that as dramatists we must try to reflect the spirit of the truth if we can know it; good research is key. But there is still a long shadow over this whole enterprise — which is that you can do the proper research and come up with a truth, but if it's not memorable or is too complicated, most people don't care, and won't see your spectacle. Barnum would've said, "They want to believe." On this rock, my career would flounder more than once.

For now, life was spectacular. I was flying high. I'd long been a comic book fan, and when the respected independent producer Ed Pressman offered me a deal to write and direct *Conan the Barbarian*, Robert E. Howard's 1930s classic creation in some twelve pulp novels, I eagerly jumped at the chance. Pressman, a toy company heir known as a producer of early films from Brian De Palma and Terry Malick, gave me confidence, but this was perhaps too much, too soon. I was thirty-three years old, single, ripe with testosterone and a roving eye; my hunger and ambition knew no bounds when fertilized by the sex and fantasy of *Conan*. Pressman suggested the experienced production designer Joe Alves, who'd done *Jaws* and *Close Encounters of the Third Kind,* as my co-director to help with the complex visuals, and I accepted; he was also offering good money if we made the film.

I set to work on an enormous canvas, foreseeing a series like Edgar Rice Burroughs's *Tarzan,* one of the most successful "franchises" (a new word then) ever created. The James Bond series was also thriving, goading me to reach higher. Why not? It was a new age in films. Fantasy was around the corner, about to boom. Robert E. Howard was a natural, nerdy storyteller, imprisoned in a small Texas town with his mother, never achieving financial success, and dying young, but dreaming so large. A new kind of hero, not easy to understand — just my cup of tea. And in the wings, Pressman had, with foresight, contracted the most famous bodybuilder in the world to play Conan, the magnetic Arnold Schwarzenegger, who'd made one film and a documentary. His Austrian accent was surreal, and to get its proper rhythm, I invited him up to my apartment to tape a reading I suggested from the comic book, beautifully illustrated at that point by the English artist Barry Windsor-Smith (whom I'd later hire for *The Hand*). I read the part of his alter ego, the fiery Valeria, who comes to save him.

VALERIA: So I have to save your ass again, you big oaf?

CONAN: I knew you'd come back.

VALERIA: The hell you did! Watch out.

A filthy monster springs out of nowhere . . . Valeria then batters a pig mutant with tusked champing jaws and a bristling snout to the ground between her lean, golden thighs.

CONAN (HIS EYES BLAZING WITH ATTRACTION, AS HE FIGHTS): I can't think of anyone I'd rather go to hell with!

VALERIA: You're a liar!

CONAN: And you're beautiful.

Arnold was *fun* to hear and clever enough to appreciate Conan. Most important, he possessed that singular quality the movies worship — charisma, which radiated from him with his ready smile and sense of humor; strangers were drawn to him immediately. One Sunday I went along with him to the Santa Monica beach to hang out; we started as two sunbathers, and within an hour, I was surprised to see twenty people had already circled his towel with their own, like smaller planets around the sun, and within two hours, there must have been fifty or sixty fellow bathers, all proud to join the orbit around the people's hero of Gold's Gym in Venice.

Arnold never lost his shrewd Austrian peasant's perception of other people's expectations. Let them underestimate him — but he knew his Conan. No Al Pacino, but then again, whoever thought he'd become governor of California? Conan, in Howard's perverse spirit, was a true pagan, as opposed to a Christian, darker than the Tarzan suggested by Edgar Rice Burroughs's Darwinian view of evolution. Howard was a precursor to the pulpish, amoral side of man; he vented the lushness and dangers of the flesh, loved the allure of money and jewels. Nor was he a patsy for a woman; he could be charmed by the opposite sex, but if she turned into a witch or whatever, he could kill her as well. His travels embraced an imaginary world of huge forests and mountains to the north and west, deserts to the south and east, through which Conan would journey in separate adventures with different tribes, ships, oceans, customs, intrigues. This world was cruel, indifferent, but an ex-slave with enough gumption could rise to the top — in that sense far more capitalistic than Burroughs's pure Tarzan apart from this world. The beauty of Conan, enhanced by his long black hair, heroic body, and, most important to note, by his Jim Morrison "fuck you" attitude, was that he remained the ultimate "Free Man."

In the first script I wrote based on different parts of the Howard lore, he rises from slave to thief to paid mercenary and killer — but not unprovoked; if you left him alone, he'd leave you alone, and if you enlisted his help, as the nubile Princess Yasmina does, he'd respond, especially if there was a treasure involved, which the princess of course was seeking to recoup from the evil sorcerer who had separated her father, the king, from his throne.

And yet when Conan wins the day, destroys the sorcerer, and brings the princess back to her rightful place as queen, he spurns her offer of marriage, not yet ready to be her king. Yet seeking more margin for his experience, he asks her to join him:

CONAN: Yasmina, come with me — into the world! You have spirit. Don't waste it shut up in a Palace in Civilization with everybody eating the same, dressing the same, speaking the same, thinking the same. Ride with me! A good horse, a band of free men, gold, adventure, plunder . . . a woman can have it too.

YASMINA: And if I came with you, Conan — would you stay with me forever?

CONAN: Forever? Always? Princess, any man who promises you that's a liar. I offer you freedom — and a chance to roam the world with me until we chose to part. What do you say?

YASMINA: I'm not so brave as I would want, nor so foolish as to hold you here. Go, my lion, go.

He goes seeking a kingdom of his own, but not through marriage. He crosses paths once more with Valeria, whom he sweeps up in his arms onto his horse.

CONAN: By fire and blood and steel — you're mine!
He kisses her as his Freebooters gather around, cheering. Valeria, like a wild lioness, breaks the lock of his lips, fire in her eyes.

VALERIA: I don't know how long it's going to last, you mercenary dog — maybe a day, maybe a month, but I don't give a damn!
She crushes him in a fierce kiss, which brings all the Freebooters flocking around with their women, cheering. Over them, Conan whirls with a laugh on his horse.

CONAN: To your horses, you lazy swine! Enough of the East and its stinking sorcery! The dead are dead, the past is past, and we ride for the West — where the merchants are fat and the seaports crammed with women, wine, and plunder.
A roar, the men breaking for their horses. End.

By film ten or twelve, in my mind, Conan, after many harrowing adventures against all types of foes and incredible females, including Red Sonja, would discover that Kingdom of His Dreams. And with it — his queen. A great series, and in Howard's world, a man's prerogative. After all, many of Hollywood's most eligible bachelors waited like kings until they aged before they either married or bore children. My script for the film, in a swoon of passion, ran to 140 pages; it was as wild as anything I'd ever written. Terrifying mutant armies out of a medieval Armageddon were at war at a time before digital effects were created.

> Out of the forest, the ARMY OF HELL comes now to the beating of the drums, steel points twinkling in the sun. First the mutants of the heavy infantry, their fangs curling up over their lips to their cheekbones and their vivid, green-horned helmets, their small iron bucklers grasped by their hairy, muscular forearms.

> THE PIG MUTANTS, bodies of men with the tusked, filthy pink faces of wild boars and pigs with bulbous snouts and small, red bloodshot eyes under Nazi-shaped helmets — wearing their chain and ball and triple irons.

> THE INSECT MUTANTS, a varied mass of beaks, prongs, shells, bat wings, goggling eyeballs, elongated snouts, scalloped ears, some with horns and snaky tails.

> THE HYENA HEADS come on their tough, swift ponies with whips and lassoes — they ride, stark naked without saddle or bridle, supple and lithe, and rising upwards to the sky above this mass of maniacs.

> A legion of FLIES and WHIRRING INSECTS buzz in a darkened poisoned cloud — blackening the sun, oppressing the senses and the very soul.

MURILLO (HIS EYE TILTING UPWARDS INTO THE LIGHT): Conan, this is the end! The end of the world.

Conan glances at Murillo with the fatalism of the true barbarian.
CONAN: Well, maybe it is and maybe it isn't, but let's take as many of these bastards with us as we can.

The resulting battle I wrote is one of insane chaos. The filmmaker Ralph Bakshi (*Wizards, The Lord of the Rings, Fritz the Cat*), who became involved after I'd given up the idea of directing it, might've achieved some of this mood with his brilliant animation, but how, without drawing it, could we pull off visions out of Hieronymus Bosch? It was clear after several technical meetings with the best in their categories that it would cost more than $100 million and was still problematic. No one was willing to go there in 1979.

My prime hope was the British newcomer from the world of commercials, Ridley Scott, who'd done the brilliant *Duellists,* where he'd shown us the terrifying true power of the saber. He was now working on a movie in England called *Alien,* from Dan O'Bannon's brilliant script and H. R. Giger's macabre vision of the world. We met in London, and though Scott had more than encouraged us in our previous meeting, he was straightforward in his impersonal turndown: "Sorry, guys, but I want to finish *Alien,* and there's something else" (*Blade Runner*). "I really like *Conan,* but I can't commit. This is a giant spectacle." I was once more, as with Friedkin, downtrodden over my false hopes, and on an impulsive rebound told Ed Pressman we should rest our hopes instead in John Milius, who'd expressed to us several times his passion to do it.

John had made *Big Wednesday,* a 1978 surfing film, and was a likeable egomaniac. He could talk colorfully, grandly about himself, as well as his love of the gun, the hunt, the feel of the sword and the smell of the leather, or his friendships with Coppola and Spielberg, for whom he'd written parts of *Apocalypse Now* and *Jaws* — famously Robert Shaw's "*Indianapolis* speech" about the ferocity of the sharks that killed so many survivors after the Japanese torpedoed their battleship in the waters of the Southwest Pacific. He drooled at the idea of *Conan* — the blood and the crack of the bone; he worshiped the broadsword with a Japanese samurai's monasticism. In the subsequent script he wrote:

THE MASTER: For no one in this world can you trust. Not beasts, men, women ... [pulling his broadsword]. This you can trust. Let shamans and fools brood about Crom. He doesn't care. Pain and suffering amuse him. Learn the riddle of steel ... and your sword will be your soul.

In this philosophy, I disagreed with John, as I felt Conan's soul was more supple than steel. For him, Conan was the bringer of death. ("What do you do?" "I am a slayer of men.") The motif of "eternal war" was the nature of Milius's world, and I was never quite sure if he was really serious when he'd say things like his hero was General Curtis LeMay with his nukes, or Genghis Khan for all the wrong reasons: "I see nothing but pasture for my horses. People are horrible. Dogs are good." John respected me for having been in combat, but I don't think he ever understood my resulting love of peace.

He told James Riordan — who wrote a biography of Jim Morrison (*Break on Through: The Life and Death of Jim Morrison,* 1991) and then one on my life (*Stone,* 1995) — of our first meeting: "I had a Claymore mine on my desk and it was facing so it would explode toward the door. I used to click the trigger all the time when I had to meet with agents and studio execs and they had no idea what it was. But Oliver just went right over to the desk and said, 'Hey! You got a Claymore! Wow, I was nearly killed by one of these.'" He thought of me as a contaminated "crazy liberal," too soft and weak. And perhaps he was right. In his terminology, I was nothing next to Spielberg, whom he so admired. He told me why: "No one knows it, but Steve is Stalin ... steel. He'll do *anything* to come out on top!" John worshiped power at its most naked.

The very night when Ridley rejected us, we agreed to meet Dino De Laurentiis at his London flat. Dino, the legendary Italian producer (*La Strada, 20,000 Leagues Under the Sea, Ulysses, The Bible*), was now enjoying an American third act and had been chasing *Conan* for some time. After less than an hour of his salesmanship, we agreed to sell the rights to make *Conan.* Ed Pressman would recoup from it the large amounts he'd invested in the project as well as some good profit — and I would get a generous, yet limited, fee for my efforts. And Dino, vowing to respect our script with the idea of trimming the costs, had Milius under contract to do his next picture. It all fit. We were comfortable saying yes. But later, walking back together through Hyde Park, Ed and I shared the uneasy feeling that we'd rushed it.

And we had. The moment the deal was signed, John Milius had no real interest in a collaboration. He took what he wanted from my script, characters, and sets, and made it into a strange hybrid of a spaghetti western and a "sword and sandal" saga, using Dino's techniques from his Cinecittà cost-cutting days. The film would lack a great set designer, cinematographer, and composer. The cast would be a strange mix of John's surfer friends, stuntmen, and over-the-top actors wandering around without much direction. It'd be shot in Almería, Spain, where many counterfeit westerns were filmed on the cheap. Even the rocks looked fake to me.

John Huston, with whom he worked on *The Life and Times of Judge Roy Bean,* was one of Milius's heroes, and John imitated Huston's breathy, melodramatic way of speaking. He would summon me to his office when I was out at Universal to come in and listen to what he'd just handwritten. Sometimes it was only a page, but he'd be so taken with his own words that he'd roar with pleasure and then look at me for approval. ("You killed my snake . . . We raised that snake from the time it was born. It was almost twenty years old. Why? Why would you do such a thing to me?" Or, as Valeria dies, "Hold me! Hold me close so that my wounds bleed into yours — kiss me — let me breathe my last breath into your mouth. I'm so cold — so cold. Keep me warm.") I did my best to smile and enjoy the experience; at least, I thought, a *Conan* film is going to get made. John's villain was essentially the leader of a Charlie Manson cult who likes to hypnotize and bluster, determined to prove that steel is no match for the power of his mind. Of course he's dead wrong and finds that out from Conan after a lot of boring mystical talk. I think in John's view of the world, the hippies and drugs from the '60s were to blame for most of the world's ills.

In the end, *Conan the Barbarian* (released in 1982) was very much a Dino De Laurentiis production and met a Dino fate. The gross was okay worldwide, and it established Arnold as Conan, but I, and many others, were disappointed. It was silly and so far from what was once conceived. Dino went on to make an even cheaper sequel, *Conan the Destroyer* (1984), with his favorite director from the 1950s, Richard Fleischer (*Barabbas,* 1961, being his best), and although Arnold held the center, it died a dog's death at the box office; after just two films, the *Conan* series was officially dead, cannibalized by Dino. It was heartbreaking. There were at least ten great tales in Robert Howard's opus. It could've been magical, so far ahead of its time, pre-digital before the *Lord of the Rings* series. It was sad to see something so full of life and possibility die. But that was the norm in Hollywood, in which, after my magical introduction, I was now getting an unsentimental education.

In this period I wrote another script for Ed Pressman, "Demolished Man," from Alfred Bester's classic sci-fi novel, which I thought was the best thing I did after *Conan,* but it was equally difficult to film. A story of "ESPers" who could communicate through various degrees of telepathy, it was also an Oedipal detective story of murder. I changed the main character from a male to a female detective, but it had so many technical complications, it required a firm directorial hand and a new technology of sound. Although admired in some quarters, the script faced the usual slow death of the unrealized film. Also in this period, I wrote "The Clerk," my idea for an adaptation of a French film from Michel Deville, *Le Mouton Enragé* (in English, *Love at the Top*), a biting dissection of French bourgeois society, which didn't work in English; the ironies didn't translate.

I lived now in an intense fantasy world with a bachelor's apartment above Sunset and an Oscar on my shelf; suddenly I had more "friends" than I'd ever had, and there were constant parties, girls, screenings, premieres, mushrooms, drugs, and drinking. I'd gone from a nobody to a somebody, which didn't mean I could flaunt it, but more that "Wow, I'm experiencing life on a level I never have before — is this the way it really can be?" A sense of wonder, I suppose, and naïveté, my eyes following the beautiful women, without seeing the realities, into all sorts of jams. Jim Morrison quoted William Blake's "The road of excess leads to the palace of wisdom" to justify the need for all experience. I too wanted no limits, no laws; as Jim said, I was "testing the boundaries."

My agent, Ron Mardigian, thirty years in the business, put it this way to Riordan: "Hollywood is weird, and the movie crowd in those days was about the weirdest it ever got. Oliver ran with the cutting-edge crowd; you had to be using the drug of choice, the language of choice, and the activity of choice. Once in a while I would say, 'I think you're going out with fucked-up people,' and that was as much as I'd get into it. That was about all I could say." Ron was what I'd call a very "straight Pasadena person" who couldn't possibly understand how many circles of fantasy and madness there were in this lotusland we were inhabiting. There was no single crowd but rather crowds of people doing all kinds of crazy things, all young, all chasing a dream of money and fame. Nonetheless, despite varying intakes of alcohol and drugs, I kept a sober side, and no matter how hard the night before was, I'd always write the next day, like a metronome — six days a week.

All this time I was looking for "that woman" who would either save me or, frankly, condemn me to hell — salvation or torture. Elia Kazan talks at length in his memoir *A Life* (1988) about his long marriage to his wife, Molly, whom he characterizes as a product of a white Anglo-Saxon culture, and how his sense of inferiority as an immigrant from a Greek minority in Turkey fueled his belief that she was the right woman to help him find "the American way," as well as to mother his children. As you read it, you wonder — Did he truly love her? Or was he really just seeking her elusive approval? Thirty to forty years go by like that, and then one day she dies abruptly of an aneurism. His subsequent life is deeply contemplative as he comes to terms with the sense of his own emptiness. Getting to know what love means to him seems to take place more through its absence than its presence.

I bring this up because during this tumultuous period, I met and married my second wife. My first, Najwa, had been coffee-skinned, exotic, Lebanese. Elizabeth Cox was equally "other" than me — a blond American "goddess" that I, as a Kazan-like outsider, would never attain. We met while I'd been dating a young woman also named Elizabeth — a stunning black-haired Texan — who invited me to a party at the house where she lived with five other Texas girls in a sort of sorority atmosphere. All six girls were wannabe somethings checking out Hollywood — to my mind, not too seriously.

When I saw my date Elizabeth's "best friend"(Elizabeth II, I'll call her), my breath was literally taken away. Many of us remember such moments.

Does your breath literally stop? Yes, it does. This is *the* one! I remember turning to another guest and actually saying, "Now that's a classic beauty!" I couldn't take my eyes off her. Her smile. Her gentle, angelic quality. An essential goodness. A light in her. She was also everything I'd dreamed of in a *Conan* fantasy. Gorgeous Texan country face, light freckles, blue eyes from her German ancestry, and yellow cornfield hair sidling down her back — big white happy teeth, and a flawless body despite a heavy cast she was wearing on one leg from a roller-skating accident. I couldn't take my eyes off her, and the other Elizabeth noticed, somewhat irritated. Elizabeth II knew it too. I knew it. There was clear disappointment in her expression when the black-haired Elizabeth I guided me into another room. My mind couldn't stop churning.

Elizabeth II remembered that moment with the same excitement I did. She told Riordan she was instantly attracted to my "Mongolian eyes," and noted that I "wore black a lot; even to the beach," where I'd wear a black coat, pants, and shoes. And that I was in a "very black mindset, because I'd written *Midnight Express*." This was a woman who could've been my therapist, as she instantly, perhaps because of her great beauty, gave me the feeling that she could understand me, no matter what tortured complexity I presented.

I saw the black-haired Elizabeth I on one more date before, basically, the exchange happened. Now these two were best friends, I was told, and yet the transfer was smooth, almost destined. Elizabeth I could, with a wig change, have looked like blond Elizabeth II, and was not at all happy to concede defeat; she remained privately furious at her "best friend," and as far as I know, they never saw each other again. But I could be ruthless in those days. I was a star. It was 1980 in a cocaine arisin' Hollywood. *Midnight Express* had made "Oliver Stone" one of the most sought-after. I wanted what I wanted, and before long, I was seeing Elizabeth II regularly, and within a short time, exclusively. She was twenty-nine, had been a paralegal and a secretary, and had had a few relationships, never been married. Most surprisingly, later when we filed Freedom of Information Act requests on ourselves, my name came up blank, whereas she had a long record in the FBI files as a radical. It turned out she'd been a Socialist Party member in San Francisco and had attended many protest meetings; Ron Kovic had met her when he was protesting the Vietnam War. She ran for some kind of city office but was defeated. She reminded me of Jane Fonda, who at that time was for me the personification of the female heroine.

Around this time my father came out to visit. I put him in my bedroom and slept on the couch in the living room. He was slowly breaking down physically, couldn't walk far, and wouldn't give up smoking after almost forty years. I introduced him to some of the pretty girls of Hollywood I knew, who all seemed to adore him. It was like that curious scene in *La Dolce Vita* where Marcello Mastroianni brings girls for his father, who then, while having a great time, suffers a heart palpitation. My father was notably impressed with Elizabeth because she was pretty, blond like Grace Kelly, and made him laugh. But with his customary sardonic nature, he reminded me before he left, "Oliver, before you marry a girl, meet the mother first 'cause one day she's going to turn into her." I'd ignore that advice. But he also said thoughtfully, "You know, I was wrong. I think you can make a living at this movie business. It's got a future . . . Kiddo, I'm happy for you," which meant a lot to me. My business-minded cousin Jimmy Stone later affirmed to me how proud my father was of *Midnight Express*. He'd been skeptical until he opened a paper and saw it was actually being advertised. He thought it might be another grade-D movie or something. And the fact that I was a writer and could make money doing it was quite a turnaround from where I'd been; he felt, for the first time, that he needn't worry about leaving me any inheritance, which he didn't have anyway. I hinted that I could help him out with some money, but he was a proud man and would have none of it. By this time his income had significantly dropped off, and his monthly investment letter, his life's great satisfaction, was about to be canceled because of its falling circulation. His visit was a sobering Saul Bellow kind of scene of humor and warmth and, at the same time, a feeling of a void that couldn't be crossed. He went back to New York and continued to go in to work every morning in midtown, where he was happiest, until almost the end.

Dad was right. The movie business in the late twentieth century was going to take off to a stratospheric level few could imagine. Orion Pictures, with Arthur Krim, Bob Benjamin, Mike Medavoy, Bill Bernstein, and Eric

Pleskow in partnership, was serious about my both writing and directing for my next outing — if I could control the budget, write not a *Conan* but something on a scale I could handle. I chose a comic novel, of all things, because it was different, unexpected, shades of *Midnight Cowboy* ten years previously. *Baby Boy* (1973) by Jess Gregg, set in the deep South, was about a lower-class loser on a chain gang who's let out into the real world when his sentence is up. He fails miserably on the outside, and commits a crime to get caught and sent back to the only home he knows and the only friend he has, another lovable illiterate — naturally, with tragicomic results. I asked Ed Pressman to produce with me, in part to protect me and teach me, and we traveled to numerous southern prisons, shocked by the medieval conditions in Mississippi, Louisiana, Alabama, Georgia, and the especially harsh rules of conduct in Arkansas, meant to break the spirit of any man.

As I was writing my first draft, I grew worried whether I could pull it off. As often becomes the case, the source material didn't correlate to the reality of the prisons I'd seen. The book, written as a fable along the lines of *Of Mice and Men,* was really the product of another era, more the '50s or even the '60s — but with the large-scale arrests owing to Nixon's War on Drugs, and the increasing cruelty in the militarization of prisons and police, it no longer fit. It was also so dependent on the kooky bond between these two inmates that the film seemed excessively fragile, easy to break. If I was going to make my first real studio film, I needed red meat, something to glue the viewers' eyes to the screen with tension, like *Midnight*. I tortured myself with doubts when I read what I'd written. I recognized and hated that inner voice, like a superego telling me, "It's not working!" — but I knew it was the truth. Guilty and blunt, and without even showing them the script, I told my partners at Orion, "This film is just not commercial to me," which I found is an acceptable exit plan in the Hollywood system.

I asked them to transfer my commitment, at no additional cost, to adapting *The Lizard's Tail* (1979), a psychological thriller by Marc Brandel, based in part on his own recent divorce. The plot revolved around the illustrator of a successful comic book who loses his drawing hand in a car accident caused by his wife's nervous driving (the result of their argument); he emerges traumatized and, by nature jealous, grows increasingly possessive, to an extreme, of his yoga-loving young spouse who's drifting away from him. She wants to move out of Vermont back to New York City. Unable to draw his own comics, he is replaced by another, younger artist. Gradually he creates a monster in his mind — his own phantom drawing hand, which returns from the Beyond to destroy, in small steps, everyone around him, and ultimately himself. This includes his young mistress at a small rural college in California, where he goes to teach, and a professor who's psychoanalyzed him too astutely. Finally he turns on his wife, which sets off a murderous climax with our protagonist ending up in a psychiatric clinic, quite insane, watching his own hand crawl out of a vent and down the wall as his female psychiatrist calmly explains to him why the hand exists only in his mind. End of story. A rather macabre and grim one, but powerful.

It was tricky material, along the lines of Polanski's *Repulsion.* I wanted to make it as realistic as possible, but there was always this issue of, how far do we go with the hand? Thinking it more dramatic and commercial, I changed the title from *The Lizard's Tail* to *The Hand.* By doing so, I entrapped myself in the expectation that we would see a hand as the real monster here — not the man himself. In fact, there were only glimpses of the hand in the book. But in the quest to create "the Hand," more and more money and attention had to be invested in it. It had to be subliminal, frightening but real, so with Orion's encouragement, we contracted the special effects wizard of the moment, two-time Oscar winner Carlo Rambaldi (*King Kong, Alien, E.T. the Extra-Terrestrial*), to build what turned out to be several different hands, most of them radio-controlled, with the ability to creep, crawl, climb, tighten, grip, scamper, and so forth, in addition to several "puppet hands" that Carlo would manually control. He was an intense Italian craftsman, like Pinocchio's Geppetto. He explained that with *King Kong*, he'd had plenty of room to build the interior mechanisms, but these hands were tiny in comparison and gave him little space for his engineering; additionally, he kept insisting my chosen cameraman, a young King Baggot, was not lighting his hands properly. There would be several fights between the two.

Although Ed Pressman was my producer, chosen in part to protect a first-time director, Orion didn't view him that way. Ed, who looked like one of the wizards in *Conan,* was physically unimposing, with a soft, whispery, cerebral voice of not much impact on a roomful of hard-boiled men. Mike Medavoy, the active West Coast boss, wanted to protect Orion's investment of approximately $4 to $5 million and, not trusting Ed, brought Jon Peters to the project, subtly describing him as one of those guys who "makes things happen." I knew Jon socially through his relationship with Barbra Streisand; this added to his "clout," as he'd also produced with her, as I've said, the troubled, expensive *A Star Is Born* (1976), which became a financial success; tellingly, it was rumored that the director had been stripped of his power in the editing process.

Jon was a street fighter from the hairdressing world, a supposed role model for Warren Beatty's character in *Shampoo,* and he went on, after splitting with Barbra, to make a fortune of his own with Peter Guber in *Batman* and other films, and later as the co-boss (with Guber) at the Japanese-owned Sony Pictures. He was the definition of a rough-hewn nouveau riche American powerhouse, and I accepted him as a second producer because I thought it could only help smooth this voyage with Orion. I was wrong, as I was about the Oscar-winning star editor (of *Apocalypse Now* among others) from the East Coast whom Mike also suggested to me; this man turned out to be impatient and arrogant and was basically using our film to switch his East Coast editors' union membership to the West Coast. We never got on, and I quickly learned to watch my back very closely in the editing room while neither crowding nor overburdening our editor. It was a delicate balance, as was almost everything else on this "little" film. Medavoy further suggested a young, precocious James Horner, who would later go on to great renown as a composer (*Titanic, Braveheart*). Unfortunately, I never felt in sync with James. In the future, I'd learn to choose only those I could truly connect with.

Actors passed — Jon Voight, Chris Walken, Alan Bates. I forget who else, with the exception of the worst meeting I'd ever had up to that point — a 7:30 breakfast at the Westwood Marquis with Dustin Hoffman. Breakfast meetings are like waking up with somebody you don't know. What do you talk about? In this case I began to sweat as I nervously went on — and on — overexplaining my protagonist's character and, worse, the reasons why it would be attractive and commercial for Dustin to play a crippled, frustrated, possessive, and angry artist who kills people with his missing hand. At 7:30 in the morning? Better left to the twilight hours. It was, frankly, embarrassing. When I met Dustin in later years, I don't think he ever connected me to that miserable, sweating neophyte director in 1980.

Michael Caine came on board for a hefty $1 million fee, and we began shooting in the summer of that year at the hallowed Culver City lot where *Citizen Kane* and parts of *Gone With the Wind* were filmed. His presence bought Orion further insurance. I'm sure Michael sometimes felt upstaged by the Hand, yet he was superb to my mind, subtle, even believable in his climactic fight with the creature. In fact, I found him convincing all the way through; when he ends up in the loony bin, he's frightening. But I still had this original dilemma. I wanted this to be a suspenseful psychological thriller, and Orion and Jon Peters wanted it to really scare people; they wanted more horror, and Jon would be there on set sometimes, or in the backrooms, to consult on how to employ our special hands, or suggest new approaches. The strain was enormous for me. How to marry two different styles? How do you debate how to scare somebody? It's frustrating. The tension and fear were in the novel by Brandel, but with our money going into the special effects of the Hand, my vision was losing its perspective. I was trying to force these scares, which a master like Hitchcock or Polanski, or for that matter Brian De Palma, would never do. Worse, I was losing my confidence.

Frank Capra, whom I deeply admired, in his excellent autobiography describes his inherent engineering ability and his quick-fix gizmos that often broke new ground in 1930s Hollywood — and although I never had a natural penchant for science or engineering in school, I really worked hard to understand the technical aspects of shooting this complicated film. I didn't want to be a writer-director who ignores that aspect, as many do; after all, you can write complex problems, but can you solve them in real time? I took great pride in trying to, and continued to do this on each and every film, which always seemed to have a unique engineering problem of its own. But *The Hand,* I can say now, was as tough and self-defeating a first studio film as I could've made, putting me unknowingly in a deep and dark hole.

We used the unwieldy new snorkel camera, designed with a periscope-type lens to access hard-to-reach places, to follow the little creature almost everywhere. We built trenches into the floors to shoot low-level. We had to schedule reshoots for some of the more complex moments that hadn't worked on a first pass, but the forty-day shoot, with a later second unit in New York, was wearing on everyone's nerves as we called on the Hand to do more and more difficult things, such as being badly stabbed and reacting as if it were a living animal. Rambaldi did his very best, but as talented as he was, he grew defensive about his own shortcomings, which frustrated him, and as a result kept yelling about the lighting, and then the frustrated director of photography would scream back. I calmed each situation as best I could but was disappointed in myself, feeling I was becoming more of a "fixer" like Dan Petrie than a visionary like Billy Friedkin.

You learn a lot from pain, mostly in retrospect. And at times, much against my principles, when I was up to here in worry and uncertainty and dissension on the set, I'd sneak off to the back of the stage with a trusted crew member and do a hit of cocaine; this was reassuring. But more often, I took a quaalude (tranquilizer) to ease my nerves. And then, as the shooting intensified, I began doing a quaalude every morning before I got to the set. This, although not that significant yet, was the beginning of an addiction which I did not see coming, a need — a need to have a drug in order to work.

The heavy-lidded Michael Caine was anxious to finish but was uncomplaining and dry of wit. One time I asked him to try and convey a certain feeling on the next take; he tartly replied that he'd "done it," and I'd "see it" when I watched it, really meaning that if I looked closely at the rushes, I'd see that he'd already done what I asked. I was annoyed with that response, but when I looked at the dailies, Caine was right. He'd given me what I asked for, just not in the way I expected. It was indeed the first rule of acting as defined by Laurence Olivier's "Look at me, look at me" anecdote. He was economical in all his gestures, while I sometimes would talk too much; directors often feel the need to explain when they really need to say little.

There are many approaches to dialogue with all types of actors. This is an art of communication, of reaching for a middle, a balance. When you travel to foreign lands, to communicate with the locals, you act in certain ways. Each film is like that — another land, another language, new faces and situations. There is no one way to do this — except to avoid talking too much. Over the years, I've seen several directors actually avoid talking to their actors, as if it's an endless bog. In some cases, I believe they're right — actors often know what they're doing, and you can get there with signals — but sometimes they're mistaken or confused, and the director has to have the confidence to step in; many don't give concise direction, and to my mind call for more and more takes till the actor wears down. Al Pacino and Tony Hopkins are two examples of actors at a very high level who never objected to my corrections, and were always open to trying something else. When an actor knows you're "seeing" him, catching him, he comes to respect you much more deeply, and I often feel this is the true "soul" of the moviemaking process.

Michael Caine was certainly becoming the character of the illustrator, who was transferring the fury he'd given his Conan-like comic book creation into his rage at his wife, played by Andrea Marcovicci in a strong performance, as well as two people he murders — the offbeat Annie McEnroe as his young mistress, and his fellow professor at the run-down college where he goes to teach, the excellent character actor Bruce McGill. Rosemary Murphy was Michael's agent in the movie, and Viveca Lindfors, as the climactic psychiatrist, rounded out a terrific, authentic cast of pros. I still enjoy the film. With the actors, it feels assured, but when it wanders too far into the realm of the Hand, it loses its way by becoming too absurd. Although it is a movie, the concept of a severed, independent hand is more than bizarre; in fact it was wacko, and was duly mocked at the time. One of the few positive outcomes for the film was that the shy Ed Pressman met Annie McEnroe, which resulted in a satisfying forty-year marriage and a brilliant son.

In any case, the why of it — why had I made this movie? — still puzzled me and lay uneasily on my mind. Why, after the hurtful failure of my first horror film, *Seizure*, did I go back to make a more or less similar film some seven years later? Hoping for better, I'd based it on a realistic psychological thriller. It was all laid out with the husband's latent jealousy over his wife, from which he becomes a monster who's quite believable as played by Michael Caine. But it was nonetheless a self-destructive tale I was telling.

What was it in myself I so loathed that I wanted to destroy my protagonist? I sensed well in advance that neither character, in *Seizure* nor *The Hand*, was the type of person a universal audience could sympathize with; they were too complicated and negative, both fucked-up thinkers — with strains of myself in them. The success of *Midnight* should have taught me to trust in a beleaguered protagonist with whom we can empathize. Why then did I feel this attraction to these weak central figures in both movies? They would've let me direct another film in the same budget range. Why did I choose this? Was it the same thing that had made me back away from being an actor? What was in me that was hiding? Or was it that, not having yet defined myself, I could speak only as a writer but not yet as a director or filmmaker?

Around the time *The Hand* opened, I gave an interview to the *New York Times* discussing the film and, referencing my Vietnam experience, said, "Sometimes I feel like the bad luck will catch up. You look over your shoulder. That's what 'The Hand' is about. That unconscious state. That time you do something you're not even aware of. Who knows whether one day you'll pick up a gun and blast your own brains out, without expecting to do it?" Interesting quote in that not only does it reflect so many problems in the Vietnam veterans' community, but also it suggests running from something I could not identify — just as Michael Caine was in this nightmare of a movie.

I made another error in judgment at this time, not apparent until later (they never are), when I left my solid and loyal writer's agent Ron Mardigian at William Morris to follow the siren call from the head of ICM, its competitive rival. Jeff Berg was the fresh creative juice, a young wunderkind whose mantra was the seductive "You need to direct what you write — and I can do that for you." After all, Berg represented some of the best directors in Hollywood. And at William Morris, I felt frustrated that my agent was limited to handling writers and was useless in my struggles with Orion and Jon Peters. Before I left, the head of the film department, the powerhouse Stan Kamen, called me into his office and tore me to shreds in a painful one-to-one, reminding me of William Morris's faith in me since my Robert Bolt days. Of course they'd help me to direct. It was embarrassing to me, but I'd made my decision, and I couldn't go back. It wasn't personal, I assured him, but that was meaningless to him, and it never is, is it? Stan had heard every excuse in his life.

In the ensuing years, of course, nothing happened with Jeff Berg. His ICM was a strange wasteland. I was at the bottom of his call list of famous directors, yet he'd return all my calls, listen empathetically, reassure me endlessly, leave me feeling great — and then, as I gradually found out, despite his intellectual brilliance, his knowledge of books outside film, his contacts, and his high-mindedness and appreciation for the art of conversation, our relationship yielded no upgrade in my status as a writer only. It all seemed like sand dribbling through my fingers.

Elizabeth was the one stable constant in my life. I separated her from her five chatty girlfriends, renting her an apartment a few blocks from mine; I preferred solitary women. The cast came off her leg, and I'd given her a small speaking role in *The Hand,* which didn't register at all. As beautiful as she was, she just wasn't an actress. I knew this right off, and no amount of acting school would change that. Although she'd had many jobs, I employed her primarily as my typist (at ninety words a minute), and also as a sounding board for ideas. Jon Peters, who considered himself an expert on women from his hairdresser days, warned me against thoughts of marriage when he casually said one day, "Forget it, man, she's nineteen fifties," meaning she was "square," outdated. A short and brutal comment, it did not endear him to me, but it stayed with me for years.

But then I wondered, who was Elizabeth really? She'd studied psychology and had an interest in counseling; her voice could easily quiet my internal fires. She had the Jane Wyatt quality of *Father Knows Best* TV, the soothing wife, and I felt she'd be a good mother, as my father had said of my mother. Or was she that secret Jane Fonda radical spitfire whom the FBI had put under surveillance? I saw no sign of it yet, but her anger was deeply buried, and perhaps she didn't want to show it and scare me off.

I visited her family in San Antonio, a military town, her grandfather having served in the cavalry in the Philippines and out west. Her father, a lanky, handsome officer in photographs, had been killed in Korea when

she was too young to remember, apparently while trying to escape from
a prison camp. Her mother, Pat, was attractive in a short-haired, leather-
skinned golf woman sort of way, but lacking warmth. Tart and somewhat
cynical, she reminded me of Mercedes McCambridge in *Giant* (1955),
who'd seen enough of Texas life to allow herself to retire from it, drink,
and golf, and not think too much. After all, Pat, who was Catholic, had a
son and a daughter by her late husband and then five more children with
Elizabeth's stepfather, a rich, taciturn Texas banker named Barney. Her
duty was done.

I wasn't knowledgeable about Texas, only enamored of the legend, but
this sprawling family seemed impersonal to me. Conversation at the dinner table was either laconic and dull or else nonexistent. After Thanksgiving lunch, Barney would retire to the den to watch football games with the
boys. Pat, meanwhile, was drinking. At one of our first meals at the local
steakhouse, she asked about my background, "You're Jewish, aren't you,
your folks come from Russia?" vaguely implying I wasn't quite American.
I clarified that my father was Jewish, his ancestors having come over from
Poland in the 1840s, and my mother was from France and came over in the
1940s. "Oh," she said, sharing a look with Barney, who didn't like the idea of
asking too many questions about anything or anybody — which was an accepted parsimonious style in a state where talk can become dangerous real
fast. But the doubt in Pat's voice bothered me. What was her all-American
daughter doing with this screenwriter guy?

I can't say my communications improved over the years with either Elizabeth's mother or her stepfather. There really seemed to be two families
under one roof here, Elizabeth and her older brother being one side of it,
the rest of the kids and their father the other, with the mother neutral in
between, basically exhausted from giving this man more babies; judging
from her short haircut and the way she dressed, the thought of more sex
with men probably lacked appeal. She never once mentioned her original husband to me, which made me wonder how Elizabeth grew up. I'd
also heard from her that it was Barney, who was quietly right wing, who'd
actually initiated the FBI investigation into his stepdaughter's socialism.
I'd never enter into a political discussion with him, as I knew it would be
fruitless. And it was impossible to talk to the mother, as she'd already hit

the booze by lunchtime. Except for a few moments here and there, I never adapted to San Antonio. The futility of the Alamo, sitting in the middle of the city, only enhanced that feeling, as I viewed it the opposite way from most Americans — as a land grab by the settlers against the Mexicans. I didn't talk about that to her parents.

The year 1980 marked a radical change in American culture. In fact, out of my disappointment at the promise and then the ineffectiveness of the Carter presidency, I actually voted for Ronald Reagan, the charismatic conservative movie star ex-governor of California. When he was elected president that year, it was his kind and relaxed manner, his sense of humor that eased my spirit; he marked a return, I believed, to that habit of reassurance we absorbed as children watching television shows like *Father Knows Best* in the 1950s. His campaign promised optimism the way Obama later promised "hope." And he was certainly an endearing president, despite all the ugliness going on out of sight of the cameras. I fell for it; many did. But we hadn't read the fine print, and suddenly the old rules were back. Vietnam had been "a noble cause," and he warned that "we're in greater danger today than we were the day after Pearl Harbor . . . Our military is absolutely incapable of defending this country." The Cold War, the Soviet Union, anticommunism became once more our dominant themes — and soon the possibility arose of nuclear war. "This country is going so far right, you're not even going to recognize it." That's what John Mitchell, Nixon's attorney general, said a few years before he was sentenced to prison in 1975. Who would ever have suspected he was right?

I had other concerns. Back in Los Angeles, I shot some difficult retakes, of a technical bent, for *The Hand* and finally finished it. We test-screened it in Los Angeles for a sample audience, and the reception was disappointing, slightly below average, the equivalent of a B– or C+ report card. I recognized it needed more work — including fewer appearances from the Hand. Directly afterward, at an urgent midnight meeting in Orion's offices, in front of ten or so key participants, Jon Peters was treating the film as an unspoken disaster that needed saving, and telling us how to re-cut it; it needed *more* terror, more "Hand." I disagreed and fought with him, it grew uglier, and Jon, always the drama queen, his ego challenged, exited then and there, taking his name off the picture, no doubt tainting us in Hollywood's eyes. We kept working the film, steadily improving it, but Orion was known to bury its own films without distribution to save money. After weeks of tension, not knowing what would happen, I was enormously relieved when Krim and the others went ahead and released the film through the strong Warner Bros. distribution network in April of 1981 — unfortunately on the weekend when the clocks were moved ahead for daylight saving time, which prompted our potential audience to stay outdoors longer and invariably cut down on movie attendance. But it didn't matter, because it wouldn't have "opened" anyway. It was "neither fish nor fowl," as they liked to say — thriller or horror film. It cost around $4-plus million and made about $2.4 million domestically that weekend, which was considered "DOA" — dead on arrival. Nonetheless, I chased the film, promoting it in various cities, at times even buying tickets to the shows, as if that would make a dent in the gross. It was superstition really. It was also pathetic.

I suffered with it the most powerful sense of failure — raw, naked. I couldn't hide it. A failure always seems worse than it is. You think everyone is seeing it at the same time, and that everyone thinks the same way, which isn't true. The Orion partners were quite used to failures, as they measured everything against their giant successes with their Oscars at United Artists for *One Flew Over the Cuckoo's Nest, Annie Hall,* and *Rocky*. At Orion, they had *10, Caddyshack,* and *Arthur*. They simply shook their heads and wrote it off that first weekend, which meant no more promotion. On top of that, Warner Bros. Foreign decided *not* to release it at all abroad, which was final and insulting. Mike Medavoy's relationship with me quickly cooled. The heat was gone.

This was also the year after United Artists released my ex-professor Marty Scorsese's film *Raging Bull,* which stunned many with its virtuosity. What had I done in comparison? The Hollywood community, given the nature of the town, seemed to delight in *The Hand*'s failure. At least, that's how I felt. After all, I'd come out of nowhere and won an Academy Award for *Midnight Express*. Did I deserve one? So many people wanted to direct in Hollywood that the cynics were happy to see the comeuppance of someone already successful failing. Still, I was able to take some comfort in a few excellent reviews, including Vincent Canby's in the *New York Times:*

> A suspense-horror film of unusual psychological intelligence and wit. Mr. Stone has constructed a screenplay that can be taken two ways with equal grace. At its most obvious, "The Hand" is a horror film, one in which some not easily describable "thing" terrorizes the countryside. It's also about anger so profound that it goes unrecognized, being accepted as an aspect of what might be called "normal" behavior until it gets out of control . . . [T]here is mad method at work as well as extremely dark humor. Mr. Caine's performance . . . is scary for being so utterly reasonable. "The Hand" suggests that [Stone is] also a director of very real talent.

But many reviews brutally ridiculed the idea that anyone could take this film seriously. By comparison, in that year Lawrence Kasdan, off his screenplay for *Raiders of the Lost Ark,* had delivered his first film, the impeccably atmospheric *Body Heat.* First films need to get attention right away. There's no mercy in comments like "almost there" or "not bad." There's just one chance. I'd blown it, and it hurt. The truth was, I was not ready to succeed.

Contrary to the cliché, success is something you *can* learn from. Among other things, it teaches you how to behave in a public relations industry like movies, and how to handle money, people, public speaking — and also gives you the capacity and desire to grow as an artist and a human being. If I had not had this success, I never would've been able to expand my knowledge of the world. And eventually, it taught me how to make movies in a better and more effective manner. Failure, however, taught me how to feel my pain, the rawness of my anger and hurt; it also taught me bitterness and the desire for revenge and its uselessness, and in the end, it taught me resilience, strength, and detachment. Failure is so painful and magnified by the slings and arrows of a fishbowl business in which multiple failures lacerate the soul until you either go mad — suicidal — or lose your will, or change your style. Or it teaches you compromise in another way — by removing your vocal cords and your conscience until you are a dog who cannot bark any longer. At which point the butchers in the slaughterhouse eviscerate and discard you onto the dog food heap — as useless. I was now "Oliver Stone," the guy who'd written *Midnight Express* and had a spot of sunlight on his face — had his moment in time. A peak moment when he'd won an Academy Award at the age of thirty-three. And that'd be it.

In Buddhism, they say the first arrow is painful, but that it's the second, third, and the other arrows we shoot into the same wound that create the worst suffering. The thing I most noticed was that my momentum stopped. Things went silent. I felt it. At the talent agencies, the people in restaurants, the way they looked at me. Depressed, haunted, I took refuge in some friends, most of them European, who made me laugh and treated the debacle as just another pit stop in this life. Perhaps they were right. They were sophisticated and fond of cocaine and other drugs, sometimes heroin.

I started to use cocaine more frequently to numb the pain. Elizabeth joined me. We'd moved to the beach in the Venice area, to a rented town house. Every day the sound of the waves pounding the shore — the sameness of that ocean began to grate on my nerves, like in Edgar Allan Poe's "Tell-Tale Heart." I bought a special set of curtains and blacked out the sun. A quaalude to kick off the day's writing and coke to prolong the energy through the sunlight hours. Down and then up; then back down. Less at night actually, unless I partied, because I'd have to restore my energy to relaunch the writing process the next day. It becomes a destructive cycle you cannot see, because it seems to be going well with the drugs tied into a fixed writing schedule. I wasn't a messy cokehead, I was turning out the pages each day, but what I needed most now was "the high," which was this combination of "up and down," contradictory motions in the mind. The downer and the upper create friction, which is excitement, and sometimes brilliant insight (or so it seemed). Wake up in the morning, breakfast, close the curtains and plunge into the cave. Break at midday for a run, then back into the cave. I can see the patterns of my father's discipline merging with my mother's indulgence. Both extremes had synthesized into this torn human being, trying to be "moderate" in his contradiction.

I was much enjoying writing "Wilderness," a *Deliverance*-type tale from the hard-boiled crime writer Robert Parker about the New England mob ending in a bloody chase through the Massachusetts outback. When I finished the first draft, my producer, Michael Phillips, the highly respected co-producer of *The Sting* (1973) and *Taxi Driver* (1976) among others, seemed to have reservations about it. We disagreed. I saw him as too much the intellectual for this kind of gritty film. Later on, when I read the script again, objectively as I could, I heard "the voice" writers don't want to hear. It's Humphrey Bogart's rant in *The Treasure of the Sierra Madre*—"Conscience. What a thing. If you believe you've got a conscience, it'll pester you to death!"—or call it the voice of Mara, who haunted Buddha all through his life by raising doubts. And this voice was whispering, "It's not good enough. You can do better." And then, the real killer, "You're not really writing with the same . . . what? Intensity of feeling, passion? Something's missing! What?"—and then the most horrifying thought of all: "Cocaine's doing this to me! It's dulling my mind. It's taking my brain!" This was a quiet but devastating knowledge because . . . because I *loved* my cocaine like a baby does a toy or an adult his ice cream, and didn't want to give it up. I was hooked on cocaine. And hooked is when you need it to operate, to work—that is addiction, when you're controlled by something other than your willpower. You're non-human. That's why I shrink from junkies and mad people in the street. They scare me. They come up to me, zombie eyes, and you suddenly realize that nothing you do or say can reach their mind. It's a mirror of your own fear of losing control. This was the first time in my life I'd ever been hooked—on anything—needing to have it at any cost, at any time. And the fact was, my "Wilderness" script really was not good enough, and I couldn't go on and make it better. I was bereft in my head. I'd lost something. Brain cells? I knew so intuitively, and with no further changes, I delivered the draft perfunctorily, backing away from the film, which was never made. A "wilderness of pain," as Jim Morrison wrote, was really a place where I found myself.

Elizabeth was coking as much as I was by this time. Monster time. She'd get up in the middle of the night, unable to sleep, and disappear downstairs for a couple of hours, tooting and dreaming, drawing things, writing wisps

of stories, calling them ideas for screenplays. The mornings would be particularly depressing. I was crying inside. By this time, it seemed anywhere
I went in Los Angeles, a sizable minority of the acting and creative population, along with many agents and young executives, were doing cocaine
— or was this my paranoia? There was a shocking report in the *LA Times* in
1980 that an estimated 40 to 75 percent of NBA players were using it. There
was a glamorous restaurant on Sunset in West Hollywood called Roy's with
the latest in Chinese-Italian fusion cooking, with coke being done at the
tables or in the restrooms — it was great fun. Hundred-dollar bills were
used to snort and tip.

Two of my European friends were far more involved than I ever suspected when they were both, shockingly, busted. One was unfairly sentenced to prison for ten years, and the other did something like three years
— but they'd left me with a pound of heroin in my closet to hold onto until . . . ? Although I was now a slave to coke, I wasn't hooked yet on the
other one, but I sure was ready. I'd snorted it several times over the last two
years and liked it too much; it went down so easy, and you could top it with
coke to go the other way — easy as an elevator ride.

That was the devil in my closet. I see it still. A Pandora's box staring back
at me every day. Do not open. In a film, it becomes a woman, then a snake
or something else, shape-shifting. This is what I was doing in my wasted
life. As a writer, as a druggie, I was shape-shifting. I eyed that pound of
heroin for two weeks, beautiful waxy brown wrapping paper, string-tied,
ready to open. I never did. I resisted, and at my request, another friend
picked it up and, as I mourned, took it away forever.

I knew in my gut that the only way that I — and Elizabeth — could break
this chain was to get out of a town where most of the people I enjoyed being with were into cocaine, quaaludes, and other drugs. You can't possibly
shake this addiction without changing your daily habits, the faces of acquaintances and friends, and the insistent pressures of a business driven to
make money. On a larger scale, I was looking at a forced exile from my new
home in paradise. Three short years before, I had thought LA was it. But
now I was scared of it; in fact I hated it, the sunshine, the sea, everything!

Some experts say shame is at the root of addiction. Perhaps so; self-loathing is part of that. It'd been evident in my first two horror films, *Seizure* and

The Hand. I'd started taking drugs in Vietnam with marijuana to relax the internal pressure, and I felt the natural tensions of the situation gave me reason. And now I could argue the pressure of Hollywood was driving me. But there was a deeper shadow. Shame and fear, yes, but it was a longing for something I could not reach spiritually in my heart. It would take years to come to terms with this. For now I was in hell.

The climax to this destructive cycle came, in a strange sense, with my marriage to Elizabeth Cox in June '81 in San Antonio, just two months after *The Hand* opened. I wore an ostentatious white tuxedo, which was not my style and made me look like a lounge singer in a *Godfather* film. But it was my second wedding, and the fact that my first one had been civil and simple now made me want to go for it. I was bonding with the real American heartland, the wealthy white country club society I had never felt comfortable in. As Elia Kazan had once been accepted into his wife's world as a Greek immigrant, this was my acceptance day. And yet the truth is I don't even remember the moment we exchanged vows under that flowery bower in the garden. The simple "I do." I had smoked grass, taken a quaalude, and snorted some cocaine beforehand, and I don't remember a thing, because the real wedding only began at the big party that night out at the rented mansion in the suburbs with cars, mariachi band, a beautiful porch, strings of lanterns, merry young people. Although I was partying hard, I was thinking about how Elizabeth and I could make love afterwards. We had to have sex on our wedding night, it was part of the mythology. But cocaine left me with a semi-paralyzed orgasm, often belated, if at all, and in the end, unsatisfactory. She insisted on staying up with her friends, and I don't even remember going to bed that night. Elizabeth was as smashed as I was. As a result, the ceremony was meaningless.

Nor do I remember much about our honeymoon on Bora Bora in the South Pacific except that we stayed at a high-end resort. I was reading, of all things, Tolstoy's *Resurrection* and was unbearably restless and, like all addicts, hated that feeling too. I'd shut myself in to write while my bride, unaccompanied, explored the island on a bike. We'd hook up later at the end of the day in what I liked to call the "wine light" and go for a long swim. But even then, my thoughts couldn't help but drift to America's nearby nuclear testing in the 1950s, and how poisoned these waters were, and the local fish we were eating contaminated.

Such was the end of this rather volatile three-year period. It'd gone by fast but numbly. I'd been numb after Vietnam too — maybe I wasn't all here. Maybe that's what *The Hand* was about? Maybe I was separated from myself and didn't even know it. I was materially happy with myself, my position in the world, my marriage to a beautiful woman, but I was miserable inside.

6

Waiting for the Miracle

With a moonshine smile and another "deal," Marty Bregman called me unexpectedly; he could've given Elmer Gantry a run. Back then, on *Born on the Fourth of July*, it'd been, "Oliver, I bought this book. It's about Vietnam. It's sensational" (Marty's favorite word) — "great front-page book review in the *New York Times*. You heard about it?" That was the Ron Kovic story. Now it was, "Oliver, y'ever seen *Scarface* with Paul Muni? Al saw it the other night — and thinks it's *sensational!* He thinks he can do it. And you know how impossible he can be . . . this one's for him. All we need's a screenplay . . ." etc. That's exactly what he'd said about *Born*, but now apparently Mr. Pacino had just seen Muni in 1932's *Scarface,* written by Ben Hecht and directed by Howard Hawks, and was excited about reenacting the role loosely based on Al Capone. It sounded big, attention-getting, commercial, but phony — I wasn't really interested. I was "off" Al at this point because of the *Born* debacle, and another Italian mob movie after the two *Godfather* films and their imitators had satiated any desire to compete.

Marty was disappointed, but never taking "no" as no, he called several weeks later to tell me, "Hey, Oliver, Sidney's [as in Lumet] got an interesting take on this *Scarface* thing. You know him and Al are close — sensational team . . . He wants to do it modern using Cuban 'Marielitos.'" This was a twist; it was different. America would never get over the independence of Cuba. We'd tried everything — assassinations, terrorism, a land invasion, a crushing trade embargo; we offered all forms of irregular asylum to any kidnappers, criminals, even terrorists who'd break out of Cuba and get onto American shores. In the latest iteration, responding to America's pressure for freedom and human rights, Castro, in economic hard times, was glad to offload some 25,000 dissidents out of the Mariel harbor on boats to Miami. Among the people were concealed some 2,500 "criminals" and "deviants" who, when discovered in the US, garnered a massive amount of negative publicity, as if Castro had once again outfoxed us.

The timing was good and gave me a reason to get away from LA. Miami was a new world, and after all, I knew a thing or two about coke, which would be what booze had been to Capone, besides which I was being offered close to $250,000 *if* the picture was made, which for that era was one of the largest sums ever paid for an adaptation, based in this case on an older film. I accepted, and with Elizabeth left LA for what would become a long "exile."

In the original, the Italian Tony Camonte (Paul Muni), an ambitious newcomer ("do it first, do it yourself, and keep on doing it"), messes with the Irish gangs on the North Side of Chicago. In the war that breaks out, he massacres them. At the same time, he keeps hitting on his Italian boss's mistress, which leads to the boss trying to kill Tony, who kills him instead. Meanwhile, his beloved sister (Ann Dvorak) falls for Tony's top hit man (George Raft in his first role). Overly possessive of his sister, Tony kills the Raft character, and she then tries to shoot him as the cops close in and kill them both. In a false note, insisted upon by the Production Code of that time, Tony is supposed to die a miserable coward, firing off his new model Thompson submachine gun underneath a giant lighted billboard that reads "The World Is Yours." The hint of incest, based apparently on the Borgia family of Renaissance Italy, was one of the reasons *Scarface* was banned in several cities and states, and withdrawn from circulation by its producer, Howard Hughes, until after his death in 1976. It was a film reviled in its time for its excesses, though nonetheless a landmark, one of the first gangster films.

Lumet, in New York, made it clear to me that what he was looking for in the film was its contemporary realism, its immigration and drug war issues, and its politics, reaching up into the higher levels of our government. The Colombians, reportedly more ruthless than the others, were taking over the drug trade from the old pre-Castro Cuban gangs. The Jamaicans and Dominicans, with their connections in New York and Jersey, were tearing off a piece; a lot of blood was being shed, but this wasn't something the Italian mob could get a piece of; this was a "new deal," with new faces and new codes.

Bregman provided introductions, and I hung with the cops at county and city levels, corrupt and straight; this town was a kaleidoscope of mirrors. Jurisdictions were labyrinthine: there was Miami, Miami Beach, and Miami-Dade Metro, with these three overlapping with the Organized Crime Division from the sheriff's office in Broward County (which covered the hot Fort Lauderdale market). This was in addition to the Department of Justice's federal prosecutors and FBI, and to make things even more complex, the newly formed DEA (Drug Enforcement Agency) with its separate jungle of bureaucracy. All this to cover a vast area of mangrove swamps and hundreds of inlets concealing countless landing spots for incoming boats and seaplanes.

It was Vietnam redux — navy, army, air force, and marines, and do you think they ever really talked to one another? Hardly. Each agency for itself (somewhat similar to our security apparatus pre- and post-9/11). As America found out in the 1920s when it tried to prohibit alcohol, it was impossible to stop the flow of a substance in popular demand, and the resulting black market profits created a huge new criminal class.

After a long depressed period when the old Jewish mega-hotels like the Fontainebleau and the Eden Roc had died off from their worn glamour, Miami was now jumping with big new real estate money along Brickell Avenue and above Biscayne Bay — high-rises, huge cranes, glass mirrors booming upward into a blue Florida sky fleeced with perfectly white clouds. South Miami Beach, by day a lower-income Jewish retirement community, a shtetl with palm trees, was metamorphosing at night into a stunning tableau of exotic, half-naked crops of young, tan people from the Latin countries in their elegant new clothes and jewelry, cutting across the wide streets to the disco music of "Celebration" or "Get Down Tonight" banging out of the clubs, past slow-moving, sleek Bugattis, Lamborghinis, and even Corniches honking for attention in their nightly parade down Ocean Drive.

Of course, the homicides were also blossoming, and "Scarface" types were becoming known to the cops, who were still trying to figure out who was who in the game — Spanish names, hard to decipher, desperate hit men, sometimes just punks on motorbikes up for the day from Colombia, driving by and shooting someone they didn't know for a few hundred bucks and flying back home the same day. The families of the dealers were now fair game — six or seven people slaughtered in a house in Coral Gables, four people in a wild shootout in broad daylight at a shopping mall.

When *Time* magazine ran a Miami cover story "Paradise Lost?" in November 1981, it was highly sensationalized, American tabloid journalism at its worst. But Americans love their violence, and America was at war again, its favorite theme. And the cops and Feds liked the attention too, exaggerating their enemy's terrain as a new 1930s Chicago. All America seemed to want to be in a movie again — or at least in their own version of a "reality show."

Hanging out at the Mutiny Hotel and Club in Coconut Grove and a half dozen other night spots, I learned everything I could over a period of two or three weeks but wasn't getting deep enough into the criminal side. A renowned and very rich lawyer had recently been murdered in his office after hours by one of his clients probably for fucking him over in one of the indecipherable ways drug dealers and their lawyers interact. These lawyers couldn't reveal much but advised me to go over to Bimini, some sixty miles off the coast of Miami, which was the closest port for the sleek "cigarette boats" running nightly at speeds up to 90 to 100 mph, able to outrace any of the Coast Guard boats, and then slowing down to almost nothing, like whispers in the night, no sound to their engines, depositing their goods in the coves around Miami. The lawyers implied their clients there might loosen up and talk to me, as it was rumored that the Bahamian government was on the cartel's payroll, turning a blind eye.

So with my wife as my cover for a Hollywood screenwriter wanting to make some kind of glamorous movie, we checked into the ritziest dockside hotel on Bimini, which, by the way, had been one of Hemingway's fishing haunts for the melancholy *To Have and Have Not*. We were still coking, so we were authentic in that sense. And within an hour, I was deep in conversation at a crowded bar with three Colombians I would call "middle management" — not the bosses, who kept their distance, nor the "mules" who actually carried the stuff. These men, wearing tailored suits, supervised the operations. There was so much volume in coke by this time that a few loads confiscated meant nothing to them. Things were more "in the open" here in Bimini than in Miami. These guys were cool; we drank and circled the subject. They were interested in this "Hollywood thing," and me with it. We adjourned to one of their rooms in the same hotel where we were staying.

By eleven that night, we were high, intense, sharing coke and kicking back rum and Cokes. When talking about my travels in Miami, I casually dropped the name of a defense lawyer I'd hung with. The name was electric. The lead guy's expression changed; he stood up, heading for the bathroom, subtly signaling for his number two man to join him, leaving Elizabeth and me with the third, least intelligent guy. I didn't like it — not at all. I'd missed a step, and I knew it. I'd found out in Vietnam that when trouble is near, it generally comes quietly, awkwardly, even stupidly, when you least expect it, when you get sloppy, and it's never that dramatic. It's just a dull shot that goes off and penetrates you — and before you know it, it's lights out. It's simple, and I had been sloppy. What were they doing in that bathroom? Talking about it. About the lawyer I name-dropped. As high as I was, I traced my mistake. My contact had obviously started in the US Attorney's office before becoming a defense lawyer, where he could make bigger money, but these guys didn't know this. And it was this lawyer who, as a former prosecutor, had put away the guy who was now in the bathroom, telling his compadre how I must be an undercover Fed.

Jesus! Elizabeth didn't have a clue; she was out of it by this time. But this was serious. They could walk out of that bathroom right now, guns pointed at me and her, and take us somewhere, torture us. Then, once they got whatever information I had, they'd shoot us, and dump us in some swamp to be devoured by crabs and other beasts. "Oscar Screenwriter and Wife Murdered in Bimini" would be the one-day headline.

There was nothing to be done. The third guy was with us, wondering at my discomfort. Well, when that door finally opened and the two Colombian dudes walked out, my eyes penetrated theirs for the verdict. It wasn't clear, except they didn't have their guns out, which was a relief. But I took it moment by moment. They were acting decidedly differently — cool, not friendly or unfriendly, more like "Let's cut the conversation bullshit." They had to get going. I agreed, of course, and keeping a friendly face, ushered my unsuspecting wife out of the room.

This didn't mean we were in the clear. Nervously, I walked Liz back to our room dockside; they knew where we were and could visit us anytime tonight. I explained the situation to her, and we lay there all night, listening to the sound of the cigarette boats gunning their engines, accelerating out, voices in Spanish coming and going. It was a very long, sticky, tense night, especially on coke with no desire to fuck. If I hadn't been so paranoid, I might've recognized that it would've actually been quite messy and embarrassing for the Bahamian government if two white Americans on a "tourist island" were murdered and disappeared into some swamp. There was too much at stake for them to risk messing up their big money operation.

The "rosy-fingered dawn," as Homer liked to call it, when it finally arrived, never looked better to me. We were gone by late morning. But the sheer tension and fear of meeting these people was imprinted on my mind, and became the model for the notorious motel room chainsaw scene early in *Scarface,* where Pacino is nearly dismembered.

Moving to Paris, my mother's city, in the later fall of '81 and staying into the winter was the best decision I could've made in regard to drugs. The cold temperature, the excellent food, the memories of my youth and family, as well as supportive friends, were the significant factors. Most important, none of my French acquaintances there did coke, which never really caught on in France. I actually got tired of it myself and didn't want it anymore. I came to realize that coke was mainly a "feeling," and essentially a feeling that got repetitive, like liquor, like sex, like gambling, like anything. Ideas last longer than feelings.

The moment I left Miami, I went "cold turkey," not touching cocaine, or anything else beyond grass, for almost three months. Elizabeth as well. It's not that I was giving it up permanently, no, but that I stopped being addicted. In retrospect, I was never a big abuser of cocaine itself, but I did mix it with downers and alcohol to get as high as I could. My doctor later pointed out to me I had a deficiency of dopamine in my brain (the natural pleasure chemical) and tended to overcompensate. But compared to the coke users I knew, I was no more or less than a 5 or 6 on a scale of 10. After Paris I would do coke again socially, but out of choice, never out of need — an important distinction.

I wrote up what I'd researched in Florida in an elegant three-room apartment not far from the Bois de Boulogne, where I'd run vigorously five or six days a week. I'd work a morning session from approximately ten to one, take a run after lunch, then write a stronger session from four until eight or nine in the evening; that was the climax of my day, probably because I'd built up a head of steam over the hours, and there'd be a certain guilt if I didn't deliver on the day when I'd sat there for so long. I was happy to return to this kind of regimented life, like the one that had been imposed on me, much to my discomfort, over four years at the Hill School in Pottstown, Pennsylvania — competitive boys in freezing cold winters, with hours of homework, and demanding sports, and horrid Dickensian food — where I was molded into a miserably unhappy young man by a harsh discipline that now saved me from my indulgent side.

My new version of *Scarface* would be about Tony Montana (in homage to Joe Montana, the champion 49ers quarterback of that era), who would have a Cuban Marielito prison background; he'd be outrageous and sassy, bigger than life in his hunger for everything. Quickly, he hits on his boss's mistress, Elvira (Michelle Pfeiffer), who's been treating him like shit, right there on the dance floor at the Babylon Club.

TONY: . . . Why you got this beef against the world? You got a nice face, you got great legs, you got the fancy clothes and you got this look in your eyes like you haven't been fucked good in a year. What's the problem, baby?
ELVIRA (LAUGHS, ANGRY): You know you're even stupider than you look.

Let me give you a crash course, Jose whatever your name is, so you know what you're doing around here . . .

TONY: Now you're talking to me, baby!

ELVIRA: First who, where, why and how I fuck is none of your business, second don't call me "baby," I'm not your baby, and last, even if I was blind, desperate, starved and begging for it on a desert island, you'd be the last thing I'd ever fuck. You got the picture now — so fuck off.

She walks off the floor. We cut to the next scene driving home with Manny, Tony smoking a cigar.

TONY: That chick he's with . . . she loves me.

MANNY (DRIVING): Oh yeah, how you know that?

TONY: The eyes, Manny — they don't lie.

MANNY: You're serious? Tony, that's Lopez's lady. He'll kill us.

TONY: What are you kidding — he's soft. I seen it in his face — booze and a "cuncha" tells him what to do.

As he promises, he takes over his boss's drug operation and his mistress with it. He remains in conflict with his disapproving mother and becomes insanely possessive of his adoring sister (Mary Elizabeth Mastrantonio), now tempted by the rich American lifestyle. His friend and hit man Manolo (Steven Bauer) has the hots for his sister, but Tony warns him off.

The richer and more successful Tony gets, the more outrageous, disregarding the first rule he learned from his boss's mistress: "Never get high on your own supply." But does he listen? Do any of us listen? Of course not. "The World Is Yours," as in the original film, appears on the Miami skyline, spelled out under a giant helium balloon. Although Tony now has real enemies all around him — rival gangs, a supply-side Bolivian drug lord, his own bankers and lawyers, and the cops — his real problem is his conflicted nature. The Feds finally nail him in a money laundering sting, which he figures he can buy his way out of.

The pressures mount, and it looks like he's going to jail for tax evasion when the drug lord, Suárez, who practically runs the country of Bolivia and is politically connected to the CIA, offers him a way out with a deal: the charges against him will be dropped if he offs a troublemaking diplomat in New York who's trying to expose the drug lord's backstage control of his country. No problem for Tony — except on the day of the assassination (based on the 1976 car bomb murder of Chile's Orlando Letelier in Washington, DC), the diplomat, who was supposed to be alone, turns up with his wife and children accompanying him in his car. Tony goes soft (for reasons of his own — a desire for family, for mistress, sister, all wrapped in one confused mind), and he can't kill the target with his family. Instead he blows out the brains of the assassin-in-chief.

It's ironic that when Tony tries to do the right thing by not killing a mother and her children, he meets his downfall; he's crossed the line with the Bolivians and he knows it. Tony unravels quickly after that, doing more and more coke. Back in Miami, he finds his sister with Manolo and freaks out, killing his best friend before his sister screams they were just married. She then tries to kill him. The final shootout, with the drug lord sending his hit men to Miami, is bloody, Tony resorting to a rocket launcher ("Say hello to my li'l fren'!") before being slaughtered, along with his sister, in an operatic climax.

Yes, it was too big, too long, too messy, but I *knew* this thing could work. It was also vital; it had that 1930s spirit of the Great Depression, with its gangsters born from poverty and desperation. In that spirit, *Scarface* in the early '80s featured an antihero gorging, front and center, on his American dream of materialism, reveling in it. It'd be a social satire, if you will, imitating and mocking the American desire for wealth at any cost. It would precede my work on *Wall Street* and, later, *Natural Born Killers*, both of which depict misshapen offspring of capitalism run amok. I packed my script with all the energy, the grit, the transgressive anger, and the crude one-liners I could muster:

"This town's like a great big pussy just waiting to get fucked."

"All I have's my balls and my word, and I don't break them for no one."

"I kill a communist for fun, but for a green card, I'm gonna carve him up real nice."

"You know what capitalism is? Getting fucked."

"In this country, you gotta make the money first. Then when you get the money, you get the power. Then when you get the power, you get the women."

"Say goodnight to the bad guy. You're never gonna see a bad guy like me again."

I intended to outdo the '30s in my "fuck you" attitude toward the authorities because now I could get away with it; the production codes were breaking down. My language was highly inflammatory. According to one fan, the word "fuck" appears 183 times, and actress Joan Collins, known for her quick wit, quipped, "I heard there are 183 'fucks' in the movie, which is more than most people get in a lifetime." In actuality, the "fucks" I wrote (I have no idea how many) were carefully placed according to a rhythm, but taking liberties, Pacino considerably upped the amount, and it didn't bother me because it accorded with his rhythm. In one of my favorite scenes, I was able to create the most complete in-your-face rejection of a civilized society that I was coming to despise for its hypocrisy. In a high-class Miami Beach restaurant based on the Forge, overheard by a rich crowd, Tony wonders aloud to Manolo and his drugged-out new wife, Elvira:

"Is this it? Is this what it's all about? Eating, drinking, snorting, fucking? Then what? You're fifty and you got a bag for a belly and tits with hair on 'em and your liver's got spots and you're looking like these rich fuckin' mummies in here? Is that what it's all about?" (He turns to Elvira.) "A junkie??? I gotta fucking junkie for a wife? Who never eats nothing, who wakes up with a quaalude, who sleeps all day with black shades on, who won't fuck me cause she's in a coma! Is this how it ends? And I thought I was a winner? Fuck it man, I can't even have a fucking kid with her, her womb's so polluted, I can't even have a fucking little baby!"

Elvira, hurt, furiously dumps her plate of food on him and exits. Tony, covered in slop, follows Manny out slowly but can't resist a stop at the door to address the stunned diners:

> "You're all assholes. You know why? Cause none of you got the guts to be what you want to be. You need people like me so you can point your fingers and say 'hey there's the bad guy!' So what does that make you? Good guys? Don't kid yourselves. You're no better'n me. You just know how to hide — and how to lie. Me I don't have that problem. I always tell the truth — even when I lie." (He starts out, staggers.) "So say good night to the bad guy . . . You're never gonna see a bad guy like me again."

These words aped my feelings when I experienced the meltdown over *Midnight Express* at the Golden Globes in 1978. I'd *felt* that many in that audience were total hypocrites when it came to the drug war, or the Vietnam War for that matter. Whatever war we're fighting. Can we ever tell the truth? Tony says elsewhere to Manny in the film, "That's the trouble in this country. Nobody tells the fucking truth!" My father, as I noted, had warned me about that. "Never tell the truth, kiddo, it'll only get you into trouble." And my mother had put it another way when she advised me through the years that "white lies are not bad. We need white lies." Perhaps we do, but look where it got my parents — no closer to their happiness. It basically led to divorce.

There's another scene close to my heart. Tony is in New York, about to assassinate the diplomat he's been sent to kill. With him is an associate, Chi Chi.

CHI CHI: What's so important about this guy anyway? What's he a Communist?
TONY: Nah, he's no Communist. He's a kinda symbol, that's what he is.
CHI CHI: What the fuck's that mean — sim-pul?
TONY: It's like when you die, your life meant something to somebody, y'know? It wasn't like you just lived it for yourself, but you did something for the rest of the human race too . . . (Tony snorts another line.)
CHI CHI: (nods his head somberly) Yeah?

TONY: Me, I wanna die fast. With my name written in lights all over the sky. Tony Montana. He died doin' it.

CHI CHI: Whatcha talking 'bout Tony, you ain't gonna die.

TONY: (doesn't hear him) . . . So I'll end up in a coffin. So what? The cock-a-roaches fire the bullets gonna end up in a coffin just like me. But I lived better when I was here. And that's what counts.

My anger throughout this period was wholly subconscious and mostly emerged in writing sessions. I was, overall, grateful to be doing well and back in the business. I had a job, I was well paid, and I was thirty-five. In my bones, I felt that I'd direct again. After eight or nine weeks, I sent the first draft of *Scarface* off to New York. Marty and Al liked it very much, no question. But Sidney Lumet told Marty it was violent and exploitive. Bregman did not agree, and to my chagrin, Sidney withdrew. I suppose Marty was expecting it, because he didn't care for all the political angles that Sidney generally liked, and he went quickly to Brian De Palma, who'd suffered a significant financial setback with *Blow Out* and saw this, like Marty did, as a big commercial comeback film. De Palma had apparently tried earlier to make a deal with Marty on a draft (written by David Rabe) using the 1932 version, but bowed out.

I returned with Elizabeth to New York from Paris early in the winter of 1982, reconnecting with the city I'd abandoned in 1976. Warily avoiding the dangerous temptations of Los Angeles, Elizabeth and I bought an apartment on a high floor overlooking Madison Avenue in the East 90s, which allowed us to run our two new Labradors around the reservoir in Central Park. Blessedly, Liz was off the coke too and back to a healthy lifestyle. We wanted a child, and we consulted a doctor, who couldn't imagine what the idiot doctor had told me ten years before regarding my fertility, haunting me with thoughts of chemical warfare. He injected me with the latest technology, quite confident that Elizabeth and I would succeed. This possibility raised my spirits enormously.

Meanwhile, Bregman went painstakingly through the script with me, with Pacino separately making incisive suggestions. We never discussed the *Born on the Fourth of July* debacle, but as I grew to know Al better, I found him surprisingly humorous, coming up with one-liners to fit Tony

Montana, whom he was evolving into with a broad Cuban accent and all. It surprised me that Al had never snorted cocaine or known anything about drugs. According to Marty, he'd had a serious problem with alcohol when younger but was now completely dry. Yet he had no problem behaving on-screen like the ultimate coke addict. Al definitely belonged to the "Method" school of acting, worshiping the aloof Lee Strasberg, who with his wife seemed to be making a rather good living teaching theater to a new generation. Al also kept a respected acting coach, Charlie Laughton, close to him, which greatly irritated Marty, who still wanted to "manage" Al in all ways, particularly his "warped" thinking. Al, to my mind, always had one goal — the play. Nothing else seemed to exist.

I continued to refine the script, and without much delay, Ned Tanen at Universal, Bregman's friendly studio, agreed to make the movie for some $14 to $15 million, which was quite good for a violent gangster film that, even on paper, was gathering a reputation for being "over the top" — another *Midnight Express* type of extravaganza from Oliver Stone, now paired with the excessive and violent Brian De Palma, who'd made *Dressed to Kill* and *Carrie.*

Bregman asked me to take De Palma down to see the locations and meet the figures I'd come to know while researching. Brian was a cold man, like Alan Parker — it comes with the territory — but he wasn't threatened by me and seemed to want me around. So did Bregman, who stayed very much in control of the film, sitting with Brian through every casting call. At one session I attended, I fought hard for Glenn Close to play the role of Al's mistress in *Scarface,* as she'd been great in the reading. I'd written the original Elvira role as an upper-class New York girl whom I knew, slumming in South Beach with a gangster boss when Tony meets her. Marty dismissed my idea as nuts — "She's got a face like a horse!" He was married to a beautiful actress, Cornelia Sharpe, a blond, and generally had a big thing going for blonds. Marty and De Palma ultimately chose a twenty-four-year-old newcomer, Michelle Pfeiffer, who scored hugely in the film and went on to a distinguished career. But at the time, I had to grudgingly rewrite Elvira's part down to make the role more of a materialistic South Beach bimbo.

Al asked Marty to keep me on the set to help him, presumably with a director he wasn't quite sure of. At first I was glad to stay on, although I was being paid only in per diem to cover my expenses, but I regarded it as a learning experience. Al was still, at this time, quicksilver of nature, turning on a dime, very sensitive to his environment, eyes, ears, skin on fire. If he saw a new face on the set, he'd react. He was just that way. At all costs I'd avoid his line of sight when he was in acting motion lest my concentration disrupt his own — somewhat like particle waves. Billy Wilder described this sensitivity in recounting how Greta Garbo banned him from *Ninotchka* for appearing in her sightline. It wouldn't be easy to direct Al, but De Palma seemed indifferent to that; he was never really an actor's director like Lumet, whom Pacino had wanted. De Palma, it seemed to me, was more interested in the "big picture," and in that vision actors were more or less an important part of the scenery.

When the shooting finally started in South Beach in November of 1982, it wouldn't take long for problems to emerge. Each day in the early rushes, Tony Montana's "scar" would change form, even move around Al's face a little, like a living worm. This created quite a stir, as no one seemed able to fix it until a new makeup man emerged who could maintain a consistent scar; but if one looks closely at some of the early scenes in the film, that scar has a mind of its own.

We also didn't last long on location. As I remember it, we were there less than two weeks before Cuban exile community leaders managed to get us thrown out of the city. First, they started the ridiculous rumor that Castro was financing the film. And when they got hold of a script, they wanted Tony Montana rewritten as a communist agent infiltrated into the US as a "Marielito" by Castro. Above all, they insisted we were distorting their so-called "contributions" to American society, which to my mind consisted of a highly politicized anti-Castro radicalism that included financing various terrorist organizations, one of which blew a Cuban domestic airliner out of the sky, murdering some eighty people. No matter what dialogue we gave Pacino about hating the Castro regime, it didn't matter to this humorless and rigid right-wing group. Our hasty exit from Miami would make the film's already reckless image worse, but Bregman and Universal took a firm stand in positioning the departure as a planned retreat to the safety of the studio walls.

At the lot in Burbank, the film bogged down. Interior sets can do that.

The sameness, the heat and confinement make people slower, as they grow accustomed to the comfort of returning to their dressing rooms and their homes at night. You're no longer a road company, which tends to be tighter; you're back to "civilian life." I'd had a similar problem on *The Hand* — how to keep the energy going. But this was different. This was like Napoleon trying to get out of Russia, and it began to affect the mood of the production — with the exception of a short liberating journey up to Santa Barbara for exteriors set at a villa in Bolivia, as well as Tony's mansion in Coral Gables. With a huge crew and cast, we were drifting from a twelve-week shoot into twenty-four weeks — extending from November 1982 to May 1983.

To begin with, De Palma was simply not the most energetic of human beings. He was overweight, slow physically, wearing the same copy of a pressed khaki uniform that an engineer might, throughout the production. He was also, from what I gather, in the middle of a divorce from his wife, actress Nancy Allen, which must not have helped his mood. But he was, no question, brilliant; he had vision, and he'd set up elaborate shots that would pay homage to this aesthetic but also take quite a bit of time for cinematographer John Alonzo to light. Brian's opinionated production designer, Nando Scarfiotti, a funky and elegant man who'd worked for the brilliant Bernardo Bertolucci and Luchino Visconti, and who'd succumb to AIDS in 1994, was his consigliere in residence, helping to give the film an extravagant '80s Miami look that caught on. Composer Giorgio Moroder would add a slick synthesizer disco score that gave the film an underlying tension and spice, as he'd done on *Midnight Express*. The violence was stylish as well, worked out as elaborately as anything Hitchcock might do; Brian, with his macabre, chuckling grin, enjoyed shooting it, as the script called for an enormous amount of gunfire, stabbings, and whatever other mayhem we came up with, such as the interior of a nightclub being totally destroyed by machine guns, mirrors shattering all over the place, and Tony's mansion being eradicated at the end of the movie. There were no significant digital effects available at that time, so because we had to use the firing devices called "squibs" that could imitate gunfire audiovisually, the pace slackened; each squib had to be replaced if the take was redone, which often was the case, and if there were twenty to fifty shots in a violent scene, it was quite a bit of labor and debilitating to the tempo. Actors would sit in their dressing rooms or trailers for endless hours.

And there was another issue that was more difficult to see, a large one really in its implications. Al had grown into the habit of not getting "up to speed" until approximately the seventh take. Sometimes a scene would need twelve, fourteen, even twenty takes. But it was generally those first six lost takes that surprised me. No matter how fast a crew moves, you'd lose at least an hour or two of prime energy to get an acceptable take. If Capra or Ford, by example, had been the director, it would've been one, two, or three takes, sometimes more, but there was a rhythm to the shooting. Here, there was a lot of lethargy and delay, and because he was such a star at this time, basically we could not move ahead to the next piece of business until Al approved what he'd done. Given Al's questioning of everything — sometimes right, but sometimes unnecessary and born from insecurity — there was no way in hell this film could stay close to its already expensive budget.

So given Brian's methodical but plodding energy levels, we'd get only three or four, maybe five pieces of business done each day. (On my later films, by contrast, we'd get seven to fifteen pieces "in the can.") Bregman was urging De Palma to move faster but to no avail. Brian would literally disappear for forty-eight hours on weekends, unavailable even for Marty's phone calls. The reason given by his staff at his rented mansion was "Mr. De Palma is sleeping and asked not to be awakened. At *any* hour." Brian wouldn't even react when the number two Universal executive came down to talk to him in his trailer during the interminable intervals between setups.

No one ever knocked on Al's door. It wouldn't have brought him out any sooner anyway; he was sticking to his pace. Even Bregman walked on eggshells around him. He was too dangerous to be confronted. This would change in later years, as I would work with Al successfully and relatively quickly in 1999's *Any Given Sunday,* but not then. I really couldn't understand why; after all, in the theater, which Al loved and where he often worked, the curtain rises — and it's just "one take" till the end. No do-overs.

As the budget climbed from about $15 million to approximately $25 million, the first assistant director was the first to go — they always are — but his replacement, a crackerjack, couldn't move Brian much faster. Anxious about "protecting" my scenes, I was pressured to look for cuts in the script, which was torture for me because I'd written an intricate weave. Frankly, Brian didn't seem to care as much about that. He wanted the Sergio Leone opera of the story; after all, he was shooting "a gangster film," which evoked for him grandeur — and I admit I appreciate that view now more than I did then. So sometimes I'd just disappear into my small Universal office or my hotel room in Santa Monica, where Elizabeth and I were camping, and either work on changes for the script or my new Russian story (more on that later), or take meetings on other projects. But I was invariably pulled back onto the *Scarface* set. And Los Angeles was sucking me back into its gravity field.

Our film, it seemed, oozed style at the expense of sense, and I challenged Brian on several staging issues, wherein the realities of a shootout were unbelievable to a Vietnam combat vet. But that was not the movie we were making. In fact, who said we were supposed to be rational? By example, for the final scene Brian sent some fifty or more gunmen into Tony's mansion to finish him, which was ridiculous given Miami's reality. I'd imagined a minimum of hit men could terminate Tony, but Brian won that argument, and because *Scarface* is grand opera, it works in its mad style.

In other arguments Brian acquiesced, but it wasn't easy for me to play the referee role on the set; in fact, it's quite miserable if you're a screenwriter who's also a director in your heart. I felt like a beggar who gets invited to the banquet but keeps a wary eye on the back entrance. In other words, I wasn't quite sure what I was supposed to be at this party. There were times, not often, when Brian would get testy if I challenged him, and he asked me to leave the set. No problem. "Who do I fuck to get off this film?" is the famous cliché when an actor can't take it anymore. Never have I felt it more than on this film.

When the last day of shooting thankfully rolled around, a traditional wrap party was planned for that evening. After the grueling six months, I thought it would've been a wonderful night to celebrate, but when I asked Brian if he was going, he surprised me, chuckling as he often did. "Fuck no. Do you think I want to be around these people another day! I'm outta here." And he was — pre-packed and en route to the airport the moment we finished. I didn't see him again for months. He'd been a mysterious man from the beginning, and he'd remain that way.

Prior to production on *Scarface,* in 1982, I wrote an original screenplay on a fictional orchestra conductor and composer in the Soviet Union, somewhat based on Dmitri Shostakovich, who forsakes his blossoming career in a frustrating fight with the communist system, then in its last stages. With Elizabeth, I traveled to ten different Soviet cities over thirty-plus days to covertly meet the real dissidents who'd been sent to psychiatric hospitals and gulags. It was a trip that would change my thinking on many levels. Bregman, whose family had emigrated from Russia, was my biggest supporter, and he arranged for Universal to finance the trip and my script, which presumably I was going to direct under his banner. I put all my intensity and heart into it, and after Marty declared my first draft to be "shit," I took it and went back to work on a second draft with his notes, and in consultation with him. It was much better. The third draft I'd do alone — without Marty.

As I was working on the screenplay in the summer of '83, Bregman invited me to see a "rough cut" of *Scarface* but warned me that I should talk to him first, right afterwards. Clearly he was worried about my talking to Pacino, whom he knew I was close to creatively. He said if I told Al my problems, "it'll only make things worse — you know Al. He'll go *nuts.*" I knew Marty's tricks, of course, and I knew he was looking to censor my reaction in advance. Al had also called me. He'd seen it, he was worried, and he wanted to talk to me right after I'd seen it. Something was up between Marty and Al, and suddenly I was cast in the middle.

When I saw the "rough cut" one morning in a typically small, crummy New York screening room, I grew massively depressed. All our work seemed to have gone up in flames. Now, it's true that I hadn't had much experience seeing directors' rough cuts, but at two hours and forty-nine minutes, this was not that, which would've been in the four-hour range. It had clearly been worked into a "finer cut" stage with some added effects, music, and so forth, but this was a mess. The beginning and the end were going to be okay, but the middle needed a tremendous amount of attention. I understood that, as a screenwriter, you can't attach yourself emotionally to the outcome of a film, but how else could I have written it? The overall sluggish pace, the lack of cohesion and meaning overwhelmed me.

Marty, suddenly and suspiciously, took to his bed sick for three days. He was unreachable. I think he knew that I'd have "problems" with it, and he knew Al would be on my case. Al did call right away — and invited me to his Upper East Side apartment. He was disturbed, and the fact that I hadn't seen the rough cut till now further agitated him. He told me Marty and Brian had apparently discredited us to each other, saying, "Oliver knows nothing about film" and "Al is a lunatic." The truth was that Al was smart, savvy in what works or not in drama, and it was a good idea to listen to what he had to say. Al did have good ideas, and sometimes, like many of us, when he sensed resistance to his idea being thought through, he'd be upset. Yet he also could be obtuse and difficult. I decided I'd try to help the situation by presenting notes on the rough cut to all of us.

Which is exactly what Marty did not want me to do. I wrote roughly five or six pages of notes, addressing almost every scene, and presented them to Al at the same time I showed them to Marty and Brian. This, as it turned out, was a huge mistake. Marty, rising a little too quickly off his sickbed, went ballistic, castigating me on the phone and then in person. I was a "traitor," I was leading a revolt against his authority, I'd jeopardized the film, and so forth, and Brian was 100 percent in agreement with him and very angry at me.

It was easier for Marty to pick a fight with me than with Al. And looking back, I realize if I'd been the director, I too would've been furious about my screenwriter talking directly to the star, undermining my authority. But this was a different dynamic. In this case, I had worked on the script far more closely with Marty and Al than with Brian. And it was Al who'd asked me to step in as a co-counsel in this dispute. Yet it's my impressionAl failed to defend me when Marty came down on me for betraying him. I'd trusted him to do so, wrongly. He was weak, evasive in that way, and I probably should've stayed out of this husband-and-wife storm, because ultimately, as is often the case, I was cut out as the friend. Al, over the years, maintained his love-hate relationship with his mentor/father figure Marty, while my own deep relationship with Marty ended harshly, and with it any prospect of doing my Russian dissident film. I wouldn't see or talk to Bregman

My dad, Louis, in newly liberated Paris, 1944. That first fresh flower of peace — with romance in the air.

My mom, Jacqueline, graduating from her lycée on the eve of the German occupation of France.

New York City, 1946 — a New World dawning.

Mom's parents, Mémé and Pépé to me, in their Sunday best, Paris, 1947.

Dad and his father, Joshua, boardwalk, East 80s, New York City, 1948.

French poodles were the rage then. I thought I was the child of one.

As a teenager traveling in Europe with Mom.

My boarding school yearbook, 1964. I was anxious to fit in and to succeed.

Hill School tennis team, spring 1965. A young gentleman headed for Yale . . . that is, until I took an unexpected three-year detour.

Here I am teaching at a Catholic secondary school in Saigon, 1965.

Two years later, back in Vietnam, this time as a GI, from September '67 to November '68.

With Dad in Hong Kong on my R&R from Vietnam. I'd just been wounded a second time and was dreading going back in five days.

Getting used to the jungle. Hauling an M60 machine gun. Hard to see much in the bush.

On my last mission — after ten days stuck in the rain in the Ashau Valley. It still reminds me of turn-of-the-century coal miners.

Oh, happy day! Back in the USA, November '68 — numb and dumb. I thought I was "home."

With Najwa, my wife, 1971. She was from Lebanon and worked at the UN while I went to film school on the GI Bill at NYU.

Wishing I could be Godard. Directing a short project at film school.

My first movie, a dream that turned into a nightmare. It wound up distributed on a double bill on 42nd Street. THE EVERETT COLLECTION

Brad Davis as young American tourist Billy Hayes denouncing Turkish justice when he's resentenced to thirty years for drug smuggling in *Midnight Express*. THE EVERETT COLLECTION

Brad Davis (left) and the real Billy Hayes (right) on the set of *Midnight Express* in Malta. They were rebels in spirit. THE EVERETT COLLECTION

With Lauren Bacall, the night in 1979 when I won an Oscar for screenwriting at thirty-three. Top of the world. GETTY IMAGES PHOTO ARCHIVES/WALT DISNEY TELEVISION

Directing my second film, *The Hand,* with Michael Caine.

Here Michael Caine is visited by the hand he's lost. Other complications follow.

THE EVERETT COLLECTION

Liz and me, our wedding day, San Antonio, June 1981.

John Milius directing *Conan,* his epic homage to sword and steel, 1981. THE EVERETT COLLECTION

Arnold, never to be underestimated, may not have been a great actor, but he sure knew it was an act.
THE EVERETT COLLECTION

Hiding out in France, writing *Scarface.*

Al Pacino, *Scarface,* 1983.
"Say hello to my li'l fren'."
THE EVERETT COLLECTION

De Palma and Spielberg
share a funny anecdote
as I wait . . . and wait. Six
months of apprentice-
ship. *Scarface* set, 1983.

Lonely winter in East
Hampton, Long Island,
1983–84, writing
"Defiance" and *8
Million Ways to Die.*

Michael Cimino, here with Mickey Rourke, on *Year of the Dragon,* resurrected my *Platoon* script.

PHOTO BY BENOÎT GYSEMBERGH VIA PARIS MATCH ARCHIVE/GETTY IMAGES

Journalist Richard Boyle, a man in perpetual motion, my creative inspiration for *Salvador* — and a real rascal.

Salvador was my third film, and I believed it was my last chance as a director. In Mexico, *Salvador* set, 1985, with Jimmy Woods (as Richard Boyle) and John Savage.

Rehearsing Elpidia Carrillo and Jimmy Woods, lovers in a desperate relationship.

Conniving to squeeze out a little more money to keep the cameras rolling . . . Here on the *Salvador* set, from left to right: John Daly, Gerald Green, and Derek Gibson.

Action! A child's dream of making a movie. I got to blow up a whole town in Mexico.

Hard-won satisfaction. With my son in Paris on the Champs-Élysées, 1986.

Chris Taylor (Charlie Sheen) returns to his platoon after his first wound. COURTESY OF METRO-GOLDWYN-MAYER STUDIOS

The essential conflict between two Americas at the heart of *Platoon* — Philippines, 1986. From left to right: Tom Berenger, Mark Moses, Willem Dafoe. COURTESY OF METRO-GOLDWYN-MAYER STUDIOS

Mixed feelings. We burned their village to the ground, but we escorted the women and children to "safety."
COURTESY OF METRO-GOLDWYN-MAYER STUDIOS

Betrayed within. The murder of Elias (Willem Dafoe) became our poster image.
THE EVERETT COLLECTION

The Philippines jungle: "I have three hours left, and I need to get five more shots, but maybe I could do it in four if . . ." This is when you decide what you need, not what you want.

The platoon got smaller and sadder as we sent each actor home once his character was killed or wounded. From left to right: Arnold Kopelson, Charlie Sheen, Tom Berenger, Willem Dafoe, myself, Dale Dye. COURTESY OF METRO-GOLDWYN-MAYER STUDIOS

Chris Taylor (Charlie Sheen) bids farewell to a friend (Keith David) who is returning to "the world." COURTESY OF METRO-GOLDWYN-MAYER STUDIOS

Taylor/Sheen hunts down his sergeant. A life choice to be made. THE EVERETT COLLECTION

A night to remember. *Platoon,* Oscar for Best Picture, 1986. Who ever thought I'd be here?

It doesn't get much better. Left to right: myself, Arnold Kopelson, Tom Berenger, Mike Medavoy, Willem Dafoe, Arthur Krim, John Daly

until *Born on the Fourth of July* surprisingly came around again six years later. And then the tables would be turned.

Ultimately Al persisted, and some of the notes I wrote were addressed, some not. I would hear things about the film in the coming months, about the Ratings Board giving it an X in October of '83 — a rating that would've doomed the film commercially. Marty and Brian went back more than once with recuts, particularly with the chainsaw scene, and when Brian reportedly protested that he would go no further, the board acquiesced to giving it an R rating. There were publicity campaigns and premieres and so forth, but I had no contact with them or, for that matter, with Al, who never bothered to call me. I was as cut off as I'd been on *Midnight Express* — the typical fate of a screenwriter who cares too much.

The film opened on December 9, 1983, and by the expectations of the industry was more of a flop than a success; it ultimately made $66 million domestically. Over time, though, with foreign revenue and cable TV, and then all the ancillary deals, it yielded a great deal more revenue to Universal Pictures and to the "gross dollar" participants Bregman, Pacino, and De Palma. As a fixed "net gross" participant, I received only union "residuals" from television and video sales, ultimately a tidy sum, but hardly what they called in the film industry "a payday." The audience reactions at the premiere, I gather, were mixed. For many it was "too much."

Reviewers like Roger Ebert out of Chicago, the leading TV and Middle America influence, and the quirky Vincent Canby of the *New York Times* were very positive, but most were generally negative and sometimes cruel, separating their cult-like devotion to De Palma, who had a semi-Hitchcock status with them, from Pacino and myself — that violent writer. "A De Palma Movie for People Who Don't Like De Palma Movies" read the title of Pauline Kael's review in *The New Yorker*. "He's stripped of his gifts. His originality doesn't function on this crude, ritualized melodrama; he's working against his own talent . . . a long, druggy spectacle — manic yet exhausted, with De Palma entering into the derangement and trying to make something heroic out of Tony's emptiness and debauchery."

Her review typified a new kind of self-conscious film criticism, and it darkened a lifetime of going to the movies for me. A sort of super-fandom wherein the critic, putting himself or herself between the movie and the audience, reveled in his or her subjective, specialized knowledge of the filmmaker, as opposed to just watching a movie without knowing who made it — as when we were young. The audience, for the most part, might not know who directed it, and it shouldn't matter. A film exists on its own merits — no cheating allowed (reviews, money thrown at it, promotions, etc.).

I saw the film for the first time in a packed theater on Broadway with a paying audience, mostly Latino and black, which gave the film street cred, and right there I knew it was a better movie than the film crowd thought — and that it would *last.* I knew it from riding the New York subways. I knew it from hearing people talk on the street. I knew it from the people who shouted back at the film, who'd repeat the lines and laugh on the playgrounds and in the parks. These people knew it in their gut. The War on Drugs was bullshit from beginning to end, a fraud sending them to prison in massive numbers. These people knew that Tony Montana had a code of honor of his own, and as fucked up as he was, he was true to his nature till that end. He was a free man. I heard from his family years later that Pablo Escobar, the emerging king of cocaine at that time down in Colombia, adored it and screened it many times. And within a couple of years, the white folks who knew the drug world came to appreciate it. Michael Mann plunged right in with the TV series *Miami Vice* (1984). He saw the power of it, acknowledged it to me, and cashed in more than we ever did. By the time I made *Wall Street* in 1987, the young white guys down there were quoting it back to me at viewing parties.

The film would live on strangely in my life, an inside-the-park home run, an entrée to a certain wild, transgressive sector of our society. For years, people would congratulate me and quote me lines from it. Gangsters and their ilk would buy me drinks, champagne, in such faraway places as Egypt, Russia, Cambodia. I could've made a great deal of money by accepting a sequel, but my "gangster" thoughts were ready to explode into the new milieu of Wall Street.

Scarface was not *The Godfather.* It lacked the family and the sense of a tragic arc. But it was a juicy, crude opera of a drug dealer's life set across a slimeball American materialism flowering in South Florida, the madness of a dream that always wants "more . . . more . . . and even more." Greed was indeed good. The '80s had arrived.

The truth was, I was heartbroken by *Scarface* and its Hollywood reception for much of that year. My career was at a strange standstill. With the money from *Scarface,* Elizabeth and I had bought a modest converted potato barn on an acre of land in Sagaponack, Long Island, to which we commuted from our New York apartment in a Volvo on weekends like old-line New Yorkers — the two Labradors, faithful companions panting in our ears from the backseat, eager to run down the fields to the ocean two blocks away, where we'd all plunge into the cold North Atlantic. It can get so lonely out there as the fall sets in. I'd read about Jackson Pollock, Robert Rauschenberg, Lee Krasner, and the abstract painters and novelists of the 1950s, inspired by the solitude, sticking it out through the long winters when there were fewer people on eastern Long Island.

It seemed a perfect place to rewrite my Russian script, which was about courage and isolation; now it would take that courage to write it as it should be written. If I could do it right, it'd be a powerful comeback movie from *The Hand.* But I could also see the madness of that dream. I needed hope that I would direct a film again, but my strongest patron had now abandoned me. Marty Bregman was a street fighter, and he would certainly hold a grudge, bad-mouthing me in the business as a troublemaker. "Defiance," as I called my Russia story, was dead in the water. I knew that it wouldn't be made — at least in this coming phase of my life. Nonetheless, I persisted, thinking if I could make it excellent, it would somehow get done in spite of the opposition. I would write it with the same concentration and tenacity of those protagonists I'd met in Russia, their eyes reflecting the despair of the hospitals and prisons, the simple pain of existence through which they were still able, occasionally, to laugh. They gave me a new sense of inner strength I'd never felt before.

This third draft of "Defiance" would become as crucial to my development as my scripts for *Platoon* and *Born on the Fourth of July* and my work with Robert Bolt on the unproduced "Cover-Up." It was a strong, in fact riveting, statement of dissent against authoritarian power of any kind

— but in this case, my timing was way off. When I finished and submitted the script, there were no comments coming back from anyone, just a check. Bregman wouldn't even call to acknowledge the reception of it — and the screenplay would disappear into the Universal vaults. And then, within a few years, Gorbachev would come to power, rendering my script a period piece. The dissident movement would take a new shape, even in my own country, and in many ways I would become one of them. I was prepared to be alone, to be isolated by my beliefs. But I *also* began to believe, like many exiled writers, the worst about myself.

Stanley Weiser, who was at NYU film school with me and co-wrote *Wall Street,* later told me that for him as a young screenwriter in Hollywood, I'd represented a standard of rebelliousness on how to break the rules and get away with it. He'd heard exaggerated stories of my fighting off intrusive executives, rejecting offers, etc. Yes — and I'd also gotten intoxicated in Hollywood and drugged in public, with stupid, immature behavior. I'd flirted with and teased pretty women, sometimes in front of jealous men. I was at times rude, arrogant — yet I'd say colorful too, the kind of guy who you don't know what he'll do next. And I would do something, never violent or intentionally harmful, but often outrageous, to make the moment less boring. This is the dramatist's inclination, to act out the scene from his head into real life, to go for that line of dialogue that has more impact, not thinking about the consequences of it to the person who's listening. There were a few "Oliver Stone stories" that I'd hear, bounced back at me, often with unbelievable outcomes. But there was truth there too. Gore Vidal had turned on me once at dinner and, in his inimitably ruthless, elitist manner, snapped, "What is it with you, Stone — is it that metal plate in your head again?" implying hypothetical damage done to me in Vietnam. Only Gore could be so vicious and blunt but decisive; that was his virtue too — to call everything, including our government, into question.

It all now seemed to gather in a paranoid storm cloud above me that thundered, "Too much." I was guilty. I was alone, in exile, my agent cold and soulless, in Russia somewhere with no friends, the snow and the trees closing in on me, no child yet in my wife's belly, month after month of silence. And when Elizabeth would menstruate, it felt like a death knell. Our expensive treatments weren't working for her or me — and it was depressingly unclear in whose reproductive system the problem lay. The medical world was a guessing game as well, but we loved each other still, and there was no blame. The guilt was mutual but unexpressed. Kubrick's *The Shining* (1980) with its insane writer protagonist was too close to home.

The only interest, ironically, in my writing a screenplay came from the notorious "bad boy" producer Don Simpson, who was a powerhouse in Hollywood off *Flashdance* and the soon-to-be-released *Beverly Hills Cop*. Simpson was known for his huge appetite for coke, big ideas, and macho behavior. He saw in me, because of my Vietnam experience, a fellow traveler, and his story idea was from a magazine piece about US naval pilots in training near San Diego that would become, after many drafts, *Top Gun*. The money he offered was big, and my agent implied I should take this idea very seriously. My problem was the content. Knowing Simpson and his instincts, I could sense this was going to be a big commercial picture about our hotshot competitive fighter pilots. The young Tom Cruise would be perfect. But after writing *Born on the Fourth of July*, I had strong doubts about military worship, and turned down the project. To Simpson and his partner, Jerry Bruckheimer, it was a potential huge moneymaker, but it didn't matter to them that when they ultimately made the movie off a series of expensive screenplays, directed by Tony Scott, that *Top Gun* literally ended with these jock pilots eagerly heading off to start a war with the Russians — to World War III, in fact, which would probably mark the end of our civilization; in other words, Don, no more "hits," no more money, no sex, no coke, just nuclear winter — fun *not*.

In this 2020 climate, I wonder, has anything changed in the American "boy hero" character? "It's only a movie — right?" They're making *Top Gun II* as I write this. I can see so clearly the way success blinds one to the content of the message. Patriotism sells. Defeat, as in Vietnam, does not. And sure enough, *Top Gun* became the highest-grossing film of 1986 ($177 million at the domestic box office). But sadly, Don Simpson would die, bloated and prematurely, of heart failure at fifty-two in 1996; it was reported that he was sitting on a toilet in his mansion, alone, reading James Riordan's 1995 biography of my life when he keeled over. I do hope he was at least enjoying himself. I always felt a certain kinship in his dancing eyes for the madness of this life.

One shining, bright, cold winter day I bought a cooked lamb and, in a bizarre homage to Odysseus and other characters in Greek drama, laid out its severed parts on my lawn, offering it with fire, incense, and prayer to the gods to wipe clean whatever I had done to offend them. I begged forgiveness, especially of Pallas Athena, the goddess of wisdom. It was a strange and solitary ceremony, witnessed only by my two ravenous dogs. I meant every word I chose judiciously, my heart so earnest to end this self-inflicted pain I was feeling as a frustrated writer, dramatist, whatever I was. When I finished, I allowed the dogs to devour the offering. After all, what did the Greeks do with all those fine oxen and sheep that were sacrificed on Homer's pyres?

Perhaps Pallas Athena was listening.

Shortly after, "out of the blue" as they say, without any introduction, Michael Cimino called and asked me to come to Manhattan. I'd met him in passing, but in person he conveyed an enormous passion for my shelved screenplay *Platoon,* which he confidently said only I should direct. Having been down that road too many times, I dismissed the possibility. But he insisted that "Vietnam would come around again," that Stanley Kubrick was cooking up a Vietnam film based on a book by Gustav Hasford titled *The Short-Timers,* which would be released in 1987 as *Full Metal Jacket.* Michael's was a voice in the wilderness to me, faint but inspiring. He'd made a deal with Dino De Laurentiis, who'd botched up *Conan,* but Michael made it very clear that he was in charge, not the scoundrel I feared in Dino, and that he would personally produce my film. Even after the epic failure of Cimino's *Heaven's Gate,* whose budget had skyrocketed from a reported $12 to $40 million and had contributed greatly to a backlash against the independence of the '70s directors, including Friedkin, Coppola, Bogdanovich, Scorsese, and David Lynch, Dino badly wanted Michael to direct an adaptation of the book *Year of the Dragon,* by ex–*New York Times* reporter Robert Daley. Dino saw this as another New York cop hit, like *The French Connection,* or his film *Serpico,* co-produced with Bregman. But this would be about Chinatown gangsters and heroin.

Michael asked me to co-write it with him; he'd loved *Scarface* and wanted that brazen street attitude to infuse this heavily researched history of the triads originating in Hong Kong that were quietly raking in a fortune off the opium-heroin trade. Daley's book was built around a fictionalized detective and his frustrating years-long chase after a Chinese mobster. I liked the idea, yes, and no doubt I was flattered that someone like Michael wanted to work with me.

And Dino was once again a charmer when he wanted something, inviting his future wife Martha, Michael and his partner-producer Joann Carelli, Elizabeth and myself, Frank Yablans, the head of MGM at that time, and his partner, the writer Tracy Hotchner, to an end-of-year celebration in the South of France. He took us to his favorite casino, where he won $50,000 on the first spin of the wheel, then lost it on the next. That was Dino, the consummate gambler. In his heavy guttural accent he told me, "Oliver, your last film [*The Hand*] Warner Brothers kill in distribution. I know you can direct a film. But you need a producer. Very important this time that you make a *success*." He was very convincing, but in rereading *Platoon* he warned me that I should "take out the dirty words. I don't want to make *Scarface* again." The proposed deal was that I would accept half my *Scarface* screenwriting fee to script *Year of the Dragon,* and Dino would in turn, with Michael, produce *Platoon* without stars and with me directing at a price of no more than $7 million. We celebrated the agreement at Le Pirate, a renowned French restaurant in the hills near Cap-Martin on the Italian border where, *Zorba*-style, we broke three hundred plates and two hundred glasses and ate lentils for good luck in the new year. We danced on the tables, then in a conga line, throwing bottles and dishes wherever we wanted, slicing open champagne magnums with swords, behaving like insane children running out onto the beach into the flares at midnight. It looked like it was going to be a wonderful 1984, Orwell's prophecy notwithstanding. I would finally get to direct a movie I loved, and what could be worse than 1983 with its tensions over *Scarface* and "Defiance"? I was so looking forward. The plates piled up in the corners with the empty champagne magnums — it was almost too good to be true, and I kind of knew it, but I had to believe in it. I had no alternative.

Now there was *Year of the Dragon* to make. Michael, who'd already done *The Deer Hunter,* was dogged about Vietnam and, unlike in Robert Daley's book, wanted to give our detective in *Dragon* a Vietnam backstory, which presumably I could supply. What he wanted was a combination of *Dirty Harry* and *The French Connection,* a kind of vigilante cop who'd break all the rules like Tony Montana, and wreak fire and destruction on Chinatown. Discussions and note taking followed in his giant production office on Union Square, then solo writing sessions in my apartment uptown or in Sagaponack. Michael was a driven soul, priding himself on his monasticism, not unlike his detective hero, whom I renamed Stanley White after a colorful Polish American LA homicide detective I'd grown friendly with. Michael became obsessed with the real Stanley, who was an authentic ex-marine Vietnam vet and, like many LA cops, sometimes a great bullshitter; but his heart was in the right place. He'd worked undercover narcotics, yet understood a guy like me from the other side of the fence who smoked dope and generally distrusted cops, especially narcs. We enjoyed arguing our worldviews.

Michael, however, seemed humorless in his intensity, overdoing it, I thought. He'd call our young Chinese production coordinator, Alex Ho, at 3 a.m. and say things like "Meet me in Staten Island at X location at five. I want to see the sun come out," or "Give me a full location board on this or that, or a timeline, or a clothing history," or whatever struck him in the moment; there were so many insane demands for knowledge that he'd ultimately never use, but he'd need to know. He also needed reassurance that, after *Heaven's Gate,* he could still command armies of people to work for him — like a caricature of Napoleon, whom, at five feet, three inches or so, heightened by the black boots with lifts he always seemed to wear, he resembled.

But he was our leader, and he seemed to be in control of his destiny. He could, if I was going to direct *Platoon,* provide the ballast I would need against Dino's mindset. I worked hard to give Michael what he wanted. And like many a screenwriter working under a demanding director, I would convince myself he was right. With Alex's help, we went to meet everybody in power who'd talk to us in Chinatown. The Chinese are exceedingly polite, but there was no admission whatsoever of any crime or wrongdoing. I had a different problem here than in *Scarface,* where the Miami and Lauderdale police forces were open about the enemy. In this case, no one in the New York police force or DA's office, or the DEA, or the FBI knew *anything*. It was quite stunning, and also frustrating.

In search of any knowledge, we attended several formal, dull three-hour dinners at the five-story tong associations in Chinatown. These are social organizations, and here they would endlessly toast one another, as I gained a great deal of weight on rich Chinese food but learned nothing from these wily bosses. Even the notorious street gangs, who did a lot of the smaller dirty work, were unavailable to us. The "slave" factories, wage laborers, waiters — nothing. We took the famous all-night buses down to Atlantic City to mix with the Chinese laborers after work. Here they'd gamble their wages away and return literally before dawn to start their lunchtime service jobs. It was devastatingly sad to see how tough it was to make it as another Chinese worker in America without connections.

But Michael was a bloodhound and kept coming back, for diminishing returns. No detail was too small for his attention. He prided himself on needing little sleep — a cat-napper. I didn't feel I had to emulate his pace, nor did I, but everyone on our growing workforce was on call 24/7 as Michael was now building a giant replica, in exacting detail, of a New York Chinatown street at Dino's new taxpayer-funded studio in Wilmington, Delaware. The costs were high, but Michael always wanted "more" and "better"; it was his nature. There was no doubt that the parsimonious Dino would cut him back anyway; Michael would ask for fifteen hundred extras when, with clever use of the chessboard, eight hundred would do. At times he'd anger his team with his arrogance or, let's say, lack of appreciation, which I found to be a common characteristic among many directors in that era. Michael, for instance, so admired De Palma's mirror-shattering nightclub scene in *Scarface* that he constructed his own nightclub and shattered even more mirrors in a *Year of the Dragon* shootout. He'd spend an extraordinary amount of money filming a Thai drug lord meeting in the real highlands of Thailand, and rehearse for hours on the correct way to smoke an opium pipe. These were things that De Palma didn't particularly care about unless it was a tool for malice — a Hitchcock thing. Michael's was a blunter documentary director's approach in the name of realism, but it was expensive.

We did finally manage to gather some insights into the style of these

192 · *Chasing the Light*

Chinese big shots. Eddie Chan, who'd been a Hong Kong police sergeant at the origin point, and fit the profile of a major importer of heroin, now owned one of the largest Chinatown banks, and he invited us to his elaborate office. A new symbol of prestige at the time was employing on your payroll huge bald black bodyguards with shoulder holsters, which I think was inspired by the '70s black exploitation films. Thus two bodyguards would accompany Eddie everywhere we walked on the streets, one twenty feet in front, the other behind. Eddie also carried his own pistol in a well-concealed ankle holster, which would certainly not fit the image of a successful Manhattan banker. But he was most amiable and seemed to know someone in every store, restaurant, or movie theater we passed. And everybody seemed to know "Eddie." Everybody owed somebody something in Chinatown.

We learned the most from a mild fellow named Herbert Liu, who was a "dissident" out of Fort Lee, New Jersey; he'd fallen out with the boys and was sufficiently pissed off to tell us some things that confirmed what we suspected was going on. There were no real busts at the time, except occasionally of the violent young gangbangers who were killing people here and there — no big money, but dangerous. Everything was below the surface, like most of Chinatown. When I asked Herbert (which is not phonetically or otherwise a Chinese name) how he got such a jarringly proper British name, like Clive or Terence, he shrugged and replied in his tough Chinese accent, "out of the phone book," which made me laugh as I realized this is what most Chinese with indecipherable names did when they got to the New World. They were inherently street smart and suspected that the truth would never be their friend, New World or Old World.

Which was a key point in the climax of the film. In the book, the American detective finds a way to finally bust his Chinese nemesis when he discovers that he's still married to his original Chinese wife in Hong Kong, as many Chinese were. Not caring that much about Western customs or laws, he'd simply married another Chinese wife when he came to the West. No big deal; it saves money and, most important, "face" — respect for the original wife. It seemed to me, after all the violence and cat-and-mouse back-and-forth, that the book's denouement provided a brilliant solution.

Our detective, Mickey Rourke, would finally get Joey Thai (John Lone) on a bigamy charge. After all, Capone had gone down not for murder but for tax evasion. Michael liked it — but Dino hated it.

"What is this? Bigamy? Is no good! American audience will hate it!"

As ruthless as he seemed, Dino was a true Italian Catholic, faithful in name to his vows of marriage. His point was that audiences for the movie were there to see violence between the two men in the end, and sexual marriage issues should not cloud this pleasure. So I went back to the boards with Michael and wrote a train wreck of a shootout near the end.

What can I really say about *Dragon*? I tried, but I was forcing it. The Stanley White character's rants, some quite racist about Asians, though leavened by favorable dialogues about the nineteenth-century contributions of the Chinese to America, didn't play the same out of Mickey Rourke's mouth as they might have with Al Pacino. Why? I think because Michael, as a director, loved excess, like De Palma, but in this case, the rants came out flat and bigoted — without the irony they needed. Was it the script? Partly.

But again, as with Alan Parker, after I'd satisfied Michael with the screenplay, I was not invited into the inner circle; Cimino was a "control freak" like Bregman, no question, but his request for authenticity at any hour of the night, at any cost, was in the end "surface," not content. He should have had the writer at a table reading, at the very least, with the actors in the room, and forced us to deal with the screenplay in the traditional way, which is to read the lines, hear them, rehearse them, if necessary change them. It works. And to my mind, it's unbelievably sloppy of any film to commit vast sums to production without at least a minimum of rehearsal and revision, even if last-minute. I'm sure I could have improved the script if I'd been encouraged to hang at the set, catch the inflections, relate to the actors. But Michael would not allow that. Nor would Mickey Rourke; unlike Al, he wouldn't even acknowledge me as a participant. Michael was the only god he served — or, really, cult leader. I don't think I've ever seen such loyalty as between Mickey and Michael. Nor, for that matter, would Dino, in his cheapness, ever have paid me a per diem to do so; and having been through the demanding experience of the *Scarface* set, I wasn't inclined to volunteer. But even if I had, I doubt Michael would have accepted my services. After all, he was a screenwriter too. Instead he told me, "Go back to *Platoon*. Get it ready."

And so I did. Our line producer, Alex Ho, whom I'd promoted from production coordinator, had by this time been fired by Michael as the *Dragon* budget started climbing into the twenties; these were still fairly alarming numbers at that time. Dino asked him to work with me instead and also asked for a revision on the *Platoon* script. I made a few changes, resisting most of Dino's clichéd thoughts, and we hired a casting director. I traveled to the Philippines with Alex for my first trip back to Asia since 1968. It was a homecoming. The caress of its soft winds, its greenish seas, gave me a longing for my past. Sailor, soldier, teacher, traveler, I'd found a new home out here after my first family came to an end, and although I had no claim, I felt welcomed back. People smiled with genuine happiness; there was such a thing in life as joy, and it could be had — here and now, it need not be delayed. I plunged into rainforests outside Manila with a small Filipino crew under the local producer, Jun Juban. We knew with our budget we'd have to be a guerrilla version of *Apocalypse Now*, which had experienced well-documented problems in the Philippines, among them trying to shoot in the typhoon season. But the jungle itself was pure, and I could imagine cutting trails deep into it, leading actors down into the riverbeds and up into the valleys. I fell in love with the landscape and the people.

My spirits were buoyed when I returned to New York, where I auditioned and cast some twenty young men without committing to contract. Emilio Estevez, Martin Sheen's oldest son, a quiet, inner-directed young man, was my choice for the protagonist. Young actors like Bruce Willis, Willem Dafoe, Woody Harrelson, and John Turturro passed through our office, and at occasional meetings with Dino, we'd discuss script and financial issues, but his mind was usually elsewhere, often on *Dragon,* his manner gruff.

Waiting for *Platoon* to go, out of that sense of independence I'd learned at NYU — that is, no one's going to help you, do it yourself — I went ahead and optioned a book with my own money, *Eight Million Ways to Die* by Lawrence Block, about an ex-alcoholic and private detective, Matt Scudder, who knows New York and its darker corners well. My own anxieties were relieved whenever I could sit and write. With insiders, I visited the Lower East Side drug gangs coming into prominence; Brooklyn was teeming with crack houses. The city was hopped up with a new kind of fever, which I tried to blend into the script and its characters. My opening voice-over for Scudder, not in the book, started:

> New York in the summer is like any other tropical port — Saigon, Rangoon, Hong Kong. It swelters and moves, and sometimes I think there ought to be palm trees growing along the sidewalk — they'd fit right in with the whores and the hustlers. Some nights, I feel Africa's in the city, the natives with their cutoffs and tank tops, flesh for sale in the land of Ugladu.

In the same vein of making life decisions, I decided to divorce myself, at last, from Jeff Berg at ICM. Our relationship, based on trust, was simply false; without trust, nothing can last. I did not pay Jeff a visit in person but chose to write him a long letter, which kept it impersonal, as our relationship had been. He called twice the next day, but I didn't return. No talk was necessary. It'd been a cold alliance, and now a cold parting. As in politics, self-interest rules. A few days later, Jeff responded in a terse note reminding me that we had a binding contract for another year in which he would be collecting 10 percent of my fees. Fine.

I signed on with my third agent, for a short time, at another, smaller agency. He was a well-meaning man, but the chemistry wasn't there for me, and I left him after several months — and returned to Berg's ICM (I was still paying them a commission anyway), but with a younger, more responsive agent there. That didn't work either. Now I was very confused.

My father, meanwhile, was still going to his office in the mornings in midtown with his shrinking clientele, still defiantly smoking and drinking scotch every day — but going to doctors and hospitals more frequently for heart and other procedures; no question he was breaking down. How quickly was the issue. Mom, who was still living half the year in Paris, now moved into the guest bedroom of my father's apartment to help him through these difficult months, bringing with her a sense of French gaiety along with various guests and friends, remixing her own life with his as it once was in the 1950s. It was a bit of a relationship renaissance, as it was clear she really cared for him in spite of all the heartbreaks she'd suffered. And Dad, for the most part, enjoyed her company more, although he'd lash out at her whenever she crossed his privacy line. Mom even talked of their remarrying after all these years, if for no other reason than that it would help her keep his large rent-controlled apartment with a terrace overlooking Third Avenue in her name. It seemed right to me, a rightness to it for our fractured family — a coming around again from 1945 to 1984 — thirty-nine years of a life "somewhat" together.

Nineteen eighty-four was turning out to be the special year I'd prayed for. With the help of a new, upbeat doctor, his attitude crucial in convincing Elizabeth and me that this would finally work — lo and behold, in April, Elizabeth called me to announce, triumphantly, she was with child. It was glorious, the best news I'd ever wanted, as real as *Platoon* ever could be. As the months drifted, it was exciting to watch her belly grow; we didn't want to know the sex, we wanted to enjoy the mystery of it. When I saw the sonogram, a little half-inch tadpole with its heart going two hundred beats a minute, I felt I was in a paradise I'd never known. Yet her pregnancy remained delicate from month to month, and we took care of her in every way to avoid a miscarriage. With prednisone shots given to assist this pregnancy, Elizabeth had grown into a far more motherly figure than the blond tomboy who'd been my partner whenever we traveled. Dad wanted to see any kind of grandchild and told me he'd hang on.

And then, just as everything seemed to be clicking — Elizabeth pregnant, *Platoon* being born, *Eight Million Ways to Die* growing into another possible film, my mom and dad semi-reuniting — things turned south again.

Dino, according to his associate Fred Sidewater, was meeting resistance on *Platoon*. More than he'd ever thought. I couldn't believe it at first. Dino's best "in" was at MGM; they were going to distribute the forthcoming *Dragon*. He asked us to cut *Platoon*'s budget, so Alex and I did, painfully. And then, a month later, he asked us to cut it again. Something was definitely wrong. We went a second time to the Philippines to fine-tune our plans, but each day I was on eggshells as Alex would take tense middle-of-the-night calls from Sidewater in New York. The gist of it was that Dino was offering to fully finance the film, originally at $7 million, now $4.5 million and dropping — if only MGM would commit a minimum of $3 million in prints and ads. There was a formula at that time with the burgeoning video market which required a minimum guarantee of advertising to ensure return on the risk capital. That formula eventually disintegrated, as all these things do, when more and more people abused it. But in any case, the answer was no. Dino, not a man who gave up easily, went, I believe, a little lower in his request, but the answer was still the same — no. I never heard the word "no" so much as I did in those years. I hated the word, still do.

Dino's "friend," which is a euphemism in this business, Frank Yablans, the man who supposedly ran the MGM studio and with whom we'd shared dinner that crazed plate-smashing New Year's Eve, was saying without saying it that the real problem was political. Alexander Haig, who'd been secretary of state for Reagan, and Henry Kissinger, Nixon's German-born doppelganger on Vietnam, were both on MGM's board of directors, and they would not want to see a movie like *Platoon* made by their studio. "That's such crap!" I protested. I doubt they even discussed it, because as is often the case, it was your so-called proponent — in this instance Yablans — who dropped the ball without doing anything lest he come under tighter supervision. People like him, in my estimation, don't even want to go to the mat with the board because they think they already know the eventual answer, and thus it isn't worth using up their political capital. But since when did we have to go to a board of directors to get approval to make a movie at a cost where Dino was the only one taking a risk? I'd never heard of such a thing. It exasperated me. What else could I possibly do? Cut the budget to shoot in Central Park?

And I have to admit, Dino *was* surprised too. He suddenly realized that with *Platoon*, he had a political hot potato that he didn't know what to do with. He'd never been in this situation before. He was already taking a chance by financing David Lynch on *Blue Velvet* for around $6 million, and that film was violently erotic. There was plenty of new video money available in the marketplace, which insulated *Blue Velvet* with MGM willing to distribute it. But my film? No. It didn't matter. Nothing mattered. We were done. The same thing was happening to *Platoon* that had happened to *Born on the Fourth of July,* and before that to *Platoon* at its origin. Realistic Vietnam films were simply not possible, although unrealistic ones, *First Blood* (1982) and *Rambo: First Blood Part II* (1985), with their retelling of Vietnam by Sylvester Stallone, were huge successes, as was *Missing in Action* (1984), with Chuck Norris saving our MIAs. America, with Reagan as its president since 1981, was in an era of renewed military buildup. Beyond resurrecting the Cold War against the Soviets as an "evil empire," Reagan said of the Vietnam War, "It's time that we recognize that ours was, in truth, a noble cause."

As to Cimino's promise to personally produce *Platoon* for me, he had his hands full with *Dragon,* and when I needed him, he disappeared in pre-production at Dino's studios in Wilmington. So much for film promises. To watch my cast crumble was a heartbreak for me, as was watching our own carefully crafted plans for how to shoot in the Philippines in the most economical way go up in smoke. I'd promised myself after *Born* never to take on Vietnam subject matter again, but I'd fallen for Cimino's seduction, which had prompted me to resurrect *Platoon* from the closet.

In the long run, Cimino was right about the subject of Vietnam as a topic, but now I was furious, crazed. I did understand that Dino had truly tried to make the film. I couldn't fault him for that. But as a month, then another month, then a third month went by, I realized there was another problem, a big one — my *Platoon* script now belonged to Dino. And when I asked his company for my rights back, it wasn't that simple. The lawyers would say, "This is a business. Dino's spent money on it . . ." etc., etc. Although Dino could be charming, he was also a bandit, pure and simple, Italian-style. There was no law. "Keep what you get. Never give anything back." The rules of the movie jungle.

Adding insult to the injury, Dino was holding back the last payment on my delivery of the *Dragon* script, a fee that had been cut in half anyway. So with limited money, I had to take on Dino De Laurentiis, who, like Donald Trump, dealt with lawsuits as if they were parking tickets. I couldn't use my lawyer, Tom Pollock, because he also represented Dino — and obviously Dino was a bigger client than I. So I moved over to the law firm of Greenberg Glusker, whose Bert Fields was known as the top litigator in the movie business. Fields turned me over to a six-foot, four-inch hunk of a man, a gunslinger with the appropriate name of Bob Marshall, who looked the part of a legal breaker of balls — Dino's balls, I hoped. But this, as is true of most lawsuits, was a messy affair that would drag on.

My dad, meanwhile, was dying. He was in the hospital, a breathing tube in his nose, a pincushion of IVs in his arms, a catheter between his legs. This once handsome, imposing man — who'd come home every day at 5:30 and be met, tail wagging at the door, by our big black French poodle, Jenny, who'd cleverly snatch the evening paper from his hand with her welcoming jaws — was a shock to my eyes. He'd been on a dialysis machine, his kidneys not functioning, passively resigned with a deeply unhappy look on his face. His sense of humor was helping, as he managed to say, "Jesus, kiddo, you think this is any fun? Wait till you end up here." He weighed 125 pounds or so, down from 175, just flesh hanging off the bones, no muscle at all. This was the man I once called "Daddy" who was so strong. It was nightmarish, as if I was seeing myself in the future.

The nurses removed the breathing tube and we talked. He was druggy and trying to be coherent. Happy to see me, sort of — that's the thing, isn't it? I'm not sure I could say he really enjoyed seeing me, as I could never measure up in his mind. But that was my paranoia too. Perhaps I did? But even with an Oscar, I couldn't feel that I was a successful man. Here I was, in a legal morass with no less an adversary than Dino De Laurentiis; I was a victim again, helpless — as miserable as Dad, who, unlike me, was dying.

I had to interrupt my visit to return an "important call" at a set hour to Bob Marshall in Los Angeles. In a phone booth down the hospital corridor, we talked urgently. Because Dino, insofar as he could get away with it, had the bad habit of paying his bills months late, a common practice in the film business to make some extra money with the bank, had made a mistake by not paying me in full on *Dragon*. As a result, my lawyer, the frontier lawman, told me we were going to go for an injunction against *Dragon* because our contract with Dino on *Dragon* was legally linked to *Platoon*. If we could scare Dino by jeopardizing *Dragon*, we might coerce him into returning my *Platoon* script. A bold move, it would get not just Dino's attention but, more important, the distributor, MGM's. With nothing more to lose because I could never force Dino to do *Platoon*, I said yes, go. The shit was now going to hit the fan.

I went back to Dad. Jesus, what a mess I was in. It showed on my face. I'd had it all at thirty-three — fame, a future, money — and now I was practically finished, and I was only thirty-eight. I looked at Dad. He was so helpless. This was the end, the real end. What were my problems compared to his? At least he'd had a life, and as much as we can be, he was prepared to die. I felt sorry for him. He wanted more than anything to get out of there and go home, drink a scotch, smoke a cigarette, and have a friend, preferably in high heels and nylons, come over. I kept encouraging him to trust in the doctor and take care of himself so he could see his grandchild in a few months. But did he really give a fuck about that? He didn't want to live. He was on a suicide run, and maybe one day I'd understand him. "But you *don't,* kiddo," he'd say. "You don't understand me, because you haven't lived my life." As sick as he was, the old rebel in him roused himself, breathed his fire. "I had a good life, kiddo. I spent it all. Don't expect anything from me . . . and you should tell your mother she's got the insurance policy and that's it. If she thinks I'm going to remarry her, tell her she's nuts." Stark talk from a father. Quite memorable.

I remember leaving the hospital resenting, even hating him. Why was he always so selfish? I already had to deal with Dino, who was the worst, I thought. And here my own father was fighting Mom and me both — on money, on his will, on transferring the apartment to Mom, etc. And his blood, my blood, was soon to come freshly into this world. But he'd warned me, it's true. He'd wiped out most of the family trust. He'd lived well, didn't regret anything, and had burned through his money. He paid, as he promised, for my education, but now I was on my own; nor did I know if my mother would be able to make it through the coming years with her finite amount of insurance unless she remarried — and then what? She'd look to me. I had no brother or sister to help.

All those plans and hopes from Dino's fabulous New Year's party in the South of France had come apart. The people who'd been there hugging and kissing were no longer talking to one another. *Time* magazine had a cover proclaiming Orwell's *1984* prophecy had not come to be, implying that Orwell was a phony prophet. I thought it was just the opposite — that we as a nation, brainwashed by our media, were increasingly descending into a box from which none of us could escape. What kind of world was it to bring a child into? *Platoon* had fallen apart, and my father was dying before he'd see our child. It'd been a tough year, perhaps a terrible one after all.

Waiting impatiently at Elizabeth's bedside in Los Angeles, to which we'd returned to have the baby, I went out to get a pizza, eating it back in the hospital room, watching my beloved San Francisco 49ers with Joe Montana take on the New York Giants of Lawrence Taylor fame in a December '84 playoff game. The smell of pizza so nauseated Elizabeth that she screamed suddenly in a voice as terrifying as Linda Blair's in *The Exorcist,* "Go! Get the hell out of here! Now!" Which I did.

The game was close, and it became incredibly exciting when I was ushered back into the room. One of the nurses was speaking calmly and urgently. "You're ten centimeters. You're ready to push, Elizabeth. Start pushing." The other nurse, a kindly older woman, told me that "in one hour, she went from four centimeters to ten. She skipped the transition stage." It sounded significant to me, like the earth was about to give way to some kind of volcanic eruption. The three of us attended as she pushed, sitting up on her knees with difficulty and in grueling pain, using an oxygen mask as the two nurses kept telling her gently to "push, push, Elizabeth. Come on, come on, Elizabeth." I was the third party watching, trying to help, holding onto her for dear life. No sporting event was ever so violent as this woman's effort to *get this "thing" out of her before she died of pain!*

A flattened head was now suddenly peeking up through swollen vagina lips. It hardly looked human — a trick of the eyes. "There it is! Come on, Elizabeth," the younger nurse was saying, and then with one last heave, the baby sailed out fast, arms in the air, in a great torrent of blood and placenta, muck and fear, along with the thunderous roar of a gravel landslide; it sounded like the birth of Zeus (only in my head, I'm sure). Our baby was a seven-pound, five-ounce, nineteen-inch-long fat little Buddha-type baby, crying his lungs out, healthy as a bear cub. I was scared it was dying because of the screams. But no! It rolled aikido-like on the mat, revealing his umbilical cord and little penis. I was shouting at Elizabeth, "It's a boy!" as she suddenly snapped back from the pain to consciousness; she was her old self again, alert, sober. We clamped the cord on the baby, who looked eyeless, a beauty, pink-red; he turned a normal color right away. So much black hair, a crown for a king!

This was that important moment in any life — your first child. What it means, well, a young mother and father had no clue. No one knows. In that glorious uncertainty, 1984 ended.

7

South of the Border

New Year's Day 1985 embodied all the rollercoaster changes in my life. Lying on the white-carpeted living room floor making googly faces at my mom was a four-day-old baby worm, whom we called Sean after the dashing Scottish actor famous as James Bond — why not? A straight, clean name, easy to remember, but not as dull as John — a boy who could be liked. The Labradors were running in and out through the sliding doors into the backyard of our newly rented house, high in the canyons of the Santa Monica Mountains in Brentwood. Elizabeth was resting in the bedroom, tired and depressed from the birth, which was the reason we'd quickly hired a nineteen-year-old Swedish nanny without much experience, which theoretically would allow my mother, who'd flown out to see her first grandchild, to take charge. So she thought, but at sixty-four, Mom was still too restless and young at heart to fulfill the exclusive obligations of motherhood.

When I crawled up close to the baby, he looked right at me, wide-eyed with wonder at who this giant face belonged to, breaking into a big smile and goo-goo sounds. "Yes," I goo'd back, "I'm your daddy!" as the worm reached out so trusting with his tiny fingers, and touched my face with the awesome sound of new discovery — "Unh . . ." If ever there was proof we are born with a sweet nature, this was it; the veils come later. Sean looked so strong to me, stout like a little Herakles, whom the Greeks claim, with their vivid imaginations, strangled a threatening python in his cradle.

I'd never been so happy, even though Dad was failing in New York. Mom told me distraught stories of him being discharged from the hospital, re-fusing all medications — and then breaking all the doctor's orders by be-ginning to smoke and drink again. And on top of that, he asked an "old friend," Laura, a sexy thirty-year-old Latina devoted to my dad, to visit him every day for a few hours; probably paid her to do this, but her heart was indeed big, and Dad would laugh with her, enjoying the last of his life. Mom, who was staying in Dad's guest bedroom to take care of him, was naturally ill at ease.

We got Dad on the phone that New Year's Day, but he was either foggy or loaded on scotch and couldn't remember if the child had been born yet. We reminded him — four days old. But then he didn't remember the kid's name. Or was it a "her"? We told him we'd be bringing the baby to New York soon. Then Tom Selleck and *Magnum, P.I.* came on, his favorite show after *All in the Family* expired, and we said good-bye.

Soon, our other Los Angeles houseguest came roaring in from some-where in a used rented car, in his usual rush, itching all over from his skin allergies. I'd deepened my relationship with Richard Boyle since meeting him with Ron Kovic on the Venice boardwalk that July of '77 when I'd first been so inspired by Ron's book. Richard had participated in many of Ron's Vietnam protests, and in the early '80s taken him on a wild car ride to Vietnam and Cambodia that ended with Ron fleeing to the airport back to the US. Though generally his life was a catastrophe, Richard was that rare individual who never acknowledged his limits, one of those people who go on losing everything and finding something else to replace it — possessions, assignments, counterfeit credit cards, driver's licenses, girlfriends, even a wife and a child. Cash was hard to come by for Richard, a commodity that eluded him with a vengeance, and when necessary, I'd reach into my pocket and help him out, trusting, however, that he was resourceful.

A few weeks before Sean was born, with my mind in the downspin I've described at the state of my career, I'd gone up to San Francisco to sup-port Richard in his run for public office on the city's Board of Supervi-sors. Promising reform and socialism, he would come in thirteenth out of fourteen candidates in that election, but with great enthusiasm, we tooled around the hilly streets in his ancient patched-up MG, unpaid parking tickets stashed in the glove compartment, hanging out with his colorful supporters, talking up a storm of future plans, and of course drinking beers and rustling up voters. Richard had been thrown out of Vietnam in 1969 by the Vietnamese government for his peace-organizing activities on behalf of the Buddhist "Coconut Monk," but sneaking back into the country, he covered the mutiny of American troops at "Firebase Pace," writing a solid book about it with *Flower of the Dragon* in 1972. He'd then been one of the last journalists out of Phnom Penh before the Khmer Rouge closed it off to the world. He'd reported out of Nicaragua during the '79 Sandinista Revolution, parallel to his adventures in the ongoing Salvadoran civil war of 1980.

He'd also managed to keep company with the IRA before moving over to Beirut with the PLO during Reagan's ill-conceived 1982–83 Lebanon mission, which ended in a terror bombing taking more than two hundred US Marine lives. Now, like me, he needed a boost. A few months earlier, his wife had escaped from their small Tenderloin apartment back to Italy with their newborn son when any means of support had dried up; they would divorce. Most people would consider Richard a troublemaker, a drunk, a freeloader, and wonder why would I hang with him, but I found him a treasure chest full of surprises — funny, at times outrageous, shrewd, a brilliant political streak in him, with the compassion of an Irish underdog. He was newly smitten with a girlfriend, whom we went to visit near Santa Cruz in her broken-down trailer. I suppose this was real life. Esther, not at all what I'd pictured, had the television turned on midday to game shows with her six-year-old blankly watching for want of anything else to do. But he cared for her madly; I just didn't see much feedback. But that was Richard, always building up in his imagination what he believed in.

When he drove me out to the airport on my last day, I spotted in the tiny backseat of the MG, beneath a bunch of unwashed clothes, an oil-stained manuscript. I casually asked what he'd been writing, at least a sign of some activity beyond his partying and politicking. "Oh, those are my Salvador stories," he said cheerily. "You should read it, man. It's great stuff!" It was a set of sketches he'd tried to sell to magazines here and there, but there was not much interest in Salvador. I was curious and took the stories back to LA. And I read them. And I knew right away, from the uptick in my excitement, that this was it. Somehow, this was going to be a movie. This was exactly the energy I needed to get outside myself and on with my life.

According to Boyle, in Salvador there were labor leaders, teachers, Irish nuns, and liberation priests fighting the landowners, the church, and the "system." Many of these folk were being tortured and killed; the cruelty was extreme, truly barbaric, but Richard's story had a kind of buffoonery at the center of it — a journalist in the gonzo Hunter S. Thompson mold — selfish, lying, self-promoting, with plenty of sex and drugs thrown in, but on the side of reform and justice. Richard's antic energy and Irish humor would make it cooler than a film like *Under Fire* (1983) with Nick Nolte, about courageous US journalists in the Central American wars, and it'd be funnier than anything I'd written, and Boyle could provide the anecdotes. I didn't know how I'd get it made, but after my frustrated detour into mainstream films, I'd make it myself at a bargain basement price. I'd mortgage my place on Long Island and my two apartments in New York and LA, and I'd get a loan from my bank through Steve Pines, my business manager. For what — $300K maybe, $500K? Somehow I'd pull it off NYU-style, the same way we did my first horror film, *Seizure*, in 1973, which cost about $160,000 all in. "Do or die!" was my reality.

On that basis, I brought Boyle down immediately to LA on my dime, shared my plans, and of course he was game. What else did he have going? We set to work like demons, several hours a day, myself writing and structuring, Richard talking and describing — two, sometimes three scenes a day, much as I'd done with Ron Kovic, except faster, a lot faster. Whereas Ron had a painfully pinpoint memory, Richard might make it up — but always with an element of truth, the spirit of having been there. The story shaping up in my mind would be about a fuckup journalist whose wife splits in the first scene with their child. He scrounges money to get back to Salvador, where there's a hot war going on and he can make a few bucks through his contacts. Once there, he hooks back up with a local girlfriend, for whom he develops stronger feelings as he runs into sticky situations and some old enemies — and before long, he's getting squeezed to a pulp, and things get deadly. Would Boyle and his woman and her child make it out of there? Something like that.

In 1980 Boyle had reported on the rape and murder of three American

Maryknoll nuns, who'd been threatened and then killed by "death squaders" because of their "liberation" work with the poor; he'd known them and
especially mourned the fourth victim, the young lay worker Jeannie Don-
ovan, who was killed alongside them. He'd interacted with Major Roberto
d'Aubuisson, the leader of a fascist political party called ARENA, who was
reported to command a far-reaching "death squad." He'd also known the
reputable American ambassador, Robert White, and said that he'd been at
the battle of Santa Ana, where the rebels had almost turned the tide but for
the last-minute intervention of the US on behalf of the Duarte government.
He also claimed he'd been close by when Archbishop Óscar Romero was
murdered in his own cathedral in San Salvador in 1980. The more I read,
much influenced by *New York Times* journalist Ray Bonner's controversial
Weakness and Deceit: U.S. Policy and El Salvador (1984), and saw on video,
I realized how ugly and unknown this Salvadoran war was. Having heard
only the US media's antirevolutionary reportage from Central America,
I was confused, and Boyle suggested we take a two-week trip to the region. I agreed to this, but only after we'd put our first impulses down in an
outline.

Richard and I were now heading off to El Salvador in a few days. Elizabeth and my mother thought I was nuts to go off with this lunatic Irishman. But with high hopes, I'd persuaded Alex Ho to join us in Salvador
and draw up a first rough budget at less than $1 million. I was making this
decision, of course, with a great deal of bravado. My financial situation
and career prospects were, to say the least, fragile and remote. Here it was
December 1985, with an infant child, a wife, a mother, and in my mind,
time running out. Few directors succeeded after forty. I'd made *Seizure*
at twenty-seven and vanished, *The Hand* at thirty-three and was derided.
Now or never. NYU had taught me this foundation — to make filmmaking
"personal," that is, it matters to you, your passion, and if you're in touch
with your emotions, you recognize its power even if it's leading you off
a cliff; you have to have the madness in you to follow it to the end. It was
in the same spirit that I'd gone off to Vietnam, or dropped out of Yale and
written my novel. Not that any of these things had been successful, but it
was passion and instinct that had driven me, and I was still young enough

to take another shot on that instinct. And if I failed . . . so be it. I'd adapt to another way of life. But how much longer could I do this?

That first night of January took an ominous turn when Stanley White, the homicide detective, whom we'd based much of the *Dragon* character on, came over for an early supper. Stanley played for us a horrible twenty-minute audiotape from a serial killer case he was working on — an actual murder these two psychos recorded of a young girl in their van pleading for her life; her loud screaming went on and on, such as I'd never heard. Elizabeth left the room, sickened. Then, as we unpacked the takeout Chinese, my mother screamed from the living room; a huge three- or four-inch black scorpion had crawled in from the garden onto the white living room carpet, in close proximity to the baby, who looked at it without fear. We froze when we saw the size of the creature, something out of a horror movie. I yelled out to my mother not to move, while Boyle, quick-witted under fire, chased the creature, equally frightened of us, out through the patio doors and back into the night. Mom grabbed Sean into her arms and rushed him out of the room.

Dinner turned more medieval when Stanley, drinking and growing blustery about his homicide adventures, excited Boyle's rebelliousness and, I suppose, visceral distrust of all cops; he'd certainly been in jail enough times. Consuming copious amounts of whiskey, beer, and wine, Boyle, with one eye on impressing our Swedish nanny, who by this point must've thought all American males were violent homicidal madmen, challenged Stanley to a barroom game of "knuckles," wherein the drinker smashes his knuckles as hard as possible into the other fellow's knuckles to see who'll cry "uncle" first. It made little sense, a relic of Celtic culture, but Richard's knuckles were quite large and tested, and Stanley knew better than to engage a man at his own game. The conversation moved on to knives, at which point Richard whipped out a hunting knife from his boot and slashed his forearm to show how fearless he was of pain, upon which Stanley followed, grinning, making his own deeper cut. Elizabeth, who'd returned for supper, had had enough by now and left the table for good. My mother was taking care of the baby, as the nanny and I watched the blood begin to flow. I was drunk too, so I'm not sure where it ended, but nothing, of course, was decided; it never is.

Stanley went home eventually, loaded, to his detective wife who probably slapped him around, and soon left him because he was just too nuts for her. Richard, on the other hand, continued drinking until I left him in a rocking chair in front of the TV with the lights fully on, beer bottle in hand. I heard later he made a lame pass at the nanny, who told him she was turned off and disgusted. She went to bed.

An irate Elizabeth shook me out of my sleep the next morning. "I want him out of the house!" is what I heard. "Today! Take him to the motel, I don't give a shit, I don't want him around Sean!" Apparently she'd woken up around six for the baby and found Richard still passed out in the rocking chair, empty bottles littering the floor, mouth open, his face now a greenish color. When she went to the refrigerator for Sean's baby formula, it was missing, and when she found the empty plastic bottle on the living room floor, it was clear that Richard had consumed it along with a dozen beers; that did it. When she flashed her Texas rattlesnake temper, I quickly yielded and escorted a shaky Richard to a local motel, where we'd continue our work.

So now my life was complicated by Elizabeth's intense dislike for Richard, and here I was mortgaging all the assets we had as a couple to make this harebrained scheme of a movie. And I was actually going to "Salvoland" with this Irishman who subsisted mostly on liquids. When I finished the outline with Boyle a few days later, he took off as an advance party, and I followed on a jammed 2 a.m. "banana flight" to San Salvador. Elizabeth acted like it was the last time she and Sean would see me.

Alex Ho had joined me for the awful flight down, and we found Boyle at the San Salvador airport in his element — "I love this fucking country. No yuppies, no computer checks, you don't need a driver's license. I hate efficient countries!" And yet Richard was arguing that we had the infrastructure here to make the film? We moved into an inexpensive but clean Ramada Inn that had no connection to the Ramada chain, with a Chilean military delegation staying in the nearby rooms, all six of them in uniforms, efficient-looking torturers, no doubt teaching their Salvadoran counterparts a thing or two they'd picked up under Pinochet. Boyle, with his bootlicking Irish rummy act, struck up conversations with them, in fact with anybody who'd talk to him. He was great at blarney, and people seemed to like him at first. Boyle had prepared a bogus two-page treatment in Spanish for our script, intentionally skewed toward the Salvadoran military as the good guys, and picturing the rebels as homicidal communists. The scheme was to get the Salvadorans to cooperate with our production. Boyle took us to meet his old friend Lieutenant Colonel Ricardo Cienfuegos in the Defense Ministry, a public relations character known to the press corps as "Ricky," who seemed to like the "script" when he read it right there in front of us; he said he'd get us to General Blandon, the chief of staff, for a quick answer. Wow. Boyle was impressing us after all, as he explained to us how, since the military ran the place, the civilian government would bend over. Of course, there was great irony in that the "bad guys" were really the military, aligned with the notorious right-wing death squads and the anticommunist Reagan regime in the US. After we'd gotten the Salvadoran hardware for the production and shot the battle scenes, our plan was to rectify this misperception by going to Mexico to shoot the guerrillas in their battle scenes as the real agents of change. It was a bold plan, very risky, but if it worked, it would be genius. Such was the power of my desire, I frankly must've been nuts to think this could actually work.

When we met with Blandon, who had a tough guy reputation, he was most impressed by our newly hired, bilingual, elegantly sexy secretary, Gloria, whom Boyle had wisely taken on for a few bucks. He read the treatment on the spot, or pretended to, and said he liked it, though we needed to get a sign-off from General Vides Casanova at the Defense Ministry. Vides was the kingpin. No one mentioned José Napoleón Duarte, the president, but on a roll, we dropped in on him at the palace, where we were blocked by the spear-carriers and shunted off to the Ministry of Tourism and Commerce. Boyle got Gloria back to work on the phones at our hotel, and she was good, and got us in to see the tourism minister, who was a key guy close to Duarte; he liked the treatment. "Anything you want, we want for you," he said. "It'd be good for tourism here." What tourism? The city was dirty and poorly paved. Maybe in the countryside, where the war was raging? But with a strong military in charge, he explained that life here was safe again.

So we went to the leading insurance company of Salvador, and the chairman, a small mustached man in a purple suit and tie who'd been contacted by the Tourism Ministry, assured us, although he'd never done a film, that a deal could be made to insure our enterprise. Perhaps it was all fantasyland, I thought, as we wandered out into the street, where there was a giant demonstration in progress, organized by an agricultural co-op; the angry, determined faces of the strikers looked right out of Kazan's *Viva Zapata!*

Boyle, promising consultancy fees to many and acting the big shot, was talking mostly to right-wing journalists, who were giving us their scoop, and occasionally a worried young left-wing journalist struggling on the edges of a threatened newspaper. The Americans working there for NGOs confirmed to us the meager prospects for this country, even with Reagan in office. Boyle went back to see Cienfuegos, who now wanted us to check with the air force general about our borrowing some of their helicopters. It was all doable, Boyle told us, he was sure of it. "We just have to work our way through the studio system here. We can pull off an *Apocalypse Now* helicopter attack on the guerrillas for less than fifty grand!" All this inside our projected $500,000 budget from my US bank loan, which I was presumably going to get. Why not? Alex Ho was quietly cynical but nodded that it was conceivable. I had visions now of an eight-man documentary crew and two vans scooting around the countryside. This script we'd started in December — less than a month ago — was actually coming to fruition! Sometimes when you really want to make a film, you just start, and sometimes it catches up to you.

Word was getting around about us, and we dropped by the political clubhouse of the fascist ARENA party in a well-protected cuartel (a small military fort or village), rimmed with barbed wire. We were warmly greeted by d'Aubuisson's number two, Francisco Mena Sandoval, whose magnetic killer eyes fascinated me — as he, in his way, was fascinated by me, the writer of *Caracortada*. Finally that film was serving a practical purpose for me, if not in Hollywood. Mena set up our visit to the National Assembly for the next day, and invited us to the inner sanctuary of the ARENA party meeting in five days' time. Here I could meet "Major Bob" — Roberto d'Aubuisson — the party leader, the highest honor of all. We acquired all kinds of ARENA paraphernalia that afternoon, the Central American equivalent of Nazi emblems, and drank tequila toasts with tough-looking hombres sporting guns in holsters on their hips, slapping me on the back as they acted out their favorite scenes with toasts to Tony Montana — "Mucho co-liandes!" (Lots of balls!) "Ratta-tat-tat! Kill the fucking communists!" I was "muy macho"!

We drove out to Puerta del Diablo, the "Devil's Door," a set of cliffs on the outskirts of the city where lovers once rendezvoused and death squads now dumped their victims, a haunting reminder of the truth behind the smiles. I wondered why the Salvadorans were so cruel in their ways of killing, and Boyle, mixing up Mesoamerican cultures, speculated, "Like the Aztecs, you know, when they chopped each other up and made dinner." We met several foreigners — military advisers, CIA types, various riffraff, and journalists at the infamous Gloria's whorehouse, where drinking went parallel to any investigation. It was Boyle's favorite hangout, and for three nights in a row he vanished with one or another of the ninety girls working there. At $30 per girl per night, he managed to blow the $300 we'd entrusted to him as scouting money. Plus the "poppers" (amyl nitrite) and whatever other pharmaceuticals he could procure. Three nights running made his face redder and his temper quicker. We fought. He told me to go fuck myself, he'd make the film without me on video, it was his story! He was a proud Irishman and he'd take no orders. I reminded him again that I was the boss, and either we worked as a unit or not at all, and he backed down. Alex Ho, who'd labeled him a "con man" from the beginning, was growing very dubious of his ability to play himself in the film, much less organize anything. Conversely, I was annoyed with Alex for his skepticism, insisting that in Salvador we were through the looking glass, and that he should trust me — and at least give Boyle the "b.o.d.," a popular acronym at that time for "benefit of the doubt."

I gave Boyle more cash, and we drove north in our rented car, closer to the still active rebel areas. At Punto de Oro, the Bridge of Gold, we walked out past government soldiers onto a huge bridge blown in half, twisted cable suspension wires lying useless, the wind blowing through an eerie silence, the sound of distant government artillery bringing back a feeling of war. We drove on across a railroad track over a rickety bridge into San Vincente, home of the 5th Infantry Division. Boyle's old "friend," a Captain Nuñez, a US Airborne–trained officer, was now in charge of four hundred elite troops — hunter-killer units known as "cazadores" — who told us that ten regular troops had been killed the day before on patrol; in Vietnam that was significant, but here, life seemed cheaper. He also told us a train had been blown up farther north, leaving thirty civilians dead, and there was heavy fighting in the area. This war was definitely not over in 1985. We went on to an air force base, where a Colonel Novoa didn't remember Boyle and despised reporters, so Boyle assumed his "I hate reporters" routine and flawlessly produced a yellowed clipping from a newspaper article he'd written years before, reminding Novoa one more time of his heroic role "in the great '69 Soccer War against Honduras!" No matter how insane Boyle seemed, there was a method to his madness, because Novoa now liked Boyle and invited us to dinner, sharing colorful, probably highly exaggerated stories with us. We were still waiting on the military honchos in the capital, but, according to Boyle, it was all looking great.

We drove over to La Libertad on the coast, an old surfing spot known in the US, where Boyle had met "the woman of his dreams," Maria, who'd since taken refuge in Guatemala; often poorer Salvadorans without "cedulas" (proper identity papers) would get into trouble with the authorities and, fearing death from the right-wing paramilitary, would flee the country if possible. The town itself was dreamy — the surf, the little shacks on the beach where we'd lie out on rented hammocks, the seafood, the drooling "Tic Tack" monsters walking around town like zombies, their brains blown on the cheap national rotgut called "Tic Tack"; we also visited an orphanage for some two hundred children run by tough Irish nuns, who remembered Richard's big heart fondly.

But Boyle was now drinking in the daytime. He brought back a scrungy hooker he'd met the night before, introducing her as his "secretary," as well as his "translator." Ho was warning me again, "He's going to be a problem, Ollie!" Boyle's eyes were consistently glazed and watery. I scolded him once more. He said it was the cortisone shot he'd taken for his itchy skin, which was all blotched, and this could have been true, plus all the pharmaceuticals he'd got ahold of every time he saw a drugstore. Who knows what he was on? I was amazed he still had a liver.

He cracked the fender driving nearly 100 mph down potholed streets, ripping through the gears, yelling at "this shitmobile," cranky over Maria having disappeared — "no pussy, nothing, deadville!" I was worried — no further word from Gloria in the capital, no real progress. Mosquitos were hitting on me through the night in my grungy room, where I had no desire to entrust my body to the sleazy sheets. I went looking for Boyle at daybreak and found him with the "secretary" and another hooker and a bottle of cheap rum. I didn't say a thing; my eyes said it all. As we sipped harsh coffee in the littered square of this ratfuck town, the vultures chewing on whatever they could find, I gave him one more chance, a test of self-control. Three days. Show me. No booze — or no film! He promised, but words didn't mean the same thing to Richard as to me. He'd stay relatively clean for a few days, but as my father said, a man may veer left or right but always returns to his basic nature in the end — and Richard was a bighearted, well-meaning alcoholic/druggie/Irish whatever. Could I live with that to get this film made?

Alex Ho, now wanting nothing to do with Boyle and doubting the film would ever happen, retreated back to New York, promising me at least a basic budget. While we were waiting for further news from the Salvadoran military, Richard and I had planned to check out Costa Rica, Honduras, and Belize as alternates and then Mexico on our way back north. I didn't care for San José — no weaponry and way too civilized to stand in for a location like Salvador, with a lot of US intelligence spooks in civilian clothes pressuring the leftist Óscar Arias government to crack down on any reform movements. Honduras was another world. The presidential palace in Tegucigalpa was a flamingo-pink candy box out of Gabriel García Márquez. An agricultural protest was in progress not far from it, its leaders closely supervised by a suspicious and tough police force. We ended up at the central cathedral, where laborers were lined up for food supplied by organizers, who told us the facts of life down there — essentially that they had to *earn* every cubic inch of their freedom. Honduras presented a more overt battle between rich and poor than Salvador, with a banana republic coup d'état atmosphere out of a Graham Greene novel. At the ugly Hilton Hotel, all the foreigners — the traders, the spooks, the con men — were, like Richard, circling for a piece of fresh news. Who was who? It was a game they loved to play; it reminded me of the covert buildup in Saigon early in that war when I was a teacher there. I had to cover Boyle on his lies to two

"Margaritaville"-type dudes in loud Hawaiian shirts who said they'd just come from canoeing in some rivers upcountry. "Whatcha up to?" Boyle asked.

"Catching parrots. We're into parrots. Selling 'em in the States. What's your M.O.?"

"Uh," Boyle responded, "we're making a wildlife documentary," which of course ignited a bunch of follow-up questions that I answered for Boyle. Anybody could be anything here.

We weren't far from the border with Nicaragua, where the United States was gearing up to overthrow the government, possibly even intervene militarily. You could feel it in the air. There were US uniforms everywhere in the streets of "Tegu," and a lot of white yuppie civilians attached to the US embassy; the females stood out, long-legged, porky, pink cheeks, alongside the devastating brown-skinned poverty in the streets. At the hotel coffee shop where our GIs in uniform hung out, I asked an Okie sergeant Boyle was trying to pick up if she had any thoughts about Vietnam. She replied robotically, "Sir, I don't have an opinion on that," as if advised to say so. They'd clearly learned their lesson from Vietnam via the Pentagon and carried a major hard-on for the media or anyone they thought might be from the media — like us. It kept becoming clearer to me why I wanted to make *Salvador.* Because it could have been about me at twenty-one, naïvely going to Vietnam for my own curiosity and sense of importance to intervene in another population's civil war, which turned out to be not such a good idea.

We moved on to Belize, another bizarre situation; it was defended under an old treaty by professional British troops who seriously believed they were there to prevent the possibility of a Guatemalan invasion from the west. Everyone needs an enemy. We toured their impeccable camp and training areas; maybe we could shoot *Platoon* here, but it bore no resemblance to Salvador. Through Boyle, we met with a man said to be the incoming prime minister, but that seemed unlikely as our get-together took place in the small backroom of a store at 9 a.m. A one-light room, shadows. Whoever he was, I told myself, perhaps he was connected to the government closely enough to ease our path. His cunning-looking assistant brought him in once we were seated. A big man, black as night, strong-faced. "What you want?" he asked in a melodious Caribbean accent. I explained, but it worried him. Boyle would've done it better.

"You not gonna make a movie about some Central American revolution and whip up my people here? We just come to power. We want to keep it awhile. You gonna give these people ideas?" No political figure's been blunter in my experience. We assured him, "It's not about revolution, but a civil war in another country that looks very different from yours."

"Okay, so what's in it for us?" he asked. Boyle then fawningly explained that we wanted to shoot a piece of it here because we saw beautiful Belize as a respite from the wars in the region; plus there were all the jobs that would come in with us. The man liked that. Money changing hands was not discussed, but it was clear that if we were serious, he was getting a cut. "Write a letter," he said, his points made. He noted our names and addresses, no business cards, and walked out. Much later, when I researched it, I saw that this man had no resemblance whatsoever to the mixed-race prime minister of Belize.

Boyle, meanwhile, was in the midst of a fight with the State Department over his passport, his problem arising out of a "violation" in one of the many far-flung countries he'd traveled to as a "war correspondent." Trying to con a new five-year passport out of the US consulate, he settled for a "temp sheet" instead that got him across the border to Mexico, which, after the chaos of Central America, was yuppie heaven with US-style amenities.

Gerald Green, owner of a film servicing company, hosted us in Mexico City. He was a polished and charming operator with a weak face, a perpetually worried frown, and a lot of Alec Guinness from *Our Man in Havana* in him. Surprisingly, he'd become a key figure in my life, but unlike Boyle, Gerald was operating in a gentlemen's league with his ascots and English accent (he was originally from South Africa), imbibing martinis and other cocktails along with Boyle, yet never overtly drunk. Coming from a supposedly successful British advertising career, he'd produced several B-films in Mexico, and because of his Mexican businesswoman wife, Patrizia, benefited from government subsidies and favorable banking arrangements. He'd coordinated the shooting for De Laurentiis on *Dune* in 1984 and for Carolco, a hot new independent company run by Mario Kassar and Andy Vajna, for *Rambo: First Blood Part II,* substituting Mexico for

Vietnam. He was passionate over my script for *Platoon,* which he'd managed to read somewhere along the line; he very much wanted me to give him a free option, promising he'd get it made. Green also respected my ideas for the unwritten *Salvador,* which was a natural for Mexico, where we would have the benefit of his studio space at Churubusco, equipment deals, working generators, crews, casting directors, and experienced actors, as well as the possibility of using extras from a cooperative Mexican army that wasn't fighting a rebellion — in other words, a true infrastructure. In terms of cash, Gerald was lacking, nervously smoking, almost nonstop, always chasing the next "deal" like any indie producer. In that regard, he had the perfect hangdog face of a basset hound, so whoever he dealt with always seemed to be "squashing" him, which of course was not true, as Gerald was pretty clever at getting his way; in fact, I developed a real soft spot for him as he dragged me through hell for the next year. He asked if his "friend" in LA, Arnold Kopelson, a successful independent lawyer and foreign salesman of films, could read *Platoon.* Of course, what did I have to lose?

Excited by these new possibilities, I flew back to Los Angeles to write the script, while Boyle went back to "Salvoland" to push our military scheme there. Breathing the heady atmosphere of Central America, I tore into the story newly possessed, and soon Boyle returned to help me toward a first draft. But I was living way beyond my means. I'd have to support not only my family and myself but also Boyle while the script was being written. My 1984 legal injunction against Dino De Laurentiis's *Dragon* had succeeded when Dino and MGM finally paid me the balance of my fee and gave my script of *Platoon* back, free of debt and all expenses (trips to the Philippines, scouting, casting, etc.), but my hopes of optioning the screenplay again for cash were not in the cards.

I did manage to make some additional money on a six-month option to a vivacious forty-year-old Beverly Hills producer and former "star" agent on the script I'd written about a New York City detective, *8 Million Ways to Die.* And, after several bumps, this seemed to be proceeding to production under the direction of Hal Ashby (*Harold and Maude, Shampoo, Coming Home*). Ashby was nearing the end of his career and, sadly, his life; he didn't reveal his cancer, but I was surprised by his lack of a real filmmaker's excitement for the project. His production designer — the one who designs the overall look of the film, builds the sets, oversees the decor and costuming, and dozens of other details — was his good friend; like Hal, he was a '50s California beatnik type, but amazingly he'd never been to New York City in his life, not even out of curiosity, and moreover had no interest in going with me to visit the streets of the Lower East Side, where I'd based the story. How could I object? It was money, and I needed it.

The dazzling producer who'd sweet-talked me into the deal was as nuts a man as I'd ever met, a complex schizophrenic who returned phone calls days later, sometimes screaming, sometimes sweet and placid, and lied about most everything because he couldn't help it; it was his nature. Elizabeth noted he had two voices — one with a natural Jewish accent, the other affected Beverly Hills; he owned a spotless house that felt unlived in, and had a terrorized blond trophy wife, two perfect children, and a revolving set of nannies and servants. Despite his glamorous name-dropping and picture-perfect life, he was also a major coke fiend and way over his head in debt. Finally, one day he evacuated the house, divorced his wife, and disappeared for a stretch. By this time, however, the film, which I'd written as a $2 or $3 million picture for myself to direct, was being funded by a new foreign sales company, PSO, for an astounding $18 million with Jeff Bridges in the lead. And the story would get even stranger.

My manager, Steve Pines, to whom I was paying 5 percent of my earnings, was having his own set of problems. Surprisingly, he'd become addicted to cocaine, as I'd been, and his main client, a movie star and also a serious addict, had just left him in a sea of accusations about embezzled funds that turned out to be false, but it looked awfully bad. In fact, my lawyer, Bob Marshall, and my agent at the time counseled me to drop him. But Steve's mind was still sharp, and I trusted him. He'd be most professional on the phone and on top of things in the office, but there would be gaps when he just wouldn't be around for me to speak to. This never actively hurt my relationship with him, but given my own past difficulties with cocaine, I was concerned. Then again, he didn't have to write; he just had to do the math, run money, and generally pay attention to everything, which he could do, it seemed, even asleep.

Nonetheless, when I pressed Steve on my proposed bank loan for *Salva-*

dor, he came to the house and laid it on the line. He didn't think the bank would go $500K, as it would be difficult to sufficiently collateralize my New York properties out of state. I could apply for a loan on my American Express credit line, but I'd need living money while I was making the picture. Maybe he could squeeze $300K out of them — but that wasn't enough. "And besides," Steve argued, "the picture gets made, Oliver, and then what? Suppose it flops? You owe the bank the principal plus interest at what, fourteen, fifteen percent? You'll become a slave to projects you won't like for the next five, seven years of your life. You've got a new baby, a wife. It doesn't make sense. We'll get the money somewhere else." He reminded me that my monthly carrying costs with rents and mortgages were now a steady $20,000, approximately $240,000 a year, plus of course the ongoing expenditures for Boyle's motel and rental car. From a cokehead, this was awfully clear thinking; Steve separated his clients from his habits, and I admired him for that. It took him a few years to get away from those clients who were also supplying him, but he eventually did, and to this day, he's still my manager and as much a friend as you can be when you have no intellectual interest in or critical judgment about movies — for which I love him.

Still, I needed to dream. I couldn't fail, I had to get *Salvador* made. But the news from El Salvador was not good, with Gloria telling us the army wanted a contract giving them approval over the finished film. Boyle went back down (the 2 a.m. flights were immigrant cheap on the inimitable TACA Airlines), and he persuaded Colonel Cienfuegos to waive the contract if Duarte's government itself gave us permission. Boyle was most optimistic, but I started thinking about Mexico seriously; Gerald Green was now estimating we could make the film there for $750K — a sum that was actually in our ballpark — which he also thought he could raise.

Meanwhile, Richard and I kept at the screenplay, feverishly enjoying the madness of it all. Without that preoccupation, I would've been overwhelmed by doubts. My father was weakening, his mind erratic on the phone, and he went back into the hospital. There was no more talk of remarriage to Mom. We promised to bring Sean to see him as soon as the screenplay was finished. It didn't help matters when Boyle brought Esther, his unemployed girlfriend, and her daughter down to Los Angeles to live with him. He tried to install her in our guest bedroom to save money, but

Elizabeth, horrified at the thought, was adamant. For one thing, she now suspected that Boyle had fucked our Swedish nanny late one night in the bathroom at the other end of the house. When I talked to Boyle about it privately, he hinted that the nanny had provoked him; but you couldn't really know what the truth was with Richard. He was also in the middle of an insurance deposition on a $15,000 claim for a back injury from a supposed car accident in San Francisco.

I shunted the three of them to a motel close by at $200 a week, where we kept working, excited. *Salvador* was my new baby, alongside, of course, Sean. I'd wake up nervous, at four in the morning, and read for two hours. Sean, liking the feel of my skin, would cuddle quietly on my chest. I'd never had such close contact with a child before. Then I'd tuck him aside, roll over, and gently make love with Elizabeth. She was smooth, beautiful, accessible in these hours. Still in her postpartum stages, she'd grow very grumpy at times during the day, asocial, disliking people like Boyle, who were part of my life now. She wanted me to make *Platoon,* not *Salvador,* which she thought amoral and disgusting, like its main character. I had to get her back on my side; I couldn't make this movie with a house divided. I took her to dinner alone and we tried talking out our noticeably growing differences — her "yuppiedom," my type-A personality, aggressiveness, impatience — and we came to a rapprochement: I'd try to be more considerate in every way, and she'd try to understand my *Salvador* dream and actually help me, not just with typing the script but in spirit as well. This was the important thing to me.

Arnold Kopelson, Gerald Green's friend and foreign salesman, came to my house to convince me how much he loved *Platoon,* even talking it up as an Oscar-type Best Film. I hated this kind of unctuous Hollywood hype and thought he was way over the top, and naturally he asked for a free option. I knew he had the money to pay something, but he didn't offer it. He was clearly shrewd, and I weighed the possibility that he could be helpful. He told me I had a reputation for being impossible, opinionated, wanting things my way. Well, considering how most directors were cut down in the business, I'm not sure it was such a bad thing to defend your integrity. In the end, I gave Kopelson a ninety-day window to run with the script.

Remember, by this date, "The Platoon" had been rejected several times in 1976, again in 1983 by De Laurentiis, and now by the B-movie indie producers without money. I felt Cimino had misled me in resurrecting it; it was just a way to make money, and I expected nothing more would come of it.

In the meantime, there was another "chap" in Gerald's wheelhouse whom he introduced us to at his company's two-floor town house just off the Sunset Strip in West Hollywood. He was an east Londoner with the classic name of John Daly who'd apparently been one of the promoters of the Ali-Foreman "Rumble in the Jungle" in Zaire. Gerald didn't tell me then that Daly had been jailed after the fight by the Congolese authorities over unpaid "taxes" of one type of another. More important to me, Daly had a small independent company called Hemdale that was beginning to get "hot"; he'd been involved in the original Jim Cameron *Terminator* as an executive producer, and was making *The Falcon and the Snowman* with the director John Schlesinger and actor Sean Penn. He was looking for more projects to expand in America. He'd started as actor David Hemmings's chauffeur and, as in a Harold Pinter parable, ended up first partnering with Hemmings, and then owning their company outright.

I liked Daly's unpretentious Cockney manner and his slangy way of talking right off; he had that "Long John Silver" gleam in his eye, which didn't take life too seriously, and although he may have been a pirate by nature, he seemed more civilized to me than many of the brutish producers I'd run into. I talked with him about my passion to make *Salvador,* and Gerald had already passed him *Platoon* to read. I left his presence exhilarated; I sensed something had clicked between us.

In early March, our 140-page screenplay for *Salvador,* filled to the brim with energy, explosive violence, sex, no limits, was finished. Gerald Green and John Daly both read it, and when I returned to see them at the town house, John literally said in his cool, detached manner — and I shall never forget his words, because only once in a lifetime does a filmmaker hear something like this — "It's bloody great, Oliver, I love the material . . ." (pause). "So which one do you want to do first — *Salvador* or *Platoon*?"

I couldn't believe I was hearing this! A choice? Considering the hells I'd crossed to get another shot at directing, this was an unbelievable affirmation. "*Salvador!*" I answered without hesitation, because if I did *Platoon,* now twice dead, I feared it was cursed and would again fall apart. *Salvador* was as fresh as my newborn baby. I departed John's office with the wings of Mercury on my heels. A screen test for Boyle was next. I'd been rehearsing him to be natural, as well as his "friend" from San Francisco, "Dr. Rock," a glib, fast-talking Jewish know-it-all and supposedly notorious underground DJ who claimed he was or had been a professor of rock 'n' roll at Stanford, where he also claimed he got to meet a lot of girls. Dr. Rock had never been to Salvador, as described in our script, but he was definitely cowardly, and in our dramatic structure would be a humorous foil who was just as fucked up as Boyle, managing to annoy him constantly while on their journey. You'd think, how can *anyone* annoy Boyle, who usually got under everyone's skin, but Rock managed it.

I put these two stooges in my Mustang convertible, and a young cinematographer, Jim Glennon, who'd worked on the independently made hit *El Norte,* shot them trolling around Brentwood blocks reciting dialogue. I thought it worked, or was starting to work — "coming off the page," as they say. Glennon thought it was quite funny, and Boyle was glowing with a sense of achievement. His girlfriend was there and loving him again; Dr. Rock in awe of his own merit. There'd been some issues, of course. Richard had been in some kind of fight the night before and had all sorts of bite marks on one arm, a scratch or two on his face, and although we reprinted the test to a more realistic and flattering color, Boyle's skin tone would change, overly red on one block when the sun hit it, and then green on another block when the sun came from an oblique angle. He'd been drinking the night before, probably out of nerves — but the truth I couldn't face was that both men were one-dimensional, self-conscious, and lacking the edge a trained actor brings, making ordinary life dramatically bigger in the moment. But it was all about potential at this point, and I felt they could do it because I wanted to believe.

I asked John and Gerald over to my house to watch the test. Daly, easygoing at all times, was laughing at Boyle's performance — he knew the type and loved the Irish "go for broke" madness in him. Gerald was less impressed: "For $750,000, you need a proper actor," he warned. John's eyes drifted over our nanny, who happened to pass through the room; I introduced them, the bent "Long John Silver" charm of John amusing to watch.

Then he was saying, "This Boyle's a real character, Oliver — he might . . . might not work — but don't kid yourself, you're going to be happier with an actor who'll really play Boyle." He left it at that, but gave me a feeling the money would be there. Then, casually, he said, "I think the script's great but too long and needs to be cut down. I also think it's going to cost more than $750,000." These two thoughts began to play a gigantic role in the ensuing events, but at the time they didn't bother me at all.

On the way out, John twinkled, razor sharp, and said, "I hope you live up to your reputation." He meant — be who you are, "the lunatic," which apparently he'd heard about from my days in London on *Midnight Express*. Alan Parker and David Puttnam had certainly done me no favors. But John was saying confidently, "I want *that* Oliver, not their Oliver."

Elizabeth and I were waiting off the lobby with Sean, now two months old, napping in my lap; children were not allowed to go upstairs in this cozy little Doctors Hospital with its 1930s New York furniture and atmosphere (now Beth Israel on 87th Street and East End Avenue). I'd been born here, and my dad had once welcomed me. Now he was suddenly standing in the doorway, looking at us. I was shocked. It was as if Death had entered the room, all the flesh now gone from Dad's face, the skeleton look of Dachau, the eyes protruding, the ears standing out sharply against his skull. He seemed happy to lay eyes on Sean, whom I nudged awake, and grandfather and grandson looked at each other with lolling tongues. They made sounds, but Dad couldn't take Sean's weight, only touched him. "Where's the other one?" he whispered, probably thinking of his childhood brothers. Although he was generally lucid, he couldn't seem to place my wife.

I visited his room the next day with Mom, where Dad lay with an oxygen mask close by. He was in a better humor, still calling his ex-wife "a silly goose" like in the old days; she did look a little bit like a goose when she got excited. What was there to be done now? Nothing, really. All I could do was kiss him warmly on his old, cold cheeks as we left. It felt to me that death was a process that you sank or melted into; you're not even aware anymore you're dying. You approach it with half steps quietly, at times in great pain, but you numb it out. After all the thinking we do about death, it seems almost anticlimactic, like "Okay, we've been there already." Déjà vu — no big deal. Truthfully, I wished he'd get it over with; there was no more point in hanging around. That's the way my father saw it too. No sentimentality.

The next morning at Dad's apartment, where Mom was hosting us, the *New York Times'* front page grabbed my eyes with a stark shot of a Salvadoran rebel flag draped over a body on a tennis court in San Salvador. I knew instinctively it had something to do with us, which it did. It was the body of our go-between, Colonel "Ricky" Cienfuegos, shot at close range by rebels who'd somehow walked up on him at his country club. There went our deal. Boyle had just gone down to see him again; I tried to reach him, but he'd checked out. When I finally found Gloria, our unpaid coordinator, she told me the Ramada Inn would not allow Boyle to return; he'd last been seen the night before, drunk with two whores, scratching all over (his allergy issue), and the other guests were up in arms and complaining about his skin disease as well as his behavior. Nor had he paid his hotel bill. Complete disaster.

I reached John at home and thought I had the wrong number when my Swedish nanny's accent came through. "Yes, John Daly residence." She was at it again! The moment was decidedly awkward but businesslike, no comment necessary. When he came to the phone, John made nothing of it. Nor, for that matter, was the murder of Colonel Cienfuegos as much of a concern as the figure his people had just budgeted for the script of *Salvador* — $3.5 million! Far higher than he'd expected. Gerald Green had separately re-budgeted the production at $2 million. Me, I was still at $800,000 with Alex Ho's estimate. But John, an earthy man, was considerate about my father's worsening condition, so we adjourned the conversation.

I later went to the hospital alone, thinking this would be the last time. He was in intensive care. "Where's Mr. Stone?" I asked a passing nurse.

"That's him." His face was now quite swollen on a respirator, straining eyes huge in his head, fluttering, barely recognizing me. I pulled up a chair and talked gently to him, intimate things. How I always respected him all his life for his integrity, hard work, intelligence, and finally, how I really loved him though he was a tough SOB.

"I know what pain you're going through, Dad. I wish I could help, but it'll be over soon," and I kissed his forehead. Downstairs in Carl Schurz

Park bordering the East River, where I'd played often as a child, I cried —for him, for the past, for the march of time.

Elizabeth, Sean, and I left for Sagaponack, where it was still cold and wintry. I'd experienced such a sharp loneliness in this house writing that Russia script that I could only associate it now with the feeling of working without hope on a project that would never get done. Now Dad was sinking, Mom was losing the disappointing love of her life. What do you feel but bittersweet? My business manager of seven years, my rock, was still hung up on cocaine, *8 Million Ways to Die* was in jeopardy of not happening, and with Boyle missing in Salvador and the budget too high, I was at deep risk. I had to go back to LA quickly and try to salvage the situation.

I stopped off one last time to say good-bye to Dad; no, not really—to have a last look is more accurate. It was the most unemotional meeting. They'd put a stomach pump in him and cleaned him out, so he looked better, but he didn't really react to anything I was saying. I was a little bored. Had he heard anything I'd said during my last visit? In my head, I was preparing notes for his obituary, then the memorial service, all the procedures, the body too diseased to give to science as he'd once wanted; cremating him. Maybe his brain could go to the doctors to study. It was a good brain. But what of his heart?

He was always tough, my dad, and as much as I admired him for it, I also hated him, yet I loved him, but damn, he had no fucking heart! — or he did and he couldn't show it. Dad could be a cold, hard man, mean in money matters, selfish with Mom and me, and he knew it. He'd always hardballed me, said more or less, "Fuck you if you don't like it!" This was the rebel side to his nature, even at the end. Yet I admired him for that freedom of spirit. A strange code. Louis Stone, 1910–1985. The end of an era for me.

At the end, things don't change like in the movies. There's no forgiveness or redemption, just the end. Although he was still alive, I did fly back to LA with Elizabeth and Sean — it was the same day that Gorbachev became the new chief of the Soviet Union. Huge, good, world-shaking changes were in store. At 6 a.m. a few days later, the phone rang. Elizabeth, the early bird, answered in bed, handed me the phone, and said, "Your father's dead . . . at seven forty-five eastern time. His heart stopped." Mom came on the line, numbed. I don't remember our words. Tired and grateful for Dad that it was over, I went back to sleep till 9 a.m. I needed it.

Despite the budgetary issues, the pace on *Salvador* was steadily picking up. Creative Artists (CAA) was a relatively new talent agency in existence since 1976, and two of their young agents, Paula Wagner, energetic, tough, sexy, and Mike Menschel, balding, gentle, and unassuming, wanted to get me away from ICM. They dangled actors for *Salvador* while ICM slept. I knew at this point I could not make the film with Boyle as the actor; it'd be suicide. Excited, I met with Marty Sheen, the quiet, almost self-effacing protagonist of *Apocalypse Now*. He liked our script and agreed to do it.

Then I had dinner with James Woods for the supporting role of Dr. Rock, which he was not right for. Jimmy was type A, whip-smart, fast-talking, charming Elizabeth with his attentions at the dinner table. He was also intensely real and had a reputation for not compromising his performances in any way (*The Onion Field*, 1979; *Once Upon a Time in America*, 1984). In Jim Riordan's biography of me from 1995, Woods is quoted as saying:

> I think Marty's a great actor, you know, but hell, I'm up for a role here so I'm going to cut his legs out from under him if I can, do what I have to do to get it. So I said, "Martin Sheen, huh? Oh, he's a great, great actor. He's kind of religious, isn't he?" And Oliver goes, "Well, yeah, a bit." And I go, "Gee, I'm surprised he didn't have a problem with some of the language here. It's pretty strong." And Oliver says, "Well, he did have a few things that bothered him." So then I say, "Oh . . . I see. I thought you were going to do this thing for real . . . go all out. I mean, if you're just going to do another bullshit Hollywood picture."

Woods had hit a nerve, as I was already questioning my choice of Marty for the Richard Boyle part, which, at its core, had to be sharply abrasive, vulgar, living on the edge of his nerves, qualities that, in truth, couldn't be identified with Marty. Boyle was the clown on the surface walking into hell, looking for the quick buck, but in the end his nobler ape, under severe pressure, would emerge as a true human being who was also a hero. At least, that's the way I saw him.

Sheen, a strong Catholic, was now also hedging, saying first that he needed to work it out with his wife, and then that he wanted Alan Arkin to be his Dr. Rock as well as his "spiritual guru" for the movie. He confided he was worried that he'd "drift back into the darkness again," by which he meant the demons he faced during the filming of *Apocalypse Now*. He was truly grateful when I gently suggested he exit the film, leaving no bad feelings on either side.

Gary Busey came to lunch for the Rock role. He was a fascinating, massive mountain of energy, but he kept going to the bathroom every few minutes — a telltale sign in those days. Mike Menschel suggested I watch his client Jim Belushi, the late John's younger brother, in a *Saturday Night Live* skit, which caught my eye with Jim's witty version of a white man's rap. He was funny in that same crudely nimble way as his brother. He was not the image I had of Dr. Rock; he was thicker and beastlike, but he would be a strong contrast to the skinny, nerve-wracking Woods, who now seemed perfect for the Boyle part. I liked it. So did Daly.

Menschel brought in the adorable Cindy Gibb, who looked the part of a Westport, Connecticut yuppie playing an aid worker who'd be brutally murdered by a death squad; her sweetness would make it all the more shocking. Woods suggested his friend John Savage, from *The Deer Hunter*, for the role based on Zen-like war photographer John Hoagland, who was killed in that war.

Salvador was beginning to take on a momentum of its own, with others invested in its success. I was no longer alone, carrying it myself. We'd decided to film in Mexico, with Gerald's professional infrastructure supporting us. The budget kept changing — from $2.2 million to $2.5 million, then closer to $3 million — and I was heavily grilled more than once by Richard Soames, the tough, dry Australian head of Film Finances, one of the three leading bond companies; in those days, you could not make an independent movie if you were unable to get a bond in case the film went over budget. There were many contingencies to this, and Daly, in the end, would override the bond company's stringent objections by putting more money into the budget and not asking the bond company to cover it, that is, not "calling them" on their bond. Still, Soames, who wore a black eye patch and looked to me like the Grim Reaper, had no sense of humor and was the headmaster you don't want calling you to his office.

His verdict was clear. "You cut the script, or we don't make the movie." And then he more or less said that I'd given him a 120-page script, but with my typographical tricks for making big things look smaller, Soames counted it out to 141 pages. Whoa. This was nothing in comparison to what was coming. Green had told me, of course, to lie. "You're smart. Make him happy, and that gets us the bank money." Well, I lied as much as I could, and kept squeezing the script down, which I hated doing on the principle I'd rather shoot more and find out whether it works than cut first. Some twenty pages were already gone when Boyle and I lied our way through the E&O insurance policy, which is jargon for "errors and omissions"; it essentially says, "Nothing in this film is close to reality, and we can't get sued by real people." But who knew? Boyle was totally unreliable, and I had no idea how many bodies were buried there. "Just lie," I told Boyle, echoing Green. Which was no problem for Richard.

When Boyle finally met up with Woods at my house, it was a disaster. Two type A's rubbing up against each other. First of all, Jimmy was taking Richard's place, of course, and second, Jimmy at that time was a sexual magnet; women in public really seemed to like his fast wit and direct, masculine approach. And when Jimmy threw some glances at our Swedish nanny, and she clearly was responding (no surprises there), Boyle, who was still hitting on her despite his girlfriend's presence, grew Irish jealous.

Complicating things further, Jimmy thought the real Boyle was way too "sleazy" for him to model himself after: "Oliver, they'll hate this guy. He's got to have some nobility, something good in him. He goes there to make a quick buck, sure, but along the way, he finds a truth that's more important." I was now worrying that Jimmy, the guy who'd called me out on making a "Hollywood movie" with Marty Sheen, was now sanitizing the shit out of Boyle. And Boyle fully agreed. We had to keep pushing Woods, who, by the by, mentioned to me weeks later when we were shooting that he'd had a great time banging our nanny on our couch when we were out of town. I spared Elizabeth that knowledge, but when I eventually shared it with Richard (to torture him for something he'd done to me), he was astounded that her taste had, to put it in Shakespearean terms, "battened on this moor." Or, in Richard's words, "How could she fuck him!" Indeed, I later got back at Woods by telling him, whether true or not, that Boyle had already visited the nanny too. I think it got to him, which was the point. My God, this film would show me so many sides to the human face, I would never quite be the same earnest soul I had promised to the movie gods.

Salvador had ninety-three speaking roles in two languages in two countries and thousands of extras (this was before digital enhancement techniques were available); we had a horse charge, tanks, planes, choppers, and seven weeks to shoot it all. Gerald Green ran the Mexican production in the strangest covert way, always on an adding machine, refiguring how to make seven into nine. And then there was Soames and Film Finances, who kept breathing down my neck, visiting the set, watching my moves, counting how many extras and takes we used, trying to gauge my mental condition, etc. It was a surveillance state. The third stressor was Daly back in LA with his international financing, which came from the Crédit Lyonnais, which was a French bank but operated independently in Holland under the financially sophisticated banker Frans Afman, who was also a bit of a rascal and close to John. He supported several Hollywood independents for years, until he was double-crossed by a greedy Italian mogul and went to jail for a while. But he reemerged to live a good life, while the mogul went on to bankrupt MGM. I very much grew to like Frans, who made *Platoon* and *The Doors* possible.

In the end, all the haggling between Green's Mexican contingent, Soames's completion bond group, and Daly's international moneymen was staggeringly confusing, with much time and energy wasted; looking back, I wonder if it was all kabuki theater meant to keep me in line and pressure me to squeeze the screenplay down to a legitimate 115 to 120 pages. As the director, I flattered myself in thinking I was keeping the film alive among these supposedly warring parties, but I was truly the last to know anything, including the actual budget, which, like a thermometer, would go up and down weekly, scaring me with thoughts of erasure and death. "Cut three days. We're over by $220,000" ... then it was "over by $800,000" ... then "over by $1.2 million ... We've gotta cut!" These were the declarations I feared daily for months. *Salvador* aged me, no question. I was already growing thin on top, but the loss of my hair accelerated — just as I was getting what I wanted after all these years. The sacrifice, I realized, was going to be high.

We planned on shooting in Mexico first, which, although it had strict unions, was not paying American scale; then we'd do the US locations in San Francisco and Las Vegas at the usual actor and labor rates. We found dozens of extraordinary locations in Guerrero state, around Acapulco, and in the state of Morelos, close to Cuernavaca, as well as in Mexico City, with a magnificent cathedral (where we'd use a thousand extras to re-create the murder of Archbishop Romero). With the charmed help of the Morelos film commissioner, Katy Jurado, the exotic 1950s movie star who crossed over to American westerns like *High Noon* and *One-Eyed Jacks,* we struck location gold — classic old towns like Tepoztlán, and roads with their rock faces out of Carlos Castaneda's Don Juan adventures. This was rough backcountry Mexico. One day we'd pass a cow just hit by a car, men with machetes already chopping up its carcass for meat. The next day we'd drive by again and see only a skeleton with a head, wild dogs licking its soup-like entrails. Dead dogs were everywhere along the roads.

We planned for two weeks in Acapulco, four in Cuernavaca, and one in Mexico City — a total of seven — and then one closing week in the US. But Gerald, a consistent doomsday type, predicted we'd need an extra week in Mexico, which we didn't have in the budget. He was right. He was already having multiple problems; for our big finale, the battle of Santa Ana, I'd wanted two hundred soldiers, and he was saying that, given the cost of making uniforms, seventy-five soldiers was our limit. And the Mexican army was jacking up its price per man for logistical help from $65 a day to $115 — and they were no longer going to rent us their planes and choppers at a discounted fee. (Later we discovered that President Duarte's administration in Salvador had asked the Mexican government not to cooperate with the film, since it reflected badly on their country. Clearly, someone from inside El Salvador had betrayed us.)

Gerald asked me to check out Santo Domingo with him as a cheaper alternative to Mexico. On a lightning-quick scout, I looked everywhere and rejected the possibility. Nothing really fit. The US had invaded the island in 1965 under President Johnson and screwed any real chance for reform or democracy, turning the Dominican Republic into an armpit of very rich and very poor. Meanwhile, in Los Angeles, Orion Pictures now definitively rejected our *Salvador* script as simply "too much." So had almost every major distributor; it was either because of politics or the violence, we weren't sure. Furthering my paranoia, our foreign sales through Arnold Kopelson were coming out flat — "too violent, too much sex." He could no longer guarantee $2.5 million in overseas sales. Though Daly stuck it out, we felt totally at the mercy of Film Finances, which effectively became our overseer. I was called in for another torturous three-hour meeting with the gloomy Richard Soames, promising to cut more and show more storyboards for our final battle scene, the cost of which worried them. I promised them a "documentary style" of shooting, which, at that time, meant a rougher handheld approach, which would preclude doing too many time-consuming takes, much less any considerations of refinement. Green backed me up and plied them with exaggerated guarantees of what the Mexican army would do for us at a discounted price. We were on thin ice.

Things became messier still. Mike Medavoy at Orion reportedly told Daly that they'd "partner" with him on *Platoon* now, before the cycle of Vietnam films ended, but I'd have to abandon *Salvador*. That was a devil's bargain if ever there was one, and we had no guarantee they'd keep their end of the deal. Fuck them, I thought. And then music mogul David Geffen's company called, saying *Salvador* was "the best script David's read in years," which I've found over time to be a typical bullshit opening line for people with either no memory or no shame; later Daly told me Geffen wanted to get rid of me and bring in Costa-Gavras to direct. Nice world.

But Daly was made of stronger stuff — not for nothing had he been a merchant sailor once, as I had — and through all this double-crossing wouldn't bow to pressure but stuck by me. I think he really believed that we were making a sleeper hit like the Academy-nominated *The Killing Fields* (1985), about the Cambodian genocide, except that our spirit was far more gonzo. Nonetheless, he kept asking me to "reconsider the violence and the length." My argument remained "reality . . . reality . . . reality." At least change the ending, he argued; it could make all the difference. To go through all this hell for Boyle to escape to the US only to see his Maria deported back to Salvador was "a major downer." In this, Elizabeth fully agreed. I said I'd consider it, thinking if we had to, we could always shoot two endings.

I was busy putting our whole team together. In New York, Marion Billings, a highly respected publicist for Scorsese, Robert Benton, and other New York–oriented filmmakers, loved our script and was joining the film with her new West Coast partner, Andrea Jaffe. This was a great boost to my morale, an affirmation that some people of note inside the industry saw something in me and the film. Through Marion, I gained some credibility with a media that had strong doubts about my violent scripts.

After the up-and-coming cinematographers Jim Glennon, Barry Sonnenfeld, and Juan Ruiz Anchía all passed, I turned to a young, handsome, silver-haired documentary cameraman, Bob Richardson, from Cape Cod, who'd actually shot for PBS's *Frontline* in El Salvador and knew the terrain. I liked his confidence and the idea of discovering this world together; it would be like having a younger brother. We'd grow together in loyalty or go down as an entity. My production designer was the same kind of person, Bruno Rubeo, an Italian art director whom Green introduced to me as a lower-budget talent who lived in Mexico City. Like Richardson, he had no feature credits, but I took an instinctive liking to him as we scouted locations. I grew very close to both of them, and as the shooting went into its maddest phase, I knew I'd found true partners; the three of us would travel this road together — to our surprise, for quite some time.

The Mexican film industry was a treasury of great faces — the best "bad guys" this side of Huston and Peckinpah for my death squad roles. They'd long ago learned how to draw attention to themselves, but I didn't mind in this case, as we were making a broad, larger-than-life film about a character like Boyle, and only once in a while did they have to temper their natural hamminess. Dozens of accomplished professionals appeared in the smallest of roles, partly because the local industry had been in a slump for several years.

Elpidia Carrillo would be our Maria, a fresh-faced twenty-four-year-old from Michoacán; raised in poverty, she smoldered with class resentment at the way race-sensitive Mexicans treated her. Elia Kazan once argued against any restrictions for a director exploring personal limits with his actresses, and I wanted badly to get down with her. She was more than willing, giving me signals when we were alone, sometimes hugging me good-bye in that lingering way that makes the need to depart a question mark. But I convinced myself that repression, in this case, would make a better film. At any rate, Boyle, who was officially our chief consultant, was coming around often to see Elpidia, attentive as a dog with his bone. That was fine with me, as Elpidia kept him distracted and out of trouble. One day Richard and I had a terrible row, his frustration erupting when he showed up with gashes on his face from what he explained was "a fall." When I gave him hell, his pride had had enough, and he blasted me for not paying him what he was owed as a co-writer, much less a consultant. Woods was getting $150,000 in salary, and the picture was now being made for far more money than we'd imagined in the beginning — and he was right. But there was no real money. Woods hadn't actually been paid, I hadn't been paid, and Richard had at least received expenses to date, and we needed every dime until we got going; then, according to Gerald, he'd get paid. Peeved, he disappeared down to El Salvador for a week without telling me. We made up when he returned, and he continued to help me as best he could.

But then it all seemed to go up in smoke again when Daly, surprisingly nervous, called to say Jimmy Woods was pulling out of the film. It was the first of many such shocks ahead. After all this, it didn't seem possible, but it was. Our start date was weeks away. I flew back to Los Angeles to urgently coax Jimmy back into the film. He'd just stopped smoking, which, according to his agent, was making him worse. Most actors get nervous before the part actually takes hold; this was that moment. It would happen to me several more times with actors over my career. I soothed him back into the film at a diplomatic lunch where I felt like I was walking on teacups, begging Jimmy, who loved watching me grovel; he just wanted, he said, to be more "appreciated." In the process, I discovered that Jimmy was a germaphobe and terrified at the prospect of Mexico. So that's why he'd refused to go to Salvador with me and Boyle on a scouting trip. I explained to him that Mexico by comparison was a cakewalk, but that was not the right approach. Nor, for that matter, did Jimmy feel he needed much rehearsal, if any at all, as he was a "pro, not some jerk-off bullshit Method actor who has to *feel* his emotions." This put me further on edge: How was I going to deal with him?

I went back to Mexico for the final countdown without my lead actor, who'd agreed to come at the last second. Elizabeth was a godsend, lifting my spirits at their lowest when she arrived for the shoot with six-month-old Sean and the nanny. Elizabeth had fallen victim on an earlier trip in Mexico to an amoebic dysentery that had plagued her for weeks and eventually recovered in LA, but we kept this knowledge from Jimmy as best we could. It didn't take long for Elizabeth to notice the way the Mexican women handled their children in the streets, carrying them in rebozos on their backs, and soon we found a quiet Mexican woman to help us with Sean, who was becoming quite a handful. Our unforgettable Swedish nanny actually seemed quite relieved to head back to civilized Los Angeles, with our recommendation, to continue her further adventures in America. We never heard from her again.

By this time I'd wake up in the mornings, whether in LA or Mexico, in a nausea of dread. Pre-production is by far the worst of the stages. Nothing has actually been shot, everything lies ahead. This was a moment when I had to take an infantryman's perspective, put my head down, and see just the six inches in front of my face. No more thinking! Avoid the big picture, put one foot in front of the other, and take it as it comes . . .

I was suddenly missing my father more than ever. His intelligence, his manner of speaking, not his anger or his meanness, but the soft hush of his intellect and humor. I felt I still wanted to perform for him — to make this giant engineering mishmash somehow work. Mom was struggling, she had taxes to pay, and the insurance money had not come through yet. I couldn't count on any form of financial settlement for the next six months. I gave her what I could, and Mom, with wiles of her own, resumed a bond with a former lover in Paris, a rich businessman, who helped her bridge this gap. Although he was married and well past seventy, he was quite vigorous, according to Mom. All very French.

And then, of course, disaster struck once more — totally unforeseen. Two weeks before our start in Acapulco, the Mexican peso was, without warning, officially devalued against the dollar. Gerald was shattered, all his local banking connections down the toilet, valueless. In one swoop, 20 percent of our budget was gone, just like that gold dust in *The Treasure of the Sierra Madre*. Daly was apoplectic at Green for banking everything in Mexico prematurely. We needed emergency funds. Daly was our only hope now. I came to suspect, when Daly suggested it later, that Gerald had some sweetheart deal going with his wife and the Mexican bank, using the original cash reserve to finance a loan for a second, cheaper Mexican film on the side, a possible Gerald move, but this could not be proven, and I never really figured out what happened. When John visited us in Mexico, another one of those "Long John Silver" grins crossed his face whenever I asked him about Gerald, and he'd just say in wonder, "That scoundrel got hoist by his own petard this time, didn't he?" Ultimately, funds were procured by John somewhere in Europe, probably from Frans's Dutch bank, and his company promised in principal, not in cash, close to another million dollars into the kitty to make up for the devaluation. Which meant we'd still have to collect the money.

I fell terribly sick with a high fever, 102° and climbing, but I couldn't afford to lie down, except to try to sleep. A Mexican doctor attended me and simultaneously gave me the routine physical insurance exam. But when I registered at 160/120, he pronounced me uninsurable because of high blood pressure. Just my fucking luck! I'd never planned on a heart attack; we never do. At thirty-nine? I'd been eating too much, gaining weight out of nervousness, not enough exercise. I thought about Marty Sheen in the Philippines having a heart attack during the making of *Apocalypse Now*. If it happened, it might not kill me, but it could certainly slow me down or cripple me. I was totally depleted.

John had the good sense and the kindness to call and reassure me not to worry, promising, "If you run out of money, we'll be there for you." It was compassionate of him. He'd been down and out several times in his life — and he knew how it felt. I've always loved him for that. I think the moral of my relationship with this man is that a little kindness or empathy from the heart goes a lot further than a scolding to the mind.

Quietly, Gerald stepped in and fixed the blood pressure doctor, no surprise there, and this problem, as with so many others, went away — and gradually I grew back to my full strength. It brings to mind a story I always loved about Franklin Delano Roosevelt. On the next-to-last day of his life, he cabled a worried Winston Churchill about their wartime ally, Russia, "I would minimize the Soviet problem as much as possible, because these problems in one form or another seem to arise every day, and most of them straighten out." Which is really true about John Daly, the way he approached his life with trust. He created, for me, an atmosphere around himself which allowed him and others to succeed — and in fact, over many years, I've learned the power of not worrying as much as I once did, thus uncreating "problems" that would then recede somehow. I wish America's leaders and its problem-seeking media would recognize the wisdom of this strategy.

D-day was finally here — rehearsals with the full cast; even Woods had come down to join us. It went well, except that Belushi found himself disillusioned when he met the real Dr. Rock, whom I'd invited from San Francisco for authenticity purposes. After a chaotic dinner in a loud and horrible Acapulco Joe tourist joint, with Belushi and Rock sitting across the table from Woods and Boyle, Belushi came over to me seething and blurted out, "You don't seriously want me to play that thoroughly fucked-up asshole, do you?"

"No, Jim," I answered, "I don't. I mean you can use it to . . ."

"Then I don't want to see him on the set!"

"All right, Jim."

Dr. Rock, on the other hand, thought Belushi was delightful and that they really connected. I reassured Belushi and graciously sent Dr. Rock back with some money to San Francisco.

At last I'd arrived at the beginning. On Thursday, June 24, 1985, the film clapper slammed shut. "SCENE 1, TAKE 1" — but even that was fucked up because the title on the clapper for our film read "OUTPOST."

"No problem," Gerald reassured me. "I should've told you, but . . ." He shrugged, meaning there were a hundred other things to really worry about. Later he explained it was "simply part of our tax deal with the bank in Holland." Oh, okay. At this point, "white lies" were routine as long as they remained "white." But I later learned that Gerald had been involved with an action picture starring Arnold Schwarzenegger. It'd been partially funded, but when Arnold wouldn't commit fully, Gerald, no doubt illegally, transferred its financing commitment to us — and thus our title. *Outpost* we remained in all the files and trade dailies until, months later, in the editing, our title was changed back to *Salvador*. Don't ask, Oliver, just go.

Years later, when I was asked in an interview about my memories of *Salvador*, I said, with a clarity I certainly did not feel then, "I looked at it as my one chance I may get, the only one . . . and I'd take this film, and like a stone, throw it as far and as hard as I could." With this David and Goliath spirit, it began.

8

Salvador, to Hell and Back

On Day 1, my first directing experience in five years, I ran around like a hare from the hounds, shooting thirty-three first camera setups and sixteen second camera shots in one beach restaurant scene that introduced several main characters and some death squad heavies. I hardly sat down during the twelve hours. Bob Richardson and his crew were kind of shocked, flying in all directions; no one worked this fast. I had something to prove, but to do so, I rushed some shots, which were not quite working and would have to be cut. Our Mexican crew was wondering, Is this going to be our pace every day? They weren't used to the "American" style. No one was.

Reality set in at the Day 2 location, a backcountry town where Woods surprises Elpidia Carrillo (Maria), who, in a ritual outside time, is washing laundry down by the river with other women. Her baby is nearby in a blanket, unattended. After some gentle dialogue, reunited, she walks off with Boyle. "Cut," I called out, pleased.

The sweet Mexican script man came running over to me, worried, not knowing what the "gringo" director really wanted. "Señor Stone, please — didn't Elpidia forget her baby?" Oh, shit. He's right. It was still there. What kind of mother . . . ? Of course, it was a dummy in a blanket; maybe that's why she forgot it? We laughed, but this tells you a little something about Elpidia, who could sometimes go totally blank in her performance. She was accustomed to the mores of the Mexican film industry, being told everything she was supposed to do in the shot; thinking for yourself was not encouraged.

We were filming two or three scenes a day at different locations at breakneck speed — but we were still falling behind. A flash flood hit one day, washing out the dirt paths for our cars and trucks. Communication problems were constant. My second assistant director, Ramón Menéndez (who soon became my first when we fired the original), was bilingual and smart, AFI-trained in the States — but he was a native of Cuba, and when he started to order the Mexican crew around to get things moving, they rebelled, unwilling to be bossed around by any Cuban. Menéndez was an opinionated idealist who annoyed me several times in pre-production when he was loud and clear about his wanting to become a director one day. But I needed his brains too much to let him go. Soon, indeed, Ramón would go on to direct the excellent *Stand and Deliver* (1988), and on our shoot, he was without equal.

The third day, as we were finishing a scene at Elpidia's beach shack, Bruno Rubeo, our production designer, by custom went ahead of us to the last location of the day, which was miles away and was to be shot that night. We were starting half-day, half-night shoots, which I learned to prefer after finding out on night shoots, meaning 6 p.m. to 6 a.m., that much of the work done after midnight is achieved too slowly and at high cost. Starting the day (if it can be done) at 1 p.m. and calling it at 1 a.m., twelve hours later, aligns better with the body's rhythms, until, that is, we can clock our body around after two or three such days to a full night rhythm. This meant working from 6 p.m. to 6 a.m. and sleeping the first part of the day. In this case, Bruno, whose powers of concentration were suspect, had gone off alone but neglected to tell anyone *where* this night location was; satellite phones didn't work well in these rugged areas, so by the time we located him and the screaming had stopped, the crew refused to go to the night location because it was too far away at that hour. It wasn't a strike, but it gave clear warning to the gringos that "Hey, we're in Mexico here. We do things our way." Storm warnings noted.

Another night, our heavyset "government censor" was quite upset when we displayed a fabricated young boy's severed head at city hall as a warning from a death squad. She thought the way we'd arranged it and shot it was "too much," especially as she was already disturbed by the amount of garbage we'd strewn on the streets. I argued that this was the reality of Salvador, not Mexico, but she saw it as a larger issue, a degradation of Latin Americans. Woods didn't help this situation when, in the middle of a sex scene at Maria's beach shack, he needlessly teased the censor, "Why do you need to be on the set for this moment?" followed by remarks like "What do you think of your job? Does it make you happy?" Everyone heard it.

Gerald had warned me to be especially polite to the censor, because unless she approved the film, we'd never get an export license for our negative to go back to the States. I turned to our Hispanic American casting director, Bob Morones, who fancied himself a ladies' man, with the idea that he'd spend some time with our censor — and who knows? He was repelled by the idea but tried his best to get the hound off our scent. We did modify the garbage in the streets, but nonetheless, she filed several negative reports on us. The worst moment would come several weeks later.

Jimmy Woods became another issue entirely — a beast of an issue. Almost immediately, he was not just stepping on Belushi's lines but taking him aside to tell him how to say them — as well as telling him to "cut the jokes." At first Belushi bowed to Jimmy as the more experienced actor, but soon he got wise — and tougher. It wasn't long before they started screaming at each other on set.

Woods: "Whattaya mean? I'm only trying to help you, for Chrissake."

Belushi: "Fuck you, man, I know what the fuck you're trying to do! I saw the back of your head crawling into my close-up" (an over-Jimmy's-shoulder shot onto Jim). Let them fight, let the tension work in favor of the scene, I told myself; after all, Boyle had dragged Rock down to Salvador with lies and promises, and it made sense for Belushi to be upset in this mess of a situation. I was getting the results on film, even if it was not pleasant.

But I sensed there was a bigger problem. It was between Jimmy and me. First of all, it's telling that he arrived in Mexico with his new girlfriend from San Francisco, whom he was preening over, telling us how high-bred Sarah was, a horsewoman of distinction. Jimmy was deeply insecure, but he was also the "star" of the picture with the most experience under his belt; he certainly let us know that we were all amateurs and he was the professional.

I had to take him on; if he sensed anybody was weak, he'd clearly jump all over him. There was in Jimmy that paradox of being the dog who barks when he can and cowers when he can't, and I had to be kind enough that I could feed him his biscuits and keep him happy. He had that "genius" sense of superiority — no one knows movies better than me. So I inevitably ended up getting in the way of his reflection, driving him nuts, and once his uncertainty kicked in ("What does Stone really want — he's making me feel like shit here!"), he'd get really crazy or surprisingly vulnerable, and sometimes, thank God, it'd come out on camera. But not always.

Things went to shit during the Friday all-night shoot at the end of the first week. Jim Belushi, in his first solo scene without Woods, is drunk in a rat-hole cantina when he takes on five tough death squaders in the street outside. To play the scene, Belushi, frustrated by Woods upstaging him in their scenes together, drank himself into an angry stupor — call it "Method drunk" — and began screaming at the villains as he ripped his shirt off, sweaty and barefoot, and turned the scene into an over-the-top performance, losing the humor of being a victim and instead becoming the victimizer. The befuddled Mexican heavies, who didn't speak a word of English, retreated in confusion as Jim stalked forward, shouting at these big guys who could've easily taken him out. As I looked up in despair, dawn creasing the sky, I knew we had nothing we could use. We were falling another half day behind. Giant locusts now invaded the set, and the toads, croaking loudly, were feasting on them. The strong eat the weak at any hour.

The next day Jim apologized to me in tears, complaining of Woods's putdowns, telling me he wanted a true relationship with me, "man-to-man." It's painful to discuss this with an actor when he's floundering, and I tried to help him as best I could, but he had to understand clearly that he was *supposed* to be in a desperate situation, and I liked the way he was frustrated. I just didn't want him to drink anymore.

By the time we got to the end of the second week, we were dragging. Everyone was nervous about the rape and murder of the Maryknoll nuns. But Cindy Gibb and the older actresses playing the nuns were possessed of stern imaginations, convincing the audience they were terrified while staying true to their God, hoping for the best. The night was short and cold, and we had to shoot fast. I was unhappy with some of the crudely shot "grabs," which were big, slobbering close-ups of the death squaders drooling over Cindy's angelic face. After the rapes, there's a silence, marked by the sound of jungle bugs, as the nuns put their shirts back on, and we think, momentarily, they'll be let go. At least that. But their fate was a harsh one, and as in the real event, each was shot in the face at point-blank range and tossed in a mass grave. Although I was unhappy with the way I'd hurriedly shot it, it turned out powerfully.

After two weeks in the Acapulco area, we badly needed to get back to Mexico City to check the cameras and retool. On location, we'd had reports of focus problems from our processing lab at Churubusco. Woods naturally went nuts when he saw bits of the blurry dailies, which looked far worse than they were when projected on location on our old projectors off improvised screens made of bedsheets. The lab, however, was of dubious quality, printing lights that were often too green or blue, and the "timer" in charge of printing the film was having communication problems with Richardson, who was still young and would fly off the handle. When we finally checked the footage on proper screens back at the Mexico City studio, we were vastly relieved to see we had just enough focus to avoid a reshoot. By necessity, we fired our Mexican focus puller and brought down a well-paid assistant cameraman from Los Angeles. I had other problems too — with my editor. She was a newcomer whom, like much of my inner circle, I'd hired on instinct, but we were unfortunately out of sync on almost everything, so I specifically instructed the editor to cut to my wishes until she could please me. Many disagreements followed, but I'd never show the rushes before I was ready. I'd stay in the editing room extra hours, sorting out the chaos no matter how tired I was, to get it right. After my experience on *The Hand,* I was adamant about not allowing this film to get out from under my control. This was, of course, increasingly difficult as the money noose tightened.

From Mexico City, we moved for the next four weeks to a new base in lovely Cuernavaca on a Sunday. The problem was no one then worked in Mexico on a Sunday, so it was a logistical disaster; it took hours to check in, find our staff, book the actors into rooms, etc. All this wasted my energy in anger and irritation. I went ballistic on Gerald about the organizing, but then learned that on top of this, without telling me, he'd fired fifteen of our crew, including stand-ins; he told us we could use crew members who weren't working to stand in for the actors when being lighted. Why? Money, of course. Additionally, Woods was calling his CAA agent to complain that Belushi "with his Jackie Gleason shtick" was getting all the coverage, when in fact 75 percent of it was focused on Woods.

Now the agent was coming down to police us, as was Film Finances, watching my number of takes, extras, my rehearsal times, making estimates that the film, when roughly assembled, would be more than four hours, and so forth. I was now cutting the script as tightly as I could, not shooting certain scenes I wanted but that, under this pressure, no longer seemed essential to me. A US video sales company also came to watch us; so did our foreign salesman, Arnold Kopelson, and his wife, Anne, as did Marion Billings, our publicist; and then John Daly showed up (with a new girlfriend). I was under a microscope in a surveillance state, but I was in another zone now, utterly possessed by my need to "make" the next setup at whatever cost. I had no shame. My temper grew short with our Mexican sound engineer, who Green said had done "four hundred Mexican films" and who said I wasn't giving him enough rehearsal time. He quit. So did the hysterical "genius Mexican art director" who'd done some "two hundred films." I didn't care; at that time, Mexican films were not noteworthy for their sound or other technical qualities. Later, the veteran sound man came back and we made up. He told me, "You'll be a great director. I know it." And then he said exactly what he'd said when he quit: "Forty years I've worked in this business. I know."

I'd sold the film to John as a "Hunter Thompson and his buddy go to Salvador" tale that becomes darker as it goes on. And in that anarchic spirit, a highlight of the story was to be Boyle's reunion with "Colonel Figueroa" at a military cuartel near rebel territory. Boyle and Rock, having been arrested as "periodistas" (journalists) and nearly killed, are brought in to Figueroa, filthy, near naked. But in a stroke of Irish luck, Boyle once glorified the colonel in a long-ago article, and he remembers Boyle! Then they're feasting together, drunk in Figueroa's quarters with several busty, colorful whores. As I told Riordan for his book: "Doctor Rock is getting a blowjob under a table. Boyle is fucking a girl while trying to pry information from the Colonel, and the Colonel is so drunk out of his mind that he pulls out this bag of ears [shades of Vietnam war trophies] and throws the ears on a table and says, 'left-wing ears, right-wing ears, who gives a fuck!' He throws an ear into a champagne glass, proposes a toast to El Salvador, and drinks the champagne with the ear in it!"

And then, improvising, the actor playing Figueroa put another ear into a whore's open mouth!

Well, this was one step too far for our government censor, who was horrified and ran to Green, who in turn was terrified — there goes our export license! We sweet-talked the censor for the next two days, trying to keep things quiet, and I presume Gerald pulled out every stop to keep the ship afloat. Later, because of pressure from the American side over sexual content, it was all chopped up in the editing room anyway, losing impact. I believe South American and European audiences would've understood the madness inherent in this scene, but when we screened it for American audiences, it just didn't work the same way. Why? Because, as it was then perceived, perhaps less so now, audiences were dependent on categorizations. If a film was sold to them as a comedy, they laughed, an adventure, they gasped, a drama, they cried. *Salvador,* like *The Hand,* was neither fish nor fowl and would be put through this laborious testing process where I found that, if something is new or unexpected, it would generally register on the audience's judgment scale as "upsetting," "chaotic," "disturbing," etc. Neither good nor bad, just new, and not to be trusted yet. *Salvador,* in hindsight, would never make for an "acceptable" film, much less a studio film, but I didn't know it then. I thought that something new could break through.

By this time, Jimmy had been yelling so much in front of the Mexican crew that Gerald came up to me one day with his most solemn look and told me that he'd been officially warned by the Mexican government that Jimmy was "a guest" in the country and his behavior, as reported, was "unacceptable." If it continued, he'd be asked to leave the country — which meant the film would have to shut down. Gerald was very serious. They meant it; they could close down the film.

We shot one hundred–plus extras lying on the side of a steep slope on an extremely hot day amid vultures and garbage, as Woods, complaining most of the time, and John Savage take photographs of the victims of the death squads. Black smoke from tires, permissible in Mexico, permeated the air, congesting our throats. There was very little water, and it was a long, long day. I should've fought harder for the necessary water, but I was barely hanging in myself; standing braced on a slope for several hours with no even ground is most taxing. In the final film, in the background, you can hear groans and see several "dead" extras squirming with discomfort; one lady, ready to black out from dehydration, simply sat up in the middle of a shot, which I left in. After all, I rationalized, some of these victims might not have been dead.

We moved on to Mexico City for the giant cathedral interior and exterior with one thousand extras. This scene is the turning point for Boyle's character; he's been through several close calls and seems now to want to buckle down and make up for his dubious past by marrying Maria (Elpidia), who surprises him when she tells him she's not interested because he's a "schemer and a scammer." He then begs her — and takes her to church to prove that he's now rediscovered his morality; he'll receive communion from Archbishop Romero himself. The day before we shot this complex and massive scene, fed up with his behavior, I suggested to Jimmy that in addition to the scripted scene, Boyle should also go to confession for the first time in thirty years. I looked at it as a chance for Jimmy to repent. Jimmy, however, was raised Catholic, and explained it this way to Riordan:

> "Oh, really? First of all, let me tell you something, Oliver. You don't go to confession on the morning before the mass."
>
> And [Oliver] says, "Well, the audience won't know the difference."
>
> "Right — there's like 80 million Catholics in the United States, but they probably won't notice? Sure." And the irony was, they didn't. He was right. That's what's so aggravating about him! So I asked him for the lines, but he said, "I don't want to give you the lines. I want you to just look into that dark, murky soul of yours, into that weasel soul of yours, and come up with whatever you want . . ." What you saw was the first time that it came out of my mouth, just total improvisation. I just used the whole thing to get back at Oliver for stuff that happened during the

film. At one point, he'd certainly called me a weasel and a rat, so
I mentioned that in the confession and so on.

That ad-libbed scene brought, as much as anything, howls from the audience and highlighted Woods's Oscar-nominated performance.

As it turns out, just as Maria and Boyle are kneeling together at the altar, about to accept the wafer on their tongues from Archbishop Romero,
this is the moment when an assassin shoots the archbishop and the whole
church erupts in panic. It seems nothing comes easy for Boyle.

Now it was time to film *Salvador*'s most complicated scenes, the full-out
battle of Santa Ana. We shot in the picturesque sixteenth-century town of
Tlayacapan, which we set up with vast swaths of burning rubber tires and
black smoke, bombs, squibs, actors running, dying — and hundreds of fascinated locals watching from the edges. This was truly a dream day for me,
as I got to be the general in this game, moving the camera and the actors
as if I were a boy playing with my toy soldiers. The town's tough-talking
Mayor Gomez was by my side, fully supportive; he'd modeled himself on
Al Capone, and much admired *Scarface*. He allowed us to build first-story
"fronts" on the main streets and second-story structures to blow out during
the battle. He also gave the okay for us to redecorate his office in city hall as
a whorehouse, replete with plush red furnishings (a makeover he liked so
much, he left it as his office).

By this time, we were clearly well over budget and schedule. The bond
company was pressuring Green for "cuts . . . cuts . . . and more cuts." Their
toughest field man was coming down that day, replacing their previous
representative, who seemed to them too compliant with Green, who was
certainly good at evading the truth, shuffling numbers around in ways, I
think, worthy of Enron later in the century. Ominously, the day before, I
had my first real fight with Daly, who now wanted to "call" the completion
bond — that is, force them to put up their money for our overage, as he realized we could not come close to finishing on budget; it would effectively
give the bond company control of the film. I was shaken, and I told John on
the phone, in as steady a voice as I could, "John, if Film Finances takes us
over and in any way damages the integrity of what *we*" (I purposely emphasized the "we") "set out to do, you and I part company on this film and all

other projects. I'll leave the picture." John, usually calm, yelled right back at me, "I won't be threatened like this!" I didn't have a leg, really, to stand on, except the work, but at least he knew it was important to me if I was willing to walk away both on this picture and on *Platoon*. Of course, if Daly pulled the plug, any chance of a new beginning for me would go up in smoke. And so would the film — and with it John's investment; our arrangement was a case of "mutually assured destruction."

With the bond people en route and Gerald on the phone telling me he was going to get the cash from a Mexican syndicate friendly with his father-in-law, I called "Action!" and the cavalry charge began. Seventy horses, which we'd wrangled with great difficulty, were galloping at full speed with rebel riders down cobblestone streets. The riders were the descendants of Zapata from the state of Morelos, although the Zapatistas never really used horses then, nor did the Salvadoran rebels ever mount a horse charge. But fuck it! If I was going down — and this was probably my last film — fuck the bond company, I wanted my horse charge.

To guarantee it, I offered to pay for it out of my fee, of which I hadn't yet seen a penny, but was rejected because there was no real money for my fee at this point; but I'd go down in style. We shot the cavalry charge four more times. Greatness! I was so excited. A complex job achieved, all this in the face of looming disaster. We were moving to our next setup when Green quietly slithered over to me, our eyes tensely meeting. "I'm not frowning, am I?" he quipped with a sly smile. "I made a deal." A million dollars out of a Mexican consortium. No takeover. Another day to live!

We plowed on. The next day the army tanks we'd rented were a few hours late. An aerial gasoline explosion misfired on one sandbagged position, and two stunt people were burned and evacuated, but they'd be okay. (When Woods heard about the accident, of course, he turned it into another melodrama.) There was a bazooka mishap on a rooftop. Then another camera malfunctioned. Fifty of the Mexican soldiers we'd hired kept smiling at the camera. I screamed them back into reality by the third take. We'd hired a small plane, repainted it with army markings to strafe low over the street where Woods and John Savage are taking photos of the battle. Jimmy was especially nervous about all the explosive squibs. He was heavily wired to the squibs in order for him to get shot in the leg. A Mexican pilot, who didn't speak English, was going to fly a single-engine plane real low right over Jimmy, who was talking nonstop to calm his rattled nerves.

I suddenly heard an explosion of words out of Savage, who never lost his temper, his soft voice raised at Woods, who was now apparently giving John some kind of advice or instruction. "You don't talk to me! You don't talk to me, you hear!" John screamed — after which Woods went ballistic, threw his prop camera bag to the ground, and yelled, "I've had enough of this shit!" Our plane was circling overhead, losing gas, and then I heard Ramón, our AD, yelling over the radio, "Woods left the set!"

"Don't let him have a car!" I said, reading Woods's freaked-out mind. A few minutes later, I heard Woods was already "three miles down the road!" Ramón was now walking alongside him pleading, "Jimmy, Jimmy, don't leave! Come on, man, we need you. Don't do this. It's a good film. We'll work this out. You'll be safe." Nothing doing. I instructed all the production people and Ramón to get ahead of him and tell anyone on this road in the middle of nowhere not to stop under any circumstance and pick this guy up. Jimmy had a prop gun in a holster around his waist. "Tell them he's a crazy gringo with a forty-five looking for a ride."

Eventually, Ramón cooled him down. The plane had to go back to refuel, another hour of daylight lost. We got Woods back to the set, and John Savage graciously apologized to Jimmy, who accepted it, and then started ranting at me. I wanted to kill him — strangle him, actually — up close, personal. Rarely has a human being brought out this desire for violence in me. I repressed my urge, and the plane returned, and in the course of things we got the shot without injury. Ten Mexican businessmen brought out by Gerald were watching the whole thing — quite an impression of our business they must've carried away.

By 6 p.m., with the sun dipping lower, we got our last aerial from a private chopper, rigged with an M60 machine gun and rocket, swooping into our tight frame and shooting Jimmy down in the same shot, wounding him; this was a miracle. Although the helicopter was about thirty feet above his head, Jimmy would claim it brushed his hair.

We'd made it. Or had we?

Early the next day, our Mexican crew solemnly called a strike. Gerald implied that something was not working out with his consortium. I shrugged. I just didn't give a shit anymore, and I walked over to a bombed-out prop car in the cemetery and gratefully fell asleep in the backseat. Some two hours later, Ramón woke me. "We're back." We were? I didn't need to know why anymore. I was ready to accept anything. I couldn't blame the crew, and we went to work like automatons and finished the day.

But there was no question our production was being hunted by the furies; it was in the air. The rumors were building through the office staff and crew: "We're closing down." Mexico was turning into a surrounding army of creditors, people everywhere not paid, angry, and we were at the Alamo. We'd also lost four rolls of film from the battle sequence when our camera loader, out of fatigue no doubt, reused two rolls we'd already shot.

The next day — our forty-second in Mexico — was our last. It was tense all the way. We were shooting Boyle's execution scene at the hands of the death squaders who catch him at the border of Guatemala, trying to sneak out with Elpidia, but he's saved at the last second by a call from the American ambassador — "Stars and Stripes" to the rescue. Naturally, Woods, before he filmed the scene, blew up at me when he claimed he'd found a real bullet in the prop rifle's chamber (I'm sure several of the crew had thought of it), and it became another great story of Jimmy saving the day from the incompetent morons around him. We finished again at a roadside cantina, chasing the setting sun at 7:30 and making it by about thirty seconds before losing the light. It was done — we were finished, the end of Mexico! And I accepted defeat. It was an ignoble end, but I felt we had to get out while we could. Say good-bye. No sense of having "achieved" this film. Everyone seemed depressed, fatalistic.

We still owed five more days of opening scenes in San Francisco, and three days for the crucial ending in Las Vegas and the surrounding desert. We heard from Daly that first he wanted the negative, work print, and sound out of the lab and out of Mexico. Though Film Finances had apparently paid the lab, they "didn't give a damn about the beginning or end"; they were furious at Green and told him, "You've done nothing but lie! . . . Now deliver the picture as per contract!" When I called John to talk about how we could finish the movie, I reminded him that I hadn't shot the film's opening or close. We had the middle for sure, but . . . In his detached Cockney accent, he interrupted, "Oh, fuck. Well, can't you just cut the beginning?" Turbulent, I pleaded, "Are you crazy? You love the beginning, remember?" He grudgingly admitted he did.

The next day in our editing room in Mexico City, as we were packing to move, Gerald was telling me with his hangdog eyes that he was "fucked," as if I was the only one left in this world, next to his wife, who might still believe him. "I've lost my shirt, Oliver." Shock on his face. "I owe a lot of money to a lot of people. My father-in-law thinks I'm a con man . . . I'm facing death here. This is bankruptcy." I genuinely felt sorry that I had contributed to his despair, but with Gerald, his expression was so sad sack that I had to suppress a laugh, wondering if he had yet another card up his sleeve.

I never did figure out how our picture was paid for; it was a secretive poker game among three parties that was way over my head. I asked Daly years later what really happened, and I remember his Cheshire cat grin as he said, once more shaking his head with delight, "That Gerald — my Lord, what a rascal!" And so it remains — a mystery.

We got out fast, grateful to cross the US border, where we rested and prepped for the finale in San Francisco and Las Vegas. Bob Richardson went to the hospital with a serious salmonella infection, which set Woods off, going hypochondriacal about the parasite he now pictured, as large as an alien, in his intestines. Boyle, who'd been drinking way too much and again looked like a bloated red toad, wanted to continue collaborating with me and start working on a new film — we'd call it "Beirut," or "Boyle Goes to Beirut" — about his previous adventures in the Middle East. Of course, in this story, he crosses Arab-Israeli lines and falls "in love" with a local beauty, then manages to find himself in the middle of the terror bombing that took 217 US Marine lives. John surely would've staked us. Yes, Richard was a pain in the ass, but it was worth the result. But there I went again, dreaming of another movie with Boyle. First I had to finish this damn movie, *Salvador* — and then closely supervise the cut. I wasn't going anywhere right now, and Daly reiterated he wanted to make *Platoon* early the next year. He'd even do it the same way we'd made *Salvador,* with or without a distributor. Daly even wanted to make the Russian script, "Defiance," that went to cold storage with Marty Bregman; he'd buy it back from

Universal. I had my doubts about any of this happening. And I was still out $30,000 in out-of-pocket production costs I'd incurred, among them subsidizing Boyle.

Year of the Dragon had finally opened that August of 1985 and, costing approximately $24 million, would make $19 million domestically, not the number they wanted. In the theaters, where I saw the film twice, my feelings were enthusiastic but mixed; the film polarized the audience. The main character was a loudmouth, and Mickey Rourke, mesmerizing in his way, lacked an overall charm. Did it have racist strains? Sure, it had elements of insult. Marion Billings in New York reported a negative reaction from her film circle. On my thirty-ninth birthday, my frequent critic Pauline Kael in *The New Yorker* called out both Cimino and me as "still living in a cave . . . one [a] brazen vulgarian — both xenophobic — bring[ing] out the worst in each other . . . so neither one knows when he has become a public embarrassment." Another notch in my career belt. In *New York* magazine, David Denby actually separated the two of us, sparing Michael his rod in order to punish "the dread Oliver Stone."

In any case, *Dragon* would never be, as we'd hoped, Michael's comeback film, and he would troll along for years, demanding, difficult to work with, and expensive to finance. He would remain a mystery not only to me but also to his macho buddies like Mickey Rourke and my detective friend Stanley White, whom he loved to hang with; they would have a hard time telling you who he was. Michael enjoyed the cloak of his own enigma, and transforming or cross-dressing, whatever, he died relatively young, without ever really becoming more of the artist he was when he made *The Deer Hunter.* He ran, I believe, headlong into his own demons — hubris, arrogance, a classic Greek flaw — when he made *Heaven's Gate* so costly, and this in turn was the checkmate of a film that mortally wounded him. I'd face a similar reckoning in a few years.

We trudged up to shoot our San Francisco opening — Boyle and Rock zooming across the Golden Gate Bridge in their battered Mustang, yapping about their woes with women on a perfectly blue day. I used my son Sean as Boyle's screaming baby in the opening shots set in Boyle's broken-down apartment in the Tenderloin. While we were shooting, Elizabeth burst in, and seeing Bob Richardson's smoke infesting the small set, started screaming at me like the angry mother she was. "No smoke! You lied to me! This is it! It's his last shot!" It seemed like everyone was screaming as we grabbed our classic opening. I guess, like Richard, I'd always be rushing and screamed at, but no matter what, fuck it, for a good cause my son could swallow a little smoke.

We checked into The Dunes in Las Vegas for our grand finale. The last of three days of shooting began on Saturday, August 31, with the temperature hitting 115° in the desert. It was fitting that I was leading a caravan of one hundred–odd people in fifteen or twenty vehicles on this insane movie on its very last day — with no idea where we were going; I was a one-eyed general leading an Army of No Money. The two previous days had been grueling and long, and now we were on to the crucial last scene of the movie — Elpidia and Jimmy and her kids on a Greyhound bus, heading north past the Arizona border, safe back in the USA. That is, until the cops suddenly pull them over for an immigration spot-check that becomes a nightmare. I hadn't scouted anything out here on US 95 out of Vegas, where it was all flat high desert anyway with no shade at all.

After twenty minutes of driving surrounded by protective police cars, their roof lights soundlessly flashing, I called the caravan to a halt when and where I felt lucky; after all, I'd gone on instinct up to now. I had three and a half pages to shoot, mainly inside a crowded sauna of a bus. Rehearse. Light. Shoot. Work it out. Block it. Block it some more. A line of dialogue here, not there, then rise, move, turn, speak here, then not . . . and so on and so on, twenty to fifty beats to every scene. It was so hot inside the bus, extras and actors needed constant water. It didn't look like we'd make it in time, but between 3 and 7 p.m., we finally got a "roll on," a sailing or surfing analogy, I think — you get the wind and you go, because the wind can change at any second. Moviemaking is very much like sailing, in that every moment is fraught with change.

Chris Lombardi, our stalwart assistant camera/focus puller from Los Angeles, went down suddenly with heat prostration. This was serious, his pallor reminding me of soldiers in the Vietnam jungle — in danger. No one else could keep the focus while Bob was operating a handheld in the small, intimate spaces of the bus. Now we were fucked. I begged him to try to stand. "Chris, you can do it! I know you can. This happened to guys a lot in Vietnam, but we always made it . . . And you know — think about those guys in the Foreign Legion. What they went through! You can do it, Chris, I know you got the guts!" Richardson later told me he couldn't believe I'd invoked the French Foreign Legion, but for me it was a life-and-death situation; there'd be no next day! Chris was a big guy with deer-in-the-headlights eyes, but, bless his soul, he groaned, probably to get me out of his face, pulled himself upright, and made it through this monster last day.

The two immigration cops quickly figure Elpidia and her two kids are illegal, and they drag her off the bus as Jimmy passionately pleads with them in vain. The worst kind of separation at the border — loved ones — except that these three poor people were headed back to a war zone in Salvador, where memories of her involvement with Boyle could endanger her life. With the sun a minute from inching down behind a far-off mountain, we rolled our last shot, from a crane above the bus, of Elpidia and the two kids being led to the cop car and driven away to detention as Jimmy watches in the foreground, forlorn.

This was what Elizabeth and John wanted me to change to a more hopeful ending. But what was Boyle's real life about but disaster and defeat? In my heart, this was so right even if I had to pay a price for it. Any other way would be dishonest about what our government was really doing in Central America.

The film was over — here, now, finally. I just couldn't believe it, and sat down at the side of the desert road, stunned with fatigue. Jimmy came and sat next to me, and in my diary I have him saying, "You know, it might've been my best performance. You kept me off balance, confused enough that I let things happen I usually don't. You made me vulnerable. Usually, I'm in complete control . . . You're not going to believe this, but I really love you, and I think you made a great film. I want this to be the one they put on our gravestones. The one that we're most proud of." Although it would still take me a little time to trust him again, these were big words from Jimmy and reflected one of his dual personalities — no doubt Dr. Jekyll. Yet I do think we actually started liking each other through this adversity we'd endured. And life does have these impossible turnarounds if you let them happen to you, and don't stay in "complete control."

Our relations ripened in later years into a mature friendship, each of us knowing the other's character from seeing the worst and the best we had to offer. Through the years, I produced the Emmy Award–winning TV movie *Indictment: The McMartin Trial* (1995) with Jimmy in the lead role, as well as *Killer: A Journal of Murder* (1995). And I cast him ten years after *Salvador* as the dread H. R. Haldeman, the president's chief of staff, in *Nixon* (1995), followed by his turn as a corrupt football team doctor in *Any Given Sunday* (1999). Jimmy, to this day, remains a bachelor who seems to have the most fun playing high-stakes poker; he tells me he's "one of the top five in the nation." Of course. Jimmy is Jimmy, larger than life, and how can we ever know the truth?

The battles of production are not to be confused with finishing a film and winning the war. The two most treacherous stages of this process are (1) the editing, and (2) the marketing and distribution of the movie. I would come to realize that it's in the marketing and distribution where the game gets even more intense; it's where the money is. And we directors, actors, writers, producers, outside studio control, might be the colorful buccaneers of olden times who captain the ships and steal the treasures, but it's the empires that still control the seas and the trade routes — and the banks. And that's where the fate of the film lies.

Editing the film over the next four months would be both tedious and terrifying, in that I seemed almost always to be on the edge of losing control of it, either to Daly's distribution needs or, more insidiously, to the forces of convention. Case in point: the ending, wherein I resisted consistent pressure to change it to a more upbeat finale. I could have finished the film with a ride into the sunset with Jimmy and his new family on the bus without any ugly surprises from the US Border Patrol — and no reshoot would have been necessary. Another stark example was a contentious five-minute conversation set in the garden of an exclusive Cuernavaca country club. The scene is all dialogue, as Boyle lets loose on a CIA agent, undercover with the State Department, and a Pentagon colonel, who are trying to recruit him as a journalist to spy on the rebels. Boyle's argument is anti-interventionist. The technocrats believe they're fighting communism. "You guys been lying about that from the fucking beginning," Boyle says. "You never presented one shred of proof to the American public that this is anything other than a legitimate peasant revolution. So don't start telling me about the sanctity of military intelligence, not after Chile and Vietnam." They argue back, but he counters, "What are death squads but the CIA's brain-child . . . but you'll run with them, because they're anti-Moscow, you'll let them close the universities, wipe out the Catholic Church, kill whoever they want, wipe out the best minds in the country, but as long as they're not commies, that's okay. That, Colonel, is bullshit. You've created a major Frankenstein, that's what."

The scene built to a powerful close: "So that's why you guys are here, looking for some kind of post-Vietnam experience, like you need a rerun or something? Turn this place into a military zone. Pour in another $120 million so they can get more chopper parades in the sky? . . . All you're doing is bringing misery to these people. For Chrissake, Jack, you gotta take care of the people first, in the name of human decency, something we Americans are supposed to believe in, you've at least gotta try to have something of a just society here!" This was all rendered relatively quickly in machine gun dialogue from Jimmy, somewhat similarly to what I did later with Donald Sutherland's sixteen-minute near monologue in *JFK*. Because it was wordy and "on the nose," there was resistance to it. But I fought for the scene in its entirety, because I thought it would probably be my last shot at saying what I believed about our government, Vietnam, and Central America. It would be my gravestone speech that would forever distinguish me from the scripts I'd written in the past but whose contours, as directed by others, concealed murky liberal sentiments at their core. If this was my last film, which I was now expecting it to be, I did not want it to be, once again, misunderstood.

In that same vein of taking stands, I decided to leave the ICM agency after these four unsatisfactory years and try this new CAA. I'd still be paying ICM for another year, but Paula Wagner and Mike Menschel, accepting that economic arrangement, had already been on set in Mexico; no one from ICM even asked to come visit. I went into CAA for the "final sale," a meeting with the notorious Mike Ovitz, whose reputation was fast-growing as the new "gunfighter" in town. I found him to be a master — in psychology, certainly. He was sure of himself, aggressive right off the bat, keeping me in suspense as to what he was going to say next. His secret was that, as the meeting goes, he's creating the suspense, not you. He started with "You're a mystery to me, Oliver, your career . . . You're a talent here . . ." (his hand indicates a high bar) "of the highest plane — with Robert Towne, Elaine May, but you make films here . . ." (with another gesture, he indicates a lower bar) "another level of people. You know, I met you years ago," which I didn't recall. "I find you very changed — calmer." This, of course, put me in sensitive territory. Jesus, how bad was I? When I mentioned my relationship with John Daly, he made it clear that although he was okay with that, they only "half-believed" in Daly (he was, after all, outside CAA's ecosystem, hardly a big buyer) — "but I think we can get you alternatives." With his whispered confidences and strong body language, Mike left the room with the same sense of mystery with which he'd entered — and left the impression that he could have been a leader in any field if he so chose. The only obstacle, I came to believe, was that he made too many people jealous. The nature of the business beast. Not to make others jealous. This is perhaps one of the hardest and most subtle obstacles anyone, especially in the film business, faces, but it's true for every facet of life. Jealousy is an underrated emotion, an invisible land mine really, a barrier of energy that would trip me as well, time and again.

I looked forward to visiting the Malibu set of *8 Million Ways to Die*, which was finally filming. Deep in my own troubles in Mexico, I had not paid any attention to its progress, as there was no further money coming to me because a fellow writer, Lance Hill, was co-credited. A third writer, Robert Towne, who remained anonymous, called and, in his gentlemanly way, told me he'd done a four-week rewrite, "purely a matter of economics" in that, at the request of Ashby and the company, he'd transposed the story from New York to Los Angeles. He shared sympathy with me in that he knew the feeling of being "robbed of my script." By the rules of our Writers Guild, it was kind of him, as neither Ashby nor the producers had bothered to notify me that I was being rewritten. When I looked at the script and hardly recognized anything I'd written, I should have taken my name off. But there were residuals and possible profits due. With *Salvador* in the heavy liability column, I was in no position to rebel.

Mine was a strange visit to the Malibu location, given the contrast to my *Salvador* experience. I rode up in an elaborate elevated tram to a cliffside fantasy glass house lit by giant arcs, almost like a candy box; the night lighting itself cost a fortune. When I got off the tram, the location parking lot was filled with Porsches, Maseratis, motorcycles, all kinds of stylish transpo fit for a well-paid LA crew. The starting "call" had been for 5:30 p.m., but no one seemed to be around or in a hurry. Dinner (in this case called "lunch") was being prepared on the scale of ancient Rome — shrimp, pastas, steaks, anything you wanted off white tablecloths set on outdoor tables.

"Where's Hal?" I asked.

"He's in the trailer with Jeff." When I inquired doing what, all I could get was that he was "rehearsing" and/or "talking." "He's been in there for an hour."

I didn't want to interrupt. I learned that the line producer was pissed at Ashby and had left the set. Apparently there'd been a lot of this "rehearsal" going on, with Ashby being indecisive about his shooting plans.

In any event, I enjoyed the dinner, talking with the intelligent and delightful Rosanna Arquette and the gracious Andy Garcia in his first film role, who described a movie to me where there were no more hookers, no New York City, no urban density or grit. It was a completely different film from what I'd written, with a somewhat unreal climactic shootout between Garcia and Bridges on the very tram I'd just come in on. The sixty-day shooting schedule was going to seventy days, the cost, I gathered, was at $12.5 million and climbing. I could've made three *Salvador*s with this. No rush, either, as Ashby came out with Bridges for the first shot at 11 p.m., hardly knowing who I was. Bridges was polite, shy. I went home bored, depleted. Farewell, *8 Million*.

Some nine months later, I slipped into Broadway's Criterion Theatre in New York and walked out in disgust, not believing what they'd done to my script, my character. How bad could it be? The reviews had been mediocre, dispassionate. It didn't hurt my career or help it; it was another forgotten film. But if you knew the inner workings of that screenplay, they'd left nothing of value in it. How could Ashby and Towne, two pros, have done this? It was offensive, like seeing your own baby aborted bloodily in front of you. I was out of the country when they released it, but if I'd been able to screen it, which they hadn't offered to me, I would've used a pseudonym — "Huckleberry Twist" or something — in the credits.

Eventually I saw the film again on video and found it simply meaningless and dull, and I thought of that $16 to $18 million churned up out of the ether — for this? PSO, the producing entity, would soon go belly-up. All that angst and that crazy psycho producer with his two accents, trophy family, and grandiose cocaine dreams, and how upset I once got — all that was gone, a legacy of ashes. No hard feelings, in fact no feelings at all. I'd been paid well — and that is how I believe many Hollywood people feel in the end, on their way to a grave at Forest Lawn.

Although we'd finished *Salvador* in Las Vegas on the last day of August, John Daly now wanted the film ready for a Christmas release for his new Hemdale distribution company, which, through its new chief, Peter Myers, had a distribution arrangement with MGM, supposedly worth $4 million in prints and ads. MGM, on shaky financial ground since the mid-1970s, had become more of a rent-a-distributor outlet. But they were better than none. So there was hope.

I had to move fast — too fast. The film, when roughly assembled, was three hours and forty-five minutes, but I knew it could work, because the Woods character was exciting, magnetic, even if sometimes repulsive. Jimmy was on fire. Working intensely, we cut it down to two hours and thirty, then, with great difficulty, to two hours and nineteen, then, in deepening pain, to two hours and eleven minutes, and finally two hours and five minutes. To keep pace with my mind, I supervised a system of editing with multiple editors in different workspaces. I brought our second editor, whom we'd been using throughout, up from Mexico, along with a third in the US who was really an assistant editor but who followed my instincts better than my first editor, with whom I still was having difficulties communicating; something in our natures was as allergic as cat and dog. It was a painful, self-flagellating process, like cutting out my own flesh. But I was driven.

Daly dropped into the edit room each week, looking over my shoulder, and we had several confrontations over the rape of the nuns, the sex, the violence, the ending. I soon gathered that John had a reputation for being heavily involved in the editing on his other productions, which led to some public battles, notably with Jim Cameron on *Terminator*, as well as with others on *At Close Range* and *Hoosiers*. I did have some leverage with him in that I had repossessed my *Platoon* rights; the free option I'd given to Arnold Kopelson had expired. He'd struck out and been unable to finance the film. Of course, Daly did not have to make *Platoon,* though he still wanted to. Additionally, since I had not yet been paid for *Salvador,* I still theoretically owned the underlying rights to it. All this, in the end, was a negotiation over my right to cut the film I'd directed the way I wanted. John joked with my lawyer, Bob Marshall, in reference to my stubbornness in editing, that "Oliver has a bullet in his head, which got lost in there somewhere, no one knows. You can tell from those mad eyes of his." Shades of Gore Vidal's "metal plate." Deep down, I think John respected me for fighting back so hard, even if he sensed the film might be a losing cause. He once told me his father had been a boxer in England and had always taken in strays, dogs and cats and such, and that had left a deep impression on his mind. I think, in a way, I was his "stray."

We had a public screening in LA in early November for 160 people. There was little laughter, a lower-than-average score, the film too vulgar and gross, a turn-off to the middle range in the market. One woman in the focus group afterward was screaming out her hatred for the film, which marked me. Joe Farrell, for many years a professional screener and researcher for the studios, whom I came to trust, described it as a "hesitant audience . . . a reluctant liking." I saw hope in this; I too believed they wanted to like *Salvador,* and that it was my job to fix it. I kept trimming, squeezing, shifting, improving.

But by mid-November, the boom came down when Mike Medavoy and an Orion-invited group of twenty people, including some directors, screened the film. I wasn't invited. Daly went, and it turned out worse than I could've imagined. Medavoy apparently cut off the screening at the midpoint, and they all walked out! As Daly told me, they "loathed the film" for its "unsympathetic characters, its excesses of violence and gore." Not only did Orion not want the film, but also they pulled out of their vague agreement to distribute *Platoon*. I was stunned, deeply wounded, growing paranoid that I had enemies everywhere, and that an underlying reason for

Medavoy's displeasure was that in his neoliberal view of the world, my film was "communist, revolutionary," and overly critical of US policy in South and Central America. It was around this time too that the Reagan administration was making another hard push to legitimize the barbaric "Contras" against Nicaragua's leftist government. And it didn't help when the Mary-knoll Sisters, without having seen it, sent a letter stating their concern over the depiction of the rape and murder of the nuns from their order; they threatened legal action unless it was made clear that the victims had "no political involvement there . . . [but were] solely religious, and must be so portrayed." For the record, it had been Alexander Haig, Reagan's hot-tempered secretary of state, who actually described the nuns as "pistol-packing" as a way to possibly exonerate the motives of the killers. Still, I cautiously removed an actual reference to their order from Cindy Gibb's lips.

A series of harsh letters followed from Daly to my lawyer, reasserting his right to re-edit in these circumstances. He specified twelve cuts, saying about the film, audiences "want to like it, but you make them stop and hate it." Some of his ideas seemed reasonable to me. Negotiations followed between John and my lawyer Bob Marshall with Arnold Kopelson, our foreign salesman on *Salvador,* helping to negotiate a settlement in which I agreed to make a certain number of cuts, and Jimmy Woods, of all people, would be the third-party arbitrator. My views of violence at that time, it's true, could be extreme. When Kopelson told me he'd shown a part of the film for buyers abroad where a soldier's face was blown off, the buyers objected vehemently. To me it was a story point, a cold revenge execution at close range.

While all this was going on, Alex Ho came back into my life and returned to the Philippines with me to plan a shoot for early the next year. All of this was financed by John because, as I say, he liked *Platoon* on its own merits, unrelated to *Salvador.* My old "friend" Dino had even weighed in with John, wondering in his guttural English, "Why you wanna make *Platoon?*" As if John had to have his mind checked out. And why, I had to wonder, did these people persist in haunting me? A good part of my life's anxieties had come from trying to outrun my ghosts. In my favor, it certainly helped that Stanley Kubrick's Vietnam epic *Full Metal Jacket* was beginning to shoot (for an entire year, it turned out), and John Irvin's super-patriotic Vietnam film *Hamburger Hill* was also set to go. The competition in this case stoked the fires.

And after Alex rendered a budget for nine weeks at $5.6 million, Film Finances, stipulating that they'd never bond Gerald Green again but trusting Alex, rather promptly said *Platoon* was "a go" for February 23, 1986. Holy cow! Unlike *Salvador,* this was going too smoothly to really believe it, and for the next weeks I took every day as it came, one by one, trusting nothing. Although I wanted to work with Gerald again, I had no interest in making *Platoon* in Mexico, where his money was. John, with an extraordinary generosity of spirit, asked me if I wanted to let Kopelson back in as the producer on the film. No doubt he was favored by Film Finances, and his foreign sales might help in the overall structure of the film. So I said yes, but this would end badly for John in a bitter lawsuit from Arnold. And right away, Arnold made his weight felt in his refusal to accept Alex Ho as his equal, seeing to it that Alex took "co-producer" status instead; this would lead to many unforeseen problems.

John also made it quite clear that he would back *Platoon* 100 percent, with or without the Orion distribution deal (Orion had turned down *Salvador*) and that I would have "final cut" in that if I didn't accept Hemdale's cuts, I'd have the right — if Hemdale did not then want to distribute the film — to go out and sell it myself. It was a risk I was quite willing to take to preserve my vision of the film. Damn the consequences. Full steam ahead. Even though I still didn't think *Platoon* was going to be made, John's confidence was deeply reassuring and during these four months helped me get through the turbulent uncertainty over *Salvador.* In fact, it was a dream moment. Why? Why with all this pain on *Salvador* did John still believe in me? He told Riordan in 1995, "Oliver puts 100% of himself into a film. It all goes up on the screen. For *Salvador,* he waived his salary, he waived his expenses. I think he would have given up his house. For him, it's the film. And that is why, whether he gets things right or wrong, there is an intensity up on the screen that could only come from a man with absolute passion." Bless him, his boxing father's spirit resides in him, and no matter how critically some people speak of him, I've always known John as a man of generous heart who cared very much about the things we did together.

Sadly, Gerald Green would never be bonded or work again with Film

Finances. *Platoon,* which he'd first discovered and brought to the attention of both Kopelson and Daly, would've changed his life, but he had to drop out. He went on to make other films, none notable, and for years afterward always told me *Salvador,* although it had cost him his reputation and his financing base in Mexico, was the film he was most proud of. Years later he was convicted under idiosyncratic US laws of bribing Thai government officials, and after a stint in prison, he ended up, with his wife, under house arrest wearing an ankle monitor. When I visited him during this incarceration, despite his Graham Greene frown, he was the same cool James Bond–ish "Englishman," not one dry martini different. You'd think, despite all his worrying, what more could go wrong for him? Maybe he'd relax a little more. And maybe he did. I hope so. He "shuffled off this mortal coil" in 2015 at the age of eighty-three, not long before the late, great Richard Boyle passed on, well worn at the age of seventy-four. Two rascals without whom *Salvador* would never have been born.

I kept at the *Salvador* cut, making it tighter, funnier, the usual "sweating" that goes on for most filmmakers overly doubting and questioning their basic sanity — and then going over it again. Rewriting is something I learned, taught to me by others like Robert Bolt, Marty Bregman, and my father, and when you think about it, film is such an elastic medium that editing becomes another form of rewriting. First, you write solo — it's in your head. Then when you direct it, you're exteriorizing it, sharing it with all; you're acting it out. And when you're editing it, it's your last chance to be alone, to rethink and rewrite. Most every dialogue can be cheated in or out of the film; new dialogues can be written, off camera, or looped into an actor's mouth. Significant cuts can be made, or linkages you never saw before you shot the film, and some things you thought so crucial to tell in the script now become unnecessary or redundant. The edit becomes as expansive as your imagination. But at a certain point you do go public again, partners looking on as you try different things, some of which don't work at all, and you bleed in front of others. To edit is to suffer because it is always difficult to close the book.

I went over the film with John reel by reel, slowly, torturously — at first with Jimmy as third party, and then just me and John. And honestly, the more closely he looked at the film, the more difficult he found it to cut this or that after all. We all share in judging another's behavior, but the more we see something, the more we understand it; the less we see it, the harsher we can be in cutting it. Empathy is born from understanding, and yet sometimes our empathy leads us astray. I venture to say that it's better to err on the side of saving what you love rather than cutting it. Because if you cut it, no matter what you're thinking, you'll always miss it years later. Find a way to make it work. I must say, to his credit, we cut less than John had planned.

Georges Delerue, the French composer who'd allied with François Truffaut for many years, had moved to the US, and Budd Carr, a canny and tasteful music industry executive who'd become my music supervisor on all my films, introduced us. We shared the French language and its humor, and that November, for very little money, Georges produced a magnificent, sweepingly romantic score, which lifted *Salvador* at least 25 percent but came too late for the people who'd passed — which now, unfortunately, included MGM, which was backing out of its vague distribution arrangement with Daly's Hemdale. Four million dollars in promotion and advertising gone.

We brought our film to its bloody conclusion just in time to make the Christmas date to validate Daly's tax shelter for the 1985 fiscal year, which required *Salvador* to be shown in an American theater before the end of the year. In any case, I couldn't "touch" the film anymore — we were out of money. Hemdale chose, of all places, Elizabeth's hometown of San Antonio, and opened it, for legal purposes only, with a minimum of advertising. For the real opening, Hemdale planned a small six-city release starting with three theaters in New York in March of '86, then other cities depending on bookings, and Los Angeles in mid-April. Not the kind of broad-shouldered release I'd had on *The Hand*, by any means.

Elizabeth, Sean, and I thus headed to San Antonio for Christmas — but there was to be no fairy-tale ending. The ten o'clock weekend show at an upscale theater held maybe a dozen people, while next door, Spielberg's *The Color Purple* was packed, as was Sydney Pollack's *Out of Africa*. How do I describe the tight knot in the stomach or throat when you walk into a theater and find only a smattering of people spread around large, empty spaces? I kept reminding myself that this wasn't the real opening, nor was this a test for sample size; nonetheless, it was a hard comedown for Christmas. And for that matter, it was becoming clearer we weren't going to register much when we opened officially the following year.

I was not comfortable with parts of my movie; it was crude and, yes, at times choppy. But what it had was power, vitality, originality, and something not seen often in American film — some critics would pick up on it — a radical and dramatic political commitment reminiscent of some young playwright of the 1930s or 1940s, a Clifford Odets or an Arthur Miller, bursting to tell a truth in a blunt, dynamic way.

I also realized two things, both painful: (1) although I'd been deeply involved for a year in Salvador the country, not many people in my own country cared at all about this small nation, this "shithole" we were helping to ruin; and (2) I'd overestimated my film. It was exciting, fresh, made in spite of overwhelming odds, but it was not "great" — and that fell heavily on my own shoulders. But I was proud of it. I'd achieved what Marty Scorsese had asked of us in film school: "make it personal." I'd made the Salvador story mine. I knew the effort we all made, and I knew there was a classical worth in this film that could not be denied.

In my mind, I was no longer "only a writer." I'd grown, finally, by fire, into a director. Michael Cimino told the press, "I don't think Oliver wants to direct. He prefers writing." But maybe Michael missed the fusion in me of two different parents that was coming into being — a father who was a writer, a mother who was a director, a giver of parties, a bringer together of diverse elements. Why not? Actors exteriorize our scripts. So do directors. From inside ourselves to outside. But perhaps because Mom and Dad, France and America, had been so different, this contradiction had grown inside me so intensely that I was now what Homer said of his most self-conscious Odysseus — "double-minded."

I dedicated *Salvador* to my father, who I wished had lived a little longer to see it. Even he would've laughed at the madness of Richard Boyle. And maybe even come to believe that his "idiot son" had not turned into "a bum" after all.

9

Back to the Jungle

My Christmas present for 1985 came in the form of Steve Pines telling me I was "cash broke." Suspicious that he was still a victim to his cocaine habits, I was furious at first, then frustrated. How could my last reserves have vanished so quickly while I was making the one and only film that I really wanted to make? It was not fair.

Back in the early '70s, when I was "broke broke" and married, I still managed to borrow $5,000 at, as I remember, a 23 percent interest rate from Beneficial Finance to pay my pro football gambling debts. But after separating from Najwa, I was "really broke" — 20 bucks on a good day, sometimes not even bus fare, and late-night walks to a bed across scraping cold streets, my mind given to fantasies.

Now I owned properties, but as Steve explained, I had no cash, just liabilities. There's a big difference, as most Americans who live on credit know; so Steve finessed a small advance through a bank to get some cash, and fortunately, in January 1986, the production money on *Platoon*, managed by Alex Ho, started to flow. It had to, because there was no way to build our sets to be ready for a late February start in the Philippines on a movie that all of a sudden *other* people wanted to make as quickly as possible. Every film is dictated to by its own logic, and for once the film was carrying me instead of me it; it was a bizarre feeling. Nothing like this had ever happened on my three previous outings, when I'd grown accustomed to an abiding state of fear and uncertainty.

Orion had been in and then out of *Platoon* when Mike Medavoy called me up to his office, wanting to "clear the air" on *Salvador*. As I'd been hurt by his turning off the film mid-screening, he apologized by way of blaming John Daly for having told him he was seeing a finished film — which was rubbish, of course, intended to excuse his behavior. Perhaps the mood on Vietnam was shifting in our favor. I have no idea why, but Mike now cautioned me to make *Platoon* "better than *Salvador* . . . non-gratuitously . . . don't rub our noses in the violence; make each character an involving human being for the audience." He cited Kubrick's classic antiwar film *Paths of Glory* (1957) as a model. There was a charm to Mike, a political animal through and through. He was like Bill Clinton — handsome, "liberal" in spite of his "eyes in the back of his head" slipperiness, but it was charming that he never thought of it that way. His was simply the "politics of life." Deceit or prevarication, in his world, was required to survive, and with savvy and cunning, he did so. And if I wanted to go on in the film business, I was realizing that, by its standard, Mike was actually one of the "good guys," and I, by that standard, was "a radical"; but I could be a radical with a job as long as I had an understanding of Medavoy's needs — Orion's needs. I guess this meeting was an audition to see if "the strong-willed, hard-to-control Stone," who'd made the infamous and "bloodthirsty" *The Hand*, which had lost money for them (the ultimate humiliation in Hollywood), would "play ball"; in which case Orion was suddenly back in the *Platoon* business as our foreign and potentially domestic distributor — pending, of course, my parole. I welcomed Orion's partnership.

Charlie Sheen, the younger brother of my first choice, Emilio Estevez, three years before, reminded me with his dark eyebrows of a young Montgomery Clift in *A Place in the Sun* (1951); there was a kind of puzzled gaze to him that I'd also had as a young soldier new to Vietnam. He'd been interesting in Penny Spheeris's *The Boys Next Door,* and although I was seriously considering John Cusack, who had more experience as an actor and projected ambiguity, John felt older. I wanted an innocence Charlie projected but didn't possess. Daly backed my choice, but at the last minute, before deals were signed, Arnold Kopelson and the dreaded Richard Soames at Film Finances asked me to meet with Keanu Reeves, another up-and-coming star, as there'd already been rumors of Charlie's "partying" and a possible lack of seriousness. Reeves was exciting, sexy, and seemed perfect — perhaps too perfect. We made him an offer but he passed, telling his agent he "hated the violence in the script." Considering what he would go on to do in films, the mindset behind this decision is confusing, but Keanu seemed in search of himself; some people say he still is.

For the role of the ultra-realist Sergeant Barnes, Jimmy Woods, to whom I returned in spite of my frustrations and concerns, passed. I could imagine his reaction: "A Philippine jungle with Oliver? Yikes! More dysentery, bugs, reliving his nightmare? No thanks!" His agent told us by way of explanation, "Jimmy doesn't want to play an antagonist anymore," which means "he wants to play a protagonist," which means the lead, preferably a "hero" — and Barnes was definitely not that. A young Kevin Costner, Bruce Willis, Jeff Fahey (the future star of Clint Eastwood's *White Hunter Black Heart*) also passed, as did Scott Glenn. What's wrong with this role? The late Chris Penn, Sean's younger brother, did want it, animalistic in his excitement, proposing to lose twenty pounds and threatening to "terrorize the other actors." I loved his defiant spirit, but he had to withdraw suddenly because of a hernia that required rest. This is where the Fates stepped in. Tom Berenger was "there," he'd always been there, unassuming, polite, but just not exciting like the real Barnes had been. Tom told me, "I was born to do it," but he was still, in Hollywood terms, a "pretty boy," a possible romantic lead, but that really wasn't him. I sensed in him a raw, seething backcountry quality that could be unsettling, and at the urging of our mutual agent, Paula Wagner, I went with Tom, albeit with hesitation. And he grew day by day, with the skillful help of Gordon Smith's realistic prosthetics and makeup scars, into an approximation of the real thing. If he survived that war, I've always wondered if the actual "Sergeant Barnes" ever saw the film and recognized what Berenger was doing?

We'd looked at many Native American actors in 1983–84, and again in 1985–86, but couldn't find a Hispanic Apache for Sergeant Elias, who looked like a young Jim Morrison, to whom I'd sent the earliest version of *Platoon* — called "Break" — in 1969 but never heard back. Deeply disappointed, I shifted my perspective for the role, and when I saw Billy Friedkin's *To Live and Die in LA* (1985), I was intrigued by its villain, Willem Dafoe, with his prominent cheekbones and strange, intimate voice. He was of mixed European origin with a flat Wisconsin intonation, but there was a "soul" in him, a gentleness that could radiate from those eyes. He was a hunch at best, but as with Berenger, I felt "something." In a way, perhaps, I didn't make "the choice" as much as "the choice" made me — and as we went along, I felt better and better about both men.

Pat Golden, an independent casting agent out of New York, led us to several new faces in Kevin Dillon, Paul Sanchez, Richard Edson, Mark Moses; and among our African American actors, we found Keith David, Forest Whitaker, Tony Todd, Reggie Johnson, Corey Glover, and Corkey Ford. Roughly 15 percent of my three combat platoons had been African American, so we pulled several more youths as background extras from Nigerian students in the Philippines. In Los Angeles, we cast a small role with a handsome newcomer who had "movie star" written all over him but was still raw — that was Johnny Depp from Kentucky. In general, I wanted a southern and small-town American look, as well as some Hispanics, and accordingly, several colorful new faces drifted in on both coasts — Francesco Quinn (Anthony's son); Chris Pedersen, a surfer type from California; David Neidorf, a roughneck with attitude; a dozen others — twenty-five or thirty in all, ready to work out of the country for the first time in their lives. It was exciting, like assembling a pirate crew to sail with; who knew where we were heading?

I was apprehensive as well. Could I really do this after so long, remember the innumerable details, actually pull this off? Had I shot the film too many times in my head, written too many revisions of the script? Cimino had once warned me, "Don't leave the game in the locker room," by which he meant a director can overprepare a film, take the life out of it before he shoots it. And I was tired, as I'd hardly had more than a day off here and there since shooting and editing *Salvador*. In truth, after all my past up-and-down excitement, I approached the actual shooting detached and somewhat emotionless, a workmanlike director, trying to keep a steady course. Perhaps because *Salvador* had been so overly dramatic.

The Pentagon's Deputy Director of Entertainment Media had rejected the script for their assistance, describing it as "wholly unrealistic," citing the language, the treatment of Vietnamese civilians, and the "fragging" (killing of fellow soldiers). No cooperation was possible; in fact, they put out an advisory in the Philippines at the Clark and Subic Bay bases against

US troops participating in any filming activity. Although I'd served with distinction, I never kidded myself that the Pentagon was in my corner. I'd seen the pseudo-patriotic war movies to which they'd given millions of dollars and equipment. Instead, I hired a thrifty ex-marine with some twenty years' experience, Dale Dye. He actually hunted me down from an announcement about the film in the trade papers and insisted on presenting himself at my *Salvador* editing room in his jungle fatigues, as I remember, with a knife and pistol on his belt. I was struck by his "Missouri-mule-in-a-hailstorm" bent as much as his avid hunger to "get Vietnam right for once!" He was a strong, silver-haired, take-charge guy, thoroughly right wing and in conflict with my views, but I knew what I wanted and I wouldn't be deterred by Dale's theories on staging combat shots. What mattered was that he was a "detail freak," and that's what I needed. He'd train the shit out of the cast, maintain a military discipline throughout the shoot, and stretch every dollar we had to its breaking point. He brought on three young military veterans to help him, and I added my Los Angeles cop friend Stanley White from *Year of the Dragon,* also a Vietnam marine, to the mix.

By early February, after a turbulent fraudulent election in the Philippines, things were changing unpredictably, and our production plans were suddenly in jeopardy. By mid-month, the country was at the edge of civil war. The dictator, Ferdinand Marcos, in power more than twenty years, and his outspoken wife, Imelda, had lost to Cory Aquino, the widow of an assassinated political reformer, but were not about to give up that power. The military was reportedly split in two. Clearly it was time for Marcos, who was sick as a dog with a kidney infection, to leave. Would he? Kopelson and Soames at Film Finances were worried. Agents were calling. Several of them had already rebelled at the terms of our non–Screen Actors Guild contracts, which required their clients to complete a two-week, 24/7 training course with Captain Dye. But in the US, per their SAG union contracts, actors were guaranteed a twelve-hour day with a full twelve-hour "turnaround," including travel (the interval between exiting and reentering the workplace). That was an impossible condition if we wanted to make a realistic war film in the fifty days we had, but on top of that, we had parents calling about their "babies" going out of the country to who knows what revolution on some ill-fated island. We were in a bind. It would cost a fortune and probably kill the film to relocate. The best solution was to stall, not panic. Amidst the political turmoil, we pushed the start date some three weeks later to March 20, which would cost us significant money, though for once we had a real contingency fund of 10 percent to tide us over.

Nonetheless, several actors dropped out, and I recast these roles from a list of alternatives I'd accumulated over the years. Tensely we followed the daily situation. Several participants, including Bob Richardson and Willem Dafoe, were already on location, telling us the streets were intermittently chaotic. Rumors were flying: some whispered that Marcos had already fled, which was not true, others that he was preparing a counter-coup. Once again I felt powerless, everything out of my control. *Salvador,* which I was promoting in New York to open on March 7, was not going at all the way I'd hoped, and now *Platoon* seemed to be falling apart *again* — two films so dear to me dying at the same time. It was as if the Fates were mocking my hopes with this crashing catastrophe.

By February 22, with mass media in the US calling for Marcos to leave, President Reagan was quietly shifting US support away from him. And on February 24, Marcos finally abandoned ship with some $15 million in jewels, gold, and cash to a secure base in Hawaii, never to return. It was later learned that after years of corruption, billions of dollars were missing from the Philippine treasury. At the presidential palace, which was overrun by the "People Power Revolution" in the streets, they'd found three thousand pairs of Imelda's shoes, which became an international headline and the highlight of a museum tour.

The tension of waiting was agonizing for me. The February New York weather had been crisp and clear despite eight inches of packed snow on the sidewalks. It came as another body blow when the Cannes Film Festival rejected *Salvador* as too "action-packed," which meant to them "commercial," which meant popular — yet it clearly wasn't that either. It would fall in between. And it would be the first of several Cannes rejections under Gilles Jacob, the French "mandarin" in charge of the festival for many years. He always seemed to look down on my films as somewhat crass, and I thus characterized him as one of those "chief priests" trying to control the culture by persecuting those of us who were rebels. How could they turn their backs on a film bringing attention to real human rights violations during a cruel civil war? Films critical of the "Establishment" had, in the past, been recognized at Cannes, particularly *Z* and *The Battle of Algiers*, but the French intelligentsia in the mid-'80s was subtly changing and becoming more "Establishment" itself. It was a strange turn of events. *Salvador's* French distributor, a small company led by Annie François in spirit, still fiercely believed in the film, but one of France's best-known leftist newspapers, *Libération*, had blasted *Salvador*—which they hadn't even seen—as far back as December, describing me as "a madman of the right" and dismissing *Midnight Express* (which had a record run in Paris) as simply "merde" (translation: shit). *Salvador, Libération* opined, would no doubt be "Stone's chance to kill nuns!" It can get really ugly on the front lines of the print world.

But there was something bigger going on in Western media that began in the late 1970s and solidified around Reagan and Margaret Thatcher in England. It was a sort of manufactured intellectual "neoliberalism," worshipful of capitalism, which could be identified with empire, NATO, and the Western military alliance, strongly tied to the World Bank and IMF economic controls. It not only was chasing down the dying Soviet empire but also was attacking any supposed revolutionary offshoots in Latin America and elsewhere. The "neo" in "neoliberalism" meant, I believe, that in no way did it resemble true liberalism.

The defiant part of me was yelling back at these ideologues, "Fuck you! People will see this film in spite of you!" Arnold Kopelson, for example, was succeeding more and more in the mainstream with foreign sales on *Salvador*—$250K in Italy, $200K in Spain, $55K in Indonesia, all proof that I wasn't alone and others believed in this film too. Yet Germany and Japan, two of the biggest buyers in the world, were still hedging. As a result, my interviews with the press were growing angrier, defensive, and more political: "Central America has a right to be what it wants to be. If a Russian nuclear sub can be fifteen miles off the coast of New York Harbor, what difference does it make if the Russians are in Nicaragua [another false rumor at the time] . . . [I]t's not a question of capitalism or communism when your kid dies of dysentery or diarrhea. American government officials don't seem to realize that revolution is a response to social and economic conditions, not a Cold War game. It's a North-South conflict, not an East-West one." Even my late father would've agreed with me on this one.

Ginger Varney of the *LA Weekly,* a respected alternative weekly that had a large film following, ran a positive cover story on *Salvador* ("Oliver Stone: Cinema's Low-Rent Lord Jim"), fascinated by my perceived evolution from '60s conservative to '80s "liberal" ("Hollywood still has no idea what to do with Oliver Stone"). *American Film* magazine, widely read in serious film circles, said that "Woods was brilliant" and Stone "the master of the kick them in the stomach screenplay." Sides were being taken, the film polarizing. Some American liberals were disgusted by the Boyle character; others noted that it was unlikely that National Guardsmen prisoners were killed in cold blood by Liberation Front rebels at the battle of Santa Ana, nor for that matter had there been a horse charge there. This was true (certainly about the cavalry), but in showing the execution of the guardsmen, I'd been looking to balance the film, as I suspected it would be slammed as "communist" and pro-revolutionary. Boyle had told me it was well documented that some rebel units had executed captured prisoners, especially officers with known death squad connections, but that for the most part, prisoners were unharmed and sometimes released. This had a powerful propaganda effect of making government troops more willing to surrender, knowing they wouldn't be harmed. Seeking this balance, I now think, was a mistake on my part.

Jack Kroll, the esteemed veteran critic from *Newsweek,* took the film seriously, saw it twice, talked at length with me about it — and would write a thoughtful review that had no meaning at the box office. Janet Maslin, the new second-string critic for the *New York Times,* told Marion Billings that although she "liked it very much," unfortunately for us, she was going on maternity leave the week of our release, and she further advised us that the *Times* was turning "neocon" in general under the direction of Arthur Gelb and Abe Rosenthal.

Although the film was opening in New York on March 7, there were no trailers, posters, billboards, or TV spots ready — a disastrous situation, according to Marion and the gentlemanly Arthur Manson, who joined our team last minute as an independent marketing adviser; he'd been in the business since the 1950s and knew all the exhibitors, but it was very late in the game. The signs were all pointing to a commercial disaster in March–April, roughly the same time of year when we'd released *The Hand* in 1981, a parallel that kept reverberating in my brain. My anger was internalized at first until it erupted at one point during an interview with the prominent left-wing journalist Alexander Cockburn, a man who loved to provoke his subjects, and I told him:

> I'm so depressed by the power of a few ignorant assholes to determine the course of the political debate on Central America —Jesse Helms, Robert Dole, Reagan, Bush—this whole Mafia of cold warriors that has existed since my birth. I'm beginning to think that the only solution is a war that involves Americans, because it's the only way this country is going to wake up to what is really going on down there. I think America has to bleed. I think the corpses have to pile up. I think American boys have to die again. Let the mothers weep and mourn. Let the mothers fucking wake up to what's going on. Because they don't give a shit about the 100,000 Guatemalans that got killed because of our technology, but when an American dies in Honduras, they're going to get upset. I tell you, I'm never going to let my kid go. I'll break the law, I'll go to Canada. I'll take him out of the country. The only problem would be if he decided he wanted to go.

These are strong words, and I'm sure I crossed the line with a lot of people who would never go to a movie made by a proponent of such revolt, which to the normal American mind is inconceivable. But I was fighting a losing battle, going on TV interviews, talking politics, history, anything to get the sleepy public aroused about Central America. The ancient Greeks had a wonderful word, "idiotas," to describe the private person who has no interest in public affairs, whereas "the public man" garners respect. But my timing was terrible, because Reagan was making a serious second push to renew the failing, US-backed "Contra" rebellion against the left-wing Nicaraguan government.

Elizabeth, who'd once been an FBI-surveilled radical, was furious with me. "You can't go on fighting this war, Oliver. You can't go on TV having political debates. It won't bring people in. You've made the movie! Enough. Everything is said . . . Make *Platoon,* and it'll bring attention to *Salvador* by its connection to the subject." She was right, and I was too emotionally involved to be clear and effective, and I stumbled in my naturally defiant way to expend my energies in fighting, hoping, despairing, and fighting some more. It's an endless torment of the soul, because it's your demon, and you're engaging it and making it worse. But sometimes a fighter cannot be logical; he just has to gut it out. I remembered my black-and-white TV in the 1950s and watching Carmen Basilio taking a huge beating at Madison Square Garden from the great Sugar Ray Robinson. Watch Carmen's eyes and imagine the punishment he endures. In my heart, I knew the futility of what I was doing.

When my mother said she'd come to Los Angeles, "but I know you're busy, I won't take your time," I knew she meant she really wanted to see Sean and Elizabeth. "What have I become?" I wrote in my diary. "A Macbeth of workaholics. I've worked straight 17 years, two scripts a year, etc., and what has it brought me? Never been able to relax, but must. I'm always running like a mad rabbit down an Alice in Wonderland hole, always getting bigger or smaller and never knowing what will happen next."

With two weeks until our New York opening and three to the start of our *Platoon* shoot, I flew to Manila in a plane filled with returning exiles, some of whom had spent decades out of their homeland, in their way paralleling my own long journey from Vietnam in '68 and now returning to re-create the war in my film. The exiles were met at the gate by a triumphant and loud press corps. I was happy for them, but I had numerous problems of my own to be dealt with on the film front. In the government changeover, the Philippine military had canceled its contracts with us, though our in-country fixer and "Dragon Lady," Nguyen Win, who was married to an ex-CIA station chief, was able, over three weeks, to arrange for a new relationship with the military, which no doubt cost extra. But for the time being, our cast of thirty young actors were sitting in their hotel rooms in a foreign country with little to do except get in trouble with the local women, until Dale Dye got his "training camp" set up on a local military base in the jungle.

We also had a burgeoning problem with Bruno Rubeo, our production designer. He was behind schedule. We were three weeks away, and bulldozers were still clearing a three-kilometer road into a hilly jungle area. We had a village to erect, an old French church, a base camp on a plain, and a tunnel complex (which we were constructing aboveground) to build. Most damningly, before I'd arrived, there'd been a collapse in that tunnel structure, and a young Filipino worker was killed. It was awful — his family's grief, a formal ceremony of apology, reparations made — and, disturbingly, Bruno was deflecting the blame onto his local construction coordinator. Alex Ho angrily rebutted him on several points, and I was inclined to believe Alex because of Bruno's finger-pointing. As much as I loved Bruno's warmth of soul, and how impressive he'd been under fire on *Salvador,* he'd not won the respect of his work crew.

Relieved to be working at something physical again, I plunged into the jungle, going deep down into almost impossible-to-shoot ravines and up mountains, searching for remote spots that would look exotic but would require arduous, backbreaking labor to haul our cameras and lights a considerable distance from the "safe" base camps film units prefer. Alex's grimace of displeasure gave me special delight. I didn't want to be the typical film director, settling for the convenient. I wanted to make something different, like *Apocalypse Now,* but on a small budget, and I had confidence we could take this strain because *Salvador* had been a killer training ground, and Bob Richardson, our cinematographer again, was more than up for it. After *Salvador,* what could be worse?

I tried to be philosophical from across the Pacific about the upcoming March 7 opening of *Salvador* in New York. But we never had a chance. Besides the paltry advertising, the initial reviews were, for the most part, detached, unhelpful; the third-string critic for the *Times,* Walter Goodman, a neocon politically, wrote a "damning with faint praise"–type review; he described it as a warmed-over Costa-Gavras fantasy propaganda piece, saying that I had a hard time distinguishing between fact and fiction. The *Daily News* and *New York Post* were simply dismissive. And when I called

Elizabeth to get her point of view, she said, "Well, it's the good, the bad, and the ugly," and read me the *Village Voice* piece from David Edelstein. He'd told Marion he'd liked the film but now wrote, "I loved the film the first time, then thought about it. I've been had"; the picture was "pumped-up outrage." Elizabeth called it "the worst review I've ever read." There were some positives. Roger Ebert, out of Chicago in syndication, gave it three and a half out of four stars, although his TV partner, Gene Siskel, gave it a "thumbs down." *Newsday* of Long Island, the Gannett chain, and Kitty Kelley on TV ("dazzling!") all liked it. The critic for the *Hollywood Reporter* wrote, "Too early to tell, but possibly the best film of the year," and *Variety* described it as "disturbingly different, as raw as its protagonist," but without the *Times* (why, oh why, did Janet Maslin have to take maternity leave that week!) and with little promotion, we were DOA in New York. All that work—gone in one weekend. The wind was knocked out of me. Oscar Wilde had summed up this moment for all almost a century before: "My play was a success. The audience was a failure."

I had to keep going now. I thought of the dissidents in Russia I'd known, the POW accounts in Vietnam I'd read. Self-pity is not possible. You must be stronger than your captors—or your critics. My fears for *Platoon* mushroomed. It could sink under the weight of this. What possible women's audience could there be for *Platoon*? Daly would certainly be thinking this now. My sense of violence was too realistic and harsh for most Americans. Maybe I was just too different, "fucked up" by Vietnam. My very nature was unacceptable in the fantasy world of moviegoers.

Without revealing any of this to my crew, I went out to the actors' training camp and slept on the jungle floor, away from it all, as in Vietnam— just me and the stars. But it was always there, burning in my brain. A year's effort. Boyle, thankfully, joined me, and we belly laughed about the journey like two veteran prospectors who'd survived—Boyle the "disgrace to his profession," me the "cartoonist"—as the gold dust blew away between our fingers. We'd started with nothing, hadn't we, only fourteen months ago, and it'd been one hell of ride into those Mexican mountains. And after all, we'd gotten out *alive*, hadn't we?

Even if there was no peace for me up there in those stars, I was reconnecting to the real world. I was no longer a young, sensitive soldier with his life (and death) right in front of him, with nothing mattering except making it through the next mission and getting back to base camp, a shower, and a hot meal. Now I was a harried, frustrated writer, director, husband, father, and businessman trying to survive in a strange jungle world from decades before, where I felt like I'd gotten myself stranded at third base with *Salvador* and I couldn't get home. The only way to score would be to hit a home run with *Platoon*.

The actors, in training, were gradually coalescing into a real platoon. At first they ragged Charlie Sheen for the package of goodies his mom sent from Malibu, which they grabbed and divided among themselves. Whenever he heard "Oh, man, I gotta call my agent," Dale Dye would yell, "You know what, a'hole? *Sin loi*" (which is Vietnamese for "tough shit"). "There's no fucking phone within twenty miles of your sorry ass!" Soon they were busy with tough hikes, blisters on their hands and feet, machete cuts, ant bites, neck burns, sprained limbs, fevers, and even broken teeth. On my second visit out, I joined Dale's night ambush at about 3 a.m. We played the roles of NVA soldiers, terrifying the actors by setting off explosions all around the perimeter. "War games" again — but unknown to the actors and my crew, I was fighting a different war, more desperate, trying to survive as a civilian. I'd arrived at a turning point. Everything now depended on the results of *Platoon*. I really tried to lift my spirits, but I just couldn't. Every day there was new and disheartening information to deal with.

The box office numbers out of New York were not good. A small artsy film from England, *My Beautiful Laundrette,* had done giant business and wiped us out. And just as we started our screenings in DC, Reagan was finally winning Congress over on Nicaragua. Nothing was going well. A John Hughes comedy, *Pretty in Pink,* with Molly Ringwald, was suddenly getting big attention. There were no follow-up press articles on *Salvador*. I could do nothing. Yet to my amazement, there was no sign of Hemdale actually closing *Platoon* down.

Arnold Kopelson arrived on the set with gloomy Richard Soames from Film Finances, who, with his one detailed eye, minutely examined our operation and surprisingly they found themselves satisfied with the efficient way Alex Ho was running it — unlike the supposedly dishonest, maligned Gerald Green in Mexico. Alex's parents were from Guangzhou province, and he lived up to the Cantonese reputation in that he was disciplined, practical, money conscious, and tough. He knew what it meant to bleed for something of value. Alex was not particularly interested in culture, his choppy Queens-accented American vernacular often making me laugh at the way he'd get so wound up and emotional; no movie dialogue could do it justice. He brought with him a beautiful blond American girlfriend, which was status to Alex, and he dressed quite stylishly in the latest Barneys fashions from New York, a cheroot to be seen in his small, sharp beak of a face, dominated by his black spectacles. I felt deeply protective of Alex and always defended him when others criticized, because he was "my find," and we bonded on this film. On the other hand, he was carrying a lot of hidden resentments from his Cimino days, when he'd always been the guy sent to do the errands, the delivery boy treatment he deeply hated.

Alex and Bruno were butting heads a lot — locations not quite ready, costs seeming to rise. We tested our explosives, flares, and lights for the nighttime jungle scenes, of which we had many, as well as the daytime red dust, which I insisted on importing in sacks from Vietnam to match the real location. (It would have a significant impact on veterans because of its believability.) We realized the daylight exposure in the deeper parts of the jungle started dropping markedly at 4 p.m., which was going to be a problem. Still, Bob Richardson was growing into a force of nature, reliable whenever others seemed shaky, also a friend with an easy laugh and a teasing humor. With his skill as an illustrator trained at the respected Rhode Island School of Design, he also helped me considerably with the storyboards to economize in advance on the number of shots we needed. A director and a director of photography can sit there and talk through any scene, cut out superficials, and hone the thinking behind it — but still, it always comes down to the "Day Of" the shoot itself. Be it Day 23 or Day 54, it will be the day when all of this will be decided. Years of prep, drafts of the script, how it looks all go into one thing only, the "Day Of," which takes on the aura of a gunfight — exciting, definitive, and we either get the shot or we don't. You commit it to film, and then you . . . well, move on to the next "Day Of" without a break or much time to think — and rarely any chance to do it over.

I brought out the same Irish editor from *Salvador*, Claire Simpson, who seemed to be doing a better job of reading my mind at this point, and her first assistant, David Brenner, who would later become my chief editor. The sound man, the armorers, the second assistant director, and the special effects team came out from England for less money than their Hollywood counterparts — all of them top people, especially when compared to my experiences on the semiprofessional levels of *Salvador*. Gordon Smith, for example, our young special effects makeup man from Canada, solved the heavy facial scar issue on the Sergeant Barnes character. Applying a deformity like that would normally have taken two or three hours each morning, killing our schedule. But using a collodion compound that he'd evolved to last in the brutal jungle humidity without burning or leaving aftereffects on Berenger's face, Gordon eventually got the process down to a twenty-minute or so makeup job each day — and it looked spectacular. Even so, after a few weeks it did begin to burn, and Berenger was in pain but rarely complained. He impressed me, growing through his training with Dale Dye into the rock at the center of the platoon, which was what we needed.

I closely watched Charlie Sheen's progress; like a genuine new combat soldier, he couldn't do much right, carrying too much equipment with that same lost look I once probably had. But as we shot, week by week, he was adjusting, uncomplaining, a goat in the jungle now, light and graceful on his feet from his baseball background, pulling long distances. But he was also growing harder, meaner. It made me think, Is that the way I changed over there? Did I become more callous, angrier, darker? What would I not do? I'd find out if I had any sense of goodness, decency, right and wrong — or if I had rotted in the heat and pain. In the person of Charlie, Vietnam was becoming a mirror of my own soul.

All the actors were growing, learning what soldiering meant with new respect. The more Dale asked of them, the more they seemed to like it; never had they experienced something like this before — or would again. Throughout, Dale was a great teacher and backbone, first up, last one down, never bitching, leading, a soldier at his best. Except when he veered into his subjective directing mode with the actors. "What happens when you look down at your buddy and he's dead? What do you feel? I'll tell you how you feel —" and then he would. Or when he saw any "gooks" on set, among them our Vietnamese Dragon Lady fixer, Nguyen, or any of the other Vietnamese she brought on to work with us; Dale definitely had some sort of Vietnamese "issue," but in time, he seemed to get over that.

On March 20, a Thursday, he marched this unit of thirty "soldiers" out of their overnight bivouac right into our first setup at 8 a.m. on a river with a ravine and deep wet jungle behind it, backlit by the sun. It was a stunning opening shot. We kept moving down the river. The men behaved not like actors but like soldiers, snapping to attention at Dye's off-camera bark. He'd trained them well. He was embedded in their nervous systems in spite of their now going off to sleep in our local hotel each night, and sometimes on weekends to Manila, an hour and a half away. Elizabeth and fifteen-month-old Sean had just joined me for the shoot, again elevating my spirits as they had on *Salvador*. She was shocked when the actors first walked out of the jungle, not even recognizing them. These men were grim, dirty, exhausted from lack of sleep. That'd been our goal. That real tiredness would make them understand our GIs' casual feelings of brutality, our stoicism in the face of death.

We were finally off and running. We got some twenty-four setups in that jungle on the first day. The next two weeks successfully set the pace of a grinding shoot, nothing taken for granted; I was smarter with a camera than on *Salvador*, not cramming in as much to get as many shots, going more precisely for what I wanted. We kept moving. The temperature, usually in the 90s, sometimes hit 100° in the afternoons with high humidity, frying our brains if we let it. I came down with a high fever but stayed on my feet, as every day counted. I was now more vulnerable, at forty years old, as well as overweight, eating cloves of garlic, feeling my joints and my wind more than I ever did as a foot soldier. I didn't want to whine, but I was a long way from being twenty-two again.

The nights were killing in the jungle. We'd wait three hours for the crane or the lighting to be moved, the rain towers to be adjusted, or the water trucks to be brought out by the local fire department, often late. We worked till five in the morning with red ants and mosquitos biting our ankles and necks. It was slow. Time dragged. People got meaner. And by Week 3, the crew's infighting was getting worse, with the veteran chief grip, an Irishman from Queens, leaving the set early, which of course upset Richardson, who was in bad shape with an ear infection. Two Filipinos took pistol shots at each other one night. Elizabeth, a dog lover, grew very upset when she saw a barbequed dog skull; the Filipinos enjoyed it as a delicacy, while she was thinking it could have been one of her beloved retrievers.

In my experience, it's the unforeseen problem that usually turns into the nightmare. The antagonism, unknown to me, between Arnold Kopelson and Alex Ho had been festering since Los Angeles, with Arnold digging deeper into the account books, now questioning every one of Alex's moves as a producer. He enlisted Soames, who telegraphed us out of LA how "furious I am at this unplanned overage." I didn't see a problem at that time. I thought we were doing pretty well keeping to budget, and that Soames was just being his nasty *Salvador* self again. We were a little behind schedule at the start, but we'd get going, it was under control, and frankly, with our contingency fund, we could afford fifty-four days of shooting instead of fifty. Regardless, Kopelson and Soames were united at the altar of money, and as a result, I started to mistrust Arnold. I was "shooting far too much footage," according to Soames. "It's imperative now to stay on a fifty-day schedule" was his Captain Bligh mentality. As first mate of the ship, I bridled at his authority, a Fletcher Christian in the making. I was growing more confident in asserting my rights as a director. "The money" had bullied me around on all my films, but now I wanted more control over my fate.

Alex, in his pride, didn't handle Kopelson well, dismissing him as a "pain in the ass" who would cost production more money because Alex and our "Dragon Lady," Nguyen, had already favorably remade our military deals after the recent revolution. Kopelson was now questioning a "done deal." "You don't come clean in the Philippines like that, what the fuck does he think he's doing? He's going to wreck everything, going back to these military guys. Trying to do *what?* Upset the apple cart is what! What's he gonna tell 'em — 'we wanna renegotiate!'" Alex would mutter on in his pissed-off broken Chinese version of American curses, which was hilarious to hear.

Maybe Alex was hiding something financially, but if so, it was peanuts in comparison to what we were achieving as a whole. Arnold was being petty, to my mind, in order to bust down an overly arrogant young co-producer. They even used to talk about Jewish versus Chinese, each trying to outdo the other with his "how far does my civilization go back" kind of superiority. As if to end the matter, Alex told me, "Don't worry about it, Arnold's a schmuck in over his head. We're holding all the cards. Shoot your movie the way you want to." I liked his defiance, but at the same time I knew there was trouble ahead.

The irony was that as *Platoon's* fortunes were under new threat, *Salvador's* were miraculously rising. I'd been told there'd been fervent applause from a large crowd at the Academy in Los Angeles, where the audience now loved Woods's performance and laughed instead of being revolted by him. And *Salvador* was hanging on in fourteen theaters in New York, received four stars in Boston, was doing okay in San Francisco and Washington with good reviews, and was still in five theaters in Los Angeles, where it was selling out! Ecstatic, Woods faxed me I should be there to see it, the cheering at the Westwood movie house. He seemed genuinely happy and proud of the film. The *Los Angeles Times* reviewer wrote, "A film that sings and screams . . . it's alive, it broils." I was amazed, of course, but confused. Coming off the convulsive journey I'd taken on *Salvador,* I was adopting a gambler's detachment and temperament.

The West Coast was turning out to be our best market, more receptive to the plight of El Salvador, which had sent us so many refugees already. We made $21,000 in three days in Westwood, and we were opening in seven to ten more cities in a week, with a slow rollout in Toronto in June. Then out of nowhere, David Denby in *New York* magazine came in with a rave, calling it "an electrifying tour of hell in Central America." The movie, he said, "combines Stone's talent for hard-driving, sometimes trashy excitement with a new moral and dramatic seriousness." This from the critic who had once referred to me as "the dread Oliver Stone." Now he was calling me the "macho-man of the Left," who'd made "the cult film of the year — corrupt but exciting, outrageous." Quite a turnaround. Elizabeth had been telling me that *Salvador* was a success in spite of its business because it was getting respect, but I'd been skeptical. Now these acknowledgments from hard-to-please reviewers provided me with a great emotional lift and helped carry me through what would be the hardest part of *Platoon* — the endless night shooting. If *Salvador* had died in Los Angeles, I don't believe I would've possessed the spirit I most needed now.

The truth was, I was so overwhelmed with logistical challenges during the shooting that the role of directing the actors became one of pure practicality and not choices one might find in extensive rehearsal. What lives? What dies? Who is scared? Who is angry? You want to get high and dance? You want to booze and talk shit? Well, your actors all know what that feels like; in fact, younger men could probably teach me a few things. They had a ball; playing at war for most every one of them was an experience they would never forget in the coming years. As to acting, it was basic and for the most part written into the script, and the actors, now trained to think like soldiers by mother Dale, took it from there. To help make it as naturalistic as possible was my goal. Later in my career these parameters would change, but not at this time.

Our chopper work was under way with the Filipino military. The noise, the daily whine, the rotor gusts were making me loopy, and when lucky, we'd get four or five setups a day. With our money and chopper time limited, we had to go for broke, flying out of the jungle canyons in sometimes difficult air currents, shooting film as fast as we could. It was the worst week of fear I'd experienced since Vietnam, yet I felt invigorated, the years scaling off with my sense of terror. One day we were filming the evacuation by several choppers of dead and wounded GIs. The winds were getting rougher in the late afternoon as Sheen, Berenger, Forest Whitaker, Keith David, Bob Richardson and his assistant camera operator, Dale Dye, myself, three "dead" soldiers, and two pilots in the Huey were lifting off from the floor of the canyon. Too many people with too much weight, trying to do too much. The chopper, having already made multiple trips and now on its last pass of the day, rose up and barely cleared the treetops. Then the walls of the canyon were suddenly coming at us in giant close-up. Way too close-up! Having been in more than thirty combat landings in Vietnam, I knew that this might be it, and I knew that Dale, on the opposite door of the chopper, knew the same thing, because the color went out of his face. It's actually weird when you come so close to dying, how easily you can accept it. You grow very calm. Good-bye is basic, unsentimental. I don't think anyone else in that chopper realized it, but we cleared that canyon wall *by inches.*

When we returned to the valley floor, my baby boy in his mother's arms was waving to me, beaming to see his dad again. If only he knew. At that moment, I realized how grateful I was to be able to return to both of them. We need that sentiment to live, that extra tug, a reminder of why we live, for what purpose. Is it to be joined with others? Or to sacrifice ourselves, as I was willing to do? Because I also recognize that I would have done the exact same thing over again, and gone up once more into those canyon walls. Because if I hadn't, the film would've been gravely hurt. The sane solution, of course, was to spend more money to get these shots, but there was no more money, and the pilots, as good as they were, knew they were cutting corners and taking risks they shouldn't take. Everyone (with the exception of the Pentagon) is on a short leash when it comes to money — and money becomes a form of God driving us to sacrifice. And indeed, less than a year later, the inevitable happened, and one of these same choppers went down with its Filipino crew on a Chuck Norris film, *Braddock: Missing in Action III,* and several people lost their lives. Was the film good? Was it worth it? To us, on our film, it was. To the gladiator in the arena, it's what it is, and you die because it's called for. In the same vein, it's given to us to live if destiny says so. Looking back at this now, I don't agree with my earlier thinking, but I recognize that hunger and desperation breed that radicalism.

Shooting with great difficulty, we fell another day behind. I was also having editing problems, as I'd regularly extend my hours each day going through the dailies, and then, with my editor, cutting together a rough assembly of a few days' work; this required making decisions, selecting a few takes only, but avoiding the boredom of long rushes. In other words, we were creating a weekly "showreel" for cast and crew — and Hemdale in LA. On typical films of the time, "rushes" were shown to director and crew, sometimes everything shot the previous days, which means many "takes" of the same thing. By creating a "showreel," I was cutting days of shooting, let's say two hours of film, down to twenty-four minutes, with smoother transitions and fewer repeats. On the other hand, this method required that I start to edit a rough feel of the film in my off hours, a lot more work for me and the editor. In all my films after that, I dispensed with "dailies," as I found that, on location, the crew is usually tired and the rushes become insanely repetitive. If necessary, I'd bring a few selected crew to the editing room if there were problems that required immediate attention, whether in costume, cinematography, sound, whatever. This actually worked better and saved everyone good energy, which we needed on a grueling shoot. I did this on every film after *Platoon,* as I now came to feel the whole process of viewing dailies was a loss of time.

Thirty-two days into the shoot, I lost my temper when our Filipino production manager, whom I already distrusted because of his continual excuses for the water trucks arriving late to our locations, moved the gigantic cherry picker we were using to position a giant arc for our jungle lighting after I'd specifically told him the night before to leave it where it was. We were now going to lose two whole hours trying to move it back to where it should've been. Two hours of our shooting time was invaluable, and in the end I knew it would have to come out of my script. With me seeing red and his blank, unresponsive stare, I lost it and kicked him in the ass as he walked away, and two minutes later he came back, slammed me in the chest with his purse (a small Filipino carry bag), and yelled, "I am a soldier. You no kick me!" Later someone told me he had a gun in that purse. The crew struck in sympathy with him, claiming it was not the first time I'd been abusive. I'd put my finger on the chest of another crew member, hectoring him, and now this. I heard the threatening murmurs that "Stone's history now!" and that there was a contract out on my life. This was growing into a difficult situation as a result of fatigue and too much overtime. We needed a break anyway, so when the crew called a strike in sympathy with the production manager, I didn't mind everything coming to a stop.

We lost Day 33 out of the now fifty-one days we had, and Jun Juban, our patient, experienced Filipino coordinator, came out from Manila to calm the situation down. I *was* losing my temper too much. Fatigue was doing me in. Elizabeth blew up at me because, she said, I was losing the respect of the international crew as well. I'd become hard, Bogart hard, as if I were Fred C. Dobbs in *The Treasure of the Sierra Madre.* Jun settled the affair. As Kopelson put it most dramatically in his account to James Riordan: "I understand that he [the production manager] was carrying a gun and was seriously contemplating shooting Oliver, and no one was going to work until this was straightened out. Finally, Oliver agreed that in a gesture to show his apology, he would let the man slap him in front of his crew. And that's what he did. It was like something out of an old *Tarzan* movie or something . . . winning the cooperation of the tribe."

Movie people, producers included, love a good story more than ordinary reality. I apologized verbally to the production manager, and he accepted — and nothing really changed anyway. The very next day there was another water truck breakdown, as well as a large van carrying fourteen or fifteen crew nearly crashing, and we lost more time when a bamboo viper bit our camera truck driver, who was wearing flip-flops, on the foot. It could have been fatal, as he needed to be evacuated for two days. The actors and crew were coming down with fevers. Our chief grip again mysteriously disappeared for the whole day in his continuing battle with Richardson; I assumed he was getting drunk somewhere.

And then the dam burst. Kopelson, with about two weeks of shooting to go, decided to fire Alex's female production coordinator. This was a power move on the part of Arnold, exercising his authority, but it was a mistake. Many in the international crew were loyal to Alex, and they threatened to quit unless the coordinator was reinstated — and Alex added the condition that Kopelson would have to leave the set, and preferably the country. This was a daunting demand, but Alex was furious, saying things like "Push a Chinaman so far, and I'm a Chinaman . . . I love the picture, but I don't give a fuck anymore. I'm pulling the plug!" Which meant Alex was quitting and taking part of the crew with him. This was a precarious situation, and we lost a piece of another day. A mutiny was taking place, but it was unclear yet who was on whose side. It came out that Kopelson, digging in the books, had come to the conclusion that Alex had misused his position, paid inordinate bribes to some Filipinos, and so forth. But why was Arnold digging in like this? If the bribes had been paid, who cared at this point? We were making this movie, and we had to keep going. We couldn't start fighting among ourselves. When I tried to cool it off, Arnold told me to "stay the fuck out of this!" Thankfully the next day we were off the clock, so we didn't lose more time, but the chaos was growing.

From my viewpoint, it was a mistake for Alex to quit so forcefully, challenging Arnold's authority. But it was a bigger mistake for Arnold to have treated Alex like he was a production manager rather than a co-producer. Kopelson said in front of others that he'd "hold the fort down until another production manager comes in." You couldn't do this to a proud man like Alex; "saving face" in Asian culture is a crucial concept Americans often don't understand (as I didn't in kicking and humiliating our Filipino PM). Both Alex and Arnold had overstepped themselves, and both men were arrogant; as I said before, Chinese and Jewish, two ancient cultures at war.

I called John Daly in the States to help resolve this crisis, and told him I wouldn't shoot again until Alex was reinstated along with his production coordinator. It took a few more hours. Arnold spoke to Daly and said that Hemdale fully supported him, but it was obvious he was nervous, a poker bluff, sweat on his upper lip. I believe Daly told him something like "Do as you want, Arnold, but if you lose this crew for one day, are you prepared to indemnify our loss?" Soames at Film Finances huffed and puffed in support of Arnold, but he had no real leverage except with Daly. Richardson told me he'd continue to work with me; his loyalty was to the film above all. His disloyal New York grip, however, said he would leave with Alex, but the majority of the Filipino crew, under Jun Juban, would continue here. Some of the crew felt Alex was blackmailing the production, and clearly he was ready to sacrifice the film, and me, to his pride. Earlier Alex had questioned, mistakenly, my loyalty to him on the production coordinator issue, thinking that I was okay with Kopelson's decision to fire her. I wasn't and would have fought it if consulted (and probably lost), but when Alex quit, everything blew up.

Arnold, sensing my loyalty to Alex, knew this was not going down well and the film would be hurt. And so he called me late that night to say he was bowing out and going to France and the Cannes Film Festival for the rest of the shoot, that Alex's coordinator was back on the job, that this was a mature decision on his part, that in any case he would fire Alex as soon as the production was over in two weeks. I thanked him, grateful for his "wise decision," anxious to get back to work the next day. Arnold, at Cannes, would continue to supervise foreign sales. Alex would finish the shoot, but was officially "ended" thereafter, although he continued to work with me quietly in the post-production period. All this to "save face."

With hard rain pouring down at night, we didn't need mutinies. The insects coming out after the rains were as horrific as I'd ever seen. I almost stepped on another snake, which was inches from my foot when Bob Richardson yelled out to warn me. This was truly the last lap of a wild stagecoach ride. The seventy-two-hour weeks were taking their toll. The crew was dragging, as I was. Bob drifted into a fever, and Charlie Sheen's eardrums were concussed from all the explosions. At one point, forty days in, I counted 40 percent of our company ill. Rainy season, which meant possible monsoons, was pending any day now. There were eight straight days with long overtime ahead, with fatigue cutting down our efficiency. We *had* to get out of there unless we wanted a disaster similar to what Coppola had suffered on *Apocalypse Now* — an entire production wiped out for months by tropical weather.

There are times you just have to eat it, and you go for as few shots as possible. When we brought the heavy lights out into the jungle at night, it became impossible to shoot because the bugs were beating so hard against the lights that our microphones couldn't record anything else. Worse still, the lights were continuously flickering because of the swarming insects, spoiling the exposures. Bob now abandoned the big lights and decided to basically shoot everything with reflectors, small spots, and our magnesium flares, which gave him an ambient, unspecific light. He also made good use of the many gasoline bombs we detonated during the final battle scene. We started to move much faster and made up some time; a lot of the final battle ended up using flare light effectively, if crudely. Out of necessity came creativity.

Richardson and I had several disagreements over this period on how to do things. Bob thought I was reckless in laying out the gasoline bombs for the battle, but the special effects chief and his crew were understaffed and exhausted from the huge amount of work they had on their hands. So because I was directing the actors in their movements, I blew the bombs myself, several dozen over the next nights. Thankfully no one was hurt by these gas explosions, but clearly this couldn't be done in today's film world, where supervisors and security specialists are legion. But this was 1986 in the Philippines on a low-budget film. Nobody cared what you did at the price we did it for. Filipino films, after all, were being shot next door to us in the jungle for considerably less money; in the daytime we saw ninja film guys on trampolines somersaulting above the treetops next to us. It was quite a zoo. But as with the choppers, when you're desperate, you do these things.

Some of the final shots occurred just before dawn, with Charlie coming up and shooting Berenger in revenge for his killing of Dafoe. Berenger was sprawled on the ground, concussed from the five-hundred-pound bomb that'd been dropped near the perimeter, blinding everyone. Charlie stalked him, found him, hesitated. At this point, in the script, I'd written an alternate ending in which Charlie does not shoot Berenger's character, which seemed the right thing to do; it also seemed to be the usual "movie way" of doing it. The "good guy" should never shoot the "bad guy" in cold blood. But I was rebelling against everything at this point. When I wrote it originally over a decade before, I'd had the young man, brutalized by the war, killing his own sergeant. That was my gut — and this night I stuck to it. Charlie/Chris pulls the trigger. Berenger/Barnes deserves it for having offed Dafoe/Elias. We could hate *that* much. We could commit murder and call it just another shooting. That's what war could do to *anyone* — make you mad, temporarily out of your mind, crazy. And that's the way we did it.

We got the last shot at 4:30, the new day just breaking, twenty or thirty of us still standing around, stunned. Was this really over? Yeah. A few tired words from me. "So that wraps it . . . Thank you, everyone, you hung in there . . . I don't think we'll ever forget this. Thank you." A little exhausted cheer. Who in the world really gave a shit about this? Well, we did. We hugged and smiled — Bob and Bruno, Dale Dye, Yves De Bono, Simon Kaye, Susan Malerstein, my tireless first AD Gordon Boos, and the others still standing; by now we felt like brothers. Jun Juban, our Filipino crew leader, and his brown-skinned brigade of hard men who'd endured austerity without complaint now managed big grins, so happy to finish. I shook each hand with gratitude; I could remember only some names, but that wasn't as important as the eyes.

Later I wrote about our wrap in *American Film*:

> I compromise on some shots, and we finish on the 54th day . . .
> Alex Ho, the Chinese production manager with me since the
> Dino de Laurentiis days, now beaten to a pulp by cast and crew,
> comes over and says, not without some irony, "Congratulations,

Ollie, it's been a long two years." "No, a long twenty," I murmur, sad because I know that although I finished the film, a part of it will never be there, any more than the faces of the gawky boys we left behind in the dust. As close as I came to Charlie Sheen, he would never be me and *Platoon* would never be what I saw in my mind when I wrote it and which was just a fragment, really, of what happened years ago. That, too, is gone. And we move on. I don't want to party with the cast and crew — they're having too good a time and I don't want to bring my director's consciousness to bear on them — so I ride home alone with the driver as the light comes up over the paddies and the buffalo, and the peasants come out as they always do to work in the fields in that first pink light of the Asian dawn. It is just another late spring day in "the World" (as we called it in Vietnam) and nobody cares that we just finished this little "thing in the jungle." Why should they? Yet as I press my face against the window of the silently moving car, in my soul there is a moment there and I know that it will last me forever — because it is the sweetest moment I've had since the day I left Vietnam.

10

Top of the World

When I returned to Los Angeles in early June 1986, I felt the difference right away. Word of mouth about my two films was spreading faster than I could believe; like fire, it jumps water and even oceans and doesn't take long. And as I learned, not much can stop it. It was, whether I knew it or not, *my time.*

Salvador was now playing in its fourth week of a multiple run in six theaters. Not quite believing this yet, I drove past lines of people waiting for weekend shows at the hip Los Feliz theater on Vermont Avenue, my name unbelievably above the title on the marquee: Oliver Stone's *Salvador*! Wow —why not Jimmy Woods? Who knew me? I'd never felt something like this before; couldn't I just stop and enjoy this for a few moments? We were in our tenth week in Washington, DC, at the high-end MacArthur venue, as well as in Chicago, Detroit, Dallas, Austin with middling business but exciting reviews. Even when audiences could see *Salvador*'s rough edges, they understood its heart. Private screenings were being set up by Hollywood stars, always a good sign—Dustin Hoffman, Redford, Streisand, Nicholson, Sydney Pollack. There were congratulatory phone calls, letters from such as Francis Ford Coppola. I was being told we were "one-of-a-kind," "original," and "fiercely independent." The great divide is expectation. When you're a known quantity in the film community, they, the insiders, think they know what to expect, and a certain "déjà vu" indifference sets in. In this case, there was only surprise.

I was, for that brief year, the unknown one, the unexpected. Although apparently not unknown to Pauline Kael. When she belatedly came out with her review in mid-July, she not only exonerated me from my past sins but actually kicked off a whole second wave for the film in New York theaters, packing the weekend houses. Marion Billings was quite surprised, as she had deliberately not screened it for Kael on its first pass because of her past antipathy to my work. But now Kael, who cultivated her capricious taste and outsize influence, wrote in *The New Yorker*, "Stone writes and directs as if someone had put a gun to the back of his neck and yelled, 'Go!' and didn't take it away until he'd finished." If only she knew.

She uncannily sensed the dichotomy in my political mindset: "As a revelation of a gifted filmmaker's divided sensibility, there's been nothing quite as spectacular as *Salvador* . . . a right-wing macho vision joined to a left-leaning polemic . . . *Salvador* has the tainted, disreputable, hard-boiled surface we expect from Oliver Stone, and the sentimentality that goes with it . . . The Oliver Stone who made this movie isn't essentially different from the hype artist who wrote *Midnight Express* and *Scarface*, etc. . . . He's working outside the industry, in freedom, but he's got all this Hollywood muck in his soul."

She clearly identified me with the protagonist: "He uses James Woods, perhaps the most hostile of all American actors, as the hero, who is called 'Richard Boyle,' but represents Stone's convictions too." With this I disagreed. Although I empathized with my protagonist, that didn't mean I agreed with him. Richard was politically astute and, to a degree, a friend, but I never totally trusted him or liked his behavior on alcohol. With women he was actually shy and inexperienced, but Jimmy made him a lot tougher. Richard made me laugh many times, yes, but he was nothing I would emulate. Accepting the theory behind Kael's criticism would make me part Boyle, as well as my other protagonists — Jim Morrison, Richard Nixon, Jim Garrison, and the rest. But does Jim Morrison's character really resemble Richard Nixon's?

Or, for that matter, what did any of these characters have to do with the self-destructive protagonists from my earlier work on *Seizure* and *The Hand*? I was always *outside* the characterizations, and that was the creative pleasure I derived, and still derive, from writing drama — *not* to have a fixed identity, to be free as a dramatist, elusive, unknown. But it seems through the years, as you build up an identity with different works, this freedom comes at a high price and is difficult to maintain, and trying to do so eventually wore me down. From this early typecasting by critics, "Oliver Stone" became for some this persona of a macho war veteran willing to break taboos, with little interest in women — and soon to be a "conspiracy theorist."

In any case, Kael's review started that strange process of making *Salvador* more acceptable in film circles, and made a difference at the box office and in the public's reaction. The film would now start working its idiosyncratic way onto many "10 Best" lists and, to our great surprise, into Academy Award consideration. Paula Wagner's husband, agent Rick Nicita, a co-founder of CAA, summed up my reentry and acceptance in LA when he told me in conversation, "*Salvador* is a great film, but the populace doesn't want to deal with that now." He told me the opposite of what more hard-boiled agents might say: "Keep making them without compromise, and one day, it will interconnect for whatever reason with commerciality, and there you'll have a real hit. The only way is to keep turning them out. Do not change or cheapen them." Strong advice, hard to pull off, but in that year of 1986, I was, without realizing it, closing in on the bull's-eye.

I was also feeling, for the first time, a deeper connection to Los Angeles itself, because I was finally tasting the fruit in its garden. Hollywood, in its essence, is a town in search of a dream — a story to tell. There's no actual city; there's an industry, there are suburbs, there's a rich culture of highly creative people. But unlike New York or Paris, it's spread out and disparate, hard to locate. There's a certain comfort and a relaxed "hacienda" style of life in Hollywood, no doubt, but without having a story told or about to be told, I find there is little substance or satisfaction for me.

Now, offers not only to write but also to direct were coming in, and I was suddenly in a whole new league when the venerable Zanuck/Brown Company, top-of-the-line Hollywood, which had done *The Sting* and *Butch Cassidy and the Sundance Kid* with George Roy Hill, out of the blue offered me a film called *Shattered Silence,* the fascinating, supposedly true biography of Eli Cohen, an Israeli spy who'd given his life on a dangerous operation in Syria. Abby Mann, the screenwriter of *Judgment at Nuremberg* (1961), had turned in a good first draft years before, but in typical studio fashion, it had worsened in the hands of others. Dick Zanuck and David Brown had loved *Salvador* because it was "real," with "real actors"; they were smooth, like born patricians who'd done things with style, producers who didn't have to get "ugly," and through whose doors my own scripts had passed several times without being noticed. Now they were chasing me.

I was at that point in my career where I was trying to be polite and make everybody happy — return each phone call, no matter who, read every script I was offered, and certainly, if I expressed enthusiasm, I wanted to back up my words with action. I didn't want to be like the many producers who'd treated me poorly over these last fifteen years. To "develop" a script was a sacred obligation, it meant a major effort to actually make it and not waste the development money; it meant, if I didn't write it myself, that I'd work closely with another writer — often without being paid for it. I abhorred the idea, from my father's upbringing, of taking money without performing a service in return; it became clear that in Hollywood, this placed me in the minority. So later, when I told Zanuck/Brown that I couldn't do their film as my next project, they backed off, disappointed. But a week later, to my surprise, they came back and said they'd wait for me to do it as a second project. I was uncomfortable with this, and felt guilty that I'd misled them into believing that I actually wanted to do the film, which I really didn't. I'd come to think the material wasn't really as good as I'd thought when I'd first read it. I've often found that once you do more research, "true stories" turn out to be not so true — or else there's simply not enough there to justify the effort and the time you need to make a film. Feeling awful, I passed once more and did not hear from Zanuck/Brown again for several years. Incidentally, the Eli Cohen story was finally made as a six-part television series more than thirty years later and seemed to veer even further from the truth then.

The manic Peter Guber from *Midnight Express* was now back, offering me the war photographer Robert Capa's story, stretching from World War II to Vietnam ("I'm very happy for you, Oliver! Now you should do something really big . . . something huge! A *Lawrence of Arabia*–type picture"). But could I really work with Guber's partner, Jon Peters, again after *The Hand*? I passed, and Peter came back with *Gorillas in the Mist* (1988), the Dian Fossey story, which was later made with Sigourney Weaver as the brainy, sexy heroine. The piece, in my opinion, was polished and surface perfect — and at the same time a trap, because it was not me. Elizabeth pointed that out: "Don't go fishing for a woman's project like that." I needed something as gritty, chaotic, and imperfect as I was.

Ned Tanen, the former president of Universal, who'd been our studio boss during the turbulent *Scarface* saga, which I did not bring up lest it ruffle the polite surface, invited me to lunch with my agent, Paula. He offered me an open invitation to come to him as an independent producer now at Paramount, forgetting that he'd turned *Platoon* down several times going back to Marty Bregman's option on it in 1976. Nor did I bring up the subject of "Defiance," which he'd never bothered to read and was sitting in cold storage, as I was sure this exotica would be of little interest to him. Although it was all very exciting to be courted by a powerhouse, Marty Bregman was a close friend of Ned's, and I was still wary of his vengeful nature and did not push further. I'd been a screenwriter long enough to realize that doing business directly with a giant studio had its own drawbacks, such as going to "development hell," as they called it, screenwriters endlessly cycling scripts that would get literally lost in a system where executives came and went, and with it, the difficult issues of "turnaround" — getting your script back in a reasonable way, costs inflated against actual cost, etc. My problems on *Platoon* with Dino De Laurentiis were freshly branded on my mind. And the reality was that I was still in a hole financially, carrying four places — two in New York (a house in Sagaponack and a Manhattan apartment), and a rented house in Los Angeles along with my original apartment — and I hadn't received full payments yet on *Platoon* or, for that matter, *Salvador*. I was spending about $35,000 a month on rents, mortgages, my mother, food, cars, a wife and a child, and a new nanny (thankfully religious and married). Pines told me I owed future federal and New York State taxes. At three o'clock on certain mornings, lying there in bed, I felt like I was in the coils of a giant python of debt, beginning its deadly squeeze. Shades of my father.

In my mind, John Daly was still my base. I owed him my career so far. He very much wanted my next project, and he'd succumb to an occasional flash of paranoia when the possibility of my going to other companies arose. As in the boxing game, he expected me to stay with him. He thought we might do "Defiance," my Russian dissident project, which he genuinely cared for. The fine actor Kevin Kline was available to play our composer, but I was now wary of my own script. "Defiance" wasn't rooted in an American reality but was more an exotic experience, and now that I'd done two tough films back-to-back, I realized how difficult it would be to pull off the story in another culture.

Daly also liked my idea to stay with the Charlie Sheen character from *Platoon*, bring him back to the States, and follow his adjustments. I saw it as a film called *Second Life*, and I'd already written something like it years before — "Once Too Much," a dark, melodramatic version of my own re-entry, including my prison experience on my way back from Mexico in late 1968. But that story didn't fit any longer, as I was now in the world of contemporary reality and no longer living a Peckinpah movie. There were contractual complexities in this idea as well; with Sheen in it, it would be considered a "sequel," which would in turn necessitate hefty payments to Arnold Kopelson, who was already on John's case for his *Platoon* fees. Arnold, quick to spot a buck, was already vigorously trying to sell a *Platoon* TV series to the networks, which worried me. *Platoon* was hardly *China Beach*, which would go on to be the defining Vietnam TV series and made quite a bit of money off its ability to be inoffensive to almost everyone.

John seemed preoccupied with the pressure coming from his expanding company, which was flirting with "going public"; he talked of selling me Hemdale stock at an option price. Yet John already felt overextended, with too many projects in development and new producers stacked up in the downstairs waiting room of his two-story town house. In his thinking, *Salvador* was already in the past. He calmed my concerns about its lack of financial success: "Come on, Oliver, it's *seen* as a success as long as you don't open your mouth and give them numbers. Be positive. The film's done Hemdale a great deal of good on the Bel Air circuit," where movie stars and studio executives created buzz about the latest film they'd seen in their private screening rooms. *Salvador*, John said, had only "been hurt by its perception as a political film, which is why we must carefully handle *Platoon*, keep the focus broad, not let it become just a war film."

Meanwhile, there were more mundane things to address, like "Where's my money, John?" Boyle was making ugly noises to our West Coast publicist Andrea Jaffe about reporting Hemdale to the Writers Guild for not meeting its minimum obligations. John had a blithe and charming way of reassuring me: "Of course Boyle and you are gonna be paid. Just have Bob Marshall sign those bloody pages." And when my lawyer Bob finally sent some amended pages of a contract, John would grin at me and say, "My Lord, your guy must've been wearing a bloody mask when he wrote this thing, he was laughing so hard!" Which, in his Cockney accent, disarmed me.

It would be weeks, sometimes months, before anything could get resolved with John and his partner, Derek Gibson, who together were running a small factory like they were pub keepers — which, apparently, they'd once been. I'd learned this from a British producer who'd known them as partners in 1960s London's East End, where they had a pub called The Spotted Duck or something similar, where boxers, gangsters, and their cohorts would hang out; and like true publicans, they'd dole out the cash sparingly while running the beer kegs. They actually at one point sold *Platoon* video rights to two different companies, which created quite a mess. But the film business was not a pub, and they could not keep it up, and soon, with numerous lawsuits past and present piling up like bar tabs, they found themselves getting into deeper and deeper shit until their company, Hemdale, went bankrupt in 1995. And yet, amid the chaos, John was pulling out gems like *Hoosiers* with Gene Hackman in one of his best performances as a small-town Indiana basketball coach, and *Salvador,* along with *Platoon.* And among the numerous projects he was developing was this exotic, difficult-to-finance Bernardo Bertolucci film in China — *The Last Emperor,* which would actually win the Best Picture Academy Award for 1987, John's second in a row. Quite an achievement for a low-budget little town house overlooking Sunset.

And truthfully, I don't think I'd ever been happier. I had two good pictures under my belt. I had a family I loved who had been on both shoots with me. Unself-consciously, I wrote in my diary of one particular Saturday: "Great day at home, at peace in my garden, books, correspondence, Sean, Elizabeth never looked lovelier, a picture editing, going to Germany and Stockholm for 'Salvador' promotion, another picture offered — a good time, Oliver, be grateful, friends, people I love, back on track with CAA. You garden as you go, run and jump in pool."

I had another competing vision for my life. I was now forty, but it'd been there all along. I suppose it was a boy's version of adventure, of a life fully lived. It was what sent me away from university life to the Far East to teach, and then into the merchant marine, and then to write a novel, and then enlist in the infantry. It spurred me on to explore the outer and then inner worlds. It was a pirate's life I romantically saw, like Burt Lancaster in *The Crimson Pirate,* one of my favorite 1950s movies. I'd be the captain with my chaotic crew — *Seizure, Salvador, Platoon* — roaming the eighteenth-century Caribbean from Port Royal, Jamaica, to ports in Cartagena and Havana, looking for that next vessel of a story idea, then board her and plunder her and get away fast before the big guns on the ships of the empire (Britain, Spain, Fox, Warner's) could close in on me. Laugh as I sail under their noses — with speed, maneuvering, and small budgets. But I had to keep a wary eye out for those other treacherous freebooters like Dino, Bregman, Jon Peters, who'd sell you out for a pittance if there was something in it for them. Dangerous men, not to be crossed. Mine was a free man's life, without a home, really, except for the wenches in the local ports, like Sabatini's Captain Blood, who "was born with a gift for laughter and the sense that the world was mad." Thus it remains a split in my soul — the home, the hearth, and then out into the wind with your crew — Odysseus's "I am become a name." Could this be? Could I live two different lives? Like those hard men I'd worked with in the merchant marine twenty years before — six months on land, six at sea; unsettled, eccentric men who remained free in their souls yet tormented. In the next years, I'd live out this split in my natures to its fullest.

The editing of *Platoon* was going relatively smoothly for a change, with none of the interference I had on *Salvador.* A month later, I'd assembled a rough cut at two hours and forty minutes, but no one saw it except for my editors. As with every rough cut I've done, I was again plunged into despair, so disappointed with myself. Nothing outside the war action scenes seemed to work. Where were the characters? Chris Taylor/Sheen was passive, underdeveloped; Barnes/Berenger was okay, but Elias/Dafoe was talking way too much in his one political dialogue. I ran through a hundred changes in my head I wanted to try right away, but this is where you need to slow down and chip away. Cutting too radically, I've painfully come to learn, is a huge mistake — like giving up what you've written out of pure pique. Very few directors like their rough cuts; they're shapeless reminders of our powerlessness. I had to cut my own fat down — take it off my body, if necessary, but in slower stages. Flagellate myself. We chipped away, little by little. Three weeks later, I showed a new cut at 2:20 to my inner circle — John, his partner Derek Gibson, Charlie Sheen, Bob Richardson, Elizabeth, and a few others. We'd added Samuel Barber's Adagio for Strings as a "temp" (temporary) soundtrack idea to inspire our Salvador composer, Georges Delerue. It worked. The music was a knockout from the beginning, with its tragic sense of loss. John was emotional and Elizabeth was crying, and that was my meter; even John's sour-faced partner, Derek, who never smiled, was beaming. It seemed so "real" to them as an experience. It still needed work — portions were slow — but we were confident. We'd make some changes and show it to Orion West.

A week later we marched into the same Orion screening room where Mike Medavoy had yanked Salvador after a few reels, decrying "Mr. Bloodlust Stone." Medavoy and the veteran Sal Lomita, who'd been a postproduction specialist at United Artists since the 1950s, were now there with a few executives. Nervously I sat off to the side. It still seemed too slow, and I saw numerous things I had to fix. The film ended, and Sal, who'd been through so many studio battles, bless his soul, was the first to say, "Greatest war film I've ever seen!" No hesitation. "It's everything Apocalypse should have been"; they'd distributed that, but I don't think it was a fair comparison, because our intentions had been different. Medavoy, a cool customer who never went overboard in his emotions, quietly told me, "You really are a great filmmaker . . . in a class all your own," as if he was amazed that this was the same guy who'd made The Hand. John Daly and Mike Medavoy were now the two heaviest allies I had. They set up a New York screening the following week for their East Coast partners. Unlike a studio hierarchy, Orion was a real five-man team, all partners in their own right, investing in their own company. Besides Arthur Krim, the urbane, dignified Eric

Pleskow, his chief production executive, would be there; also business affairs chief Bill Bernstein, and Arthur's law partner from the old days, Bob Benjamin — as well as the icy foreign sales chief, Ernst Goldschmidt, and presumably the entire domestic and international sales force, which was in town for other reasons. "Better be good," Pleskow warned Sal.

It was climax time. We trimmed and refined and went to New York on a humid early August day and walked into a postage-stamp-sized screening room on the west side of midtown at 4 p.m. In trooped Krim and company. How many times had Krim done this since he'd first headed United Artists in 1951 then formed Orion in 1978? All those great Burt Lancaster and Kirk Douglas UA films (*Paths of Glory, Sweet Smell of Success*), the other independents — *The African Queen, High Noon, Marty, In the Heat of the Night, One Flew Over the Cuckoo's Nest, Rocky, Annie Hall, Midnight Cowboy,* and currently *Hannah and Her Sisters*. There'd be no surprises for him. Krim represented what I'd loved about movies — their independence and intelligence. If I couldn't live up to his esteem, I'd never be who I wanted to be.

His projectionist, however, was a dour, defensive antagonist who put me on edge right away. We were still on twelve single reels, not yet having combined them into the standard 1,500–2,000-footer. And sure enough, this "veteran" projectionist missed every single one of the twelve changeovers, causing the picture and sound to cut awkwardly into the incoming scene. I was miserable, furious; any director would've objected, but now I was a fatalist. The picture ended. There was no Sal Lomita there to embrace it. Arthur Krim shook my hand and smiled. "Powerful picture," he said, and retired to his office with the others. They thanked me courteously; they seemed moved, but who could tell? I was asked to come back the next day.

Back in LA, John was uncharacteristically nervous, telling me not to worry, he "could pull the picture" from Orion and take it to Paramount, where he could get a better deal. The two of us had been here before with Orion on *Salvador* and were realists who knew we might have to scrape our way through again. I screened it the next day for Marion, Arthur, Alex Ho, and others; they seemed overwhelmed. The picture was undoubtedly "working."

Then I went up to Orion and met with Eric Pleskow and the sales, marketing, and promotion chiefs. Krim was not there — was this a signal? Eric was an Austrian, warm, semi-compassionate, with a handsome thatch of silver hair and an elegant accent. He could also be very cold when he had to be. But when he compared *Platoon* to his experience of seeing *All Quiet on the Western Front,* I knew he was sensitive to the horrors of war and the change young men go through. It was "big stuff" to him, "important," and he felt it should come out in the December 18–21 "corridor," and then "let it settle in through January and February; otherwise, in November, it might get blown off by exhibitors." The marketers, Charlie Glenn and Bob Kaiser, were thinking all the top TV shows would be interested in doing pieces — *60 Minutes,* Ted Koppel's *Nightline,* and the rest. Ernst Goldschmidt, the foreign salesman, was quiet, probably not sure how this film would play abroad. I assumed Krim wasn't there because it wasn't that important a deal to him. He'd adopt a wait-and-see attitude. But he had told me "powerful picture," so I'd take it as it comes.

I came out flying, high off the meeting, in my naïveté not questioning, as a veteran filmmaker would, how widely would Orion release the film at Christmas, how much would they spend on advertising and promotion. High figures would indicate strong confidence in the film's chances, but I was just happy they liked it, and trusted to that. Later, I'd hear from a producer who'd been at one of the LA screenings that week and ridden the elevator down with Medavoy and other Orion executives; they'd speculated out loud, "I don't know. Tough picture to sell. What do we do with it?"

In other words, Orion liked it but wasn't investing much money in its box office chances. Thus a limited release in three cities, six theaters, on December 18 was planned, and then . . . we'll see. But in those days, a limited release meant quality and wasn't necessarily tagged with the "difficult film, little money" label it's come to stand for. And whatever happened in those screenings got out fast, the pulse, which was already exciting enough for me, quickened by way of the phone calls to our editing rooms, which doubled as my office, cutting into my time — no assistant to respond to notes, letters, requests.

Indeed, my life was getting crazier, and I was being stretched thin. Against my common sense, I fell in love with another project Daly wanted me to do — "Tom Mix and Pancho Villa," based on a semi-fictional adventure novel by the notorious Clifford Irving, brought to John by two German independent producers. I say I fell in love because there was such a deep romanticism in this fantasy of a young Tom Mix, later to become the star of silent westerns, running off to join Pancho Villa in the Mexican Revolution; it certainly bore similarities to my youth and going to Vietnam at nineteen. Mix goes through a hell of a lot of fighting, growing up, and loving two different beauties — one Texan, the other Mexican — on his hard-earned journey to wisdom, Mexican-style. Perhaps I was a lost cause freak; not merely the Mexican Revolution, but what else was Vietnam but a botched and not even just cause?

I wrote my draft of "Tom Mix" in eight or so weeks in this blitzkrieg period of reading scripts, meeting numerous producers, pondering actors for Tom and Pancho — and of course still editing *Platoon*. For every film I'd make, I'd find, conceptualize, and develop probably five others. Writing was and should be — but is no longer — an R&D process that allows for rumination and failure, much failure. Studios were generally able to underwrite that process, but not anymore, unless the property is an established franchise.

I liked my "Tom Mix" script, but I didn't love it. In these stages, a film is a wonderful fantasy of what you're going to do with it. You dream it, but you never have to go through that hard day-to-day reality of shooting it. It is, in its way, a modern version of the *Odyssey*'s Lotus Eaters, a dangerously tempting time, the fruit hanging low. With "Tom Mix," the *Platoon* follow-up "Second Life," and also potentially "Defiance," I had three projects with John Daly. Enough.

I'd also sparked another idea for Mike Medavoy called "Company Man," about the spooks I'd seen in places like Honduras and Costa Rica when I was researching *Salvador*; these were ex-military guys, sometimes working for the CIA, trying to make a buck buying and selling anything. The whole Orion crowd went for it with the proviso "As long as it's not anti-US. Don't rub our faces in it, Oliver." So I had yet another deal; it was exciting, but it also made John Daly crazy because he was so competitive with Orion. And it was another obligation for me, and I was already overloaded. What was I thinking? I loved ideas. I had so many pent up over the years, all those treatments and scripts — I was a fountain, awash in origin stories. But each of these ideas took time, imagination, development. I commissioned some drafts to be written by others, and a good amount of time was given over to meetings, describing my ideas to other writers. I began to see Hollywood as the confluence of many streams converging in the great river of a final product that might be the work of several creators — a collective consciousness, so to speak. It didn't often work out that way, however — in fact, quite rarely, as the outsourced drafts did not live up to what I'd dreamed. But as my oil strike was now gushing, it couldn't be easily capped. So I kept going. Make movies, Oliver. Now is your chance.

Even Dino De Laurentiis wanted me back. The owner of some three or four hundred negatives of films dating back to the 1940s, he was newly recapitalized with a distribution company of his own, and with his customary chutzpah, he invited me up to his new mid-Wilshire office, which was the size of a football field. There he was, the tiny five-foot, four-inch dictator behind his huge desk, his large, dark-green-rimmed glasses and gravelly voice and Italian accent — "You make a good movie, this *Platoon* — I make a mistake." He shrugged — that's fate. His only regret was the loss of revenue to him, not the pain he had caused me. "But you know, Oliverre, you welcome back in the family" — spoken like a true don. He owned the rights to the remake of *20,000 Leagues Under the Sea* (1954): "Action! Octopus — underwater — big story. Jules Verne. Genius!" It had been one of my favorite kid movies, no question, but it seemed far-fetched to redo an illustration that's been done well. The real thrill was in exploring new ground.

"Dino," I replied, speaking with a firmness I had not been able to muster in our previous encounters, "what's done is done. But you must realize that I've made two films now with John" — on both of which he'd called John to question his sanity — "and I'm loyal to him. I'm in his family now," which was technically not true but sounded like something a killer like Dino would understand. Not that it made much difference, as he reassured me, "No problem! I make the film with John — this 'Tom Mix' I do!" How he even knew about it was not the issue; it was his assumption that he could acquire it, as he could most everything.

We would see. Dino would cross my path again, a character for the ages, his appetite for something *King Kong*–size unquenched. Leaving his office, I realized Michael Cimino's name never came up; Dino must have already put the disappointing box office numbers on *Year of the Dragon* out of mind. For that matter, Michael never contacted me about *Platoon*. I thanked him in the film's credits and with the media, I pointed to his original inspiration for me to try again to make the film. Years later, I tried to help Cimino produce a poetic and solitary fable about a wild white stallion that he wanted very much to make. I was able to secure him a $14 million commitment from the independent producer Mario Kassar, who by then had made *The Doors* with me. It was a good amount of financing, and Michael, after the failures of *The Sicilian* and *The Desperate Hours*, needed a break to get back in the ring. But — Michael being Michael — he wanted a bigger budget, more than $14 million, and after a while, I gave up.

And then there was Ed Pressman from *The Hand* and *Conan*, who came to me with a generous offer to write and direct something we could do together about our native city, New York. I'd always had a soft spot for Ed, who'd been a gentleman, though ineffective as my producer on *The Hand*. Still, I liked him as a friend. The 1950s quiz show scandals, which Robert Redford would make into the excellent *Quiz Show* in 1994, had always fascinated me. How could these producers and contestants be so dishonest to the little people like me in my pajamas, watching huge sums of money being won through cheating? It was another ugly lie, and we'd been hypnotized by it. Because I was busy writing "Tom Mix," Pressman and I hired my NYU classmate Stanley Weiser (*Coast to Coast*, 1980) as our scriptwriter.

But soon thereafter I dropped the quiz show scandal for another story, because I realized the subject of Wall Street and big money was the new "action" in my hometown. My father's relatively gentlemanly world of investing was still there but rapidly receding; I saw this film as a collision of the old and the new. Increasingly the media were sensationalizing young entrepreneurs being busted for "insider trading." I had one friend in his early thirties who'd already made a fortune — millions of dollars, which seemed impossible then for somebody so young — who made it sound like having sex. It was vulgar, exciting. Stanley and I screened the 1957 Clifford Odets classic *Sweet Smell of Success*, and we worked closely to develop our ideas. The older, tougher guy (Burt Lancaster) in our film would be this big shot, Gekko, and the younger guy (Tony Curtis) would be the "kid" who went along — until he didn't. Stanley, a New York "wise guy," set to work on a first pass that August.

I'd previously turned down Ed Pressman's offer to adapt his *Reversal of Fortune* book by Alan Dershowitz (based on the mysterious "true" story of New York socialite Sunny von Bülow's suspicious death), but he convinced me I could make some extra money, which I needed, by co-producing the film with him. After meeting with the charming Old World agent Paul Kohner, we decided to ask his client Billy Wilder, then eighty and retired, but with the mental vigor of fifty, to direct. In person, Wilder was sardonic and tart. He hadn't seen *Salvador* but said, "You should be a leading man instead of this masochistic line," and then completely demolished the von Bülow tale we were offering him, saying it had no old-time story essentials, "twists, turns, conflicts, emotional involvement . . . Every script they bring me is a beautiful woman, but if I don't get an erection, there's nothing I can do." He shared stories of Europe in the 1920s with Kohner, and then told us what he really wanted to do . . . if we truly believed he could still direct a great film. Of course we believed! From his shelf he pulled out a coffee table book on Le Pétomane, an 1890s Frenchman infamous for his musical farting on stage. Wilder, thankfully, would never make that movie.

Ed and I did go on to co-produce *Reversal* in 1990 with Glenn Close and Jeremy Irons (who won an Oscar for his role), but of much more satisfaction to me was my continuing relationship with the Berlin UFA–trained Wilder over lunches, dinners, and much laughter. *Salvador* and *Platoon,* when and if he saw them, were likely a little too real for him, and when he'd ask me, "Now what are you going to do?" and I'd tell him, I could count on his "Oh, no! Kennedy's brain splattered all over the place again! Three hours! Are you crazy? Won't make a dime." When I later told him I was doing *Nixon* (at three hours and fifteen minutes), I wish I could've photographed his expression. "Oy vey! Career suicide!" I didn't really know what Billy thought of me, but I do think he loved, as with Le Pétomane, my shaking things up. As he would say, "Épater la bourgeoisie!"

The music for *Platoon* was struggling to be born. We'd used, rather extensively, songs from the 1960s — "Tracks of My Tears," "White Rabbit," "(Sit-tin' On) The Dock of the Bay," "When a Man Loves a Woman," "Groovin'" — that were popular with the troops. The costs for using published commercial hits at that time were still reasonable, but the more success these type of films enjoyed, the more prohibitively their costs would rise. For our original music score, Georges Delerue, inspired by *Ran,* the Kurosawa film, was delivering the rhythms I was looking for — Oriental, atonal, and eerie at times. But his theme on piano to replace our Adagio for Strings temp track was only okay, not really moving in comparison to Samuel Barber's original classic. Barber's piece is really a simple melody; Delerue's version moved around too much and sounded too manipulated. This is where friendships in the film business come apart. Although Georges was wounded, he kept working on it right up to the recording session in Vancouver, where we'd gone for budget reasons. There I rejected his final attempt and asked Georges to just conduct the original Barber Adagio himself; he accepted and did it beautifully and with heart. He would have to take his name off the film, he said, but I pushed him very hard not to do that, as I felt he had contributed several other pieces of music that enhanced the final movie. Nonetheless, it marked the end of our warm relationship after only two pictures.

Insofar as we still had the same amount of post-production money, the editing of *Platoon* was done at one of the cheapest film labs in Hollywood, Consolidated Film Industries (CFI), inside ugly, industrial rooms. Why, given the amount of time filmmakers spend in them, are editing spaces so grim? Ridley Scott, my original choice to direct *Conan,* loved *Platoon* and *Salvador,* and now advised me, "Don't do a slick mix," by which he meant the Hollywood tendency to strive to make everything easy on the ear, smooth — too smooth. This was both blessing and curse. Too many sound mixes as a result featured a sound that was unable to truly "disturb" (that is, awaken) audiences in good ways, or else was intended to disturb them in conventional, manufactured ways. As our final sound mix was done on a very tight two-week schedule, this was a delicate matter. You have three mixers, all audio experts, overseeing their giant electronic board, and if the ego of the chief mixer is fragile, it can, in the confined dark space of a couple of pressurized weeks, blow up — especially when the director changes his mind, which, frankly, he must do as he goes along. And that is crucial for any director to understand — the need to keep your independence, not to be stampeded, maintaining your ability to simply say no. I insisted, for example, on bringing to the final mix, for comparison purposes, the "temp dub," which we'd done on the fly weeks before, using music we liked, random sounds from the production shoot, and whatever struck our taste; this was our "guide track" to facilitate the editing process, and would generally annoy the mixers.

In our final version, after hours of labor, the resulting reel was sometimes so well mixed that I found it became boring, Muzak neutral, and it didn't deliver the raw edge I'd felt in the work print. Or maybe the bombs, grenades, and rifle fire tired out the ear and we needed a change; or I might prefer the original, difficult-to-hear dialogue over the smoother but less believable dialogue track the actor has dubbed himself with. There are hundreds of such details on each twelve- to twenty-minute reel, and dozens of key decisions to make each day, involving far more tension than you'd imagine, almost, I think, comparable to the pressure I'd felt on the production of the film itself. It becomes a highly subjective experience for the director, and the good directors, over the objections of their experts, must travel there, go to their subjective side, and trust it, even if it's costly or "nutty" insofar as it's outside the conventional approach. You may not be able to tell the specialist specifically what you want, but you can spot what you *don't* want — and then it's your job to say "No!" whether to the mixers, the producers, the editors, or the composer himself. I repeat this because it's important: don't put something in your film if you don't like it, because you won't like it now or in ten years when you see the film again. It will haunt you to the end of your life. "Just say no."

And even then, when you're nearing the end of your low-budget two-week stint, you've cleared out at least two days to finally see and hear a good print of the whole mix in one go. And then, well — flaws become visible in so many new ways, you may want to jump in and make fifty to one hundred more fixes. Or, as I've heard told, some directors with great clout have even fired the original mixer and started over! The mix is a motherfucker no matter how you cut it. Sound is truly a 50 percent yin-yang marriage to the picture, which separately on its own now lives or dies in the lab in the timing and coloring of the first acceptable "answer print." This process of reprinting the film can take either a week or a month or more, depending on the director's eye, but one day — finally — there will be that married "answer print" of sound and picture copulating together, and it will be the very best your film will ever be. You're now ready to ship to fifteen hundred or two thousand theaters in one mass printing.

But then you discover the distributor might make only five to fifteen "pristine" (first generation) prints for their best runs, in the largest money-making houses, and unless you watch it closely, the lab will run off inferior release prints at less cost for the multiplexes, prints that are a second generation removed from the negative. And then, after these quality-control battles, many an obsessed director must have the courage to go out and look at the film in actual movie theaters. There you may experience issues you cannot control — theater owners cutting projection light down, darkening your film to save money on the bulbs; or a lazy projectionist, running six to ten films at once, failing to correct an out-of-focus print; or simply the cranks in the audience who love to complain about the sound being too high, and because of those three people complaining, the house manager and projectionist lower your incredibly sweated-over mix to barely decipherable levels, so that you lose 30 to 40 percent of your sonic impact! I've lived through many hells in different theaters, written dozens of instructions, policed, monitored, begged to get the film out in the way we made it — to much frustration and only modest avail.

All this has changed with video, streaming releases, digital projectors replacing film, and the disappearance of release prints; this has simplified the experience by making the technology easier to control. I wish I could get back all the angry, wasted energy I put into protecting my film prints. But even now, when I go into a stranger's home, I cringe when I see a new seventy- or one-hundred-inch giant smart screen (made more for news and sporting events) replaying a film at thirty frames per second instead of twenty-four frames, which is the speed at which we make the film — and which can be easily corrected, though it never is, through the controls on the TV. If film survives in any form, it will be because of collectors, people who care with the same passion accorded to centuries-old paintings.

• • •

It was ten years since I'd stood sobered at the Statue of Liberty at that enormous July Fourth celebration in New York Harbor; I remembered my vows to some ancestral force that was guiding me through life. So much had changed since then. How much happier I was now, with my child dozing in my arms on a Saturday afternoon, my beautiful wife sliding into the room, our two smiles saying the same thing — what a treasure we had together.

We'd found a new house in the Santa Monica flats on two lots, which gave us a backyard with a pool and guesthouse. It also had a real basement of three rooms like in East Coast homes, and inhaling the moist ocean air a mile away, I could walk peacefully at night with the dogs around our neighborhood of gingerbread houses where everyone seemed to be in bed by ten. It was a far cry from New York for sure, and maybe I was falling into that peaceful middle-aged suburban slumber I'd always heard about but never experienced. How would I know? The times were changing. In the '80s, credit lines and money were loosening; we bought this house at the heady price of $1.2 million, which meant we were carrying a $10,000 mortgage each month, which also meant that Liz and I were again living beyond our means. Time was required to write a screenplay, and screenwriting yielded a poor ratio of manpower to financial reward. As if on cue, my father visited me in a dream at that time, sitting on my bed while I was sleeping, saying with his devilish grin, half-meant or not, "The last person I ever thought would come through was you . . . you moody little shit." It gave me chills and guilt; my father could instill that directly. And guilt drove me through much of my life, trying to please other forces outside myself. I *seemed* to have grown past that, or so I hoped.

I thought maybe I wanted to live the life of Robert Young in *Father Knows Best* or Fred MacMurray in *My Three Sons*. I wasn't truly sure. Inside me was the demon, waiting to go back out to sea, hating this hoopla of meeting people, selling them, justifying myself. Of course, not all was a 1950s–1960s TV show. Although she seemed healthy, Elizabeth had, from the time we spent in the Philippines, suffered serious parasite damage. Now, with the stress of a new house and the impending release of our film, an ulcer was found in her intestines. There were hidden rivers there. The internist said it would take a year more or less to cure her.

My mother came out to visit and, at a restaurant one night, clashed with Elizabeth. Having been strongly influenced by my father's Republican views, Mom had never really liked *Salvador* as a film because she couldn't agree with any of the revolutionary feelings in it; despite her loving and highly charitable nature, she reverted sometimes into a silly, reactionary older woman, who, on this night, said in admiration of my new movie *Platoon* that war was a good thing, shaping the species after a Darwinian "survival of the fittest" model: "It made Oliver stronger." Elizabeth coldly cut that off with "My father was killed in Korea," and left the table without further discussion. Mom was a paradox to me until her dying day. She loved the Reagan people for their social elegance, but her French peasant upbringing was in conflict with her own snobbishness, which was acquired in a class-conscious France. Mom believed that an "upper class" should be in charge. Elizabeth, the former radical, did not want my mom to overstay her welcome, and I eased her transition back to New York.

On my fortieth birthday, apart from the blessings of a family, nothing could have pleased me more than the *Salvador* video finally hitting the stores. Now everyone could see it. This was like the paperback book that would reach those who didn't read hardbacks. It was still the early days of video, and within two weeks, 110,000 copies of *Salvador* were sold, in addition to the rentals. This meant approximately $6 to $7 million in orders. I no longer felt so ashamed about Hemdale losing money on the film; I could be proud. The film was continuing to open in various countries six months to a year after its American release. At the San Sebastian Film Festival in northern Spain, I sat with five thousand excited young people in a giant indoor "velodrome." As the film ended with Elpidia and Jimmy being separated, the crowd was up on its feet yelling, cheering in an amazing show of support I'd never experienced before. Magic wings were carrying me wherever. It was selling out in Sweden, and at the Irish Film Festival, the hot young filmmaker Neil Jordan (*The Company of Wolves, Mona Lisa*) compared my conversion from making "previously dubious" films as "equivalent to Saint Paul on the road to Damascus." Words can suddenly balm years of pain. England would finally break down and show it in January. And it actually did great business in London off glowing reviews (though nowhere else in the UK). Japan would never give in, to the best of my knowledge, but Germany, another big market, finally opened the film on the heels of *Platoon*.

In the United States, December 1986, the date of *Platoon*'s opening, was fast approaching. I was traveling back and forth between Los Angeles and New York. The adrenaline was mounting. Waking up at 4 a.m. with anxieties, I knew it could all still backfire. The huge Academy screening in Los Angeles was packed, which indicated real curiosity in this low-budget film people had heard about, and aside from the older members for whom it was too violent, the response was enormous. That was the first signal with an audience. I don't remember going to a single test screening; I don't believe there was one. Dozens of calls and requests for meetings were pouring in from everywhere, including foreign journalists and producers, even though I still had no office and was working out of my new house. The movie had its own wings now; they were built years before in Danny's small New York apartment, where a dreamer, quite broke, wrote down this flow of ideas, based on a combination of personal experience and his love of Greek mythology. That screenplay had lasted, and it was the key to this moment, the thread through the labyrinth that had gotten me out into the light of day. I must never forget that.

Orion seemed to be more excited than before. They were talking about "nominations" and saying "it might make sixty million." I didn't want to think about that because, as my father had taught me, there's always a 1929 to wreck your hopes. Charlie Sheen's father, Martin, who'd once been slated to star in *Salvador*, called to congratulate me but asked me to reconsider my ending — "Don't let the boy shoot the guy in cold blood." Morally, he was right. But then it wouldn't have been a war, would it? Charlie dismissed his father's objection as old-fashioned, as he was now beginning to sense the change in the wind of his career, sniffing the money and power that would come with it.

My press interviews were endless, as journalists tried to strip away who this "preppy time bomb" was, "the boy who went to Vietnam because he wanted to," etc. It actually tears away at you. You're trying to be courteous and responsive and feel as if you must make the journalists happy, which can be a major mistake. Endless people, meals, mostly praise, tension self-created, all these marinate in an atmosphere of great comfort, and I began to understand what Tennessee Williams meant when he complained that comfort, not poverty, was "the wolf at the door." Especially in a movie age, it becomes a creature unto itself; self-consciousness eats at the purity of your original drive.

Needing very much to keep a focus, I continued working with Stanley Weiser on our script about Wall Street, which we now called "Greed." We visited with several top financial executives, as well as the lower-level brokers and the Securities and Exchange officials who were investigating white-collar crime. It was another world. The hidden venality and viciousness reminded me of the violent, money-hungry cocaine world of Miami. In fact, several successful Wall Streeters I met, in their thirties and forties, were snorting coke. One tough executive, whom we hired as a consultant, was working for the notorious Drexel Burnham firm, led by Mike Milken, and his language reflected their reputed attitude. He'd talk of "ripping out" someone's guts or throat, giving and getting blow jobs, and so forth. Gutter talk, but telling; we put it into our script. One young friend of mine, making millions of dollars, already had a town house on the Upper East Side, fancy cars and bikes, and was renting big-time in the Hamptons — while doing cocaine with regularity. He'd boast, "You wouldn't believe the amount of money I made this week."

I'd say, "Yeah, but nothing like what I saw on *Scarface*."

He'd scoff, "Really? I pulled a million two last year. This year, my partner's projecting eight to ten million for the firm . . . and it's *legit* — you don't have cops up your ass, or guys who'll stick a shiv in your back when it's turned . . . You know Sammy?" he'd mention some name. "I introduced you to him at Jim's garden party? He took out twenty-five mil on selling his company. Took him three years to build it up. He's going to another one now, a bigger start-up, more money. He says he's aiming for a hundred-mil buyout."

My eyes were popping. "How old is he?"

My friend said, "Thirty-two. And he's cool, too. You can do blow with him, smoke one of your shit reefers, and get down."

It was an ego business, and my friend suggested it was even darker and more corrupt than anything I'd seen in Vietnam or Miami. He warned me that a big shot I just met was "ultimately looking how to *fuck* you, Oliver. And he will befriend you to befuck you. The name of the game is, he wants to *explode* inside you." Money was sexual to these young men, and a successful act of seduction was rape. It was man as beast; these young players loved the thrashing and the blood. It was a million miles from my father's stately, sober investment world. What the hell happened to the modesty associated with having money?

We already had bidders for a script no one had read. The young, brilliant production chief at 20th Century–Fox, Scott Rudin, wanted to be in business with me. Warner Bros. vice president Billy Gerber jumped in with his proposal. This infuriated John Daly when I revealed my plans to him. He wanted to get in, but when I told him the budget for shooting in New York would run upwards of $15 million, he thought I was corrupted and losing my marbles — "Gawd's bloody 'ell, this film should be made for less than ten million" — though John didn't say how. I became more excited as I sensed this script was really going to work and get made. It became my main focus outside of *Platoon*.

With six weeks to go until opening, our marketing meeting in New York was worrisome because, in a way somewhat like the *Salvador* campaign, nothing really was ready. *Platoon* had no national trailer and an abstract poster (called a "one-sheet") that I had doubts about, and which we'd soon abandon. Also, it had become clear that some Academy members thought the film was just too brutal and preferred Woody Allen's *Hannah and Her Sisters* or the excellent Merchant Ivory film that year, *A Room with a View.* The critics, in their year-end awards, were favoring *Hannah* and David Lynch's *Blue Velvet,* which I could understand. *Platoon* was going to be on some, but hardly all, year-end Top 10 lists; it would never be a unanimous critics' choice. I'd been there before with *Midnight Express* and *Scarface.*

And as I delved deeper into the situation, it became clear that *Platoon* was the innocent victim of an old simmering feud; Orion was pissed at Daly and Hemdale for not having put up $600,000 in prints and ads on an earlier film that year, *At Close Range* with Sean Penn, which had flopped. They wouldn't approve anything until this debt was settled. The shit only got deeper, as it always does, when the story now involved Orion owing Daly payments on the foreign rights of *Terminator.* Orion was not acting overly concerned; after all, they were opening our film in only three cities, with a supposedly wide rollout later. Daly, on the other hand, gambler that he was, was quite willing to pull *Platoon* and take it to his new hypothetical "ally," Paramount. This kind of "switching" companies was part of John's modus operandi as an independent producer, but it would eventually land him in dangerous waters. If he had been a pirate in another century, which he was in spirit, he was doomed to hang from the highest yardarm.

But unknown to us, the political currents were shifting subtly in our favor. When *Salvador* had been released in the spring, Reagan was still succeeding in selling his Contra war in Nicaragua to the US public, and there was the looming likelihood that US troops would find a justification for a limited invasion of Nicaragua, as they had in Grenada in 1983 and would later achieve in Panama in 1989 to catch General Noriega. But when Eugene Hasenfus, a CIA contractor, was shot down and arrested in October on a cargo overflight of Nicaragua, the pro-Contra story began to unravel fast. Reagan's administration was deeply implicated in a secret $30 million sale of arms to Iran, of which at least $18 million was funneled to a slush fund for Reagan's "Contras" fighting the legitimate Nicaraguan government. It was actually far darker than revealed at the time, but the surface of the scandal alone would essentially undermine his last two years in office with indictments.

Salvador, condemning US support for death squads, now seemed on point, and *Platoon*, calling out the madness of Vietnam, was opening at a most favorable juncture. Not only could it be perceived as a tribute to the men who had fallen there, but also it had enough red-blooded action to satisfy the need for violence in American bones. Yes, in the film American soldiers burn down a Vietnamese village and kill some villagers, but true to the paradox of that war, we showed the soldiers evacuating the villagers to safety, in one image a child riding the shoulders of a big GI. And yes, American troops would turn on one another and kill, but this platoon could be written off as an undisciplined unit, with draftees in it, which couldn't be considered an example of an elite army unit, like the Airborne. And lastly, in our portrayal, the platoon's drug use was not overdone and didn't interfere with their combat ability — only their mindsets — and could thus be overlooked. In other words, the film was raw and provocative but, given the conditions of war, "understandable." Our timing, December 1986, was as good as it gets.

Platoon opened in six theaters on Friday, December 19, in New York, Los Angeles, and Toronto, and from the first show at 11 a.m. at the Loews Astor at 44th Street and Broadway, it was a runaway train. Arthur Manson, our fatherly marketing adviser, described a line down the block, mostly men, veterans, quiet, waiting, shuffling. He said the screening itself was muted. But the movie's effect was clear afterwards — from the men who continued to sit in their seats after the lights came up to those few crying alone. Across town, at the tony Loews on East 66th Street, it was another type of hushed crowd, mostly men as well, drawn by the reviews. It seemed *Platoon* could be both action film and critical success.

The reviews were out of this world, not just impressive but impassioned. The all-important television reviewers were near perfect, as Roger Ebert called it "the best film of the year," and Gene Siskel, who'd not cared for any of my previous work, was gushing. Richard Corliss of *Time* magazine gave us an entire page of love-hate: "A document written in blood that after almost 20 years refuses to dry." He was saying that it was going to open wounds again, it would be controversial. Vincent Canby of the *New York Times* called it "a major piece of work, as full of passion as it is of redeeming, scary irony." As for the screenplay, he said, "It's less like a work that's been written than one that has been discovered," calling the film "a singular achievement," while the *LA Times*' critic wrote, "a Goya with a camera . . . drives a stake through the heart of every Rambo clone." The *Washington Post* reviewer in January said about me, "In the past year, with *Salvador* and *Platoon,* he has gone from a screenwriter who seemed to bring out the worst in the directors who hired him to one of the five or six American directors who matter." And David Denby of *New York* magazine, who had once been brutal about my work, wrote that *Platoon* "culminates in the explosion of surreal horror that Francis Coppola labored for in *Apocalypse Now,*" calling it "the kind of Vietnam movie that many of us have longed for." Denby captured the ambivalence of the village scene when he said: "The My Lai–type massacre we have been expecting doesn't quite happen, but it doesn't need to. Stone has shown us the bottom, the worst. Appalled, we know how committing murder might feel good . . . With this movie, Oliver Stone completes his amazing transformation from bum to hero."

To be "a hero" is a boy's natural dream — but to be called out as one, while still in midlife, gave me an enormous internal thrill. All the years when I thought I was wrong, when I was told I was bad — all this time, maybe I was right. That's the kind of self-congratulatory thinking I was going through. Why not? I would soon enough experience the other side of that coin again. But for now, it was important to enjoy it all. I sensed on that opening day that this was a peak experience that would probably never come my way again. To have great notices and do business and be forty years old and in good health — it was so rare.

I appeared on ABC's *Nightline* that evening with Ted Koppel and his guests — the tall, Lincolnesque David Halberstam, who'd been an early skeptic of the war as a correspondent for the *New York Times* (and who would write a glowing review of the film); and Jim Webb, assistant secretary of defense, who'd written a great novel about Vietnam, *Fields of Fire,* and once served as a lieutenant in a marine platoon. Webb would criticize the film as an aberration. American soldiers did not behave in this way. Obviously, we differed. He'd been an officer, and as I earlier described, I had little contact with their world — or they with mine. *Nightline* turned out to be relatively tepid, as are most American television news shows, with their commercial breaks and time limitations. Also I too was somewhat superficial, trying to avoid unnecessary controversy, emotional, and, as "a hero," just grateful to have made the film. A first-timer, so to speak, in the limelight, very unlike my radical side, which had emerged during the failed *Salvador* PR campaign.

I was flying at a high altitude. Tom Cruise, even then the embodiment of a young superstar from *Risky Business* and the top-grossing film of the year, *Top Gun* (which ironically I'd been asked to write back in 1983), came to town with his soon-to-be wife, Mimi Rogers; they saw *Platoon,* and afterwards we went to dinner. The agent we shared, Paula Wagner, had gotten him interested in "Greed," which no one had actually read yet — but it didn't matter, it was simply assumed that the script would be there. My Lord, such things had never happened to me before. What a turnaround from being ignored. But because he was already committed to Dustin Hoffman and director Barry Levinson to start *Rain Man,* Cruise wanted to know if I could possibly wait for him until the fall to start "Greed." Unfortunately, there was an actors' union strike expected that June, a situation that was coloring all the studios' production schedules. I'd flirted with Michael J. Fox, a huge star at that point, and Matthew Broderick, and I'd even made a vague commitment to Charlie Sheen — more like "Do you want to do this with me?" Scott Rudin at 20th Century–Fox was adamantly against my waiting for Cruise because Hoffman was "always delayed" (which turned out to be true; *Rain Man* was shot more than a year later). But there was no question in my mind that Cruise was the right choice for my Wall Street movie. He could play brash, energetic, go get 'em at any cost, cut any corner, and unlike Charlie, he was 100 percent all there, committed to being a star.

Ironically, earlier that day in the hotel lobby of the Regency on Park Avenue, I'd crossed paths with Warren Beatty, who called out to me. "Heard your movie was very good," he said. "You writing something?" He was such a handsome devil.

"Yeah, for the spring."

"About what?"

"Money."

"Cast yet?"

"No."

His eyebrows went up. "Think of me."

I teased him, "But with you it takes two years of rewriting."

He smiled, went out the revolving door into the street.

So when I met with Cruise that night, I couldn't imagine a better marriage than Tom as the young broker and Warren as the old fox. Beatty and Cruise in the same frame at that time in their lives. Would it have worked? Made more money? Possibility is a strong aphrodisiac.

Platoon kept growing beyond my expectations. The *New York Post* ran a full page of pictures and "People in the Street" reactions: "Lines not seen since 'The Godfather' in '72!" CBS put together a special, flying three members of two different platoons I served with in the 25th Infantry and the 1st Cavalry Division to New York for a moving reunion that paid heed to the emotional needs of a country that now wanted, out of a sense of guilt, to make it up to the misunderstood Vietnam veterans by pouring out their gratitude. Or maybe it was really a Reagan-era moment when America was trying to feel good about itself again.

Time magazine, then still a major force in our culture, planned a cover story on the movie and kept Marion in suspense until the last moment on whether it would actually appear; either it was going to be Reagan's prostate or us on the cover of the January 18 issue. It turned out to be us. Now we were hitting all segments of the population. On La Brea Avenue in Los Angeles, I saw lines a block and a half long of African Americans, Asians, hip, young, old. America's darling TV host Jane Pauley was saying, "Never have I been so deeply moved." Jane Fonda, an avid antiwar activist, said she broke down and cried when she saw the soldiers leaving the burning village with the Vietnamese kids riding their shoulders. It was a unifying experience. After I did a highly successful Oprah Winfrey show, one of the producers called out, "You should run for president!"

What made this entire period different from anything I would ever experience again was the slow rollout of the film; in its odd way, it was an accident. Orion was known to make offbeat movies at lower prices, but they wouldn't distribute or spend money on them with confidence. With *Platoon,* they were caught with their proverbial pants down. Arthur Manson was upset that Orion didn't have the bookings or the materials ready to go wider quickly at the New Year. Exhibitors were already calling on the very first weekend, trying to book *Platoon,* but they couldn't get it. Manson, through his personal contacts, managed to get screens in Chicago and San Francisco for that New Year's, but still, it went very slowly. We were "leaving money on the table," he said, meaning that the enthusiasm dies down unless the movie can be seen when it's most talked about.

You could argue that Orion's Eric Pleskow was able to make tougher deals with the exhibitors on a slow rollout, and thus extract a higher percentage of the gate. And that they'd had great success this way distributing *One Flew Over the Cuckoo's Nest* in 1975. Yet I'm sure even Pleskow and Krim were much surprised when the film kept going, week after week, through January, into February, and, remarkably, all the way through March and beyond. Women began to attend in significant numbers in the third week of the run, and the film kept gaining momentum. I was naïve in the sense that I could never have imagined so many people existed in the United States, much less the world, and with the exception of fantasy blockbusters, I doubt this could ever happen again in this country, as time will never go quite that patiently again, nor will people postpone their gratification to see a movie.

On March 30, Oscar day, some fifteen weeks after *Platoon* had opened, the gross was over $100 million — and would go on into April to total a cumulative $130 million–plus domestically. Truly, for a highly realistic film with violence and no children's audience, this was a miraculous phenomenon, not only across the US, but across the world. Considering that John Daly had made the film for $6 million and owned all the rights and was releasing it with only minimal expenditure, the profit worldwide was enormous for that time, the film grossing as much as $200 million to $250 million at the theatrical box office, in addition to the sale of the ancillary rights for video, television, and such.

Naturally *Platoon* had its detractors. Pauline Kael, priding herself on her role as the Wicked Witch, poured her acid on the film, which she found "overwrought" with "too damn much romanticized insanity." She emphasized that I was "a very bad writer" but added, "Luckily, he's a better director than writer." Kael had particularly hated the "preppy narration extolling the nobility of the common man," calling it "a grown man's con" and me a "hype artist," and thus, I felt, denying me the validity of my experience partly because I'd been to a "prep school."

At the end of *Platoon*, flying over the wounded and dead, Sheen's last words were voice-over: "Those of us who did make it have an obligation to build again, to teach to others what we know, and to try with what's left of our lives to find a goodness and meaning to this life." So many people, young and old, have told me over the years how moved they were by these words that it's hard to reconcile this with Kael's contempt for the narration. Well, if I was such a lousy writer, I wanted to be a "good" lousy writer. And I wanted people to be moved by that lousy writing. Kael's criticism would become the basis of a backlash from her devotees, who constituted a small, self-referencing colony in the film world. Their spotlight was now on me, no matter what I did — and Kael had set that spotlight, well before her praise for *Salvador*, on *Midnight Express*. Another kind of reaction set in over the years, with many "film buffs" telling me that *Salvador* was their favorite of my films, conspicuously bypassing *Platoon*, which I was okay with, as long as they liked at least one of the films I'd made.

At a Q&A at the Harvard Club in Manhattan, fully packed to the rafters with its staid portraits of past Harvard presidents looking down from high wooden panels, there were polite, intelligent questions about the film's "morality" and so on until a slightly drunk, red-faced graduate raised his hand: "I appreciate the love fest and all; it's a well-made movie and all that, but I was a patrol leader in Vietnam, and your story is absolute crap! The guys over there were straight, there were no drugs in the field, they were good men. Your film's an insult to them." He was shaking with emotion, and as I went about my counterargument, he kept interrupting with "Come off it, pal! Rape? There was no sexual intercourse in combat!" And again, when I was referencing *Salvador* and Reagan's paranoia about communists crossing the Rio Grande, he cut in with "What about the Chinese rolling over Tibet!" There was big applause on that. I was going through a form of baptism by fire once again, but I was ready for it, as each argument had to be countered with the specific. To my mind, the issue wasn't about the behavior of individual units or soldiers in Vietnam, which follows human nature; it was about the corruption of a military system that had been fed on monstrous lies.

At the International Berlin Film Festival in mid-February, the reception was quite controversial. At the packed screening for some fourteen hundred journalists, I heard booing and some cries of "Scheisse" — shit! There was far more applause, but a large segment of West Germans, as I found out, despised the heavy American military presence in their country and equally detested US foreign policy; they were contrarians looking to knock down a "big shot" American film that could be interpreted as glorifying war with its music and many beautiful images.

The press conference after the film was rough. Hundreds of journalists packed into a hot hall, flashbulbs in my face, again the introductory applause and strong booing. One idealistic woman attacked immediately with "Why do you have Charlie Sheen kill the bad sergeant?" — leading her to the criminality of the American war effort. Another woman asked, "Why are there no women in the film?" A man made a statement: "This is nothing but a boring old war movie, why do you make it?" An upset Swiss journalist kept rudely cutting in, not letting me answer, grinding her axes. Simultaneous translations were going on in various booths in Italian, French, Russian, Japanese. It was a wild ride as a press conference. Suddenly here I, a dissident from the Vietnam War, was representing the USA. The film, nonetheless, went on to do spectacular foreign business everywhere without exception, even Germany.

Meanwhile, the Veterans of Foreign Wars, along with conservative celebrity icons like actor Chuck Norris, attacked the film as a disgrace to the American fighting man. Dale Dye, no friend to war protesters, responded strongly on our behalf. *Parade* magazine, a national Sunday supplement of great popularity, was edited by Walter Anderson, an ex-marine officer who told a Vietnam combat photographer, who then told me later, that this magazine would never give *Platoon* an inch of coverage because it was a disgrace — and *Parade* never did, nor in fact did it ever, cover any of my later films. There was a twenty-fifth-hour attempt to discredit me as a fraud who'd never served in Vietnam. The story, put out by some veterans, bubbled up out of a newswire service when Dale Dye, keenly on the lookout for such things, caught it fast. He was worried. "Oliver, what's going on? They're saying there's no military record for Oliver Stone?!"

This was strange. It took me a few beats to think it through. "Yeah. Because I was William Stone there." And then they found the records, and the story vanished.

In that year and the next, boxloads of letters came to me — many of them heartfelt, moving, and so many of them similar. "My husband/son/father came home quiet, never the same again, never talked about the war, never wanted to see a movie about it . . . but when we finally saw your movie, we talked/he cried/he went back several times to see it." Or sadly sometimes, more than once, a suicide followed within days of someone's seeing the film. And the relative writing me the letter wasn't blaming the film but was actually thanking me for letting them understand why their loved one possibly killed himself. On several occasions, I made telephone calls to veterans in hospitals dying from some form of cancer or war wounds.

There were letters asking for film clips to be used in criminal trials where PTSD was a defense. There were letters from nurses, grateful we'd shown the gore and toll of combat. One black author of a Vietnam book was up in arms, claiming we'd portrayed the African American troops as particularly cowardly, shirking combat, which was simply not true; each soldier, black or white, was an individual drawn from my experience.

There were surprisingly detailed letters from men asking if the bloody attack at the end of the film was based on the January 1, 1968, 25th Infantry battle at "Firebase Burt," the area also known as Suoi Kut on the Cambodian border, which it was, and amazing new details were given me, foxhole by foxhole. Our company commander, a captain I'd barely seen or known when I was in his unit, got in touch with me with his corrections — namely that he'd never called in an airstrike on our perimeter. And yes, there were other letters in which I was called out for participating in "war crimes," saying I should be charged or surrender to the authorities.

In Hollywood, I was flattered with praise, way beyond my *Midnight Express* experience. Steven Spielberg wrote me, "It's more than a movie. It's like being in Vietnam." Marty Scorsese was quoted as saying, "It's good to see our country can still produce directors like him. He has a unique style, and he's become a real personal filmmaker. No one else is doing the things he's doing. He's out there by himself." And Elia Kazan had told someone I knew that *Platoon* was "the film of the year," which was most heartening. Even Brian De Palma, normally a cold man, was quoted as saying, "Seeing *Platoon* get through the system makes the soul feel good."

Jackie Kennedy wrote me a beautiful letter: "Your film has changed the direction of a country's thinking. It will always stand there as a landmark — like Rachel Carson's 'Silent Spring,' like Thomas Paine's 'Common Sense.'" She invited me to visit her New York publishing house. Perhaps I could write something for them? I had no idea then that in a few years I'd be tramping, with muddy boots, through her manicured garden when I made a film on the brutal murder of her beloved husband. The Reagan White House, according to Orion, had shown *Platoon* four times in special screenings. Taxicab drivers in Manhattan were calling out my first name as I walked past: "Hey, Oliver! (or Ollie!) Great film. Tell it like it is, buddy!"

"I am become a name"—that beautiful line from Tennyson's "Ulysses" echoed in my memory.

While I was visiting the floor of the New York Stock Exchange for research purposes, the PA system suddenly announced, somewhat embarrassingly, "Everybody! The director of *Platoon* is down here with us on the floor, making another movie!" And all these brash, powerful New Yorkers froze for like a minute to break into excited applause. If only my dad could've seen this. The high-end Ogilvy & Mather British advertising firm, which would never grant me an appointment in the early '70s when I was trying to sell our advertising reel, was now offering me $50,000 to do an American Express card commercial. In my mind, that was the height of American praise—to be plastered all over airports and magazines. But it felt wrong to commercialize this painful collective experience, and I turned them down. Even the Polish underground movement against their Soviet-supported government reached out to me for help. It was getting to be too much.

In late January at the Golden Globes (where I'd embarrassed myself in 1978), I lost the screenwriting award, without regret, to my old mentor, Robert Bolt, for his script of *The Mission*. The picture had finally come out after more than ten years of delay, a lush, cerebral epic produced by Fernando Ghia, now overshadowed by his partner, David Puttnam, who'd produced *Midnight Express* and gone on to do *Chariots of Fire* and *The Killing Fields*. I congratulated all of them, because I thought *The Mission* was one of the great films of that year; but sadly, the theme of the Jesuits in the Amazon jungle in the early eighteenth century was not a topic for modern audiences, and the film lost money. Ending up in the red had nothing to do with *The Mission*'s quality, only its subject matter—a price to be paid over and over again for those of us who veer from the margins.

Later that evening, when Tony Curtis called out "Oliver Stone" as Best Director, I was relaxed as I glided up to the stage. The Golden Globes were now a widely televised event, and this time I was sober and prepared. I had my list of names in my head, thanking and acknowledging the Vietnam veterans and "John Daly, who gave me a shot when I was unemployable," and "Elizabeth, my wife, whose unwavering love brought me through the dark years." The strong applause surged and carried me in its redemptive glow for weeks.

When the prestigious Directors Guild Awards rolled around in mid-March, untelevised, I went out of my way to acknowledge the long line of DGA past winners. I praised Elia Kazan, who was receiving a lifetime achievement honor, and his *Viva Zapata!* as a major inspiration for *Salvador.* I spoke of "the giants of my youth ... their lights shine no less dimly as an example to us — we're in the tradition of Wyler and Wellman, Stevens and Ford, Huston and Hawks, Billy Wilder and so many others who've created a lifetime's body of work." The DGA gold plate is enormous, and holding it, I felt solid — like the writer-director I'd wanted to be since NYU. I'd arrived. I could honestly, for the first time, call myself successful.

On the plane to New York after the Globes, I saw Al Pacino. He looked beaten, older than I remembered him from our strange partnership on *Scarface,* where he'd asked for my support but never gave me his. He seemed distantly happy for me and said, "You've grown into your success ... you deserve it. You've been around." He, on the other hand, was openly sick, he said, "of getting my head cut off" — in movies like *Revolution, Author! Author!,* and *Cruising,* on which he'd had a difficult time with Billy Friedkin, who was originally going to direct *Born on the Fourth of July;* Pacino was now working on the fifth writer's draft of a picture that would never get made and would become the embodiment of all the defeats we face in a volatile profession. But Pacino was still the street Hamlet to me; Al didn't miss much with those big shiny eyes and a savagely instinctive actor's radar for the very moment he was in. I find this to be a most crucial aspect of acting. "We communicate with our eyes," Napoleon said; my own eyes were always far too small for the screen, but nature's choice pleased me.

Perhaps that's why I preferred to be behind a camera or a pen. That was changing now, as I had to become the public face of *Platoon,* and in a larger sense, the Vietnam War itself. I had to develop a more public persona, for which I had little training, having shied from debate societies in school. It was on-the-job training. In Washington, I made my first National Press Club appearance, which, in comparison to times still to come, went smoothly. I spoke, among other things, of the need to remember the war, almost fifteen years past now. I spoke of "moral amnesia." And I defended the violence in *Platoon* by defending its realism as opposed to the sanitized, unrealistic violence we see in television and movies. "The point is that violence ruins you, in some sense, forever. It takes a piece of your soul." To judge from the violence that continues in today's films, it's become even more realistic and gruesome than in previous years, but its meaning is largely lost when one American soldier on that big screen can still manage to kill ten or twenty Somalis, Libyans, or Taliban before expiring. Why can't Americans just die miserably like everyone else?

Shortly thereafter, I received "the call" I'd heard whispers about, "the call" that comes out of the blue, never chased. It comes or it doesn't. Mike Medavoy, who handled his affairs, had set it up. "Marlon Brando's going to call you," Mike said. "I showed him *Platoon* —"

"Oh, okay."

"He brought Michael Jackson and Liz Taylor."

"Oh, okay." Was I glad I wasn't in that screening room. Distracting to say the least.

"He'll tell you. You'll like him. He's a good guy."

Less than half an hour later, when that high, self-conscious, nasal-strained voice came on the line, it had to be him, but sometimes you still have to wonder if it's a prank. Brando — "Call me Marlon" — clearly grasped the root of the film and its success. "You can understand how you go outside all moral restraints" was the way he put it. *Platoon* was "a watershed film that will sweep the Oscars." He understood the dilemma that most fascinated me: Would my protagonist, myself, cross the line into immoral behavior — into sadism even? He seemed to identify closely with the village scene in which American soldiers humiliate the Vietnamese peasants.

I kept thinking: he sounds just like Brando, his voice from *On the Waterfront*, but . . . It was a long call, as he meandered to his second point. He wanted me to work with him on his pet project about the infamous 1864 massacre at Sand Creek in Colorado, an outgrowth of his passion for the cause of Native Americans. He launched into a fascinating monologue with the visceral power of the one he did in *Last Tango in Paris*, to "butter up your ass like a pig," vividly describing how US soldiers took the Native women, "cut their tits and cunts off, stretched them across the pommels of their saddles." The way he spoke was as if he was doing it himself with a skinning knife, his voice elemental with rage, clashing between his own male and female sides in his imagery of savagery, pure savage cruelty.

His anger was very real, but I knew I didn't want to do this massacre film. I'd just done *Platoon* and *Salvador;* I wanted an escape from cruelty. I suppose he sensed that, and he was blunt in suddenly asking, "You can give me a quick yes or no. A short thrust of the knife to the belly is better than a slow carve up the back." A poet of a man, resignation in his voice; he knew. I said with some hesitation, "I'm not too keen on doing it."

He wished me well on "Greed," which would soon be retitled *Wall Street.* "It's a great idea, but is it commercial?" Who knew? I didn't really think about that. I told him it "was an honor for me you called. Growing up, you were one of my idols." He laughed, I believe moved, but how many times had he heard this? We made vague promises of getting together. A legend. I never thought I'd talk to or see him again, but actually I would — in a face-to-face that was passing strange.

So I'd come to this moment in time. Success was a beautiful goddess, yes, but was I being seduced by this vindication, this proving myself to my father; was it the acceptance, the power? What did I really believe? I'd made it a moral issue that America was truly wounding itself in Vietnam with our struggle between pro-war/antiwar, right/left, Barnes/Elias, but was I avoiding the larger moral issue of the wholesale slaughter of 3 to 4 million Vietnamese people — and all that implied? What had really happened to America? It was no longer just about Salvador or Vietnam. My mind was still scared of this confrontation; it was a mind that would have to evolve further, assume greater risks. One baby step at a time.

Oscar night was Monday, March 30, 1987. It'd been so emotional that first time — seeing Cary Grant, Laurence Olivier, John Wayne, two of them gone now. This was my second date, but I was as excited about it as in 1979. No more was I the scriptwriter. I was the filmmaker. Our underdog status was long gone, and it felt, frankly, like we couldn't lose. Why feign surprise when everyone was telling me the same thing? The veteran publicity man from Warner's, Joe Hyams, informed me, "Stanley [Kubrick] just saw the picture and loved it." Joe was dead sure: "You're gonna win, kid." This time I'd keep my head to the earth. I wouldn't be spun or wooed by Oscar again into another hubristic downfall. I'd stay rooted in my family. When I'd returned to Los Angeles and seen Sean waiting for me at home and he gave me a happy hug — "For Daddy," he'd say, prompted by Elizabeth — the world at that moment would come to a fullness I've rarely experienced. That was the difference between 1979 and 1986. It was my happiness.

Nonetheless, before the awards show, I took a Lysanxia, a tranquilizer, which would help navigate this torturous three-and-a-half-hour journey. First the red carpet and the reviewing stand with the inimitable Army Archerd of *Variety* announcing each arrival. Kathleen Turner, Jane Fonda, Sigourney, Sissy, a parade of dresses, the royalty of some magic kingdom walking past the yearning masses screaming out their names — "Over here! Over here! Oliver! Oliver! Here, here!" Girls in *Platoon* T-shirts jumping up and down. Then Elizabeth and I, accompanied by my mother and her handsome gay date, producer and partygoer Andy Kuehn, were escorted to our seats in the very first row in the full glare of the TV cameras. *Platoon* was nominated for eight awards, among them my original screenplay. I was also up separately in the same Original Screenplay category with Richard Boyle for *Salvador* — that rare occurrence of competing against yourself. Richard was sitting with Esther a few rows back (she was a long way from that trailer in Santa Cruz), trying to figure out a way to cash in on all this glamour, which he did, talking his way into a professorship in film at an inland California college, a "gig" he milked for at least twenty years before he moved back to the Philippines, where life was cheaper. In another section, his former antagonist, Best Actor nominee Jimmy Woods, was glowing alongside his horse-riding girlfriend, whom he'd marry, and soon divorce. Jimmy knew he had a real shot at the crown.

Each time the TV cameras cut to me for my reaction, as if I was bound to win, it felt like a new form of public torture. Supporting Actor went to my *Hand* star Michael Caine for *Hannah and Her Sisters*, not to Dafoe or Berenger, who canceled each other out in the balloting. I lost out on both my films for Original Screenplay to Woody Allen for *Hannah*. Bob Richardson lost out on Cinematography, but we did win Sound for our British pro, Simon Kaye, and we won Editing for Claire Simpson.

As my time approached, I did get nervous and skipped out twice to the lounge area, where Elizabeth steadied me, patted me down, and I took another half pill — what was wrong with me? There was no profound answer. It was just pure fucking nerves. It would take years to steady those nerves; only repetition could do it. Would I make it tonight? I could see myself dissolving in sweat in front of millions; talk about embarrassing. I suddenly felt like bolting out of there. Liz gripped me, calmed me.

The Foreign Film award was given to a Dutch film, *The Assault* — and its director blathered on, it seemed, forever. Then Best Actress went to Marlee Matlin for her moving performance with Bill Hurt in *Children of a Lesser God*, directed by one of the exceptional female directors at that time, Randa Haines; Marlee is deaf, and her acceptance won hearts.

When Elizabeth Taylor stepped onto the stage to award Best Director, the audience hushed with excitement. She was the best, and you knew it when you saw her. My dream girl of the 1950s and 1960s, still so glamorous, the heart of the movies. David Lynch, who directed *Blue Velvet*, was sitting not far away, and years later, he revealed how much he really wanted to win "just to be kissed by Elizabeth Taylor." She began by reading the five directors' names — Lynch, Allen, Roland Joffé (for *The Mission*), James Ivory, and me. And suddenly, in one of those bizarre moments when a breeze suddenly blows through the window and your body temperature drops back to normal, I felt calm, so calm, feeling this great moment for what it was — a spot of heaven.

"And the winner is . . ."

The camera, for some reason, was on my mother's date, Andy, with his mustache, who actually looked a bit like me, and then —

"Oliver Stone!"

The camera found me. Is this a dream? And yet, I was sentient. "Kiss Liz twice," Mom was saying to me across my wife's knees. Which Liz did she mean? I kissed my Liz. My mother meant the other one. The applause sounded deafening, the gods had found me this moment — and millions of people were laying eyes on me for the first time in their lives.

Then I was gliding across the stage, and I felt cool and easy, making sure to kiss Liz Taylor on both cheeks, as the French do.

"Thank you for this Cinderella ending, but I think through this award, you are acknowledging the Vietnam veteran, and you're saying that, for the first time, you understand what really happened over there, and you're saying that it should never ever in our lifetimes happen again." There was strong affirming applause. It was a big moment. *USA Today* called it "the classiest, evocative speech." And then I went on, almost defiantly. Was I going too far now? Was I going to blow this too? ". . . And if it does, then those American boys over there died for nothing, because America learned nothing from that war they called Vietnam."

Although there was resounding applause and more affirmation, in view of the upcoming Panama invasion and the first Iraq War, how wrong I was — but at least I tried. Then I thanked my colleagues, and with Queen Elizabeth guiding me to the wings, I returned to my seat to see the next two categories coming up fast. Best Actor was presented by an aging, emaciated Bette Davis with great theatricality, but not to Jimmy Woods, who many felt deserved it — and how sweet it would've been — but deservedly to Paul Newman, a no-show who was finally receiving it on his seventh nomination for *The Color of Money.*

And then Dustin Hoffman came out. "And the Best Picture of the year is . . ." (envelope) "*Platoon!*" I know it sounds repetitious, but it bears repetition because I'd need to remember this moment when my storms came; the ugly duckling had just been transformed into a swan.

Platoon, at the start, had been a thousand-to-one low-budget shot — all those turndowns, all those years of indifference — the men of Vietnam spread all over the country tonight — it was all spinning through my heart. Arnold Kopelson came to the stage alone, as had been determined, denying John Daly his true reward, as well as Alex Ho, but Arnold wanted to be the only producer up there. I watched from my seat, and despite my fears of his going on too long and pretentiously, he offered a simple and moving thank-you.

As the show wound down, I returned backstage, where Liz walked me into the first of four media rooms and bade me good night with her movie goddess smile, and the next day sent me a bucket of red roses with a witty note, "From the other Liz." Always saucy and sexy. Endless photographs of Dustin, Bette, myself, the other winners — and into the press questions. By now I was a trained seal, and when asked for my reaction to the denunciations of *Platoon* by some conservatives and the VFW, I gave it back to them without rancor.

Then the parties, the faces, the bonhomie, Dale Dye in his full white marine uniform calling for "Bravo Two!" to form "at attention!" at the Hemdale party at La Scala. I was standing with my mother and wife and John Daly next to Arthur Krim and his wife, Mathilde. My mom, having met Liz Taylor and Bette Davis and Jennifer Jones, three of her favorite actresses of all time, was in paradise. Michael Douglas, with a mustache, was hugging me. Jimmy Woods, Charlie Sheen, Tom Berenger, Willem Dafoe, all of them — Richard Boyle, Paula Wagner, Mike Menschel, Steve Pines, Bob Marshall, our banker Frans Afman, Gerald Green, Arnold Kopelson, everyone who'd played a role — Bob Richardson, Alex Ho, even members of our team in the Philippines were calling in. I could do nothing wrong that night short of vomiting on the cake, but I held myself with dignity; I wanted to remember this happiness.

I'd been chasing the light a long time now. I'd felt its power. I was now forty years old, proverbially at the halfway point. It'd been a remarkable two-film journey from the bottom back to the top of the Hollywood mountain. With *Salvador,* I'd slung the stone hard and far, and it had given me a foothold. And with *Platoon,* I'd managed to crest into the light. Money, fame, glory, and honor, it was all there at the same time and space. I had to move now. I'd been waiting too many years to make films. Time had wings. I wanted to make one after the other in a race against that Time — I suppose really a race against myself in a hall of mirrors of my own making.

Thirty years now, I look back and realize I had no idea then of the storm that was coming, but I did know instinctively that I'd reached a moment in time whose glory would last me forever.

ACKNOWLEDGMENTS

I have David Rosenthal to thank for his thoughtful and experienced advice in editing and shaping this story. And Cassandra Jaskulski for her long days and devotion to deciphering my handwriting and sticking with me through so many drafts and corrections. Also, my agents Bryan Lourd, David Kopple, and David Larabell for finding a home at Houghton Mifflin Harcourt—and providing encouragement through these years to keep writing it.

And certainly, to my beloved mother and father who nurtured me, and my family who have helped sustain me. And my doctor, Chris Renna, too, for helping preserve my memory and my health.

Lastly John Daly, who passed away too early in 2008. Following his bankruptcy, he eventually found his way back to the movies. Financed by entities unknown to me, he directed several straight-to-video thrillers, which I gather were profitable. Next to his unique independent run as a producer, I believe directing films probably gave John the most satisfaction. To steal a line from *Captain Blood*, "He was born with a gift of laughter and a sense that the world was mad."

INDEX

BAINTE DEN STOC

WITHDRAWN FROM
DÚN LAOGHAIRE-RATHDOWN COUNTY
LIBRARY STOCK